"This book is inspiring and a journey worth taking."
— Don Hahn, producer of *Beauty and The Beast* and *Lion King.*

"A story that every parent and teenager must read."
— Dana Leu, a California high school teacher originally from Romania.

"Everyone has a story and this is an incredible story everyone should read."
— Dr. Skip Baker, behavioral specialist and one of the four doctors in this book.

"Every emotion in my body was awakened by this book. Two thumbs up Lacy!"
— Chris Magarian Ucar, television director.

"Before you date or get married you should read this book."
— Dr. Tamika Henry MD, MBA, and healthy lifestyle strategist.

"Deeply inspiring and amazing foresight."
— Mark Christopher Lawrence, comedian, actor, starred in *The Pursuit of Happyness.*

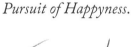

SHE
WAS
WORTH
IT ALL

BOYS DON'T KNOW WHAT MEN SHOULD

ALSO BY LACY WESTON

Transform Your Reality: Break Your Personal Chains

Available on Amazon and at other fine retailers

SHE
WAS
WORTH
IT ALL

BOYS DON'T KNOW WHAT MEN SHOULD

LACY WESTON

Requests for authorization should be addressed to:
Lacy Weston
115 W. California Blvd. #269
Pasadena Ca. 91105
lucciano@pacbell.net

Cover design by Ivica Jandrijevic
Interior layout and design by www.writingnights.org
Book preparation by Chad Robertson

ISBN: 978-0-578-51036-1

LIBRARY OF CONGRESS CATALOGING-IN-PUBLICATION DATA:

Names: Weston, Lacy, author
Title: She was Worth it All / Lacy Weston
Description: Independently Published, 2019
Identifiers: ISBN 978-0-578-51036-1 (Perfect bound) | (eBook)
Subjects: | Non-Fiction | Memoir | Adversity | Child abuse | Personal Fitness | Body-building| World Champion
Classification: Pending
LC record pending

Independently Published

Printed in the United States of America.
Printed on acid-free paper.

24   23   22   21   20   19   18   17   8   7   6   5   4   3   2   1

I dedicate this book to all of you that are
holding on to secrets,
living in secret,
or happen to be the secret.

YEAH! Hey!
When you wish upon a star. Your dreams will take you very far, yeah.
When you wish upon a dream. Life ain't always what it seems.
Oh yeah.
Once you see your life so clear,,,,, hey.
In a sky so very dear, yeah. You're a shining star, no matter who you are,
Shining bright to see what you can truly be. (What you can truly be!)

— Earth, Wind, and Fire, *Shining Star*

CONTENTS

FOREWORD

Not one life enters this world without a purpose or several purposes attached to it. As humans, it's up to us to mature, adapt, learn, and maneuver through this world and our journey with our eyes, ears, and senses turned on. Although we may be distracted by people, places, and things, it's up to us to grow and become stronger despite those distractions and rise above those distractions as best we can. If things were easy, the word 'triumph' would have no reason to exist; and if it were impossible, life would have no reason to exist, but somewhere between triumph and impossible is where life sits and it will sit closest to the word that we accept for ourselves.

It's easy for one to wish they were born into a rich family with all of the perks or born into a race of people that seem to receive favor. That reminds me of a conversation I once had with a friend as a child when he told me he wished he could trade places with a well-known NBA basketball player. A few years later, that pro basketball player lost his money, career, and relationship to drugs.

It's better to take the life we have and design it, build it, and enjoy it as best we can as often as possible, because wishing we were someone else dances too close to the word impossible, and definitely does not lead to a life of triumph. To blame others, society, and circumstances is an option. Learning to use your energy toward identifying one's potential and setbacks despite society and circumstances leads to healing, growth, and a world of continuous triumph. Don't believe me? Meet me on page one.

Lacy Weston
La Canada, California
2019

Acknowledgements

Many people over the years have helped and supported me in numerous ways, and to name them all would be an entire book of its own.

Thank you to the reporter who told me to motivate the world, and the woman at the laundromat who told me she knew I was born to make life better for others, and the child that thought I was an action hero and asked for my autograph while I was at a park doing chin-ups at age sixteen.

Thank you to director Chuck Bowman for giving me a guest appearance on a TV show when I was twenty-three, and thank you to writer, producer, and director Stephen J. Cannell for making me promise to write this book. I kept my promise.

Thank you, Russi "Minnie Mouse" Taylor for all of your belief, trust, and support over the years.

Many thanks to everyone from Class of '83 and the original rat pack before then.

Thank you readers for buying this book because I've wanted to get it to you for quite some time.

Thank you family and a special thank you to my brother Russ, "Gus", in this book.

To the three visions I saw when I was a teenager that came to be Casey, Marie, and Raquel, thank you all for allowing me to live one of my greatest dreams - being a father to all of you.

PROLOGUE

1968

Nine children and an older woman got out of the car and began walking toward a white chapel in the middle of nowhere in Mississippi. One of the sisters held the hand of the youngest boy who was three. As the family entered the small and half-filled chapel, the mother broke down crying as did some of the older children. The youngest boy didn't know why everyone's faces were leaking water but he noticed that whatever was in the black box in the front of the room was what was making people's faces leak water. Everyone sat down except the mother and the oldest girl. They went to go see what was in the box with their face leaking a lot. The oldest girl tried to get something out of the box but many people stopped her as she made loud noises. The youngest boy grew curious and had to see what was in the box. He quickly scooted off the seat as fast as he could and ran his little legs to get to that box, but someone grabbed him from behind, picked him up, took him back to his seat, and sat him down. The boy looked to see who grabbed him and noticed a robust black woman with an off-white dress and a big hat on her head. She told the boy that he should stay right there and that there was nothing up there for him to see. The boy waited for the woman to walk away, then he scooted off the seat again and ran faster than before to get to the box. As he got a little closer he was plucked up again and continued kicking his feet trying to get away, but he was placed on his seat again. Again, he looked to see who grabbed him, and he saw a light-skinned black man in a suit that smiled at him and said, "You're pretty fast but you should really stay here." He told the little boy that there was nothing for him to see up there. The boy waited until the man went away and he scooted off the seat for the third time. Like greased lightning, he ran for the box and was met by the oldest girl. She walked fast toward him, making loud noises with a leaky face, and grabbed him and took him back to his seat. She hugged the boy tightly as her face leaked and she made sounds, awful sounds. She told the boy she knew he wanted to see what was up there but it was best that he didn't go. The boy kept trying to watch the people going up to the box as the oldest girl hugged him.

After watching people go up to the box for a while, people began to leave with their heads down and faces leaking. The boy and his family began to leave. As they headed for the exit, the boy tried one more time to make a run for the box. He yanked his hand from the older girl's hand and ran between all of the people, but the mob of people stopped him. The older girl picked him up and carried him to the exit as he looked over her shoulder, trying to see the box as people walking behind them interrupted his view. As they left the chapel, they walked past many people standing around with their faces leaking, but the family kept walking quickly to the car.

Once everyone was in the car, the older woman started the car then sat quietly for a few moments before she drove off. After driving for a short while they were about to drive over a bridge, but the older woman stopped the car and let out a very loud sound and lowered her head forward as the other boy and girl in the front seat rubbed her shoulder. The little boy looked up at an older boy next to him and tugged his shirt while pointing at the older woman. The older boy told the youngest boy that the woman was scared to drive over the bridge and it made her sad.

The little boy stood up on the seat to look at the bridge and the look on his face showed that he thought the bridge looked fun rather than scary, so he appeared puzzled as he sat back down in the car and looked at the older woman. Minutes later, the older woman began driving again, and as she drove the older children looked sad while the younger children looked confused, and the little boy fell asleep.

1969

There was always a lot of energy in the house, with kids moving and running everywhere along with music playing in the background. The older girls would take care of the younger boys, and the older girl named Esta with caramel-like skin seemed to be in charge of caring for the youngest boy named Lacy. This was probably because she was 18 and mature enough to cater to the youngest boy's needs since he was barely 4 years old. There was Alexandra, 16, with darker caramel skin, and Odessa, 14, with skin like milk, banana-like hair, and eyes like the sky on a sunny day. The oldest boy was Randy, aged 12, with skin like licorice, then there was Gus, 10, with skin like Graham Crackers, Marcel, 7, with skin like Abba Zabba candy bars, and Horace, 6, with skin like sugar babies.

Everyone was in school at this time except Lacy, so he looked forward to being with everyone on the weekends because of all of the fun they would have. When the ice cream truck would come by, the older girls would go to their piggy banks and jars to get pennies for everyone to buy ice cream and candy. The other children wanted ice cream, taffy, or bubblegum, but Lacy always wanted Candy Dots because he liked pulling the dots off the paper and eating them. He also wanted the candy necklace because it made him feel like a king. His favorite snack was Barnum and Bailey Cookies in the circus-themed box with the white carrying handle. His second favorite snack was the candy necklace.

He'd run around with that candy necklace and get so sweaty that the colors of the necklace would get all over him. He didn't care about the candy tasting like sweat and ate it anyway. Yum!

This was the routine each Saturday afternoon, and sometimes the older children would pull furniture out of the house into the backyard and cover it with sheets to make a tent so they could pretend they were all camping as they ate their snacks. All of the children thoroughly enjoyed this, but Lacy was clearly in heaven with everyone and never wanted the fun to end. The older girls would tell the rest of the children when it was time to finish the candy or get rid of them so they could clean up before Mom got home. Lacy would get a little sad when the parties were over because it seemed that everyone acted much differently when evening came. As the sun went down and evening would come, Lacy noticed that the older woman would always come in wearing a white outfit, set her purse on the kitchen table, then run to the bathroom all while questioning the girls. "Did anyone come to the house asking questions?", "Did the phone ring?", "Were there any deliveries?", "Did they hear from someone named Sandrine?". As the girls answered no to all of the questions they would sort of giggle because the older woman would pee with the bathroom door open and it sounded like a strong hissing sound. She would say, "OOOH, Sweet Jesus, I had to go bad," and while still on the toilet she would yell to Esta, "Did you fix dinner?"

"Yes," Esta said. "Everyone ate."

The older woman said, "Then fix me a plate because I'm starved." When the older woman came out of the bathroom, she hurried herself to the kitchen and quickly patted the heads of Marcel and Horace, smiled at Randy and Gus, gave curious and untrusting glances to Alexandra and Odessa, and expressed her dissatisfaction with Esta. As the older woman fixed her plate and made her way to the table to eat, she said it was time the younger children went to bed, so all of the boys headed to their bedrooms and the girls stayed in the living and dining room area. As the older woman ate, she questioned the girls again and talked about her day at the hospital.

"Was June Bug over here today?" she asked.

"No," the girls said.

"What about that Michael Myers boy?"

They said, "He wasn't here either."

"You heard from Sandrine?"

"No."

"We haven't heard from Sandrine."

"Good! I don't want her calling or coming by and if she does I'm calling the police on her. The Simmons next door tell me everything so I better not catch you two lying to me."

"We're not lying," the girls said. "Nobody came over today."

"Good!" After questioning and continuing to smack her food down, the older woman told the girls how she ran around that hospital for hours cleaning up vomit, wiping smelly asses, and taking orders so she had no time for any nonsense, so there better not be any nonsense going on. The girls told her there wasn't any nonsense going on as the older woman wolfed and smacked her food down some more. This was the routine each night, and Lacy would fall asleep listening to as much of the chatter from the dining room as he could, then he would question Esta about it the next day. He wanted to know what the words that he would hear the older lady saying meant. "What is vomit?", "Why did she run around the hospital?", "What is smelly grass?" Esta would patiently explain what these things meant as gingerly as she could to a four-year-old, but there were times she would get very frustrated because Lacy was always so curious and kept the questions going. "Why did she clean up vomit?", "She don't sound like she like vomit.", "Esta? Do you clean up vomit?" Esta answered Lacy's questions then told him he really shouldn't be listening to other people talking unless they were talking to him. Lacy said he just hears the talking coming from the other room. Esta told him he should not listen and just go to sleep. Lacy said okay, but each night he would listen again and have a list of questions for Esta the next day.

As summertime approached, Esta would spend more and more time with her friends and had less time for Lacy. When Lacy asked Esta why he didn't see her as much, she told him that she would graduate high school soon and needed to complete a lot of work right now. She said after graduation she would not see a lot of her friends anymore, so they were all spending a lot of time together now. He asked her what graduation meant. She told Lacy that graduation was when someone finished a certain amount of learning and got to go to the next stage of learning. She said she finished all of the learning in grammar school and graduated grammar school, and now she was finishing high school and would be graduating high school soon. Esta asked Lacy if he understood what graduation meant. Lacy said yes. He looked puzzled for a moment then asked what would happen after graduation. Esta told Lacy that she would go to college for more learning. Lacy asked what college was. She told Lacy that college is where you go to learn a skill so you can work and make money to buy food and a house to live. Lacy asked what a skill was. Esta, slightly frustrated, explained that a skill is knowing how to do something correctly. It means you can do the job that someone needs you to do because you learned how to do it. Lacy said okay, then he asked Esta what she would do after she bought food and got a house. She said, then I'll have a family and live happily ever after. "Lacy, why are you asking so many questions?"

Lacy said, "Because! That's where the answers are." Esta looked fit to be tied but took a deep breath and told Lacy that he was absolutely right and from now on she would ask people questions to make them think and that he had made her think. She said that was a good way to teach others and help them learn.

"Thank you Lacy, you just taught me that I should ask more questions."

Lacy said, "Yeah, because that's where the answers are." He said, "Esta, I have another question." Esta's bright smile of satisfaction sort of slipped from her face as she asked Lacy what his question was. He asked her what 'absolutely' meant. She said you and I absolutely have to get going so I can drop you off next door so Shirley can babysit you.

"Absolutely means there is a far greater chance something will happen, like you going to Shirley's will happen right now."

Lacy said, "Okay, but I'm not a baby."

Esta said, "No, you're not a baby, but babysitting can be for children of many ages."

Lacy said, "Then why don't you just say people sitting?" As Esta knocked on Shirley's door, she told Lacy they could discuss babysitting later so that she wasn't late for her friends. Lacy asked Esta if she would be back soon, and she said not too soon but that she would see him that night. She always spent time with Lacy at night.

Shirley opened the door and said "HIIIII Lacy!" Lacy said hi back and smiled at Shirley because he liked Shirley. Esta kissed Lacy on the cheek and told him to be good and he said he would. Just then, Esta's friends drove up to pick her up and all yelled hello to Lacy.

He waved back, yelling hello to them, then Esta quickly ran off to meet her friends as she yelled, "Have fun!" to Lacy and "Thank you!" to Shirley.

Shirley yelled, "You're welcome!", and "Have a good time!". Shirley was 14 years old and always seemed happy and had a pretty smile. Her mother Lilly, on the other hand, was always smoking a cigarette and walking around the house in slippers with a fur ball on the front and her hot pink polyester pants, floral print top, and a floral print scarf wrapped around her head and hair. If she wasn't walking around the house aimlessly barking orders, she was sitting in a chair watching television with one eye while the other eye watched Lacy or anyone else in her view. Lacy didn't like being around Lilly because she seemed mean, cranky, and scratched herself a lot as if she had mosquito bites. It seemed that Shirley was always doing chores around the house and taking orders from her mother. Shirley do this, Shirley do that, and don't let me have to remind you again to get those clothes out of the dryer. It seemed that Shirley didn't have a day's break from doing laundry. Lacy would tag along with Shirley as she did her chores around the house or made quick trips to TG&Y, which was a store like Walmart but much, much smaller. Lacy even followed Shirley to the bathroom when she had to go. She'd look at him and say, "You can't come in but I'll be right out." He stood by the bathroom door because he didn't want to be near her mother Lilly. As Lacy was waiting by the bathroom door, he heard Shirley's brother Ari come in through the front door. Ari was about 13 years old and was always getting yelled at by Lilly each time he came home.

"Boy, where you been?" Lilly would shout. Ari said he was with friends. "Those good for nothing friends of yours better not get my boy in trouble! Now, come over here and give Mama a hug." Ari would slowly walk over to his mother with some hesitation as she would have that fiendish Grinch-like grin on her face. "Come over here boy, I ain't gonna bite cha." Ari would move a little quicker and when he got close to Lilly she would grab him by the ear and twist it and he would yell in pain. She would say, "Now tell me what you've been doing and where you've been."

Ari said, "I told you, Mama. I'm not lyin'. I was with friends and we were just talking and laughing at the park."

"You been smoking those funny cigarettes?" she asked.

"No Mama. Some people be smoking those things but I don't because I know better." Lacy would peek around the corner and watch Lilly question Ari, and Lilly would look over and see Lacy and yell at him and tell him to mind his own damn business and get out from around that corner. Lacy ran back to stand by the bathroom door, waiting for Shirley to come out as he stood in fear that Lilly would come for him next. When Shirley came out from the bathroom, Lacy asked if they could go outside and play but Shirley said she had to finish folding clothes and asked Lacy if he wanted to help. Lacy said he didn't know how to fold clothes but he could watch.

Shirley said, "I can teach you how to fold clothes."

Lacy said, "Okay Shirley." Since Esta always helped Lacy pick out clothes and get dressed, he never experienced sorting and folding clothes as he did with Shirley, and once he got the hang of it he enjoyed it. At one point, Lacy noticed some red shorts he had not seen before so he picked them up and told Shirley he thought they were funny-looking red shorts.

Shirley snatched the shorts out of Lacy's hands and said, "These aren't shorts, they're my panties." Lacy asked what panties were. Shirley told Lacy that panties were women's underwear. She said, "You have underwear that look like shorts and so do women but we call them panties." Lacy told Shirley that her panties felt different than his underwear and Shirley told Lacy she wore big girl underwear and big girl underwear was not like little girls' and boys' underwear. She said little boys and girls had accidents sometimes and your underwear needed to help catch your accident. Big girls and boys didn't have those accidents. Lacy looked at Shirley like she was his new best friend and told her that he couldn't wait until he could wear big boys' underwear. Shirley laughed and said it would be a little while before that happened but he would wear them one day. When they finished folding the clothes, Lacy asked if there were more clothes that needed to be folded because it was fun. Shirley laughed and said, "There are always more clothes but we can take a break and watch some television if you want."

"Okay," Lacy said. "Let's watch television. My favorite show is Mighty Mouse and it only comes on in the mornings when everybody's at school. I don't always get to see it because your mom comes over at that time so the adults can watch that exercise guy with the funny clothes and his dog."

"OOOHH! You mean Jack LaLanne?" Shirley asked.

"YEAH! That's the guy that they watch at the same time Mighty Mouse is on and he makes funny faces and the adults sit smoking cigarettes and say how hard the exercise is."

Shirley said, "Jack LaLanne is a very healthy man and he wants to help other people get healthy too."

"I'd rather watch Mighty Mouse because Mighty Mouse is stronger and healthier than that guy."

Shirley laughed and said, "Mighty Mouse is a cartoon, Lacy. Mighty Mouse isn't even a real person."

Lacy said, "Mighty Mouse talks just like a person, acts like a person, and does everything like a person, so how could he not be real?"

"Come here," Shirley said to Lacy. She sat him down and got some paper, a pencil, and some crayons, and began drawing pictures. She explained to Lacy that cartoons were drawings on paper that were stacked together and they were placed in a machine that made them move forward or backward. "When the pages move quickly it makes the drawing look like it's moving quickly but it is only a drawing." Lacy asked how they made the drawing talk. Shirley explained that people wrote stories for the cartoons and other people read those stories while someone recorded them reading. "Once the readings are recorded, someone else takes the recordings and plays them at the same time the cartoons or moving pages are moving, and that is all recorded on a machine that can record the sound for you to hear and pictures for you to see."

"So Mighty Mouse is just a piece of paper?" Lacy asked. Shirley said yes. "Nobody ever told me that Shirley," Lacy said, as he looked really sad. "Thank you, Shirley."

"For what, Lacy?" she asked.

Lacy said, "Thank you for telling me the truth about Mighty Mouse. I don't want to watch him anymore." Shirley asked why Lacy no longer wanted to watch Mighty Mouse and he said, "Because it's not a real person, it's just paper. I wanted to be like Mighty Mouse but if he is only paper then I'd rather be like me."

"And who are you?" Shirley asked.

"You know," Lacy said, "I'm the professor. Everyone knows that. I wear professor's glasses and I know things no one else knows."

"Hahahahahaha." Shirley laughed so hard and loud while Lacy just stared at her as if she lost her mind. He didn't seem to see anything funny about what he said. He asked why she was laughing and Shirley continued laughing and said, "Because you do look like a professor with those black-framed glasses." Her laughter slowed down and she found a sense of seriousness and said, "You do seem to know a lot for your age and speak in a way that most four-year-olds don't speak. And you ask an awful lot of questions that have to do with life and the future. Why do you want to know so much about the future all the time Lacy?"

He said, "The future is what calls me and says I belong there. There are many people there waiting for me to help them."

"How will you help these people you speak about?" Shirley asked.

"I don't know yet but I will know in the future," Lacy said.

"Don't you just want to play and be a kid?" Shirley asked.

Lacy said, "I'm not a kid, I'm a child. A kid is a baby goat. I'm already a child, so I don't have to do anything to be more of a child, and I do play. What I don't have is the future but one day I will."

"Lacy, I have a question for you."

"Okay," Lacy said.

Shirley said, "I know it's silly and I feel stupid for asking it."

Lacy said, "No one is stupid, not even mentally retarded people. We all just think differently."

"Lacy, do you always have to talk like that? Sometimes you scare me."

"I'm sorry Shirley. I don't mean to scare you, I'm just telling you what's in my head."

She said, "That's alright, it just seems so odd that you are four and you sound like you're 40. Like a 40-year-old midget." Shirley burst out laughing after she said that, but Lacy just looked at her with a serious face and asked what a midget was. She told him a midget was a very short adult that doesn't grow past the height of a child. Lacy asked Shirley if she thought that was a very nice thing for her to say to him. Shirley looked bewildered and felt embarrassed and said she was sorry.

Lacy said, "That's okay." Then he burst out laughing and said, "It is kinda funny," and laughed more as Shirley looked at him as if she could not make heads or tails of what just happened.

Lacy asked, "So what's the question you were going to ask me?"

Shirley said, "Oooh yeesss. Lacy…Do you think I'll get married one day and have a big family and a nice home?"

Lacy looked off to the side for a moment then looked back at Shirley and said, "No. You're going to live with your mother for a very long time. You want to move out but you keep coming back and staying with her." Shirley started to cry and Lacy asked why she was crying, but Shirley got up and ran out of the room. Lacy began to run after her but stopped at the doorway when he saw Lilly down the hall as she met and stopped Shirley.

Lilly asked, "What happened, what's going on Shirley? What did that Weston boy do?"

Shirley said, "I asked Lacy if he thought I'd get married one day and have a big family and a nice home and he said NO!" She cried hysterically as she said, "Lacy also said I would live with you for a long time."

Lilly slowly backed away from Shirley, put her hands on her hips, raised her head to look down her nose at Shirley and asked, "So, what's wrong with living with me? You too good to live with ya mutha after all I've done for you and that poor excuse for a brother?"

"No Mom, no," Shirley said. "I just want my own family and a wonderful life of my own and I got scared when I heard what Lacy said."

Lilly said, "You mean to tell me your ass is in there listening to a four-year-old as if he knows anything at his age?"

Shirley said, "Well, his sisters told me they ask him questions and he…"

Lilly interjected with anger and said, "SHUT IT UP! GIRL, YOU SHUT YOUR MOUTH RIGHT NOW BEFORE I SHUT YOU UP! Now you get your little narrow ass in there and finish folding those clothes and any other chores you have." Shirley didn't say a word. She just walked to her room with her shoulders drooping and her head down. When she got near her room, Lacy apologized for making her cry, but Shirley didn't say anything. She walked by him as if she didn't even see him and sat on her bed in deep thought with tears coming from her eyes. Lacy stood near her and told her he was sorry and didn't mean to get her in trouble.

Shirley looked at Lacy and tried to smile as she softly said, "It's okay. You didn't get me into trouble. She just yells all the time about everything and I hate it. Lacy, you didn't do anything wrong," and she reached to hug him and said, "you're a good boy."

Lacy said, "Shirley, you're good too and I really like you."

"You do?"

"YES! Can we go outside and play now?"

"I don't think so but I can make you a snack and we can watch TV."

Lacy said, "Okay!" As Lacy ate his snack and watched TV with Shirley, he fell asleep as he often did after eating snacks and watching TV. After a long nap, Lacy was woken by Esta to take him home. As Esta walked Lacy home, he asked Esta why he doesn't get to stay with the other children at home and has to stay with Shirley.

Esta said, "Everyone else is older and has things to do, plus *I'm* supposed to take care of you and when I can't I ask for Shirley's help. You like Shirley, don't you?" Esta asked Lacy.

"YES!"

"Did you have a good time with Shirley?" Esta asked.

"Yes! Shirley can babysit me whenever you aren't here."

"Oh, you didn't miss me?" Esta said.

"I always miss you when you're not here Esta."

Esta wiggled Lacy's hand as she held it and said, "I always miss you too Lacy," then they both smiled happily at each other.

As they entered the house, there was a lot of commotion going on. It seemed that Odessa and Randy were at it again. Those two would fight about anything.

"Go back to your room Snow White heffa!" Randy said to Odessa.

"Who you callin' Snow White heffa, Skillet Leroy, Captain Midnight, and Darkness all wrapped into one!" Odessa said to Randy. Just then, Randy pushed Odessa and Odessa took her shoe off and started beating Randy with it while he called her half breed, mistake, misfit, and heffa. Odessa said, "I'll show you who the heffa is!" as she kicked Randy in the leg but aimed for his testicles.

Randy said, "You missed!" as he slapped her across the face.

Odessa started crying and that's when Alexandra dove at Randy and tackled him to the ground and shouted, "You hittin' a girl again, huh? You punk! Hit me and see what happens." As Alexandra had Randy pinned down and was slapping his face, Odessa ran over and began kicking Randy in the legs as she called him punk Skillet Leroy.

Randy said, "Okay, okay, get off me. I give up. You win. No fair, two against one. Get off me."

"I'll beat the black off you. You have no business hittin' a girl big as you are. What's the matter with you?" Alexandra asked, as she gave him a smack-sounding slap across the face. "You're nothing but a trouble maker and you're always causing problems at home, at school with other kids, and your teacher thinks you're retarded. Are you? Are you retarded?" Just then, Randy pretended to be knocked out as he would often do to get his beating to stop. He figured if he played possum that everyone would think he was unconscious and badly hurt. Nope. It only infuriated Alexandra when he would do that so she would give him a fresh one across the face and tell him to pretend that didn't hurt, and that was when he would start crying and beg her to stop. Alexandra would stop and get off of Randy once he began to cry, but she would seal the deal of humiliation by saying, "Okay, let's leave the punk alone since he's had enough beatings from a girl. Bye punk! I'm going to my room punk! If you need another beating you know where to find me punk!" Randy would stand up and yell that he was going to tell Mama they jumped him when she got home from work.

He said, "And I'm gonna tell her that you've been calling me retarded again. Mama said I'm not retarded and those teachers are idiots and so are you."

Alexandra would just smile and sing, "Tell, tell, go to hell, and hang your booty on a rusty nail." As all of this was going on, Esta would take Lacy to her room and try to talk to him so he would not pay attention to all that was going on, but Lacy was too curious about the commotion.

"Esta, what's a punk? What does Skillet Leroy mean and who is Snow White?" Esta told Lacy none of that was important for him to know and that he shouldn't repeat any of it. Lacy said okay, then asked what "hang your booty on a rusty nail" meant.

Esta looked at Lacy and said, "I thought I told you to not pay attention to all of that and that none of it is important."

Lacy said, "I know, but if it's not important then why do they say all of those things and why does Randy cry when they say it?"

Esta said, "LACY! You do not need to listen to any of that or repeat it. Do I make myself clear?" Lacy looked shocked at Esta's tone and behavior with him since they were just holding hands and smiling together not long ago. Lacy began to cry and said he was just trying to learn. Esta said she didn't mean to raise her voice at him and make him cry but he needed to just listen and do what he was told when she told him. Lacy said okay, and looked away from her in a way that showed he didn't want to talk to her or be with her at that moment. Esta asked Lacy if she was mad at her and Lacy said he didn't understand why she got upset and couldn't talk to him like he talked to her without getting mad at him. Esta said he asked so many questions at times and it was hard to keep up with all of the questions so she gets frustrated. Lacy asked what frustrated meant. Esta said, "See what I mean? You have another question already."

Lacy said, "If you stop using words I don't understand then I won't ask so many questions. Can you do that Esta? I don't want you to get mad at me but you say a lot of different words all the time. Can you use words I understand?"

Esta said, "If I do that how will you ever learn?"

Lacy looked at Esta as if she was from Mars and said, "That's what I've been trying to tell you."

Esta asked, "What have you been trying to tell me, Lacy? What? What? What?"

"You're getting mad again."

"You're giving me a headache and making my head spin."

"That's not true. I haven't hit you to give you a headache and your head is not spinning. You're not telling the truth, Esta." Esta ran out of the room in frustration, making a grunting noise. Lacy just stood there and wondered why Esta had such a hard time talking and listening. He turned on the TV and turned the channels until he found an old movie since he always liked old movies. He was a sucker for a love story but he really liked the gangster movies because the gangsters were always dressed well and always said the same thing in every movie like "Boys, we've got to organize." When Lacy learned what the word organize meant, he once told Esta that he would be organized one day and have his own business and say, "Boys, we've got to organize." He told Esta that he would not use guns and bad guys in his business because his business would help people instead of hurt them. When Lacy saw a good scene in a movie he would call Esta to come join him and watch the movie with him. "Esta! Esta!" Esta would run in and ask what was going on. Lacy said, "You're missing a good part in the movie. Come sit down and watch the movie." Esta would sit with Lacy and they would watch the movie and talk until Lacy's bedtime. This would be the routine on the weekends. During the week, everyone but Lacy had school nearby at La Sida Elementary School or Giano High School.

When everyone went to school, Lacy was left at home by himself for at least thirty minutes before the older Abba Zabba-colored woman in the white nurse's uniform came home. Esta told Lacy that when the big hand on the clock was on the six it would be eight-thirty and he wouldn't be alone after that. Sometimes Lilly would stay with Lacy on days when her ex-husband wouldn't stop by for them to hug each other a lot. During the thirty minutes Lacy was alone, he was terrified. They would leave the TV on for him and tell him to watch all of the cartoons he wanted, including his favorites, Mighty Mouse and Savoir Faire. Lacy would put on a brave face and smile as they left but he was frightened to be alone and always felt a presence in the house and heard noises. As he watched the cartoons he could feel someone or something near him that felt like energy, a force, or a being of some kind, and Lacy refused to look away from the TV. He believed looking away from the TV and in the direction of the force or energy would cause the energy to transform into some type of being and he was terrified of that.

THE NOISES FROM THE ROOM

After thirty minutes of sheer terror, Lacy would hear the front door being unlocked and knew that was the Abba Zabba-colored woman coming home from work. She would say hello, eat breakfast, and go to bed. Lacy didn't care that she always seemed too tired to spend time with him and went to bed because he was just happy not to be alone in the house. Lacy would watch TV and play with blocks and other toys until eleven-thirty, when the Abba Zabba woman would get up and ask if he was hungry. He would say yes and she would make him a peanut butter or Devil's Food spread sandwich served with milk or juice. Lacy would say thank you and she would say you're welcome. She always seemed so happy at that time of the morning because minutes later, a man would come to visit. His name was Jasper. He was about 5 feet 10 inches tall, with a dark caramel complexion, a close-cropped haircut, and very clean-shaven face apart from his mustache. Jasper drove a green MG convertible sports car that Lacy liked but didn't like riding in it because Jasper liked going fast on curves and Lacy felt very unsafe in a car without a top. When Jasper would arrive, the Abba Zabba woman would say, "JASPER IS HERE!" She was so happy when Jasper came over that she would smile the whole time at Jasper and forget that Lacy was even there. When Jasper would enter the door, he and the Abba Zabba woman would kiss and hug but he would keep the hugging short as he would see Lacy watching, and something about Jasper's eyes and behavior told Lacy that Jasper wasn't comfortable with him watching. The Abba Zabba woman would notice that Jasper grew uncomfortable, so she would tell Lacy to watch TV then the two would go into the kitchen and have lunch together. After they had lunch, Jasper would surprise Lacy with another bag of small plastic Army men for them to play war. Jasper promised Lacy he would bring a new bag of Army men each time he arrived so they could play Army men. He taught Lacy what the word strategy meant, and told him that the military used strategies to win wars and if Lacy learned strategies he would do well in life. Lacy loved playing Army men with Jasper and never wanted to stop playing, but the Abba Zabba woman would come over to their game and tell Lacy it was time for his nap. Jasper would tell Lacy they had a good game and would play again next time, but he needed his nap so his body could grow strong and healthy. Lacy always liked what Jasper had to say and followed his directions because he trusted him. Jasper had a unique energy and presence that Lacy felt and Lacy could not understand why he spent so much time with the Abba Zabba woman. Jasper would stay with Lacy until he fell asleep but Lacy would wake up in a short while when he heard those same odd noises he had heard many times before. Lacy would sit up on the sofa and listen.

He would get up and walk toward the hall and listen near the Abba Zabba woman's room where the noises were coming from. Lacy would put his ear near the door and hear, "Mhm. Mhm. MMMHHHMM."

Lacy asked, "What are you doing in there?"

There was dead silence for a moment then the Abba Zabba woman said, "We're just talking. Go back and lay down on the sofa and sleep."

Lacy would say, "But I heard noises like 'Mhm, mhm. MMMMHHHMMM."

The Abba Zabba woman said, "We are just talking Lacy."

"Why do you have the door closed?" Lacy asked.

The Abba Zabba woman said, "You need to stop listening to everything and go back and lay down so we can finish talking. We'll be out soon, okay?" Lacy said okay, but as he walked away from the door, he turned back slowly to listen and again the noises began. *MHM, MHHM. MMMMHHHMMM,* "OH Jasper." Lacy wondered what they were doing in there but he knew they were not just talking and the Abba Zabba woman was lying. Lacy did not like being lied to about anything. Lacy once told Esta he doesn't like being lied to because it feels terrible when it's happening. Esta asked Lacy how he knew a lie was happening and Lacy said because he feels very sorry for the person, and the light around them gets a little darker for a moment, like when a light flickered. When Lacy told Esta this, she clearly could not look into his eyes and started aimlessly moving about the room they were in.

Shortly after Lacy heard the sounds coming from the bedroom, the Abba Zabba woman and Jasper came out and Lacy would ask if they finished talking. Jasper would grin and say yes but the Abba Zabba woman wouldn't grin at all and would look bothered by Lacy's question.

Jasper would leave and the Abba Zabba woman would take Lacy with her to run errands and go grocery shopping. After doing errands they would return home and drop off the groceries and anything else purchased along the way, then they would get back in the car and head out to pick the others up from school. The Abba Zabba woman never really had conversations with Lacy, she just asked questions.

"Lacy, what do you think of Jasper?"

"I think Jasper is a neat guy and a good person," Lacy said. She asked Lacy if he thought Jasper really liked her. Lacy said, "Yes, he likes you a lot, but is he going away somewhere for a long time and not coming back." The Abba Zabba woman asked why Lacy said that and Lacy said he just sees a time when Jasper doesn't come over anymore because something happened to him or is keeping him away.

The Abba Zabba woman got angry and said, "You talk too much. Be quiet! You don't know what you're talking about and always make things up too." Lacy went quiet and thought of Esta. He wished she was with him because he didn't like when the Abba Zabba woman got mad because she looked evil and seemed that way too. Lacy would try to sit very still like a squirrel does when they sense danger. He felt if he didn't move a muscle that she would calm down and pay more attention to the radio playing. As they would pick up the other children, Lacy would get a little excited because he wouldn't be alone, however, he only felt close to Esta and Esta came home later because she would work at the TG&Y store after school. Lacy also felt a bond and close-ness with Gus because Gus' energy seemed friendly, honest, and trust-worthy. Gus was six years older and always seemed to have something to do like tinker with a gadget or construct something. Once they all got home and raced out of the car, Marcel and Horace would run around the front yard pretending to be airplanes, and Randy stood in one place playing with his yoyo that was taken away by the teachers countless times. Randy always counted on the Abba Zabba woman to get his yoyo back from the teachers each and every time. Gus went into the house and began his homework, and then changed clothes so he could go to the Boy Scouts. Randy got kicked out of the Boy Scouts a while back. Odessa and Alexandra went to their room and made chains out of the silver foil wrappers that held chewing gum and listened to Smokey Robinson and the Miracles. Odessa was in love with Smokey Robinson but Alexandra thought he was just another pretty boy. The Abba Zabba woman seemed to have a very odd schedule because some-times she worked in the day and other times at night. On this day, she made dinner then went to bed early so she could work the next morn-ing. Lacy just moved about the yard and house trying to find his place to fit in but quickly made a habit of clinging to Gus before Gus' car-pooled to the Boy Scouts or got involved with homework on other days.

Lacy's place was on a very old rocking chair where he would sit for hours and think about his future, past happenings, and everything in between, while the other children went about their day. As Lacy sat in that rocking chair he would listen to the goings-on in the house, but he was more focused on the goings-on in his head and all that he saw in the future. When Esta would come home, Lacy would jump out of the chair and run to her and give her a big hug, and she would hug him tightly too. She would ask what he did all day and he would mention playing Army men with Jasper, running errands, and looking at the future. Esta would tell Lacy that he should not think about the future so much and think more about now. He told her that he doesn't think about the future, the future thinks about him, and he just sees it happening. Esta really didn't know what to say to Lacy, so she hugged him and looked off into the distance.

CANDY

The goings-on during the day and evening were quite routine. The nights that the Abba Zabba woman had to work would be the nights that the sisters would come together in the kitchen and make different snacks depending on what Esta brought from the store. Caramel candy, sweet popcorn balls, peanut butter cookies, or sugar cookies were just a few of the choices they would make, and Randy would usually do something to ruin the batter or take a great deal of the snacks when they were made and lock himself in the bathroom to eat them. The sisters would bang on the door and threaten to beat him if he didn't come out of the bathroom with everything that he took. Randy would yell through the door saying he only took a couple and that it wasn't a big deal. As he yelled through the door, it was easy to tell that he stuffed his mouth with a lot of the snacks to finish them before opening the door. When he would finally open the door, he would explain that he only had two cookies or one piece of caramel or that he had one sweet popcorn ball and had eaten half of it while the other half was in his hand as proof. The sisters weren't buying his lie. They yanked him out of the bathroom and worked him over for stealing and lying and told him not to do it again. Of course, he did it again, and again, and again. The Abba Zabba woman would hear of Randy's beatings the next day when he would slightly change the story and say that he was only helping the sisters cook and they turned on him for no reason. The Abba Zabba woman always took Randy's side no matter what and that was the way it was. Randy could do no wrong, even if the wrong he did was so crystal clear to see. The Abba Zabba woman had an idea after that. She asked Jasper to stay with them at night when possible while she worked so he could keep an eye on them and make sure they didn't get too far out of control. This was great for Lacy because his Army men pal would be over for longer and he could also learn more about strategy. Everyone liked Jasper, but Randy gave Jasper a difficult time because Randy didn't really listen to anyone but the Abba Zabba woman. She sometimes had difficulty getting him to listen but once she looked him in his eyes and gave an order, Randy would stop what he was doing and listen or at least pretend to listen. Because of Jasper's work schedule, he would have to leave early in the morning before sunrise to work as a fireman. This was the new routine for quite some time and it was great having a man around the house at night as a father figure for everyone and to keep the house balanced and in order. By the time the children woke up for school the next day, Jasper had left for work and a new day had begun.

Often, the other children would let Lacy sleep as they got ready for school, but Lacy didn't want to sleep and wanted to go to school too, so he wouldn't be home alone. Every once in a while, school would let out at noon so the other children would come home earlier. That suited Lacy just fine. Other times, one of the children might stay home because they were sick or chose not to go on a school field trip, and that was another great day for Lacy. There were times when Randy would stay home because he got suspended from school for talking back too much to teachers, playing with his yoyo in class when told to stop, or using foul language at the teacher or another student. He probably picked up some of the foul language from Lilly, Shirley's mother. Lacy thought Randy was a bit peculiar and watched him like a child watched a squirrel to see what it would do next. When Randy would stay home with Lacy during suspensions from school he would pull all types of capers around the house. Playing with matches, making prank calls, eating up the cookies the sisters made, and giving one or two to Lacy so he wouldn't take all the blame. Randy always made sure to get some-one else in trouble with him if he could so he would not be the only one to answer for wrongdoings. One day when Randy stayed home due to a suspension, he was sitting on the sofa while Lacy was sitting in the rocking chair watching TV. Randy knew Lacy liked the butterscotch candies that were in the candy jar up on the mantel that Lacy couldn't reach, so Randy asked Lacy if he wanted some.

"Yes!" Lacy said, as he got excited and looked over to the candy dish.

Randy said, "No sweat. Coming right up! Anything for my little brother. Anything you want you just tell me and I'll get it for you." Lacy didn't know what to make of those statements since most things Randy did ended up getting him into trouble. Lacy asked Randy if they would get into trouble by taking the candy and Randy asked Lacy if he was going to tell that he had candy. Lacy said that he told Esta everything. Randy said, "Yeah, well don't tell her about this." Lacy said okay, but he planned to tell Esta anyway because he always told her everything since he trusted her so much. Randy took a few pieces of the candy from the glass candy dish and went back to sit on the sofa. Lacy looked at Randy wondering why Randy didn't give him the candy. Just then, Randy said, "Lacy, do you still want the candy?" Lacy said yes. Randy said, "You can have a piece of candy if you do something for me."

Lacy asked, "What do you want me to do?" Of course, Lacy thought Randy wanted him to do something like steal cookies or light matches, but Randy had something else in mind.

Randy said, "Come over here with me." Lacy got out of the rocking chair and walked over to Randy with eyes of wonder and question in his face. As Lacy got close to Randy, about three feet away, Randy said to stop right there. Randy said, "Watch this." He pulled out his penis and started jerking it. Lacy asked Randy if he had to go to the bathroom and Randy said no. "This is what adults do when they want to feel good. Do you want to try?" Lacy said no. Randy said, "Just try it. It's not a big deal and I'm trying to teach you something. Just try it and I'll give you a piece of candy." Lacy asked why Randy wanted him to pull on his penis and Randy said because it feels better when someone else does it. Randy said, "It's just like pulling on my finger and feels the same so it won't feel weird and you'll get candy after." Lacy said okay. He pulled on Randy's penis and Randy quickly said, "If you put your mouth on it, it will taste just like this candy." Lacy looked at Randy and asked if his penis tasted like candy too. Randy said, "Yes! All penises taste like candy. Try it and you'll see, but you have to suck on it like sucking on candy to get the sweet flavor out. If you try it I'll give you all the candy." Lacy didn't say anything, he just looked at Randy as he tried it.

Lacy said, "It doesn't taste like candy."

Randy said, "You barely tried it, you have to really suck." So, Lacy tried again, and Randy said, "That's it. Like that."

Lacy said, "It doesn't taste like candy and I don't want to do it anymore."

Randy said, "Then you won't get the candy."

Lacy said, "I don't want the candy."

"You better not tell anyone about this."

"Why?"

Randy said, "Because I'll blame you and say you asked to do it and no one will believe what you say."

Lacy said, "This is why you always get into trouble. You do things you're not supposed to do and you lie all the time."

Randy stood up and pushed Lacy down and said, "Just remember what I said. No one will believe you." For the first time in Lacy's life, he felt betrayed and tricked. He got up and told Randy something was wrong with him and one day he would be sorry. Randy said, "You don't scare me, you're just a punk kid."

Lacy said, "It's not me that will scare you. Your future will get you."

Randy pushed Lacy down again and said, "Go to the devil."

Lacy said, "No, that's where you're going."

Randy said, "You don't know what you're talking about and you always say things that make no sense. I'm gonna eat the candy myself and you get none." Lacy just stared at Randy as he went back to the rocking chair. Randy asked why Lacy kept staring at him but Lacy said nothing. Randy said, "You better stop staring at me," but Lacy kept staring. Randy said, "I'm going to the kitchen to get more cookies and when I get back, you better stop staring." When Randy came back to the living room, Lacy was still staring at Randy. Randy said, "I'll give you three seconds to tell me why you're staring, then I'm gonna yank you outta that chair and hurt you."

Lacy said, "I'm staring at your life. It's not going to be good for you. You will never forget this day and neither will I, but I will be okay and you won't be." Just then, the Abba Zabba woman began unlocking the door.

Randy said, "Remember, don't you say a word 'bout this." Lacy just turned and looked at the TV. The Abba Zabba woman came in and said hi to Lacy, and Randy ran up to her and gave her a hug. She smelled the cookies on Randy and asked if he'd been eating cookies and he said, "Yes, Lacy wanted some so I got some for us." The Abba Zabba woman looked at Lacy with disapproval but didn't say anything to him as she turned and headed for the bathroom while telling Randy not to take cookies without asking. "Yes Mom," Randy said. As the Abba Zabba woman was in the bathroom hissing away on the toilet with the door open, she asked Randy what else Lacy got him to do. Randy said, "Oh, we ate cookies and he wanted the butterscotch candy but I told him no. The butterscotch is yours and we aren't allowed." Lacy looked at Randy with eyes that said "do and say all you want because your fate is sealed and I feel sorry for you."

When the Abba Zabba woman came out of the bathroom and into the living room she said, "Lacy, you know better than to ask for cookies this time of the morning don't you?" Lacy said yes. "Then why did you ask for them?" she asked. Lacy looked at Randy and Randy looked at

Lacy with an angry look. She asked again with a stronger and louder voice that she never used with Lacy before. "Why did you ask for the cookies when you know you aren't supposed to have them?" Lacy didn't want to lie but Esta wasn't there and he didn't know what was happening and why the Abba Zabba woman was talking to him like this when she rarely spoke to him.

She moved toward Lacy and Lacy said, "Because I was hungry."

"You weren't hungry, you wanted cookies and that's why you asked for them isn't it?" she asked. Lacy began to cry and said yes. She said, "Don't you let me have to have this conversation with you again. Do you hear me?" Lacy said yes as he sat in the rocking chair with tears flowing down his face. She went to the kitchen and Randy stood and stared at Lacy with a big grin because he got away clean with his wrongdoings. Lacy just stared back at Randy with tears flowing from his eyes as he dropped his head slightly while still looking at Randy. He looked at him with a look that must have scared Randy because Randy stopped grinning.

"Remember what I told you about your life?" Lacy asked Randy. Randy didn't say anything and seemed to freeze up. Lacy said, "It's already happening, and all that you're doing to me and others will come back to you like a slingshot. Laugh all you want but I will laugh later." Randy snapped out of his frozen state and told Lacy he was stupid and what he says doesn't matter because Mom believes him and always does. Then, Randy went to the kitchen to charm the Abba Zabba woman for some cookies but she told Randy to get ready for school because she spoke to the school and they said he could go back. Randy wasn't excited about that and said he didn't feel well and wanted to stay home.

The Abba Zabba woman said, "No, you're going to school and you will behave." Randy begged to go the next day instead and the Abba Zabba woman told him to hurry up and change because he was going and that was that.

Randy stormed out of the kitchen with slumped shoulders and an angry look on his face. He walked by Lacy slowly and said, "You better not say anything about what happened earlier." Lacy would not even

look at Randy. The Abba Zabba woman told Lacy to turn off the TV
because he was going with her to drop Randy off at school. After Randy
came out dressed and ready to go, he was playing with his yoyo.

The Abba Zabba woman said, "You're leaving that at home," and
Randy pitched a fit and told the Abba Zabba woman that the teachers
lied on him and that he didn't play with the yoyo in class.

He said, "They are just jealous that I have a better yoyo than the
other kids and that's why they took it." The Abba Zabba woman looked
at Randy and said if he got it taken away again he would not get it back.
Randy grinned and said okay, as he began playing with the yoyo and
walked out of the house to the car.

Army Men and the Dream

After the Abba Zabba woman and Lacy dropped Randy off at school, they returned home and Jasper's car was parked on the street right outside the house.

Lacy said, "Jasper's here."

The Abba Zabba woman said, "Yes, he's here. He's going to watch you for a little while so I can run a few errands."

"Okay," Lacy said. Lacy couldn't wait to jump out of the car and see Jasper. The Abba Zabba woman and Jasper got out of their cars and hugged each other briefly and said they'd see each other in a little while.

Then Jasper said, "Well Lacy, let's go for a ride." Once they got into Jasper's MG convertible, they were off. Lacy would look up at Jasper as Jasper drove the car because he looked like a race car driver as he made his turns. Jasper really liked driving that car but Lacy would ask Jasper if he would slow down on turns because Lacy thought he would fly out of the car. Jasper said, "There's no need to worry Lacy, you're sitting pretty low in the car and you will not fly out, but I will slow down."

"Thank you, Jasper," Lacy said. "Where are we going?" Lacy asked.

"You'll see," Jasper said. As they drove up streets and around turns for a while, Lacy heard his all-time favorite song come on the radio – "My Cherie Amour" by Stevie Wonder. Lacy started singing along with Stevie Wonder and Jasper asked, "Isn't that your favorite song?"

Lacy said, "Yes, how did you know that?"

"Esta told me."

Lacy looked around for a moment then asked, "When did she tell you that Jasper?"

Jasper said, "Oh, I don't remember but she told me."

"Why did she tell you that Jasper?"

Jasper said, "We were talking one day and she was telling me about you and how you two spend a lot of time together."

Lacy said, "Yes, I love Esta and she's great! She doesn't have as much time to spend with me like before because she's going to graduate soon."

Jasper said, "Graduate? That's a big word Lacy, do you know what it means?"

Lacy said, "Yes. Esta told me. It means you've finished one part of learning and are ready to move on to another part of learning."

Jasper said, "Wooow! That's right. Good for you Lacy. Esta teaches and helps you a lot, doesn't she?"

"Yes," Lacy said. "She's the one I'm with most of the time. The other girls spend some time with me but Esta is the only one that gives me a bath, gets my clothes ready, fixes my dinner, and talks to me before bed. She also reads to me and teaches me how to read and speak properly. I even sleep with Esta in her bed and she talks to me after bad dreams."

"Bad dreams?" Jasper asked. "What kind of bad dreams Lacy?"

Lacy said, "I've only told Esta about the dream I keep having but I can tell you since you speak with her about me."

Jasper said, "Thank you, Lacy. It makes me feel very special knowing that you will share your dream with me."

Lacy said, "Good. The dream I keep having is of me as an adult but not in the future." Jasper looked at Lacy and asked if he was an adult now in the dream. Lacy said no. "It was a long, long time ago in a different world. I am an adult man and I think I am as tall as you in my dream, Jasper. My shirt is torn and dirty and my pants are also torn and dirty. My pants stop way before my ankles and I have no shoes or socks but I am running as fast as I can through bushes and trees. I get chased by many people yelling and screaming 'Find him!' and I can hear dogs barking and guns being shot. I can tell all of the people are only chasing me as if I ran away or left when I wasn't supposed to have left. I really think the people chasing me want to hurt me so I run to get away from them but I get really tired of running and feel my heart beating hard in my chest. When I can't run anymore, I run and jump into some bushes and sort of lay down to hide so they won't see me. It works. The people and the dogs run past me and the dogs don't even know I'm there, but so many people pass by and I can still feel my heart beating so hard in my chest. As people run by, some of the people shoot their guns and one of the bullets hits me in the chest and that's when my heart beats faster making a sound in my head like 'dooooooooooot, dooooooooooot, doooooopot, dooooooooooot, dooooooot, doooot, dooooot, doooot, doooot, dooot, doooot, dooot, dooot, doot, dot, d'. Then I wake up on the last sound. I think my heart panics then stops at the end and I think I wake up before I die, because when your heart stops you die right?" Jasper's eyes widened as he just looked forward at the road. "Right Jasper?" Lacy said.

"Yes. Right. Well, not always. Sometimes the heart can stop and start again if not too much time has passed."

Lacy said, "I'm glad I wake up from the dream on the last doot because I don't know what would happen if I didn't wake up. I could die in my sleep."

"No Lacy, it's just a dream and you won't die if you don't wake up before the last doot. How long have you been having this dream, Lacy?" Jasper asked.

Lacy said, "I think it started after a funeral we all went to a long time ago, but it happens each week. I used to be really scared and scream when I woke up, but Esta told me not to be scared and that we all dream scary dreams."

Jasper said, "That's right. We all dream and sometimes the dreams can be scary, funny, or sometimes make no sense but they are only dreams."

"Right!" Lacy said. "Jasper?"

"Yes, Lacy."

"You want to know what else Esta does for me?"

"Sure. What else does she do for you, Lacy?"

"Sometimes when I wake up my eyes are glued shut because she says I get a lot of goop from my eyes that stick to my eyelashes. She gives me medicine for that but she uses a warm towel to clean the goop away first so I can open my eyes. No one else does that but Esta. She really likes me a lot."

Jasper said, "My, my, my, you two really do spend a lot of time together."

"Yes! And we're always going to spend time together because we made a promise to always be together."

"That's a great promise you two made."

"Yes. Esta and I make promises all the time. She promised that she would bring me a treat each day from work and I promised that I would practice my numbers. I can count to 100. Do you want to hear me do it?"

"No. No. That's okay," Jasper said. "I believe you. You can count for me later because we are at the surprise now." Lacy looked around and asked what a ho bee shop was. Jasper laughed and said, "It's not a 'ho bee' shop, it's a hobby shop. It's a place where you can find things that you like to do to have fun with when you're not working or learning. This is where I get the Army men." Lacy lit up like a Christmas tree.

"Neatoooo!" Lacy said, as he jumped out of the car and headed for the door.

"Wait up Lacy," Jasper said, "don't go in without me."

"Okay," Lacy said, as he looked in the store window, anxiously waiting to go in. Once they got inside, Lacy was taken by all of the model airplanes, cars, kites, and gadgets the store had.

Jasper grabbed Lacy by the hand and led him to the Army men and said, "Here we are."

Lacy could not believe his eyes when he saw how many packs of army men and other military men and props there were. "WOOOOOW Jasper!" Lacy said. "If we had all of this stuff we could take over the world with our army."

Jasper laughed and asked, "Is that what you want Lacy? To take over the world?"

"No," Lacy said. "But, we could. No one would want to have a war with us."

Jasper said, "And that's the same with intelligence. If you practice being intelligent you will have fewer problems than if you don't practice intelligence."

"What's intelligence?" Lacy asked.

Jasper said, "It's your ability to learn and remember things. That is what school is for and where you go to learn."

"I have a good memory," Lacy said.

Jasper said, "I know you do. SAY IT LOUD!"

Lacy said, "I'M BLACK AND I'M PROUD!"

Jasper laughed and asked Lacy who sings that song, and Lacy said the soul man James Brown. "You do have a good memory, Lacy. Why don't you pick out a couple of packs of Army men so you and I can work on war strategies when we get back?"

"Okay!" Lacy said. After they got the Army men, they got into the MG and headed back home, and Lacy was so thrilled to have more Army men that he didn't even notice Jasper's driving. Once they got home, Lacy ripped open the bag of Army men and couldn't wait to play. Jasper made sandwiches for them to eat while they played, and they had a wonderful time. After much time passed, the Abba Zabba woman came home and it was time for Lacy's nap and for the Abba Zabba woman and Jasper to go to the bedroom to talk as they always did. On this day, Lacy wasn't too sleepy and couldn't go to sleep, so he sat up on the sofa and just listened to the Abba Zabba woman and Jasper making their funny talking noises. So Lacy wouldn't pee on himself, he usually wore blue or pinstriped overalls with one side unfastened so he could pull the fastened strap down to use the bathroom when necessary. He went to the bathroom while listening to the adults talking, then came back and sat on the sofa and stared at the front door screen. The front door was always open in the afternoons but the screen was locked. Lacy thought to himself, *they always call me the professor so I should be able to open that screen.* Lacy got off the sofa and walked over to the screen door and looked at the handle to figure out how to open it. He pushed up his glasses and looked for the button that he had seen Esta push many times. He pressed and pushed and *click*. His eyes widened. He wondered if the door would open, so he slowly pushed the lever down and it did. He stood there for a moment, hoping the Abba Zabba woman didn't hear the door open. He was afraid to go out because he watched the Alfred Hitchcock movie "The Birds" with the other children during one of the cookie-making nights. After that night, Marcel told Lacy that when he went outside a big bird would grab him and take him away, so he better not go outside alone. As Lacy stood by the screen door he thought about what Marcel told him. After a few moments, he decided to make a break for it and walk to the school where he and the Abba Zabba woman dropped the boys off so he could see Gus. Since he and Esta would go to that school field to play, he believed he remembered how to get there. He made his move. He carefully walked out of the house and deliberately didn't close the screen door all the way so it wouldn't make a loud sound. He walked down the driveway and down the street. As he passed neighbors he waved at them as if he was on a nice daily stroll. There was a neighbor, Mrs. Sanchez, on the other side of the street that looked at him wondering why he was out alone. The neighbor who lived just a little further down, Rhea, who was much older, said to be careful walking and not to go too far, and Lacy said okay.

As he got to the end of the street, he made a left turn around the corner and walked further to make a right turn, and from there the school was about 100 yards ahead. Once Lacy got to the school he realized he didn't know which classroom Gus was in so he just stared at the classroom doors. As he stood there in his overalls with the one side unfastened, he kept staring at the doors until one door sort of sparkled with light for just a moment and the sparkle went away. Lacy decided to go to that door. As he walked down the small grass hill of the school toward the classrooms, he was getting excited because he wanted to see Gus and thought if he got Gus out of class they could play. When he got to the door he didn't waste a second. He knocked on the door and stood back a little to avoid getting hit by the door. Lacy thought Gus would open the door but instead, a woman with a big bright smile opened the door and said, "Hi, what's your name?"

Lacy said, "Hi, my name is Lacy," as he tried to look into the classroom.

The teacher said, "It's my pleasure to meet you, Lacy. My name is Mrs. Monroe. Where did you come from?"

"I came from home," Lacy said, as he tried to look into the doorway of the classroom again.

The teacher asked, "Well, where is your home?"

Lacy said, "It's down the street and around the corner and down the street and around the corner again on the right side of the street."

The teacher laughed and said, "You sure know your directions. You're much too young to be in school but I would enjoy having you as a student when you're ready. Who did you come here with Lacy?"

"I came by myself since everyone at home is sleeping." Lacy kept trying to look into the classroom.

The teacher asked, "Are you looking for someone Lacy?"

Lacy said, "Yes. I'm looking for my brother Gusty."

"Gusty?" the teacher asked.

Lacy said, "Yes, Gusty."

The teacher said, "OOOHHH! You mean Gus?"

Lacy said, "Yes. That's who I'm looking for. Is he here?"

The teacher said, "He certainly is. Lacy, we were just about to do some exercises. Why don't you come in and join us?"

Lacy said, "Sure! I watch Jack LaLanne do exercises all the time on TV."

The teacher laughed and said, "Lacy, you are full of surprises. Why don't you go next to your brother Gus and he can show you how we exercise?"

Lacy said, "Okay. Thank you, Mrs. Monroe." Lacy quickly walked over to Gus as the other students were giggling and saying hi to Lacy. Lacy wore a big smile and said hi to everybody. Once he got to Gus, Lacy said, "Hey Gus, I came to get you out of class so we could play."

Gus said, "What are you talking about? I'm in school and you're not supposed to be here and you're going to be in trouble."

Lacy looked at Gus and said, "But nobody is awake at home and I was by myself, so I came to play with you and I got here just in time because all of you are playing."

"We're not playing, we're exercising, and you're not supposed to be here."

"Are you mad at me Gus?" Lacy asked.

"No," Gus said. "I just think you're going to be in big trouble for leaving the house and coming up here."

Just then, the teacher said, "Okay everyone, out of your seats and stand next to your desks. Ready? Go." The first person in each row leaned down and rolled a bouncy ball between their legs to the person behind them, and once the ball got to the last person they would reverse the action until the ball got back to the first person that rolled it. This game went on for about three minutes.

Lacy looked at Gus and said, "Isn't this fun Gus?"

Gus looked at Lacy and smiled and said, "Yeah." Then Gus said, "You know what Lacy? I'm glad you came but I hope you don't get into trouble." Lacy never thought about the trouble part until Gus mentioned it a few times.

Once the game was over, Mrs. Monroe said, "Gus, so that no one will worry where Lacy is, would you take him home?"

Gus said, "Yes Mrs. Monroe."

Mrs. Monroe asked the class to say goodbye to Lacy and as the class said goodbye, Lacy wore a big smile and said, "Goodbye everybody, I had a good time."

Then he asked Mrs. Monroe if he could come back and she said, "Maybe we should wait until you're a little older because this class is for older children, but I'm glad I met you and hope to see you when you start school."

Lacy said, "Okay. I'll see you when I'm older."

Gus and Lacy left the classroom and as soon as they got outside Gus said, "Lacy, you shouldn't leave the house and come to the school like you did because you could get hurt or a stranger could take you."

Lacy said, "But I wanted to see you and I had no one to play with."

"I know, but you shouldn't do it."

Lacy said, "Okay."

As they walked home, Gus said, "Lacy, you know what?"

"No. What?"

"I'm glad you came to my school today."

"REALLY?"

"Yeah! You got me out of class just in time, because we were doing to take a spelling test after exercises."

Lacy looked at Gus and asked, "Don't you like spelling tests, Gus?"

Gus said, "They're okay. I don't know how to spell all of the words for this test, but now I have more time to study the words thanks to you."

Lacy grinned and said, "See! There was a reason for me to come to see you today."

Gus said, "Yeah, but just remember what I said about walking to my school alone."

Lacy said, "Okay Gus," as he looked up at Gus, smiling.

While the two were walking home, they passed Rhea and she said, "Hi Gus. Is everything okay?"

"Yes. Lacy walked to my school and my teacher asked me to take him home."

"To your school?" Rhea asked.

"Yes," Gus said.

"OOOHH! Lacy, I thought you were going to a babysitter's house or something. You shouldn't bother them at school. Shame on you."

Gus said, "It's okay. I'm taking him home."

Rhea said, "You're such a nice brother to have Gus. Lacy, you ought to thank Gus for being so nice."

Lacy looked at Gus and said, "Thank you," with a happy smile, then he looked at Rhea with concern as to why her words were coming out slurred like that and why she was outside standing around. Moments later, they got to the front door and Gus noticed the screen was slightly open.

"Lacy, did you leave the screen open?"

"Yes," Lacy said.

Gus said, "You can't do that because someone could come in and steal things."

Lacy said, "But I didn't want them to hear me leaving."

Gus said, "I don't care. You can't leave the screen open. I won't tell that you did that but don't do it again."

Lacy said, "I won't, I promise."

Gus told Lacy to sit on the sofa, the exact place Lacy was tired of sitting before he went to see Gus. Gus said, "I'm going to wake up Mom and Jasper." Lacy didn't say anything and just sat on the sofa and waited with a look of concern on his face. He could hear the conversation going on between Gus and the Abba Zabba woman as Gus explained how he was not at school because he had to bring Lacy home.

"What?" The Abba Zabba woman came out quickly and asked what was going on as she raced down the hallway and looked at Lacy. She asked if he'd been out of the house and he said yes. She asked why he did that and he said he wanted to see Gus. The Abba Zabba woman told him he should have asked her if he wanted to see Gus. She asked Lacy how he got the door open and Lacy said he pushed the button on the screen. Just then, Jasper came out and asked Lacy if he was okay and how he remembered the way to the school. Lacy said he watched as he went to pick up and drop off the rest of the children. Jasper grinned and asked how Lacy knew which classroom to go to for Gus.

"I just knew," Lacy said. "I got there and I just knew, so I knocked on the door and Gus was there."

Jasper just laughed and said, "You're pretty smart Lacy, but it's important to be careful and let others know where you're going before you go. Next time you feel like going somewhere make sure you knock on the door and wake us up and let us know." Lacy said okay. The Abba Zabba woman just shook her head then Jasper put his arm around her to calm her, then the Abba Zabba woman told Gus he could go back to school.

Gus said, "Okay, see you later Lacy." Then he closed the screen and ran off. Jasper told Lacy he could watch TV and that they were going to take a nap.

Jasper said, "Remember, knock on our door if you need anything and before you decide to go somewhere." Lacy said okay.

TRUTH

Later that day after the adults woke up, Jasper came out of the room and said, "Come with me Lacy, let's go pick everyone up from school."

Lacy hopped off the sofa with a huge grin and said, "Here I come." After picking everyone up from school, Jasper drove them to the TG&Y where Esta was working so each child could pick out a snack. As the children went to pick out snacks, Jasper spoke to Esta. Instead of a snack, Lacy grabbed a toy airplane made out of soft compressed wood that was about a foot long.

He ran back to Jasper and asked if he could have that instead of a snack and Jasper said, "Sure, but if you want a snack you can still get one, then you can stay with the others until it's time to leave."

Lacy said, "THANK YOU JASPER!"

After Lacy picked out the candy necklace that made him feel like a king, he went to the others, but noticed Esta and Jasper talking and that Esta seemed bothered as she kept looking at Lacy. Jasper noticed her looking at Lacy and Lacy looking at them, so he smiled at Lacy, tapped the counter a couple of times, then walked over to where the children were and said, "Okay everybody, it's time to go." The snacks were paid for and everyone piled into the car and headed home. When they all got home, the Abba Zabba woman told Jasper she got called into work and had to go in for a few hours since someone else had to leave work early. She asked Jasper if he could stay the night but he wasn't able to and this was clearly upsetting to the Abba Zabba woman. Jasper said goodbye to everyone without smiling as much this time and left. The Abba Zabba woman quickly got ready for work and left as soon as she was ready. Odessa and Alexandra flipped a coin to decide who was going to get dinner ready for everyone and the boys began playing and watching TV. Oftentimes when the girls would cook, Lacy would watch. Odessa once asked Lacy why he liked to watch them cooking and he told Odessa he wanted to learn because one day he would have to cook for himself. The other boys were told to do any homework that was assigned until dinner was ready. When Odessa said dinner was ready, everyone went to eat, but there would be jokes about Odessa's cooking because she made pancakes one day that came out green. Ever since, she had been teased about her cooking. Lacy liked Odessa's cooking and ate everything on his plate. After dinner, Alexandra and Odessa cleaned the dishes and the kitchen while the boys watched TV. Lacy would try to help the sisters with chores but they would tell him to just play or sit and watch. Lacy would hear the sisters complain about chores so much that he was hoping to lighten their load by helping out whenever he could because he knew the sooner they finished the sooner they could play or spend time together.

After Odessa and Alexandra finished cleaning, they stayed in the kitchen and took turns speaking on the phone while giggling to each other about whom they were speaking to. Lacy would ask who they were speaking with and the girls would say, "None of your business, now go with the others and watch TV." Lacy would pretend to go watch TV and hide behind the wall that separated the kitchen from the living room and listen to the sisters on the phone. When Lacy heard the sisters finishing on the phone, he went near the other boys and pretended to watch TV. The sisters told Marcel and Horace to get cleaned up and ready for bed since they had school the next day. Randy and Gus stayed up later since they were older but Gus decided to go in the back and play with his Hot Wheels that he and Randy often fought over. Randy would either steal or damage Gus' Hot Wheels, but Gus never stood for Randy's behavior and wrung his neck. Of course, Randy would later tell the Abba Zabba woman and Gus would have to compromise in a way that would please Randy. Since the other boys were in the back of the house, that left Randy and Lacy in the living room watching TV while Alexandra and Odessa were having a private giggly conversation at the dinner table and wanted to be left alone. A few moments later, there was a knock at the door but it was more of a slow *thud, thud, thud* that Lacy had not heard before, and the sisters looked surprised by the knock too. Both sisters looked at each other with concern and made their way to the front door.

They asked who was at the door and the voice said, "It's the Boston Strangler..." Immediately, the sisters ran from the door and got a broomstick and a mop and Randy ran to the back of the house. Lacy's eyes widened because he had heard of the Boston Strangler on TV and was terrified, but he was not going to leave his sisters to handle this alone. He asked what he should do and they told him to go to the back of the house, but he just hid behind the hallway wall not far from the front door. Again, *thud, thud, thud.*

"Go away," Odessa said, as both sisters had their weapons ready and stood with fearful emotion.

Just then, a loud laugh rang out and the voice said, "Hey, it's us, June Bug and Michael." Both girls yelled "you idiots," "dummies," and other names they came up with. They opened the door and chased the boys down the walkway, past the garage, and down the street. Just then, Randy came out and told Lacy he knew it was June Bug playing tricks.

Lacy asked Randy, "If you knew that then why did you run?"

Randy pushed Lacy and said, "I didn't run. I went to the back to protect the others." Lacy looked at Randy and didn't say a word. Then, Randy squinted his eyes a bit and asked Lacy if he said anything about earlier and Lacy said no. Randy said, "Good, and you better not, either." Since the others were in the back and the sisters were outside, Lacy sat in the rocking chair, waiting for the sisters to come back. He could hear the sisters' voices just outside because they came back and were standing near the driveway, laughing and talking with the boys. Randy told Lacy to get out of the rocking chair because he was going to sit there. Lacy said he was already sitting there, so Randy grabbed Lacy's arm and yanked him out of the chair and onto the ground and said, "Don't ever make me ask you twice." Lacy sat on the floor for a moment then got up and went to the screen, hoping the sisters were coming in soon. When he heard Randy get out of the rocking chair, heading toward him, he went outside and ran toward the sisters with Randy right behind him.

June Bug said, "Heeey it's the professor, no, it's Poindexter," as they all laughed because of Lacy's black-framed glasses. The sisters asked what he was doing outside when he should be inside.

Randy quickly said, "I tried to stop him from coming outside but he wouldn't listen to me." The sisters asked Lacy why he didn't listen to Randy and went outside. Lacy didn't say anything and just looked at the sisters. It was clear that Lacy interrupted the sisters' time with the boys, so they were not too pleased with him. They asked Lacy again why he was outside and June Bug and Michael Myers said to let him stay out here, and that he probably just wanted to play.

Alexandra said, "No, something's wrong because I know that look in his eyes." She asked Lacy what was wrong.

Just then, Odessa said, "She's right. That look in his eyes says something's wrong." Alexandra asked Lacy what happened as she squatted down to his level and looked into his eyes. Lacy looked at Randy briefly, then looked back at Alexandra.

Alexandra looked at Randy and asked in a stern voice, "What did you do to him?"

Randy said, "Nothing. I told him not to come outside and he didn't listen."

Odessa said, "Lacy, tell us what happened. You don't have to be scared because we're here and if he did something to you we'll get him."

Alexandra said, "Lacy, if you don't tell us what happened we can't help you and it could happen again."

Randy said, "He's probably going to tell you I took the rocking chair from him."

"Is that it?" Alexandra asked. Lacy said no. "What is it then?" she asked.

"…He asked me to put my mouth on his thing."

"HE'S LYING!" Randy yelled repeatedly. Odessa covered her mouth, June Bug and Michael Myers quit laughing, and Alexandra looked at Randy with an angry look as she asked Lacy if he put his mouth on Randy's thing. Lacy said yes. In an instant, Alexandra leaped and landed on Randy and began beating him with closed fists as Odessa jumped in. June Bug and Michael Myers tried to stop them as Lacy began crying because he somehow felt that this was going to come back to him in a bad way.

June Bug went to Lacy and told him not to be afraid because he was with him. But, Lacy knew June Bug couldn't be there all the time. Randy was screaming and yelling so the neighbors across the street, Mrs. Sanchez and her husband, came over, as well as Lilly, Ruth, Shirley, and Ari. Now the secret was out and everyone knew, and Lacy was terrified about what was going to happen next because Randy always got his way in the end. Lacy's concern was the Abba Zabba woman, but he didn't mention that to anyone. The neighbors pulled the sisters off Randy and asked what happened, and the sisters told the neighbors what Lacy told them. The neighbors looked at Lacy and went to him and asked if this was true. Lacy said yes. The neighbors asked if he was alright and Lacy said yes but he was shaken and tearful because of all the commotion and because he wasn't sure about what was going to happen. Mr. Sanchez, in his thick Hispanic accent, asked why

Randy would do such a thing to his little brother, while Mrs. Sanchez and the others waited for an answer. Randy broke down crying and said Lacy was lying and that he didn't do anything. Just then, Esta arrived home and saw all of the commotion and asked what happened. When she found out, she ran toward Randy to attack him, but Mr. Sanchez blocked her and said beating him up wasn't going to help anything.

"When Mrs. Nelson gets home you can all talk about this. For now, it's best to go inside and not fight, and if you want me to stay for a while I will."

Mrs. Sanchez said, "That a good idea. You stay with them, and Esta you can call Mrs. Nelson to let her know what happened."

Esta said, "Alexandra should call since Lacy told her what happened, and I'll stay with Lacy."

Odessa said, "I'll stay with Lacy too," while the other children gathered around wondering what happened to Lacy. The Abba Zabba woman was called and there seemed to be a bit of confusion during the call between Alexandra and the Abba Zabba woman as Alexandra spoke to her. Alexandra started crying a little while speaking with the Abba Zabba woman as it seemed like the Abba Zabba woman wasn't letting Alexandra finish her sentences. When they finished talking, Alexandra told Esta that Mom was coming home in a little while and no one was to harm Randy. When Esta heard that, she grabbed Lacy's hand and took him to her room and hugged him tightly and told him how worried she was that such a thing happened to him. She told him that when she got the chance she would take him away from this place, but he could not tell anyone and it was their secret and only their secret. She made Lacy promise.

"I promise Esta. I won't tell anyone because I want to go away with you and live with you."

Esta said, "I love you Lacy."

Lacy said, "I love you too Esta, but Esta?"

"Yes, Lacy," Esta said with tears in her eyes.

"When you take me with you can Gus come too because I'll miss Gus if he isn't with us."

"No Lacy, No. I can only take you so you can't tell anyone, you hear me?"

"Yes Esta, I hear you. I do. It's just that I really like Gus and I feel he is kind of like me."

"What do you mean kind of like you?" Esta asked Lacy.

"I feel Gus needs someone to be with him like you are for me."

Esta looked at Lacy and said, "You're right Lacy, he does. But I can only take you. Do you think the other boys need someone like me too?"

"No." Lacy said, "The other boys get anything and everything they want and never get into trouble."

"What about the girls, Lacy? Do they need someone like me?"

"No," Lacy said. "They are older like you and can take care of themselves but they aren't treated fairly and they know it. But, they have each other."

Esta said, "You've been thinking about this and figured it out for yourself, haven't you?"

Lacy said, "Yes. I don't feel like I belong here."

Esta said, "Lacy, I know the feeling you mean, and I understand because I feel like that sometimes too."

"You do?" Lacy asked.

"Yes. But don't worry Lacy, we will not be here much longer." Lacy smiled and asked Esta if they could watch an old movie together. Esta said, "Just for a little while because you should be going to bed soon."

Lacy said, "Neeatooo!" He hopped up onto the bed and Esta turned on the TV and told him he could watch and she would be right back. She left to make a phone call in the other room and Lacy could hear her crying so he went to see what was wrong. Esta told him she was okay and had something in her eye and for him to go back and watch TV. Lacy went back to watch TV, but he knew she was sad and he thought it was because of what happened that evening with all of the commotion. As Lacy was watching TV he fell asleep but was woken up by a loud commotion in the living room and was told to wake up by Esta because he needed to answer some questions. Lacy was barely awake as he was led to the living room by Esta and he saw the Abba Zabba woman and Randy standing near each other.

Randy shouted, "There's the rat fink liar."

All of the girls yelled at Randy telling him he was the liar. The Abba Zabba woman stared hard at Lacy and said, "Come over here." Lacy walked with a lot of fear in his face. The Abba Zabba woman said, "Tell me what you said Randy did to you." Lacy looked at Esta since she was the main person that Lacy always had to answer to for almost everything. The Abba Zabba woman said, "LOOK AT ME WHEN I'M TALKING TO YOU AND ANSWER MY QUESTION DAMNIT!" As always, Lacy drifted for a moment so he could understand the word damnit. She said, "Don't stand there like a dummy, answer my question!"

Lacy said he wanted to answer the question but didn't know what damnit meant. This made the Abba Zabba woman so much more furious than she already was, so she grabbed Lacy by the arm and said she'd teach him what damnit meant as she dragged him down the hall toward the bedroom as the girls begged her to stop. Esta tried to plead with her but she slammed the door shut, locked it, and said, "Now, it's only you and me in here and I want you to tell me exactly what you said Randy did."

Lacy was crying and he said, "Randy told me his thing tasted like candy and he would give me some of the butterscotch candy if I put my mouth on his thing."

"PENIS!" she yelled. "IT'S CALLED A PENIS NOT A THING! PENIS! CAN YOU SAY THAT?" Esta was knocking on the door, asking the Abba Zabba woman to let her in and to believe Lacy. "SAY IT NOW," she ordered Lacy.

Lacy said, "Penis."

She then said, "So, you're saying that Randy asked you to put your mouth on his penis and you did it?"

"Yes," Lacy said as he cried.

"YOU'RE A DAMN LIE AND I'M GOING TO TEACH YOU RIGHT NOW ABOUT LYING." She pulled out a belt from the closet and grabbed Lacy by the arm and began beating him as he tried to block the hits with his hand and by jumping around. "The more you move, the more I'll spank the living daylights out of you." Lacy didn't know what all of that meant but he did understand the part about how more moving equated to more of a beating so he tried his best not to move but he couldn't help it. When she finished, she told Lacy to lie on Randy again and see what happens as she tossed the belt on the bed and dashed out of the door. As she dashed out, Esta and the girls dashed in as the other boys stood outside the door looking in.

Esta grabbed Lacy and said, "I'm so, so, so sorry Lacy. I believe you."

The sisters said, "We believe you too and you didn't do anything wrong. You were treated badly by Randy."

Esta said, "I'm here Lacy."

Lacy was crying and said, "Where were you when she was hitting me?"

Esta was at a loss for words for a moment and said, "She locked the door and I couldn't get in, but if I could I would have stopped her." Lacy asked if he could speak to Esta alone, so the other girls hugged Lacy and kissed him with tears in their eyes and said they would leave the room. Once they left the room, Esta asked Lacy why he wanted them to leave. He asked if Esta would close the door and Esta did. They could still hear the Abba Zabba woman yelling from the other side of the house about working hard and having to come home to ungrateful children after washing and wiping natural ass all day.

She said, "You're welcome, now eat up because I have to leave soon." Lacy said okay. Once he finished his pancakes, Esta took him to help him get cleaned up and dressed before she left. As everyone began to leave, Esta told Lacy to sit in his favorite place and that she would turn on the TV for him. He climbed onto the rocking chair and sat like the captain of a ship ready for action, then Esta kissed him on the head and said, "I love you and will see you later."

Lacy said, "I love you too and can't wait to see you later." Moments after everyone left, Lacy got that feeling again. He sensed he wasn't alone and that he was being watched over but this time it was a different feeling. Lacy wasn't as afraid but instead, he was cautious, alert, and very curious. He spoke out and said, "I don't see you but I'm not scared like before. I think you're God. You're the one that Esta tells me about, aren't you?" Just then, Lacy felt a very good feeling around him that made him nervous. He was looking all around the room for something to appear but it didn't. Just as quickly as that energy or feeling entered the room with him, it left after minutes of being there. *Click.* Lacy jerked and was startled by the sound, thinking it was the being or energy he felt but realized it was the front door being unlocked by the Abba Zabba woman. Lacy stayed seated in the rocking chair, and when the Abba Zabba woman came in, she closed the door and walked past Lacy without saying a word. Lacy didn't say anything either. After she put her purse on the table and got a glass of water from the kitchen, she went back to the living room and stood in front of the TV. She said she knew he was probably upset with her but that he must understand lying wasn't a good thing. She said she punished people for lying so as long as he told the truth they would get along just fine. She asked if he understood and he shook his head yes.

She said, "If I were a blind person I couldn't see that you were nodding your head. Did you understand what I said Lacy?"

"Yes."

"Good," she said. "Now, Lilly is coming over soon so we can have tea and talk so you can just keep watching TV."

"Okay," Lacy said.

When Lilly came over she asked the Abba Zabba woman how Lacy was and she said, "Oh, he's fine. I took care of him last night for telling stories."

Lilly said, "I don't think he made that up."

The Abba Zabba woman said, "Now don't you start. I already straightened him out over this lying on Randy and hoped you and I could have tea and talk about other things."

Lilly looked at the Abba Zabba woman with a twisted face and then looked toward Lacy then back at the Abba Zabba woman and said, "Okay, let's have tea." As they were walking to the kitchen, Lilly said, "Hey Lacy, whatcha watchin' there?"

Lacy said, "Felix the Cat."

She said, "Yep, that Felix and his bag of tricks."

Lacy giggled and said, "Yes." Lilly leaned over to Lacy when the Abba Zabba woman was in the kitchen and she told Lacy she believed him and Randy should not have done that. She told Lacy to keep what she told him a secret as she patted his head and quickly went to the kitchen since she heard the Abba Zabba woman's footsteps heading back toward the living room from the kitchen.

The Abba Zabba woman said, "There you are. I thought you got caught up in that darn Felix the Cat that Lacy always watches."

Lilly said, "Well, that cat Felix do be havin' a pretty cool bag of tricks." Then they both laughed hard for a bit then sat down to have a conversation over tea. A little later, the Abba Zabba woman went to the living room and told Lacy he needed to play with toys or find something to do since she was going to take the small TV into the kitchen so she and Lilly could watch the Jack LaLanne show. Lacy could not figure out why they watched Jack LaLanne because they sat in chairs at a card-playing table drinking coffee, smoking, and talking about the exercises Jack was doing. This annoyed Lacy because he felt they were completely wasting time and missing the point of what Jack LaLanne had in mind. Besides, Mighty Mouse was just about to come on and that was more important than blowing cigarette smoke at the TV instead of exercising with Jack. Lacy went to the living room and colored in the coloring book Esta got for him. A little while later, Lilly had to leave because the Abba Zabba woman had to take her nap before Jasper came over. The Abba Zabba woman put the TV back in the living room for Lacy to watch what he wanted, then she told him she was going to take her nap until Jasper came over. Since Jasper was going to stay over a few days a week now, he had his own key. Later, as Lacy was watching "I Love Lucy," Jasper arrived and Lacy was excited to see him. While the Abba Zabba woman was sleeping, Jasper asked Lacy to sit on the sofa with him and spoke with Lacy about what happened with Randy. Lacy asked how he found about it and he said Esta told him. Lacy asked when they spoke since he wasn't over the night before and Jasper said she called and told him because she knew he would see Lacy today and wanted him to know what happened.

Jasper said, "I'm sorry that that happened to you Lacy, it was wrong that Randy did that."

Lacy said, "I'm glad that you believe me Jasper, because Randy is lying and he gets away with everything he does."

Jasper said, "I do believe you Lacy, and one day Randy will get caught and he will learn a big lesson."

Lacy said, "He might get caught but he will never learn a lesson because something is wrong with him." Jasper asked Lacy why he said that and Lacy said, "I just know something is wrong with him because of the way he acts and looks at people. It's as if he can't control himself and he lies all the time and pretends to be a baby when he wants his way. He's much older than me and I don't act like that. Why does he act like that Jasper?"

Jasper said, "Lacy, you're so smart and wise for your age. I don't have an answer for you but I'll think about it."

Lacy said, "Okay," then the two of them watched a few episodes of "I Love Lucy" together. Jasper sat with his arms stretched out on the back of the sofa with his legs crossed and Lacy sat right next to him leaning into him. Jasper was nodding off a little here and there as Lacy would giggle about Lucy's antics on TV. When he looked up at Jasper and saw his eyes closing he stopped giggling out loud because he didn't want to wake him.

A little while later, the Abba Zabba woman came out and saw them sitting on the sofa, put her hands on her hips, and said, "Jasper!"

Jasper woke up and said, "Oh, hi. I must have dozed off."

She said, "Yeah, you must have."

"Why didn't you wake me up?" Jasper said, "I got here and got talking to Lacy and watched TV and just dozed off."

She said, "MMMHHHMM? Okay. Dozed off. Now that you're awake do you want something to eat?"

He said, "Yes. I am hungry. Lacy do you want something?"

Lacy said, "Yes please." The Abba Zabba woman looked at Lacy as if he was causing trouble, so Lacy said, "I'm not really hungry, so I can wait until later."

Jasper said, "What? No way professor. You've got to eat too." The Abba Zabba woman looked at Jasper with squinty eyes and Jasper said, "I know that look, and you don't need to give that to me. Let's get in this kitchen and get some food going."

The Abba Zabba woman said, "Yes, let's. I want to talk to you."

Jasper said, "Of course you do. Lacy, tell me what happens with Lucy."

Lacy kept his head down and softly said, "Okay."

While the two were in the kitchen, Lacy could hear Jasper saying, "Take it easy now. I was just spending time with Lacy. I was going to come in and see you but I fell asleep." The Abba Zabba woman said he'd been acting different lately and that she thinks he's talking to someone else. Jasper said, "Between working, coming over near lunchtime, and coming back at night when I can, my schedule is all over the place. You are really getting upset over nothing." Lacy turned the TV down a bit to listen to what they were saying and was hoping she wouldn't upset Jasper and make him leave. As she continued in on Jasper about not being as available for her phone calls he got quiet and said, "Let's eat, then we can go and talk in the bedroom."

That seemed to get her attention because she said, "Alright Jasper," with a cheerful kind of voice. Then, there were a couple of giggles, and moments later the Abba Zabba woman brought Lacy a sandwich with a huge smile as if she just opened a can of happy in the kitchen. She said, "Here you go, Lacy." Lacy perked up and said thank you. He was surprised at her chipper attitude and liked it since he had not really seen it before. She went back to the kitchen where she and Jasper ate their food and spoke quietly so Lacy couldn't hear. Lacy turned the TV down a couple of times, trying to hear them talking until Jasper asked Lacy if he turned the TV off.

"No, it's on."

"I couldn't hear it so I thought you turned it off. Will you turn it up so I can hear it?" Jasper asked.

"Yes," Lacy said, with a disappointed look on his face. After all, how could he eavesdrop with the TV turned up? He couldn't. That was when he snuck over to the wall separating the kitchen from the living room so he could hear what the adults were talking about. With the loud TV and the adults whispering, Lacy couldn't hear a thing so he went back to the rocking chair and ate his sandwich. The adults stayed in the kitchen so long that Lacy fell asleep and when he woke up, the TV was on but it was turned low. He didn't hear any more talking from the kitchen, instead, he heard those strange sounds coming from the bedroom again. Lacy went to the bedroom door and asked Jasper if he was ready to play Army men.

Jasper said, "No. I don't think I'll have time to play today Lacy, but next time, okay?"

"Okay," Lacy said.

Then the Abba Zabba woman said, "Lacy, we will be out later so please don't knock on the door again. We will come out later."

"Okay," Lacy said, as he walked back to the rocking chair and sat down. As he sat down, he had that look on his face that dubbed him the name 'professor'. He stared off into space with that noggin of his conjuring up something. *It's coming, it's coming, wait for it. An idea is coming.* He grabbed the arms of the rocking chair that he could barely grasp and slowly climbed out of the chair and stood by it for a moment, listening to the noises from the bedroom start up again. He began slowly making his way to the screen door and opened it and made his getaway. He was headed up the street and the only neighbor outside this time was Rhea. She didn't notice him until he passed then she yelled, asking him if he was supposed to be out, and that was when he started running to make sure he made it to the school before getting caught. Up the street, then a left, up the street, around the corner, and there it was. Gus' school. He knew which room to go to and he knew the class and the teacher were waiting for him and that it was time for exercise. Just in time.

Lacy knocked on the door and stepped back, waiting for the teacher to open the door and...out came a student that said, "Hey Gus! It's your little brother. Mrs. Monroe, can he come in?" Mrs. Monroe said yes and told the student to bring him in. Mrs. Monroe didn't look as happy to see Lacy this time but she said hello and was nice anyway. She told him he could go next to Gus and that she would be right back. Lacy thought this was great until Gus told him that his teacher went to call home. Lacy's eyes widened.

"Why would she do that?" Lacy asked.

Gus said, "Because you're not supposed to be here and you're going to get into trouble this time and I'm gonna watch because I told you not to come up here."

Lacy looked at Gus and knew he was upset. He didn't know why Gus was so upset since Lacy was only trying to spend time with him. Lacy looked scared and a girl near Gus' chair said, "Take it easy on him Gus. I wish I had a little brother that came to see me like that." Lacy leaned forward and smiled at the girl, but Gus leaned forward to block Lacy from looking at the girl and wasn't smiling. When Lacy saw Gus' face, he quit smiling and continued to look at Gus' face until the boy in front of Gus asked Lacy if he wanted to see his Super Ball bounce.

Lacy said, "Yeeees."

The boy got up and took the ball out of his pocket and bounced it on the floor and said, "Isn't that neat?"

Lacy said, "Yeees, it's neatoooo." Just then, Mrs. Monroe asked for both Gus and Lacy to come outside, so they got up and headed for the door.

Gus said, "See. You're gonna get it now."

The class said, "Goodbye Lacy!" and Lacy waved and said goodbye and asked Gus if he was going to wave goodbye.

Gus said, "I'm not leaving stupid, you are." As they got outside, Mrs. Monroe asked if Gus would wait with Lacy until he got picked up. Gus said yes. Mrs. Monroe said goodbye to Lacy and told him it was not safe to leave the house by himself so he should not come to the school alone, all while resting her hand on his shoulder. Lacy said okay, then she went back into the classroom. As Gus and Lacy waited outside, Gus told Lacy that the girl that said she wished she had a little brother that wanted to come see her, liked him. Gus said he didn't like talking to her because she talked too much and always wanted to talk to him so he would just ignore her. Gus said, "Now when I go back into class she's going to want to talk to me all about you and drive me crazy."

Lacy said, "I'm sorry Gus. I didn't know that would happen. Can you tell her to be quiet?"

"You don't think I thought of that?" Gus asked Lacy.

"You're pretty smart Gus, I guess you would have thought of that," Lacy said.

Gus just looked at Lacy without smiling and Lacy just stared at Gus, waiting for his next sentence, but there wasn't one. Just then, they noticed Jasper speeding up the street toward the school.

"That looks like Jasper," Gus said to Lacy.

"It is Jasper," Lacy said.

Gus said, "I know it's Jasper."

"Then why did you say it looks like Jasper?" Lacy said.

"Because it's another way of saying he's here or I see him coming."

"Oh, I'll have to remember that," Lacy said. "Gus?" Lacy asked.

"What?"

"When people say it looks like rain do they mean they see rain or it's coming?"

"Yes, you got it," Gus said.

Lacy said, "Neeeaaatooo! Thank you, Gus."

Gus said, "You're welcome." That little exchange seemed to have brought the two closer and warmed Gus up a little more to Lacy with that teaching experience. Gus said, "It's time for you to go home, I hope you don't get into too much trouble. You can walk to Jasper's car alone and I'll see you at home later."

Lacy said, "Okay Gus, see you later," as he ran to Jasper's car while looking back at Gus waving, but he got a little nervous when he got closer to Jasper because Jasper wasn't smiling. "Hi Jasper," Lacy said, as he got into Jasper's car hoping for happy and jolly Jasper to say "Hi Lacy."

Instead, Jasper's face looked a bit stressed when he asked, "Aren't you supposed to knock on the door and ask if you wanted to go somewhere?"

"Yes," Lacy said.

"Then why didn't you knock on the door and ask?"

"Because I was told not to knock on the door again," Lacy said.

"I never told you not to knock on...OH, right. She did say that didn't she," Jasper said. "Listen Lacy. From now on, do not leave the house or go outside unless you get permission from an adult."

"What's a permission?" Lacy asked.

"It's not *a* permission, it's permission," Jasper said. "Permission means being allowed to do something. When you get permission, you're getting an okay from someone to do something."

"I get it," Lacy said. "Before I open the bag of Army men I ask you if it's okay and you say yes or no. Yes means I have your permission and no means I don't have your permission, right?" Jasper's face softened a bit as he looked at Lacy.

A moment later, Jasper put his hand on Lacy's head and softly shook it and said, "You got it Lacy. You're a fast learner." Then, Jasper revved the engine a couple of times and sped the car around to the driveway and headed home. As they were driving, Jasper told Lacy he wasn't in trouble, but if he left the house one more time he would get in trouble with the woman of the house. Lacy knew that meant the Abba Zabba woman. Lacy said okay. "We have a deal, Lacy?" Jasper asked.

"We have a deal," Lacy said.

"Shake on it Lacy," Jasper said as he held his hand out. Lacy grabbed his hand and they shook on it. Moments later, Jasper and Lacy pulled up to the house, got out of the car, and headed toward the front door when they noticed the Abba Zabba woman standing on the other side of the screen door looking at Lacy with a very angry look. But of course, he ruined her talk time in the bedroom with Jasper. Jasper put his hand on Lacy's head as they got closer to the door, and just as they approached the door, the Abba Zabba woman opened the door, reaching for Lacy. Jasper put his body in the way of her hand and said, "No need for that," as he ushered Lacy into the house, shielding him from her. The Abba Zabba woman asked Jasper what he thought he was doing by getting in her way. Jasper looked her straight in her eyes and said, "Lacy and I had a talk and we agreed with a handshake," then he looked at Lacy as he continued to say, "that he will not leave this house unless he gets permission to leave. Isn't that right Lacy?" Jasper asked.

"That's right," Lacy said.

"A handshake?" the Abba Zabba woman asked. "A HAND-SHAKE?" she asked again, louder. She said, "I don't do handshakes and I don't kiss ass, but I'll kick ass and I'll kick his little ass for leaving this house."

"Did you hear what I just said to you?" Jasper asked. "It's over. It won't happen again and you've got my word on that. You need your rest anyway, so why don't you go lay down and I'll join you after I finish speaking with Lacy."

The Abba Zabba woman just looked at Lacy with squinted eyes and a twisted face, her top lip hanging slightly over her bottom lip and her hands on her hips. "Okay," she said. "But! Next time I'll beat your little ass, do you understand me?"

"YES," Lacy said.

"You better! And learn how to work your snaps on the overalls." She turned to Jasper and said, "Alright, I'll be in the bedroom, and Jasper, don't you let me fall asleep before you get there."

"I won't," Jasper said. "I'll be in soon." As she headed down the hall to the bedroom, Jasper looked at Lacy and tilted his head to one side with a look on his face that told Lacy that was a close call and that this couldn't happen again.

Lacy looked at Jasper and said, "I promise I won't do it again Jasper. I promise."

Jasper said, "I know Lacy. I know."

He asked Lacy if he needed anything and Lacy said, "No. I'm fine."

"Well then, I am going to lay down and take a nap."

"I'll be right here when you get up."

Jasper grinned and said, "That's wonderful Lacy," then he turned and went to the bedroom. Lacy pulled out the Army men and began setting them up, and once they were all set up he climbed into the rocking chair and stared at the Army men for a few moments, then he began to drift into his thoughts. He began thinking about that nightmare he kept having of himself being an adult and being chased by many men. He had a clear picture in his mind of the chase and how exhausted he was before he decided to dive into the bushes to hide. As he thought about the nightmare, he believed that the adult version of himself did nothing wrong to those men and felt he was escaping their hate for him. Somehow, after escaping their hate in that life he wakes up in this life just before dying, and then the Abba Zabba woman becomes the new source of hate because it feels as if she was chasing after him with hate. As Lacy thought this through, he began rocking in the rocking chair as he often did once he figured out a problem or had an answer of some sort. He rocked himself right to sleep. Sometime later, the Abba Zabba woman came out of the bedroom and said she was going to pick everyone up from school and stop by the store, and asked Lacy if he wanted to go or stay home since Jasper would still be there sleeping.

Lacy said he would stay home, and she said, "Okay, but remember, if you go outside that door I'll tan your hide, do you understand me?" He understood that because he heard someone say it in a movie just before they whipped someone.

"Yes," Lacy said.

"Okay. I'll be right back," she said. Lacy said okay. She would usually just pick up the boys because the sisters were older and could all walk home, but they would get picked up from time to time along with the boys if they didn't stay after school to spend time with friends. After she left, Lacy spent time thinking on that rocking chair, and moments later Jasper came out.

"Did she leave to pick up the others from school?" Jasper asked.

"Yes," Lacy said.

Jasper said, "Okay. How are you, Lacy?"

"I'm fine," Lacy said.

"That's good. You know Lacy, she's really doing a lot and works many hours, so when she asks for something, no matter what it is, she expects it. If she tells you to do or not to do something and you don't follow orders, that's the same as you saying you don't care what the order was and you're not going to follow the order. Do you understand Lacy?"

"Yes Jasper," Lacy said.

Jasper said, "Good. I know you understand and want to do what's right but it's important for us adults to help you understand things better. You're a good boy Lacy, and I believe you will be a good man too as you practice communicating with others and continue to ask questions when you don't understand something. Okay?" Jasper said.

Lacy said, "Okay. Does communicating mean talking to others and understanding what they mean?"

"Yes," Jasper said, "and it's also helping others understand what you mean with how you communicate or speak to them. If someone has a difficult time understanding what you mean the first time you share your thoughts with them, then simply share your thoughts with that person in another way to help them understand. You can also ask the person to tell you the part that they don't understand so you can clear up that part for them."

Lacy said, "Okay, I understand. It's like when you're making noises in the bedroom with words that I don't understand but when I ask you what you're doing you tell me you're talking with a language that I'll learn as I get older, right Jasper?"

"Hmm," Jasper sighed. "Kind of like that. That is pretty close and I believe you've got the right understanding of what I mean," Jasper said. "I see you have the Army men set up. You did a good job of setting them up Lacy, and both sides are set up strategically as I showed you. Both sides are equally set up to protect themselves from every angle. Bravo Lacy! Bravo! In life, remember to look out for yourself the same way. You have a wonderful smile Lacy and you're always very happy. People might try to make you stop smiling and want to see you unhappy. Do what you can to protect yourself from those people just like those Army men are protecting themselves."

Lacy asked, "You mean people like Randy?"

Jasper looked at Lacy and said, "Anyone Lacy. Anyone. Do you understand?"

"Yes Jasper," Lacy said.

"Very good Lacy. You'll be alright." Just then, the telephone rang, so Jasper went to the kitchen to answer it. As Lacy sat waiting for Jasper, he stared at the Army men and thought about what Jasper just told him about protecting himself. He thought about what happened with Randy and how he could be more careful with Randy and people like Randy. As Lacy was thinking, he heard Jasper saying, "I can't, I just can't. I have to leave and take care of some business and work early in the morning. Okay. Okay. Don't be that way. Okay!" Then, Jasper hung up the phone and quickly walked back from the kitchen to Lacy. Lacy asked Jasper if he was upset. "Just a little frustrated," Jasper said.

Lacy saw that Jasper looked upset, so Lacy was very careful when he asked Jasper if it would upset him to explain what frustrated meant. Jasper just looked at Lacy and rubbed his forehead as he sat down next to him and said, "FRUSTRATED. This is a word that many people experience, so you want to really learn this one Lacy. If you or someone is frustrated, it means you or someone is upset or annoyed. Annoyed means the same thing but you can be frustrated because you heard bad news or you can't solve a problem, and if you are annoyed that is probably because someone did something that you didn't like."

"Okay," Lacy said. "Jasper?" Lacy asked.

"Yes Lacy."

Lacy said, "I asked if you were upset and you said no, but you said frustrated means you or someone is upset or annoyed. It sounds like you're upset and annoyed. Are you?"

Jasper didn't say anything and just looked forward as he and Lacy sat side by side. Lacy didn't want to upset Jasper, so Lacy just looked forward too and kept quiet. A moment or two passed, then Jasper said, "Yes Lacy. You're right. I am upset and annoyed but I didn't want you to have to worry about me being upset so I wasn't being fair and honest with you and I'm sorry. We are always honest with each other and I should have been honest with you."

Lacy said, "It's okay, Jasper. I know you didn't do it to hurt me and you only did it to see me smile instead of be sad. Thank you for being nice to me Jasper. I'm not upset with you. You're my hero!"

"I'm your hero?" Jasper said.

"Yes," Lacy said, "you're my hero because whenever you come over you're like Superman! You make things better and you know so much and help me learn a lot so that I can be a hero too."

"Wow!" Jasper said. "Well, Lacy. I feel very special to be your hero. No one has ever said that to me before."

Lacy said, "Well, I'm saying it to you so that makes you a real hero Jasper."

"Thank you, Lacy," Jasper said. "Listen Professor Lacy, I'm glad that you see me as a hero, but for you to live a very good life please try not to see people as heroes because people can make mistakes and no longer seem like a hero. If a hero no longer seems like a hero because of something they said or did, then that can hurt or be very upsetting or frustrating to the person that saw that person as a hero. That goes for things too Lacy. Some people wear necklaces around their neck or bracelets on their wrists and say that they love those things. Or, idolize people or things, which means they look up to or give great respect to particular people or things like buildings or cars because they believe those people or things make their lives better. They believe that without those people or things that their lives are not as important. You just remember that your life is important because some babies are brought into this world and others don't make it. You made it, so respect yourself and your life more than idols and people who may seem like heroes. You can be respectful of people that deserve respect because they do good things, and you can like things like buildings and cars, but love yourself always. Any questions?" Jasper asked.

"Not right now," Lacy said. "I like how you explain things Jasper, and I hope I can explain things as good as you one day."

Jasper said, "Lacy, I think you will explain things better than me and you will have a good life. And it's okay to want to speak like or do as well as someone else as long as you remember whatever you do must come from you and reflect who you are and not the person that you want to speak like. Am I filling your head up with too much information today Lacy?"

"No," Lacy said, "I like it and want to learn everything you can teach me because I think I will need it all one day. Jasper, I think a time will come when I won't see you and you won't be coming around, so teach me everything you can about being an adult."

"What makes you say that Lacy?" Jasper asked.

Lacy said, "Just like that nightmare I keep having, I keep seeing myself in this house and you're not around anymore." Jasper looked nervous and perplexed at the same time and asked Lacy if someone told him that he would not be coming around anymore. Lacy said, "No. It's just what I feel."

Jasper said, "I see. Well, we can feel things and believe things can happen but it's sometimes just a fear. For example, you are afraid of the boogieman but there is no boogieman, yet your mind tells you there is a boogieman even though you have never ever seen a boogieman. Right?"

Lacy said, "Right, but just because I haven't seen the boogieman doesn't mean there is no boogieman. And because I feel you will not be around one day doesn't mean I'm wrong. Right, Jasper?"

Jasper looked at Lacy again with a nervous half-smile on his face and said, "Anything is possible but we just need to live life and see what happens. But, let's go. We need to go next door and speak with Lilly to see if she can watch you. I have to leave soon and the others won't be home for a while because Marcel needed to get an outfit for a school play. Do you mind staying with Lilly?"

Lacy said, "Sometimes she looks at me as if she is afraid of me and other times she looks at me with a big grin as if she really likes me, so I can stay with her but I'd rather stay with Shirley."

"Well, we may not have a choice, but come with me and we can check to see if she can watch you, otherwise, you will have to stay with Rhea and I don't think you want that."

"You're right, I don't," Lacy said. "She's always laughing and talking to herself as she walks around in her robe."

"Hahahaha! You make me laugh," Jasper said. Jasper knocked on Lilly's door as he looked down at Lacy with a smile, then broke out laughing again.

"Are you laughing at the same thing?" Lacy asked.

"Hahaha. Yes," Jasper said. "It was funny."

Lilly opened the door with a cigarette in hand and her head cocked to the side as if she caught someone in a lie. "What's funny? Did he say something about me?"

Jasper said, "No. Nothing to do with you Lilly, just to do with earlier conversations. How are you?"

Lilly said, "Oh, I'm fine," as she puffed her cigarette and asked to what did she owe the courtesy of his presence since he was too good to ever visit.

Jasper said, "I'm not the social hour type but I'm happy to visit when there is a family get together with both houses."

Lilly looked at Jasper and took another puff and said, "Mmmhhmm? I bet." Lacy was just standing there studying Lilly and thinking she would make a great scary cartoon character in the Bullwinkle cartoon. She could be Natasha's friend.

Jasper said, "Lilly, I have to leave and no one will be home for at least an hour or so. Can Lacy stay with you until everyone gets home?"

Lilly puffed on her cigarette and looked down at Lacy and said, "Sure Jasper. He can stay with me and Shirley can watch him." Lacy's eyes lit up when he found out that Shirley was home and Jasper looked down at Lacy and smiled at him because Jasper knew this made Lacy happy.

Jasper said, "Great. Well Lacy, I'll see you next time, and you be a good boy okay?"

"Okay," Lacy said. "See you next time Jasper."

"Isn't that cute." Lilly said, "See you next time Jasper." Lacy looked at Lilly questionably because he didn't like being mocked that way when he was greeting or saying goodbye to someone, and Lilly was notorious for doing that. As Jasper went back to the house to lock up and leave, Lilly told Lacy he could go to the living room and she would be right there. Lacy went to the living room but watched Lilly as she stood at the front door smoking her cigarette and watching Jasper walk back to the house. She stood there until he walked back to his car and drove away.

MY CHERIE AMOUR

When she closed the door, she sashayed over to Lacy like a rat with a secret and a grin that said "I gotchu now". She took a puff of her cigarette and said, "So, that was a lot of static at your house last night."

"What's static?" Lacy asked.

Lilly's eyes squinted a bit and her grin shrunk into an annoyed smirk as she took a puff of her cigarette and blew the smoke away from Lacy. She then looked at him and said, "Listen little boy, this is not Mr. Rodgers' neighborhood and I'm no Mr. Rodgers looking to teach you every little thing. I said, static, meaning noise and disturbance at your house 'cause a tha boy Randy. He's always up to no good and I try to tell Beatrice 'bout her boy but she dun wanna listen. I'm sorry 'bout what happened to you but that boy is a problem. Beatrice knows it and you know it too, don't cha Lacy?" Lacy just nodded his head yes. Lilly said, "If I was blind I couldn't see you nod your head."

Lacy said, "Yes."

Lilly said, "Thas better. No sense in nodding your head when yo mouth works."

Just then, Shirley came in and said, "Hi Lacy."

"Hi Shirley," Lacy said.

"Do you want to help me fold clothes, Lacy? I just took them out of the dryer," Shirley said.

"Yes," Lacy said.

He asked Lilly if he could help Shirley, and Lilly took another cigarette puff and said, "Go awn. You don't want to talk to me anyway. You
act like you scared a me or sa-mmm, but you don't need to be scared a
me. You need to be scared a that Randy boy cuz sa-mm is wrong wit
him and I know thas right. Now, get awn in there and help Shirley wit
those clothes."

Lacy and Shirley went to Shirley's room and she pushed the door
closed a little. Once they were in her room, Shirley said, "I'm sorry you
had to listen to her going on and on about nothing. Sometimes she
drives me crazy."

"Is that why you closed the door a little?" Lacy asked.

"Yeah. I didn't want her to hear what I said to you."

"Okay," Lacy said.

"What Randy did was not right Lacy, and I hope Alexandra and
Odessa taught him a lesson," Shirley said.

"He will never learn from lessons," Lacy said. "He's like that little
girl Rhoda in the movie "The Bad Seed" and just like her, he will get
away will all of the bad things he does until he's an adult and the police
get him."

"Why would you say that?" Shirley asked.

"Because that is what will happen," Lacy said. "No one will stand up
to him and stop him from doing what he does except the police and
that will be his life. I can see it. I feel sorry for him but that is what will
happen and it seems like no one sees that but me. Why can't anyone
else see that Shirley? Why don't you see that Shirley?"

Shirley said, "Well Lacy, he is still quite young and has plenty of time
to change, so I don't know. You have a very interesting imagination
Lacy. I know Randy isn't always nice to you and he's a trouble maker
but don't think bad things about him because of that. He can change
and I believe he will."

Lacy asked, "Do you believe he will change because you see something in him that tells you that or because you hope for that?"

Shirley looked around the room baffled, then looked at Lacy and said, "Huh, I really don't know. I just hope he changes."

Lacy said, "That's the difference, Shirley. You hope he will change and I see he won't. I hope he will change too but hoping isn't as strong as what I'm seeing and what I see will not change because he doesn't want to change. He likes how he is and he will like it more as he gets older."

"Okay, let's talk about something else Lacy as we start folding these clothes."

"Okay," Lacy said. "I heard my favorite song by Stevie Wonder again today. "My Cherie Amour."

"You did?" Shirley asked.

"Yes," Lacy said.

"Why do you like that song so much Lacy?" she asked.

He said, "Because Stevie Wonder was telling his feelings to the world about a woman he has not met yet, but will."

"Wow! Lacy, most people just listen to that song and sing along but you listen and think about what the words really mean. You're not really four years old are you Lacy?" Shirley asked playfully.

Lacy said, "Yes, I just turned four not long ago. You can ask Esta and she will tell you."

Shirley said, "Oh, Lacy. I was joking with you. I know you're four."

"Then why did you ask?" Lacy asked.

Shirley said, "I was just joking or being sarcastic. But now you want to know what sarcastic means right?"

Lacy said, "Yes."

"I know you're four years old, but I was pretending or acting as if I really didn't know. Being sarcastic is a way of saying the opposite of what the truth is as a joke, even though everyone knows what the truth is. It's just a way to play."

"I think it's silly," Lacy said.

"Are you calling me silly?" Shirley asked.

"No," Lacy said, "I don't think you're silly. I think the word sarcastic is silly and people shouldn't do that because it's confusing."

Shirley said, "Right now it might be confusing for you but it will make more sense as you get older and you will probably be sarcastic with people too." Lacy just looked at Shirley with his professor look in his professor glasses. "Well, we better get to folding these clothes. Do you remember how to do it, Lacy?"

Lacy said, "I think so," as he tucked a pair of socks inside of each other and made a ball out of it as Shirley showed him.

Shirley said, "You remembered. Very good. Keep going."

Lacy tucked more socks and began folding tops and pants, then he saw Shirley's panties again and said, "Look what I found!" and started waving them around.

Shirley grabbed them like before and said, "Now you're being the silly one." Lacy started laughing and told Shirley he liked the color of her panties. She said, "You do?" He said yes, and asked if red panties were her favorite because she had a few in the same color. Shirley said she liked the green ones, pink ones, and blue ones too, but she just had more of the red ones.

Lacy asked what color panties she was wearing and she said, "Lacy! You shouldn't ask questions like that." Lacy looked startled and didn't know why he couldn't ask her that because they were friends and he was already folding her panties. "That kind of information is private."

Lacy asked, "If it's private information, who will you share that information with?"

Shirley said, "I meant that information is private for me to know, like my secret not to share."

"Oh," Lacy said. "I'm sorry."

Shirley went quiet for a moment, then said, "It's okay Lacy. I can see why you thought it was okay to ask since we've been playing."

Lacy said, "Good, I'm glad you see that Shirley because I didn't mean to cause a problem."

Shirley said, "Nope. No problem at all, everything is okay."

"Neeatoooo," Lacy said.

As they kept folding clothes, Shirley looked at Lacy and giggled. Lacy asked why Shirley was giggling and Shirley said, "Oh nothing."

Lacy asked, "If it's nothing, then why are you giggling? It must be something or you wouldn't be giggling."

Shirley stopped folding clothes and just looked at Lacy and said, "It's just that you act so much older than you are at times, and I keep seeing you as a forty-year-old midget and it makes me laugh."

Lacy looked at Shirley with a straight face and said, "I thought we talked about that and how it wasn't nice."

"We did," Shirley said, "and I don't mean any harm to you and I'm not teasing you, I just mean you're like a grown man at times and understand so much."

Lacy smiled and said, "People tell me that but I don't know why."

Shirley said, "It's true. You speak like an adult but you have a child's body and I don't know any other children who do that. Lacy, imagine if when I spoke I sounded like a four-year-old, wouldn't that sound funny?"

Lacy said, "No, because you do sound like a four-year-old. You sound just like me but you know more words. Your mother sounds like a four-year-old too and has trouble with some of her words."

Shirley just looked at Lacy and said, "That's not what I meant."

"Then what exactly do you mean Shirley?" Lacy asked.

Shirley said, "Let's just forget about that for now and keep folding clothes because you'll see what I mean when you are older."

Lacy said, "That's what people keep telling me. When I ask questions that people can't answer they tell me I'll understand when I get older. I don't think I have a problem understanding. I think adults have a problem explaining then tell me to wait until I'm older so someone else can explain better than they can."

"SEEEEE! HAHAHAHA!" Shirley laughed loudly and hysterically as she pointed at Lacy. "SEEEE! THIS IS WHAT I MEAN LACY! HAHAHAHAHA! WHAT CHILD TALKS LIKE THAT?

HAHAHAHA!"

Lacy stopped folding clothes, turned his whole body toward Shirley, put his hands on his hips and just stared at her through his professor glasses as if he were watching paint dry. This made Shirley laugh harder as she continued pointing at him and holding her stomach since it began to ache from laughter. Lacy looked at the bed where all the clothes were and grabbed a pair of her panties and started waving them around asking, "Do these belong to anyone?"

Shirley stopped laughing and said, "Give me those."

Lacy kept waving them around and said, "Why did you stop laughing?"

Shirley said, "Give me those panties."

"Can't answer the question?" Lacy asked. Shirley started reaching around Lacy's body to get her panties back but Lacy kept putting the panties in different hands and turning and twisting his body so she couldn't get them.

Shirley got angry and yelled, "GIVE ME MY PANTIES!" Just then, Lilly walked in and asked what was going on. Lacy quickly tossed Shirley's panties onto the bed then Shirley grabbed them and just stared at Lacy as Lacy stared at her, and Lilly wondered what was going to happen.

Lilly asked again, "I asked you two what was going on in here."

Shirley said, "I was making fun of Lacy and he took my panties."

Lilly asked why Shirley was making fun of Lacy and Shirley said, "Because he was talking like a grown man and it made me laugh."

Lilly said, "Oh, he was doing his forty-year-old midget thing again," then she started laughing, so Shirley laughed a bit too but stopped when she saw Lacy look at her. Lacy stood there looking at Lilly as if she were the stupidest adult on the planet and had no room to be making fun of anyone with her Fruit Loop outfits, raggedy teeth, and fur ball slippers that she drags around in while puffing on that never-ending cigarette with the long ash hanging from it. Shirley laughed as Lilly said, "You two keep it quiet in here while I'm watching my soap operas," then walked out as she continued to mumble and giggle all while trying to take a drag off her cigarette.

Shirley leaned down to Lacy and said, "I'm sorry Lacy. I didn't mean to hurt your feelings." Then she hugged him and said, "You're very wise. We sometimes laugh at what we don't understand and I don't understand how you got so wise and are able to speak the way you do so early in life. That probably doesn't make sense to you now, and I don't know any other way to explain it but I'm not laughing at you, I'm laughing at what I don't understand."

Lacy said, "Thank you for telling me that Shirley. I don't know what you see when you look at me or what anyone sees when they laugh when I speak but I wish you and they would stop doing it."

Shirley looked at Lacy with caring and understanding eyes and said, "Lacy, from now on I won't laugh about this anymore."

Lacy said, "I don't believe you," as he stared at her.

She asked, "How can I make you believe me?"

Lacy said, "Nothing. You laugh about this all the time like the others and you say you'll stop but you never do."

Shirley said, "But this time I promise I won't do it anymore." Promises were a very big thing to Lacy. If he made a promise or someone made a promise to him then there was no turning back.

Lacy said, "Shirley, you promised before."

She said, "I know, but I see how it bothers you so I won't do it again." Lacy looked away and began folding clothes again and said he couldn't wait until Esta got home. Shirley said, "Lacy, I'm really sorry and I wish there was something I could do for you to believe me." Lacy just kept folding the clothes. Shirley stepped back and pushed the door, nearly closing it, then she stepped forward near Lacy again and said, "You can hold my panties Lacy." Lacy stopped folding the clothes and looked at Shirley.

"You won't get upset if I hold them?" Lacy asked.

"No," Shirley said. "Go ahead, hold them." Lacy picked up her panties and looked at them, then looked at her trying to imagine her wearing them. "Why are you looking at me down there?" Shirley asked.

Lacy said, "Because I'm imagining what they look like on you."

Shirley said, "Well, I'm wearing those same color panties you have in your hands."

"May I see?" Lacy asked. Shirley's eyes widened and she covered her mouth in embarrassment as she cringed.

She asked, "What exactly do you want to see?"

Lacy said, "I want to see what your underwear looks like under your dress."

"Lacy, you shouldn't be asking for things like that at your age," Shirley said.

Lacy asked, "What age should I ask about things like this?"

Shirley said, "I don't know, but not at your age." They just stared at each other, then a moment later, Shirley looked through the crack of her bedroom door to make sure Lilly wasn't there, then she moved toward Lacy slowly and nodded her head and said okay. She slowly turned around and lifted her dress so Lacy could see her panties. Lacy's eyes widened because he saw more than just her panties. He'd never seen a girl's leg up that high before where it created the shape it did at the top of the legs. Shirley looked over her shoulder and said, "You can touch if you want." Lacy looked at Shirley and wore a huge grin and quickly put both hands on each butt cheek. As he was rubbing his hands over her butt cheeks he got the bright idea of pulling her panties down. Just as he tried, Shirley turned and grabbed his hand and said, "No, no, no. You can't do that."

Lacy said, "Okay Shirley."

As Shirley went back to folding the clothes, Lacy started folding clothes too but he was now mesmerized by Shirley and had a huge grin on his face. "Why are you grinning Lacy?" Shirley asked.

Lacy said, "Because you let me touch your panties."

Shirley quickly looked over her shoulder towards the door then squatted down and held Lacy's face and said, "Lacy, you can never tell anyone I let you do that okay? If you tell we will both get into big trouble."

Lacy said, "But it's your panties, so why would we get into trouble? You gave me permission so we did nothing wrong."

Shirley said, "You're right, I gave you permission, but adults would not understand and they would make a big deal about it and we will get in trouble so you can't tell anyone, not even Esta. You can't tell Esta or anyone. Do you promise?" Lacy looked at her and asked if she wanted him to promise he wouldn't mention it for the rest of his life or just for now. Shirley asked, "What kind of question is that and why would you ask that?"

Lacy said, "Because when I watch the old movies women always ask the men about their past and the guy always tells them the truth."

"OOOH," Shirley said. "When you're an adult you can tell, but don't say anything about it until you're at least twenty-one. Do you promise?"

Lacy said, "It's a deal. I promise not to tell anyone until I'm twenty-one." Shirley gave Lacy a big hug and kissed him on the cheek. For some reason, that kiss on the cheek made Lacy feel different than all of the kisses he had ever had on the cheek before. He didn't know why he felt different but he now saw Shirley differently than before. They went back to folding clothes but Lacy kept looking at Shirley with a big smile on his face and Shirley would look at him occasionally with a smile on her face. This was the start of the new babysitting term between Shirley and Lacy. After several weeks of Shirley and Lacy's escapades, they had gotten closer and closer and built a lot of trust between each other. Whenever a sitter was needed for Lacy, he told Esta that he'd rather stay with Shirley. There were even times when Lacy would ask to stay with Shirley when others were home. One day, Esta asked Lacy why he liked staying with Shirley and he said she taught him how to fold clothes and she helps him understand words like Esta does. "And she's funny in a goofy kind of way."

Esta said, "Yes, she can be goofy."

Then Esta asked Lacy if he liked Shirley more than her and Lacy said, "No Esta, I like you the most. You take care of me and make sure I'm okay. Shirley is my friend and takes care of me when you can't."

"So, I'm the queen and you're the prince."

"No, you're the queen and I'm the professor, who one day will be king."

"Hahahahaha," Esta laughed and said, "you're right. One day you will be king but you will still be the professor. But right now, I have to drop you off with Shirley so I can go to work but I'll see you later tonight."

Lacy got excited and said, "Okay. Let's go!" Esta looked at Lacy as he was heading for the front door and she couldn't help but be jealous. Moments after Lacy was dropped off at Shirley's house, Lilly told Shirley that she needed to go to the store and would be right back. Since Shirley knew her mom would be gone for a little while, she thought she and Lacy could play the panty game while Lilly was gone. Shirley held Lacy's hand and took him to her room. She bent down and hugged Lacy then stood up and turned around and lifted her dress. Lacy began his touching longer than before because they had no fear of getting caught since Lilly was gone. This time, Lacy began pulling Shirley's panties down and she stopped him when her panties were halfway down.

She was looking at him over her shoulder and he looked at her briefly then looked back at her backside, then *BOOM!* Lilly pushed the door with her hands and the door flew open and she yelled, "WHAT THE HELL IS GOING AWN IN HERE? I KNEW YOU TWO WERE UP TO SUMTHIN', COMEEER YOU NASTY LITTLE BOY! WHACHU THANK YOU DOIN? HUH? WHATCHU THANK YOU DOIN?" Lacy looked as scared as he did when the Abba Zabba woman yelled at him when he explained what happened with Randy. He was afraid to say anything because he thought he would get blamed again and told it was all his fault. He looked at Shirley and hoped she would say something, and that was when Lilly grabbed him by his arm and quickly yanked him out of the room while telling him he should be ashamed of himself and couldn't come to her house anymore and was going to make sure everyone knew why. She yanked him all the way to his house and knocked on the front door, waiting for someone to answer. Marcel came to the screen door and when he opened it, he saw it was Lilly. Lilly pulled Lacy into the house and asked if Beatrice was home.

Marcel said, "No she's at work, only the boys are home right now."

Lilly said, "Well you tell your Beatrice or Esta to call me when they get in, ya hear?"

Marcel said, "Okay." Lilly quickly left and Marcel asked Lacy what happened, but Lacy remained quiet because he made a promise to Shirley not to tell. The other boys asked what happened but Lacy wasn't telling. He told the boys they had to speak with Shirley.

Randy said, "Whatever it is he's gonna get spanked for it."

Marcel and Horace chimed in and Horace said, "Yeah, you better tell us because you're gonna get spanked if you don't."

"Leave me alone," Lacy said. But Horace and Marcel rarely left Lacy alone. They liked teaming up on him with negative comments and scare tactics.

"Hey, four-eyes? Too bad you don't have a brain to match all of those eyes. The baby has to walk around with his overalls unfastened so he doesn't pee on himself. One day you won't wake up from that dream nightmare you have and the people chasing you will chop you up into little tiny pieces," Marcel said. The truth was that Horace was the notorious bed wetter and Marcel was afraid of his own shadow and needed regular enemas due to constipation. Lacy would let them say their say and not let it get to him because at four he could ride a two-wheeled bike without training wheels and they couldn't. He could run like greased lightning, leaving them in the dust. Whatever athletic activity was presented to Horace and Marcel, Lacy performed with ease, which made them very angry and jealous.

This also infuriated the Abba Zabba woman, so she would often tell Lacy he had to stay in the house while Horace and Marcel played so that they would not feel inferior even though they were older and in school. Odessa and Alexandra had just come home and asked what was going on.

Gus said, "It looks like something happened at Lilly's house between Lacy and Shirley, so Lilly brought Lacy home and said he can't go back over there."

"WHAT?" both girls shouted. "LACY WHAT HAPPENED? WHAT DID YOU DO? WHAT DID SHIRLEY DO? DID YOU TWO FIGHT? DID YOU BREAK SOMETHING?"

Gus stepped in and said, "He's not talking and won't tell us but maybe you two can talk to Shirley since he's been saying we should talk to Shirley."

"Come on Alexandra," Odessa said, "let's go talk to Shirley."

Alexandra said, "What if Lilly is so angry that she yells at us?"

"Let's go to Shirley's window and try to talk to her."

"Okay," Alexandra said. "Let's go."

As the girls dashed off to speak with Shirley, Horace and Marcel began teasing Lacy again, telling him that whatever he did, they would all know very soon, and he was gonna get into big trouble. Gus told Lacy to just sit and wait until Odessa and Alexandra got back. Randy asked Gus why he was protecting Lacy and being so nice to him. Gus said, "He doesn't need all of you treating him the way you do. How would you like it, Randy?"

Randy said, "You're no fun and should mind your own business," as he played with his yoyo.

Gus just looked at Randy and shook his head, then said, "Lacy just stay right there and wait."

Randy said, "Yeah Lacy, just stay right there and wait to get your spanking. Hahahahaha." Randy laughed.

"Hahahha. Yeah. Hahahaha." Horace and Marcel laughed. Lacy looked at the three of them and wondered how he could be related to them because he would never want them to ever feel bad or hurt. He thought maybe they acted that way because it was what happened as you got older and he was concerned he would grow into that behavior too and didn't like that thought. As Lacy waited for the girls to return, he began to wander with his thoughts. He thought about the homemade tents in the backyard, goodies from the ice cream truck, and everyone laughing happily. Then his thoughts wandered to a day when all of that would change. In Lacy's mind, he saw a time when he would not be able to rely on Esta and it made him nervous. He tried to think of something else but he kept seeing a time when Esta could not help him with the things she used to help with and he didn't know how to process that thought or feeling.

He began to drip tears and look very sad. Just then, Horace noticed the tears and began laughing and said, "Oooh look at poor little Lacy crying. He knows he did something very bad and that's why he's crying isn't it Lacy? Isn't it. Say it you little weasel, say it!" Horace and Marcel just laughed and Randy smiled like a kingpin smiling at his thugs beating someone up. Lacy just looked at Horace with a look of disgust. Horace said, "Don't look at me with those cat eyes of yours. Everyone knows you have those cat eyes but they don't scare me. Look away now. I said look away now," Horace said. Lacy refused to look away. Horace continued teasing him, so now Horace would have to deal with him staring. Horace didn't like the staring so he just ran into another room yelling, "Lacy's a dummy, Lacy's a dummy." Lacy just went back to his thoughts and hoped he would not be like the other boys and be nicer to people as he got older.

"LACY! COME HERE!" the girls shouted as they entered the front door.

"Come with us," Alexandra said. They took Lacy into the bedroom and told him that Shirley told them that her mother caught Lacy touching her panties while she was wearing them. They told Lacy that was wrong and she should have never let him do that. They told Lacy that Lilly beat Shirley and Shirley was still crying. Lacy looked sad because he liked Shirley and felt like he got her into trouble and now she was in pain.

"Is she upset with me?" Lacy asked the sisters.

"No," they said.

"She's embarrassed and she is concerned that you don't like her anymore and that you think she is stupid. We think she's stupid for letting this happen and when Esta finds out she's probably going to beat her up," Odessa said.

"No. Please tell Esta not to beat her up," Lacy said. "Please!"

Alexandra asked Lacy if touching Shirley's panties was all that happened. "Did she ever ask you to take your pants off or put her hand in your pants Lacy?" Alexandra asked.

"No," Lacy said. "She didn't do that."

'Good," both sisters said.

"Well, Shirley can't babysit you anymore because of this so you will have to stay with Mrs. Sanchez," Alexandra said.

"Mrs. Sanchez?" Lacy asked.

"Yes, Mrs. Sanchez," Alexandra said. "We don't have many choices for sitters and must use what we have." Alexandra asked Lacy if something happened at Mrs. Sanchez's house.

"No," Lacy said. "She just seems angry a lot and when she gets upset with her children she tells them she doesn't love them anymore then they start screaming and crying and following her around the house begging her to love them again."

"Does she ever hit you?" Odessa asked Lacy.

"No," Lacy said. "She just yells and tells me I'm a bad boy whenever her children and I don't want to play together."

"Why don't you want to play with her children?" Odessa asked.

Lacy said, "I do play with them but when they see me having a good time with their toys they tell me I can't play with their toys anymore, so I just sit and think. When they see me sitting and thinking then they say I can play with their toys again and I don't want to then. That's when they tell Mrs. Sanchez and she yells at me and says I'm a bad boy."

Alexandra said, "Maybe you can try to play with her children and get along for a little while. Summer is here soon and we will all be home more so we won't need a babysitter."

"Okay," Lacy said.

"Are you okay?" Odessa asked Lacy.

"Yes," Lacy said.

"Then let's go to the living room so you can play while we make something to eat."

"Okay," Lacy said. When Alexandra opened the door she saw Randy, Marcel, and Horace as they ran away from the door laughing and saying that Lacy was touching Shirley's panties.

"Lacy didn't tell us he had a girlfriend and now he's gonna get the belt tonight for touching Shirley's panties while she was in them!" Randy said.

"Lacy, did you like touching Shirley's smelly panties?" Horace asked.

"What did she look like under that dress she always wears Lacy?" Randy asked.

Marcel nearly bust a gut laughing and giggled like a hyena and could barely get his words out. "L-, hahaha, La-, hahaha, Lacy, how did-, hahahahaha, how did you get Shirley, HAHAHAHAHAHAHA! How did you get Shirley to let you touch HER PANTIES? HAHA-HAHAHAHHAHAHAHAHA!!!!" Odessa and Alexandra told the boys to shut up and stop acting like animals and to leave Lacy alone. Lacy started tearing up because he told Shirley he would not tell, but now people were finding out.

Just then, Randy said, "Hey Lacy, there's a girl at school I like, can you teach me so I can get her to let me touch her panties? Hahahahaha." Then Marcel chimed in, as did Horace, repeating Randy's question.

Lacy looked at Randy and said, "Teach you? Your teacher tries to teach you and sends you home instead. You can't be taught."

Randy looked at Lacy and charged at him, knocking him over while Horace and Marcel yelled, "Get the panty monster before he gets away!" as they laughed and mocked him. The sisters pushed Randy away from Lacy and Gus called Randy an idiot for picking on a little kid.

Lacy said, "Child."

Horace said, "Yes, he's not a baby goat, he's a panty-touching child. Hahahahahah."

Lacy said, "And you're Bozo the Clown with freckles."

When Marcel heard Lacy call him Bozo the Clown, Marcel stopped laughing. He looked angrily at Lacy and said, "I hope you get beat so hard that you can't walk."

Lacy said, "You will still be Bozo the Clown," and that's when Horace ran into the bedroom and started crying and saying he was going to tell on Lacy when Mama came home. The sisters laughed hysterically at Lacy's comments to Marcel because he did look like Bozo the Clown with shorter red hair. Alexandra was always ready for a fight and would stand up to anyone, so she loved seeing Lacy stand up for himself against the bullying. However, he was concerned about what would happen when she was not around to protect him from Randy. Alexandra was not as concerned about Horace and Marcel because she knew they had many words but not a lot of confidence to go against Lacy by themselves. She told Lacy to not pay them any attention and play or watch TV while she and Odessa made something to eat.

Odessa was the peacemaker and didn't like physical contact so she didn't encourage Lacy to act like the other boys with the negative comments and carrying on with that. But, she did laugh her heart out when Lacy called Marcel Bozo the Clown and how Marcel's loud opened-mouthed laugher turned to immediate silence and shame as he ran to the bedroom crying. Lacy didn't laugh at all. It bothered him to make someone feel bad but he wanted to get Marcel's attention so he would stop, and he always knew just what to say to get the attention of Randy, Marcel, and Horace, or the hecklers of the family. After Marcel ran off to the bedroom, Randy and Horace went quiet and just looked at Lacy, knowing they were next to get what Marcel got. Lacy just sat in the rocking chair and paid them no attention, and they went about their business. Later that evening after dinner and after the younger boys had their baths, the Abba Zabba woman opened the front door and Marcel was waiting right there for her to enter so he could tell on Lacy for teasing him and about Shirley. Marcel was speaking a mile a minute so the Abba Zabba woman told him to wait until she got in and to slow down. He couldn't slow down because he started crying all over again. The Abba Zabba woman said, "Marcel, wait! I have to go to the bathroom so come with me and tell me what you have to say."

"Uh, huh, uh, huh, uh, O, O, okay," Marcel said in his crying voice with tears running down his face. As they headed for the bathroom, Randy and Horace began their quiet comments toward Lacy. They spoke softly because they knew the Abba Zabba woman would come out of the bathroom quite angry after listening to her most favorite children tell her how they were wronged. If she heard Randy and Horace joking about the situation she would yell frantically at the top of her lungs, not at anyone in particular, but as a way to release her frustrations. Randy, Horace, and Marcel could never handle her indiscriminate yelling without breaking down. As Randy and Horace told Lacy how he was going to get it, they could all hear the Abba Zabba woman sounding like a hissing snake as she peed while Marcel was trying to gain his composure and tell his version of the story a mile a minute. Alexandra and Odessa stood next to Lacy and told him to stay calm and not to worry because they would explain what happened and how wrong Shirley was. Just then, the toilet flushed. They never knew what the Abba Zabba woman's mood would be when she came out from the bathroom after working all day, but silence was never good, especially after someone complained like Marcel did.

"Where's Lacy?" she asked, as she approached the living room from the hallway.

"In here," Odessa said, as she looked at Lacy with concern. As the Abba Zabba woman entered the living room, she saw Lacy and put her hands on her hips and before she could say anything, Odessa said, "We found out that Shirley encouraged Lacy to do what he did and she's old enough to know better. Shirley said it's all her fault and they were just playing."

The Abba Zabba woman said, "You call that playing?"

Odessa said, "No, I don't, but that's what Shirley said they were doing and she made it into a game so Lacy thought he was playing a game."

"He thought rubbing Shirley's ass was a game?" the Abba Zabba woman asked.

Alexandra said, "Lacy likes playing games more than any of us, so if Shirley called it a game, I could see how Lacy would have thought it was a game."

"Is that what you thought Lacy? That it was a game?" the Abba Zabba woman asked him.

"Yes," Lacy said.

The Abba Zabba woman said, "Since you thought it was a game, why don't you tell me how the game was played?" Lacy looked at the sisters, and the Abba Zabba woman looked at him with her hands on her hips and said, "I didn't ask you to look to them for answers, I asked you to tell me what happened."

Lacy fixed his glasses and as he was about to speak, Marcel said, "Yeah, tell her how you played with Shirley's panties."

"Yeah," Horace said, "we all want to hear this." Randy just played with his yoyo while staring at Lacy with a huge grin on his face.

"You boys hush up," the Abba Zabba woman said, "now go on Lacy."

Lacy said, "Shirley and I were folding her clothes like we do whenever I go to her house."

"What? Folding clothes at her house? You don't fold clothes here, so what are you doing folding clothes at their house?" she asked.

"Yes. That's why I was doing." Lacy said.

"I know what you were doing dummy, I'm asking why you were doing it."

"Shirley washes clothes all the time and she asked if I wanted to help her fold them after they dried and I said sure."

Just then, the Abba Zabba woman let out a big *HUUHH!* "Go on," she said.

"When we folded the clothes, I saw her panties and…"

"STOP!" she said. "How do you know what panties are?"

"Shirley told me when I saw them on the bed with the rest of the clothes."

"THAT DERN NASTY TRAMP! Keep talking," she said.

"One day Shirley got upset when I was waving her panties around, then later she let me hold them. I said okay."

"Why did you want to hold them?" she asked.

Lacy said, "Because they felt different and had neato colors."

"Neato isn't a word, so stop using that word," she said. "So you thought they were pretty?" she asked.

"Yes," Lacy said.

"Keep talking," she said.

"I asked Shirley what color panties she was wearing and she said, "that's private" and she couldn't tell me that."

"So you wanted to see under her dress?" she asked.

Lacy said, "No, I wanted to see what color her panties were."

"YOU'RE A DAMN LIE! YOU KNEW WHAT YOU WERE DOING AND WANTED TO LOOK UP UNDER HER DRESS! DIDN'T YOU?" she yelled.

"No," Lacy said. "I just wanted to know what color she was wearing."

"STOP LYING!" she shouted.

"Yeah, stop lying," Randy said.

"Quiet Randy," the Abba Zabba woman said. There were giggles in the background from Horace and Marcel.

"I'm not lying," Lacy said.

"Oh, so you're calling me a liar then?" she asked. Lacy looked at the sisters because he clearly didn't understand how she thought he was calling her a liar. "STOP LOOKING AT THEM WHEN I'M TALKING TO YOOOUU!" she shouted. Lacy began to shake a bit. "Okay! Then what happened?"

"We kept folding clothes and talking, then she asked if I wanted to see her panties and I said yes, then she turned around and lifted her dress and showed me her panties."

The Abba Zabba woman's mouth opened wide and her eyes got wider as she asked, "Then what happened?"

Lacy said, "Then she said I could touch her panties so I did."

"How did you touch them?" she asked.

"I put my hand on her panties like this," he said, as he showed her his open hands.

She said, "So you were feeling her butt? You didn't want to feel her panties, you wanted to feel her butt the whole time. You don't fool me." Lacy just looked at her as if she was the strangest person he had ever spoken with. "I oughta tear your black ass up and hang you by your thumbs," she said. Lacy just looked at her because he had no idea why this woman was yelling and screaming at him and not listening to a word he was saying. He was thinking *when's Esta coming home?* The Abba Zabba woman stormed off to the kitchen as she said, "I haven't even eaten yet and I'm starved. Lacy, you stand right there and don't you move until I get back and figure out how to deal with you." Lacy just stood there. "Is there something in there for me to eat?" she asked.

"Yes," the sisters said. Randy, Horace, and Marcel just grinned and made snickering noises at Lacy while the sisters looked upset at the Abba Zabba woman's reaction and were very concerned for Lacy. The sisters told Lacy they had to do their homework but they would get their books and do their work in the living room. Lacy said okay, as he stood in that same spot while the brothers mocked him and tried to make him move from the spot where he was standing by pushing him and putting their hands in his face.

Marcel said, "You better not move or you'll get into worse trouble." The sisters came back and the boys ran off. As the Abba Zabba woman ate her food, Lacy could hear her occasionally setting the fork down on the plate as it made a clanking sound, so he knew she would be down soon. Moments later, Lacy heard the front door being unlocked and he knew who it was. He did not move from where he stood but he turned his head to watch the front door open.

Esta opened the door and said, "Hiiiii Lacy!" Lacy gave a partial wave and said a soft hello, hoping the Abba Zabba woman didn't hear him. Esta asked, "Don't you want to give me a hug? You usually run to me."

Lacy whispered, "Yes, but I'm in trouble." The sisters told Esta what happened and Esta started tearing up and threatened to break Shirley's neck. When the sisters told Esta that Lacy might get a beating, Esta went into the kitchen to try to soften things with the Abba Zabba woman.

As the conversation started, the Abba Zabba woman raised her voice and said, "If you were here this would not have happened, and now you want me to be understanding!?" Esta pleaded and pleaded until the Abba Zabba woman said, "Then you handle this, I don't want to hear any more about it. Get him out of my sight, I don't want to see him again tonight, ya hear?"

"Yes," Esta said. Esta grabbed Lacy by the hand and said, "Come with me."

Lacy said, "I was told not to move."

Esta said, "You can move now." She took Lacy into the bedroom and told him she was sorry for not being there when this all happened and said he should not be treated as if he was a crook.

"What's a crook?" Lacy asked.

"A person that steals things."

"Oh, you mean a thief," Lacy said.

"Yes," Esta said. "How do you know what a thief is Lacy?" she asked.

Lacy said, "I heard Odessa call Randy a thief because he takes people's things."

Esta smiled and said, "You've got a very good memory Lacy, but I hope you can forget what happened today and not let it bother you."

"I don't think I'll forget it Esta," Lacy said, "but I won't let it bother me."

Esta said, "That's a good start," as she hugged him. Esta told Lacy he could watch TV or go to sleep because he had to stay in the room for the rest of the night to avoid getting into trouble. Lacy wanted to watch TV and hoped there would be a good old movie on. Esta said, "Okay. Then let's get your pajamas on first and brush your teeth so I won't have to wake you up if you fall asleep watching TV."

"Okay," Lacy said. After he got cleaned up and ready for bed, Esta turned on the TV and found a good movie to watch. She sat with Lacy for five to ten minutes before she headed to the kitchen to eat dinner. She wasn't gone long, but when she returned, Lacy was almost asleep and was hugging her sweater. Lacy opened his eyes wide and sat up since he noticed Esta staring at him with tears in her eyes. "What's wrong Esta?" Lacy asked.

"Nothing," Esta said. "You're just a wonderful little boy, and I love you Lacy."

Lacy said, "I love you too Esta," then he lay back down and hugged her sweater. Esta sat near Lacy, caressing his head with a sad look in her eyes, and that worried Lacy because he thought maybe the Abba Zabba woman was mean to Esta. As he thought about why Esta might be sad, he fell asleep.

A TABLE WITH THREE LEGS

The next morning, Lacy heard everyone getting ready for school so he got up and looked for Esta. Alexandra said, "Good morning Lacy. You looking for Esta?"

"Good morning," Lacy said. "Yes. Do you know where she is?"

Alexandra said, "Yeah. She had to leave early because needed to meet someone before school."

"Who did she have to meet?" Lacy asked.

Alexandra said, "I don't know but she left in a hurry and told me to tell you she loves you and will see you later today. I have to keep getting ready for school so you can watch TV or play." Lacy looked a little confused because Esta never left without saying goodbye. He said okay, then stood still for a moment, looking around thinking about what he should do. He went back into the bedroom and sat on the bed because he didn't want to run into the Abba Zabba woman, especially if she was still upset about yesterday. When it was time for the others to go to school, Lacy stood in the doorway of the bedroom and peeked out, listening to everyone getting ready to leave.

"See you later Lacy," Gus said.

Lacy said, "Goodbye Gus."

Horace said, "Have fun watching Underdog, four-eyes. Maybe you'll touch Polly's panties. Hahahaha." Marcel said nothing and just gave Lacy an angry stare as he was leaving, and Lacy stared right back, smiling. When the others saw that smile from Lacy it meant one of two things. It meant, "you didn't get to me", or "I'm going to get to you." Either way, the others didn't like when he smiled when they felt he should be sad or upset. When Marcel saw that smile from Lacy he got moving and left.

"Lacy, don't you want to watch TV?" Odessa asked, as she walked out from the bathroom.

"Maybe later," Lacy said. Odessa was wise and knew Lacy was waiting for the others to leave, so she told him she would turn the TV on so it wouldn't be so quiet once they all left. She knew Lacy got scared when he was alone and it was quiet, but he didn't know he got scared because of the energy he would feel all around him. Lacy smiled and said, "Thank you Odessa."

She hugged him and said, "Your food is in the kitchen so make sure you eat, okay?"

Lacy said, "Okay, thank you Odessa."

She said, "You're welcome. Bye Lacy."

"Bye Odessa."

"See you later Lace," Alexandra said. "Don't worry, we'll be back in a little while so don't do or say anything to get Mom upset with you, okay?"

"Okay," Lacy said. Alexandra said Esta should be home earlier today because she wasn't going to work. Lacy's eyes lit up and he said, "REALLY?"

"Really," Alexandra said.

Just then, the Abba Zabba woman said, "Everyone in the car so we can go." When Lacy heard the Abba Zabba woman's voice he backed up a little into the bedroom out of fear.

Alexandra said, "It's okay. We're leaving, but remember what I said Lacy. Be good and just watch TV or take a nap and stay out of her way."

"Okay," Lacy said. She hugged Lacy and said bye-bye. Lacy said, "Bye-bye, Alexandra." Lacy waited by the bedroom door until he heard the front door close, then he walked quickly to the living room as he looked over his shoulder a bit in slight fear. Cartoons were on so Lacy hopped into the rocking chair and began watching. As he watched cartoons, he was wondering what was going to happen when the Abba

Zabba woman got back as she would be back very soon since the schools were so close to home. He was hoping he could say all of the right things when questioned and keep quiet when he wasn't questioned. While all of this was going through his head, he occasionally looked at the TV and remembered his favorite cartoons were on. He was hungry but he didn't want the Abba Zabba woman to return and see him eating and get upset thinking he made the food himself. She already told him he shouldn't have asked Randy for cookies the other day, even though he never did ask for them. Lacy thought it was best to wait until she got back before he ate, so he just sat in the rocking chair thinking and watching TV. After some time, Lacy heard the door being unlocked and in came the Abba Zabba woman, but she wasn't alone. Lilly was with her. Lacy thought Lilly must have seen the Abba Zabba woman as she pulled into the driveway and asked to speak with her. They both walked in, having a conversation about things they heard in the news and who did what to whom and who was in trouble with the law. They walked right by Lacy and said quick hellos to him. "Hi," Lacy said. The two ladies went right to the kitchen and continued their conversation. Lacy hoped they would stay there talking until Jasper arrived so that he and the Abba Zabba woman could go talk in the bedroom, then she'd go to sleep and forget about speaking to him about what happened with Shirley. As the two ladies spoke, laughed, and giggled in the kitchen, Lacy continued watching TV but he was getting very hungry since he still had not eaten. He thought of going to the kitchen to ask if he could eat his food but he thought one of the ladies would bring up the Shirley situation, so he just stayed in the rocking chair. Just then, the Abba Zabba woman came out from the kitchen and said she was going to take the TV into the kitchen so they could watch Jack LaLanne. Lacy said okay as pleasantly as he could, hoping to avoid upsetting her as Alexandra instructed him.

As she grabbed the TV, she said, "Lacy, are you going to eat your food?"
"Yes," Lacy said.
"Well then, come in here so you can eat."

"Okay," Lacy said. Lacy was extremely hungry and could not wait to tear into his food, so he hopped out of the rocking chair, but as he made his way to the kitchen he slowed his steps.

He quickly realized being in the kitchen would remind the Abba Zabba woman and Lilly about the Shirley situation. When he got to the kitchen he saw his food on the table right next to where Lilly was sitting. He avoided looking at Lilly and went to the chair to sit down to eat.

"Well, aren't you going to say hi?" Lilly asked.

"Don't you know how to say hello when you see someone Lacy?" the Abba Zabba woman asked.

"Yes," Lacy said. "We all said hi when you walked by me in the living room."

"OOOHH! That's right!" Lilly said.

The Abba Zabba woman said, "Ya know, he's always sitting in that dern rocking chair so it's easy to pass right by him."

Lacy noticed she looked a little annoyed as she said that. Lacy said, "Yes, that is a big chair and I'm small so it's hard to see me."

Lilly laughed and said, "I guess so...There he is," as she gestured to the TV.

"Okay. Eat your food Lacy, and be quiet," the Abba Zabba woman said. "Jack LaLanne is on."

"OOOH, there he is in his tight little outfit," Lilly said, as she took a drag off her smelly cigarette and looked at Lacy. She said, "You know boy, if you eat your food and take care of yourself you could be like Jack LaLanne. Couldn't he Beatrice?"

"I don't know about him. Marcel or Horace for sure, but I don't know about Lacy. He likes watching those dern cartoons too much to be like Jack LaLanne." Lacy was probably the slowest eater on the planet but he was really trying to speed up his eating that day so he could go back to the rocking chair and get away from the two ladies. He didn't like smelling Lilly's cigarette smoke and he didn't like how their conversations somehow always found a way to positively highlight Horace and Marcel for things they had not done or probably would never do.

"Yeah, well, if he can't be like Jack LaLanne maybe he can be like Shaft," Lilly said, "the detective that solves crimes and gets all the women. Hahahhaha. Whatchu thank Beatrice?" The Abba Zabba woman cracked a smile but no laughter came out of her. "Oh, Beatrice, you know I'm just playin' wit' the boy," Lilly said. Lacy knew Lilly's comments were going to get him into trouble for sure so he picked up the pace on his eating so much that the Abba Zabba woman noticed it.

"Slow down Lacy," she said. "You're not a kid or a baby goat, you're a child. Remember?"

Lacy said, "Yes, I remember."

"Well, goat, kid, or child that likes touching panties wit' the booty still in 'em," Lilly said. "So, there's a dirty ole man in there somewhere. Ain't that right Lacy," she asked. Lacy kept his eyes on his food and acted as if he didn't hear what she said. "Cat gotcha tongue boy?" Lilly asked. "I caught you playin' peekaboo under Shirley's dress, didn't I?" She puffed on her cigarette and cocked her head back to blow the smoke toward the ceiling. Lacy looked at Lilly with a neutral stare and stopped chewing his food.

At that moment, Lacy wished he was an adult so he could tell Lilly to go home and clean up her nasty self and stop blowing that smelly cigarette smoke all over the place.

"Don't gi' me dat look wit' those green eyes of yours," Lilly said. "Beatrice oughta tear yo little behind up like I did Shirley. I whooped her little black ass like a runaway slave and I bet she still can't sit down. Up in my house wavin' her ass around like she's Tina Turner. Well, I dun taught that little bitch who Ike is up in ma house and you should be next!" She said, "Beatrice betta not let this boy get away wit' that shit or he'll be just like my husband wontin' to grab a piece o' ass whenever the sun comes up."

"Lilly," the Abba Zabba woman said.

Lilly said, "He was trying to grab him some booty last night and I grabbed him and tried to twist it off. Bet he won't try dat again the cheatin' bastsud."

"Lilly!" the Abba Zabba woman said. "Your language."

"OOOH! You right Beatrice, I'm sorry, but this boy got to learn a lessin."

"I've already spoken to Esta and she will take care of it," the Abba Zabba woman said. "Now. Let's watch Jack."

"Esta," Lilly said. "Esta will take care of it? Esta ain't gooone dooo sheeiit. She la dat boy and pratect em'. She ain't gonna put a whoop on his bahine like you or I would."

"Let it go Lilly, just let it go and let him eat," the Abba Zabba woman said. "I think he's learned his lesson."

Lilly put her hand on Lacy's head and softly shook it and said, "You learn your lesson Lacy? Donchu let us catch you runnin' roun' here up under nobody's dress ya hear?"

"Yes," Lacy said.

"Good," Lilly said. "Now, finish ya food," she said as she took a big drag off of her cigarette, then said, "These kiiiiiids ah tell you."

The Abba Zabba woman wasn't paying Lilly any attention and constantly commented on Jack LaLanne. "He's so flexible, and look at that smile," she said. "I'd like to exercise with him."

"MMMMHHHMM? I bet you would," Lilly said, then they both broke out laughing hysterically. Lacy looked at both of them and wondered how they met and why they watched Jack LaLanne exercising and telling everyone to get out of their seats to exercise when they sat and did nothing. Of course, Lacy was happy to hear that he wasn't going to have his black ass torn up as Lilly put. She would have probably bought a ticket to see Lacy get beat because she enjoyed beating Ari and Shirley for any reason she could come up with. But, he was even happier that Jasper would be there soon and that they would play Army men. When Lacy finished eating he asked the Abba Zabba woman if he could leave the table to set up his Army men.

"Yes," she said. "Oh Lacy, you'll have to play Army men alone today because Jasper can't come over because he has too much to do." Lacy's body language showed that he wasn't too thrilled to hear the news, but he said okay.

"Yeah, that Jasper could teach ma husband soom thangs. Ma husband godda be wanna duh mos ignrent people I know and he lucky ah don't beat his ass more than ah do."

The Abba Zabba woman said, "But he is good to the children and takes good care of you."

"Oh, that he do," Lilly said, "but thas cuz ah be beatin' his ass. You see him runnin' down the driveway from me. He know who boss. Sheeeit! Remember dat Lacy. The woman the boss or she gooonen beat yo ass. Ya hear?" Lacy nodded his head. Lilly said, "Na. If I wa blind I couldn't see dat."

Lacy said, "Yes Lilly," then he went to the living room thinking, *if you were blind you wouldn't be able to find your way over to our house either and that would be great.*

As he was walking away he heard Lilly say, "Ya know, I don't thank dat boy like me much."

"Oh Lilly," the Abba Zabba woman said. "He's just a child with a very active imagination that never stops. He's in their playhing so leave em' be."

"I'm telling you Beatrice, the boy needs a treatment like ah give ma husband. *Whap, whap, whap, cawhickup.* Ya know what ah mean."

"I know what you mean," the Abba Zabba woman said.

Lacy was a little sad that Jasper wasn't coming over and that Esta left earlier without saying goodbye before school. He set up the Army men and played for a short while, then sat in the rocking chair thinking about what it would be like to be an adult and what his life would be like. He thought about the old movies he watched and how happy the couples were in the movies in their nice home. Lacy also thought about family and what type of man he would be for his children. Would he tear their asses up like Lilly or talk to them like Esta, Odessa, and Alexandra? Would he let the children treat each other like Randy, Marcel, and Horace treat him or teach them to be kind like Gus? Right there in that moment, Lacy made a promise to love his children and always talk to them and not beat them because beatings didn't teach anything except confusion and anger. Once Lacy made that promise to himself he began rocking in the rocking chair. As he was rocking with a smile on his face, the Abba Zabba woman and Lilly walked into the living room because Lilly was leaving.

Lilly said, "Whatchu doin' in here smilin' and rockin'? Thoughtchu was gooone play wit' them Aumy miiin?"

Lacy said, "I played with them and now I'm just thinking."

"Oh yeah?" she said. "Whatchu thankin' 'bout now Mister?"

"I'm thinking about my future," Lacy said.

"Bahahahaha! Future? Bahahaha! Beatrice, you need to do sumthin' 'bout dat boy. I ain't never seen no chile sit rocking the way dat boy do thankin' 'bout no future. Well, Einstein you just keep right awn rockin' and thankin' and if you come up wit' sumthin' good you make sure you shar it wit me ya hear. Bahahahahaha!"

Lacy said, "Okay." As Lilly and the Abba Zabba woman went to the front door, Lacy kept watching Lilly and saw that she would not enjoy her future because she wasted it each day on cigarettes and silly behavior. She made fun of people and things she didn't understand and liked beating people and being nasty to them. *If I could share a thought with her to help her life I would but I have nothing for her*, Lacy thought. *She will always be sad and mean and that's why her husband doesn't like coming home and will leave one day.* Lacy clearly felt that Lilly's son Ari would leave shortly after high school and not visit her much because he couldn't take the hostility in their house and Shirley would stay close to Lilly because Shirley will be just like her mom. After Lacy had these thoughts, he started rocking in the rocking chair again. He felt uncomfortable with the thoughts he had about Shirley's family because he really liked Shirley. After the Abba Zabba woman closed the door, she said she was going to take a nap and would be up later so they could do some grocery shopping before picking up the others from school. "Okay," Lacy said. As the Abba Zabba woman was heading toward the hallway to go to her bedroom she stopped and asked Lacy if he thought Lilly was strange. Lacy asked what strange meant. She said odd or different.

"You mean like a table with three legs," Lacy asked.

She said, "Yes, like a table with three legs instead of four legs. That would be different and odd."

Lacy said, "Yes, that is like Lilly. She's like a table with three legs. She is strange just like that table."

The Abba Zabba woman was quiet and just stared at Lacy with a small grin, then she asked, "Lacy, do you sometimes see things or have thoughts that just come to you without you thinking about them first?"

"What do you mean?" Lacy asked.

"I mean, when you watch TV you see things on the TV screen happening on the screen, but do you sometimes see things in your mind or in your head before you think about them?"

Lacy said, "Many times before I think of things, the things happen in my mind before they happen in the house or outside."

"Like what?" the Abba Zabba woman asked, as she stepped closer to Lacy. Lacy got nervous because the grin left her face and she seemed bothered that Lacy was saying the things he was saying.

He said, "When Jed from across the street broke his arm I saw that would happen many days before it did happen." She asked Lacy to explain what he saw. Lacy felt energy moving around him as if the energy around him was comforting him and protecting him. He felt the energy around him somehow did not want him to say much more about this to the Abba Zabba woman. So, instead of telling her that his mind saw Jed riding a bike and moments later saw him screaming in pain holding his arm days before the incident, he told her that he saw Jed looking unhappy and days later he had a broken arm.

She said, "Well anyone could have thought that. Maybe you just saw him looking sad and after he broke his arm you mixed up what happened and thought you saw the whole thing before it actually happened."

Lacy looked at her and felt the energy around him get stronger and stronger. He didn't feel he could trust her with the truth so he said, "Yes, I think that's what happened."

Take Me to Church

"You don't see anything before it happens. You just think you do because you observe or watch everybody so much that you think you know what's going to happen next, right?" Lacy did not like how she was talking because even at age four he felt she was trying to play with his mind. To avoid trouble, he said yes. She smirked and said, "Huh. Just what I thought. I'm going to bed. Keep the TV down so I don't hear it."

"Okay," Lacy said. After she went into the bedroom, Lacy felt the energy around him and his head. He felt as if the rocking chair was floating or vibrating in a way that was comforting. He felt like he was not alone, and whatever was with him or around him was letting him know that what he sees in his mind is true and real and he must trust and believe in himself and in the messages he receives. Lacy didn't know how to process this exactly but he was very accepting of this because he felt the peace and balance of the energy. He would get a similar feeling when he and the family would go to St. Martha's Church in La Puente, California. When they would go to church he would see so many people and felt so much energy there. He felt as if he should be speaking with the man that was at the front of the room. When the man spoke, Lacy felt as though he was speaking but the people were not really listening. Lacy felt the people were somehow not getting the point of why they were there. Lacy wanted so badly to stand up and go to the front of the room and tell the people that they must stop begging and hoping and let their minds feel what the man was saying. Many times when they were at that church, Esta would look at Lacy and whisper in his ear.

She would ask, "What do you feel right now?"

Lacy would just smile and say, "I feel everyone's pain and hurt and I want to help them."

She would ask, "How would you help them?"

Lacy would say, "I want to help them feel what I feel and hear what I hear and see what I see." She asked how he would do that and he said if he could talk to them and they listened and didn't treat him like a little boy that they would not have the same pain and hurt. He said they hurt because they believe the man at the front of the room will take away their pain but their pain is from their life and not him. One day when they were at church and Esta was asking Lacy what he felt, he said he felt the people's pain and hurt but he also felt her pain and hurt. She looked shocked. He asked her why she was in pain.

She said, "Lacy, I'm not in pain," as she tried to grin, but Lacy saw through her grin and felt she was not being honest. For the first time, he felt Esta was lying to him, so he looked at the front of the room so she wouldn't feel uncomfortable or get caught. She turned her head and looked at the front of the room too, then she told Lacy she had to go to the bathroom and asked Alexandra to watch him. When she got up to leave, Lacy turned around and watched her walk away and felt she was in trouble or did something wrong. Alexandra told Lacy to turn around and listen to the man talking at the front of the room. Lacy didn't like listening to that man because Lacy felt that man was tired of what he was doing and didn't want to be there. Lacy was concerned about Esta, and though she went away to cry, Esta didn't come back until church was over and met everyone by the car afterward. Lacy asked where she went, and Esta said she ran into her girlfriend Christina and that she would meet them at home in a little while. She looked a little sad, and Christina kept looking at Lacy and patting him on the head.

Alexandra said, "C'mon Lacy, get into the car."

Esta hugged Lacy and said, "I'll see you soon." Lacy said okay. Christina waved at Lacy and said goodbye. Lacy got into the car as the others did and they headed home. As the car pulled away, Lacy watched Esta and Christina from the back window of the station wagon as they walked away very quickly. Alexandra noticed Lacy watching Esta and that he looked upset, so she began talking to him.

"Lacy, do you want to play with your Army men when we get home?"

"No," Lacy said.

"Do you want to play in the yard?"

"No," Lacy said.

"How about play with your Big Wheel or the Sit N Spin Esta got for you?"

"No," Lacy said.

"Don't be sad Lacy," she said. "Esta will be home soon."

"Okay," Lacy said. The Abba Zabba woman overheard the conversation and said Esta would be going to college soon and working to help pay some bills so he might as well get used to her not being around as much. That didn't make Lacy feel any better than he did. Once they were home and in the driveway, the others couldn't wait to get out of the car to go do whatever they were going to do, but Lacy just sat right where he was, staring straight ahead.

"C'mon," Alexandra said. Lacy looked at Alexandra then looked down and started crying. Odessa saw him as she was standing at the back of the station wagon waving for him to come out of the car just before he began crying. Alexandra got out of the car and went to the back of the station wagon as Odessa was opening the back door. Odessa got into the back with Lacy and held his hands and told him everything was alright and he didn't have to cry. Alexandra stood nearby and said, "Yeah Lacy." Lacy looked at both sisters. They had no idea what exactly was going through Lacy's mind but they knew he missed Esta. Alexandra said, "Lacy you can sit there as long as you want but we're going into the house." Odessa looked at Alexandra and Alexandra said, "C'mon Odessa, let's go inside so he can be alone."

Odessa said, "Okay Lacy, we'll be inside. When you get out of the car, come get us so we can close the back door since it's heavy." Lacy said okay. Alexandra thought if they pretended to go into the house Lacy would be scared sitting alone in the car, but he watched them walk away and past the wall of the house where they were no longer in sight. Lacy kept looking at the wall of the house and caught the sisters peeking to see if he had moved or was getting out of the car. When Lacy saw them peeking, he laughed because he realized they were trying to trick him. When they saw him laugh, they walked back to the car laughing and Odessa said, "Okay, time to get out of the car Lacy."

Lacy said, "Okay, but can we do that again?"

"Do what again?" Odessa asked.

Lacy said, "Walk over there and hide again like you did then look at me so I can see you." They looked at each other and giggled and said okay. They did it and Lacy laughed just as hard as he did the first time. He wanted them to repeat this again and again until one time they didn't peek around the corner and he continued to wait. After less than a minute passed, Lacy thought they must have gone into the house. The car began to shake so he got scared and quickly got out of the car and ran toward the house, and when he got on the other side of that wall of the house, Odessa and Alexandra laughed heartily as his little legs were speeding around the corner. Alexandra caught him as he came around that corner of the house while Odessa was still squatting down at the front of the car since she was the one who snuck over to the car to shake it. She knew that would get Lacy out of the car.

"You thought we left you, didn't you?" Alexandra asked. Lacy said yes as he quickly looked over his shoulder as if the boogieman chased him.

Odessa laughed as she said, "You should have seen your little legs move when I shook the car."

Lacy asked, "You shook the car?"

"Yes, I knew you would get out of the car if I shook it because you wouldn't know why it was shaking," she said, as she continued to laugh.

"You tricked me," Lacy said.

"Yes, I tricked you to get you out of the car and it worked, now let's go inside."

"Okay, but it's my turn to trick you and Alexandra." They said okay. Once they got inside, Lacy kept sneaking up on them saying "Boo! Boo! Boo!" After doing this for quite some time, the sisters grew tired of pretending they were scared and told Lacy he scared them so much that they were too tired to be scared, which made no sense to Lacy. Of course, he had to ask how they stopped being scared because they were tired. The two exhausted sisters looked at each other and said they would explain it to him later. He said okay, then just watched them as they began to sew and knit. Much later that day, Esta came home with her girlfriend Christina and as soon as Esta entered the front door the Abba Zabba woman asked where she'd been.

"I was with Christina and my other friends."

"Well, you should have been home a long time ago," the Abba Zabba woman said.

"Christina, Esta has many things to do around here so she can't have any company today and will see you some other time."

Christina said, "Okay. Esta, I'll see you later."

Esta said, "See you later Christina," and began tearing up a little. Esta's high school graduation was getting close, so she was trying to spend quality time with all of her friends before they all went to different colleges or took on careers that would prevent them from getting together as often as they did. Esta was very upset with the Abba Zabba woman but the Abba Zabba woman didn't care one bit. It was as if she liked seeing Esta unhappy. Lacy was happy Esta was home but she was not in a good mood and wanted to be alone, so Lacy stayed in the room with Odessa and Alexandra while they sewed and knitted. Later when it was time to eat, Lacy went to the room where Esta was and asked if she was going to eat. She said, "Not right now. I'll eat later." Lacy asked if he could sit with her and eat with her later. Esta said that he should go and eat but Lacy said he'd rather stay and eat with her later so Esta said okay, and smiled at him. After everyone else had eaten and the

Abba Zabba woman went to her room for the night, Esta decided it was time to eat. She and Lacy went to the kitchen and she made a nice meal for them both to enjoy while they sat at the table right next to each other. As they were eating, Lacy told Esta he could see that she was thinking a lot. She nodded her head yes.

Lacy said very quietly, "Esta if I was blind I couldn't see that," then he giggled. Esta looked at Lacy and hugged him tightly and rocked him back and forth a little. He heard Esta making sounds as if she was crying so he looked up at her and asked why she was crying.

She said, "No baby. I just have a lot on my mind and I wanted to see my friends but I can't leave the house. Nothing you said or did is upsetting me. I'm okay," Esta said. "Finish your food because I know you're hungry."

Lacy began eating his food again, then he looked up at Esta and put his hand on her shoulder and in a whispering voice said, "It will be alright Esta, soon we can leave here and you won't have to cry anymore." She grabbed Lacy again and started rocking him, and there were more tears. Lacy said, "Esta, maybe I should be quiet and eat my food because when we talk right now you cry."

She said, "No, no, no. I just have a lot on my mind. Don't stop talking Lacy, because you have a lot to say and one day people will want to hear what you have to say. Today, I just have a lot on my mind. I have to go to the bathroom but I'll be right back."

"Okay," Lacy said. She was gone so long that Lacy went to check on her. He checked the bathroom but she wasn't there. He saw that the bedroom door was closed so he called out, "Esta? Are you in there?"

"Yes Lacy," she said. "I'm speaking with Alexandra and Odessa and will be out soon. You can wait for me in the kitchen or living room." Lacy said okay, but he didn't leave. He stood by the door trying to listen but they were too smart for him.

They opened the door and caught him trying to listen, so Alexandra grabbed him by the hand and said, "C'mon Lacy, you can watch TV or play with your Army men." Lacy walked with her but he was looking over his shoulder because he wanted to know what they were talking about so badly. He had a feeling they were talking about him. "C'mon Lacy, stop being so nosey. Ain't nobody talking about you," she said. Lacy knew when Alexandra spoke like "you ain't" or "he ain't" or used the word "ain't" and spoke quickly that she was either upset or very tired. She didn't look tired so Lacy believed she was upset about something but he didn't want to get on her bad side. He saw how she handled Randy and threw her fists into his face repeatedly when he got out of line. He also saw how she handled boys in the neighborhood if they weren't respectful. She would swing her fists while telling the boys why she was swinging her fists. It was like she was reminding them of what they did wrong while they were getting hit repeatedly in the face and chest. For some reason, after the boys had enough of a beating, she would stand over them and ask them to tell her what they did wrong and why they got a beat down. After the boys answered her question she would finish the beating with a kick if they were on the ground or a slap across the face if they were standing. So, when Alexandra said, "C'mon Lacy, ain't nobody talking about you," Lacy looked forward and didn't say a word and sat where she told him to sit. "We'll come out soon, but you stay away from the bedroom door, you hear?"

"Yes," Lacy said, "I won't try to listen."

"Good!" she said.

Randy mocked Lacy and said, "I won't try to listen…You little punk." Lacy just looked at Randy for a moment then began playing with his Army men. "Oh, now you're gonna play with your stupid Army men, huh? Let me play," Randy said as he began knocking the Army men over and tossing them everywhere.

"STOP!" Lacy said.

"Who you yellin' at?!" Randy asked as he slapped Lacy on the back of the head.

"I'm telling you to stop," Lacy said as he stood up.

"You standing up to me you punk?" Randy asked. Gus stood up and told Randy to leave Lacy alone. Randy said, "Mind your own business."

Gus said, "I am minding my own business, and if you keep picking on Lacy I'm going to pick on you."

"Oh yeah?" Randy said.

"You're not as stupid as people think. You heard me. Now move away from the table," Gus said.

Randy walked away, giving Lacy a dirty look as he knocked over a few more Army men on his way. Gus helped Lacy pick up his Army men and told Lacy to try to avoid Randy. Lacy said, "Okay. Thank you, Gus."

Just then, Alexandra came out and asked what was going on. Gus explained what happened and Randy knew what was coming so he ran into his bedroom and shut the door. Alexandra opened the door and closed it behind her and all you could hear was Randy screaming, "He's lying, he's lying, no, don't, I, ouuuu! OOOO! I'm tellin' ma OOOuuu! Okay, okay, please stop, I'll stop I won't…Ouuuu! Alexandra PLEASE STOOOOOOOOP!" Then they heard the door slam as Alexandra left the room without saying a word and went back into the room where Odessa and Esta were talking. When Randy heard Alexandra go back into the other room he crept slowly into the living room so Alexandra wouldn't hear him.

When he got there, he gave Lacy a dirty look and mouthed the words "I'll get you", as he pointed at Lacy. Lacy just stared at him with a blank expression because he wondered what Randy's problem really was and why he couldn't just be happy or quiet. Lacy once told Esta that he believed Randy's brain was like a faucet that never turned off so it fills the house and wets up everything. He told her that Randy's brain was not under his own control. Esta told Lacy not to tell anyone else that. When Lacy asked Esta why he should not tell anyone else, she said, "Just don't because it will only get you in a lot of trouble, okay?" Lacy said okay. As Lacy stared at Randy, Randy made a *PCHSHHH* sound, then walked away. Horace and Marcel had their eyes glued to the TV the whole time. Gus was watching TV too, but he was watching the interactions between Randy and Lacy in the corner of his eye. The sisters were in the bedroom for a very long time, but when they came out, Odessa told Marcel and Horace it was time for them to get cleaned up and ready for bed. Alexandra stood in the hallway by the bedrooms and got Lacy's attention. Using her finger, she gestured for him to come to her. Lacy went to Alexandra and she took him into the bedroom where Esta was. Esta and Alexandra both explained to Lacy that Esta needed to go out for a little while but she would be back later. Of course, Lacy asked where she was going. "I'm going out for a while to be with my friends, but I will be back later," she said.

"Are you going to see Christina?"

"Yes. Her and other friends," Esta said.

Lacy said, "I thought you weren't supposed to see her today or go out."

"HUUUHH! You need to really mind your own business Lacy," Esta said. "I'm going out, and Alexandra and Odessa will look after you, so be good and I'll see you later." Lacy looked confused but said okay anyway. As Esta climbed out of the bedroom window, Lacy asked Alexandra why Esta was not using the front door.

Alexandra said, "If she uses the front door she might get caught because the front door makes noise when you open it but the window doesn't make noise."

"Oh," Lacy said. "She's sneaking out of the house like I did when I went to Gus' school."

Alexandra looked at Lacy with a blank expression, then she got off the bed, headed for the bedroom door and said, "C'mon Lacy." He followed her to the living room where she sat with Lacy on the floor and began setting up Army men with him, but the phone rang and Alexandra hopped up and answered it quickly since the Abba Zabba woman didn't like being disturbed with phone calls while she was sleeping. Alexandra stayed on the phone for quite some time, so Lacy just stretched out on the floor lying on his back and began thinking. He would have sat on the rocking chair to do his thinking, but Randy was sitting in that chair, staring at Lacy every so often. Eventually, Lacy fell asleep on the floor but was woken up by the Abba Zabba woman yelling.

"WHERE'S ESTA? WHO TOLD HER SHE COULD LEAVE? I'LL SKIN HER ALIVE! SHE MUST THINK I'M SOME-BODY'S FOOL! SHE'S PROBABLY OUT WITH THAT CHRISTINA GIRL AFTER I TOLD HER NOT TO GO OUT! BOYS LET THIS BE A LESSON TO YOU. NEVER HAVE DAUGHTERS BECAUSE WOMEN ARE NOT TO BE TRUSTED! YOU CAN'T TRUST THEM WORTH A DAMN! IF RANDY HADN'T WOKE ME UP TO TELL ME THAT DAMN ESTA LEFT AFTER I TOLD HER NOT TO LEAVE I'D STILL BE SLEEPING WHILE SHE'S OUT SNEAKING AROUND BEHIND MY BACK. THAT GOT DAMN BITCH!" The Abba Zabba woman paced back and forth then went to her room with harsh words still flying from every angle of her mouth. Lacy was very shaken because he had never heard the Abba Zabba woman yell and speak about Esta like that before. He also looked at Randy and noticed that Randy was loving this. Randy had a huge grin on his face and looked at Lacy and gave Lacy the finger. Whenever Randy gave Lacy the finger, Lacy just looked at Randy's finger and wondered if Randy didn't know how to use his pointing finger and used his middle finger by accident. "ALEXANDRA AND ODESSA! GIT IN HERE!" the Abba Zabba woman ordered. As they rushed to meet her in her bedroom, Lacy moved just as quickly and stood outside the bedroom to listen, hoping to not get caught.

"Yes," both sisters responded.

The Abba Zabba woman asked, "Where's that low-down skunk of a sister of yours, and you better talk straight and talk quick and I don't want any lies, ya hear?"

"Yes," they said.

"We don't know where she went. She left but didn't say where she was going," Odessa said.

Alexandra said, "That's right."

"RANDY!!!" The Abba Zabba woman yelled. "Git me a belt! And you know the one I'm talking about."

"I sure do. Coming right up," Randy said.

"So, you two think you can outfox me and pretend not to know where that bitch went. Hahahaha. Well, that bitch might be having a good time but you two won't, I'm gonna beat the life out of both of you until you tell me where she went."

"Here's the belt you asked for," Randy said. "Can I watch?" Randy asked.

"NO! NOW GET OUT AND CLOSE THE DOOR!" she said.

Randy said, "Okay," as he closed the door slowly while grinning at the sisters. Alexandra gave him a dirty look and pointed at him to let him know she was going to beat him later.

The Abba Zabba woman slapped Alexandra's hand down and said, "I'm the queen bitch around here and I whoop ass, not you. Now, do either of you feel like talking?"

Odessa said, "Esta just asked us to watch Lacy while she was gone and told us she would be back in a while."

The Abba Zabba woman asked in a very calm but stern voice, "So, she asked you two to watch Lacy, hmm?"

"Yes, she did," Alexandra said.

"So, if she asked you two to watch Lacy that means you knew she was leaving and you didn't stop her from leaving or wake me up to tell me. DID YOU?"

"No..." Odessa said.

"We didn't. We're sorry," Alexandra said.

"Sorry my ass! You may have just as well left with her behind my back. NOW GIT UP!" Odessa started crying even before she got hit, but once she got hit, her cries were terrifying. Lacy had not heard anything like this ever before and wanted badly to rush in and help, but he knew something very bad would happen if he ran in there. "OH, you ain't gonna cry Alexandra? Okay, I'll teach you how to cry you lying bitch!" There were non-stop slapping sounds from the belt against Alexandra's body but she wouldn't break.

She held back the crying sounds until one hit must have hit her in a very vulnerable place because she let out the loudest scream and shouted, "YOU'RE WRONG FOR THIS! I WISH DADDY WAS HERE!"

The Abba Zabba woman said, "Well, he's not here. He's dead. Remember? You have me and I have to put up with your lying asses."

"LACY'S OUTSIDE THE DOOR LISTENING," Randy shouted. Lacy quickly made his way to the living room and sat by the table with his Army men.

The bedroom door flew open and the Abba Zabba woman raised the belt and gave Lacy a fierce look and asked, "DO YOU WANT SOME OF THIS?"

"No," Lacy said, as he could hear the cries coming from the bedroom.

"Stay away from the door Lacy," Alexandra said.

"YOU SHUT YOUR DAMN MOUTH AND DON'T TALK UNTIL I TELL YOU TO TALK," she shouted at Alexandra. The Abba Zabba woman looked back at Lacy and said, "Don't you be spyin' on me unless you want me to beat your little black ass raw," then she turned and went back into the room and closed the door and continued the beatings. When Odessa couldn't take any more of the beating she told her where Esta was. The Abba Zabba woman made Odessa call whoever she had to call to reach Esta. Once Esta was reached, the Abba Zabba woman got on the phone and told Esta to get home quick. Esta was so concerned about what was going to happen when she got home that she brought one of her friends with her to help explain to the Abba Zabba woman where they had been and what they were doing.

When Lacy saw Esta enter the front door, he wanted to go to her so he stood up but didn't move from where he stood. When he heard the tone of the Abba Zabba woman telling Esta's friend that she was not interested in lies and excuses and should leave, Lacy knew it was not the time to run to Esta. When the girl left, the Abba Zabba woman closed the door and began to beat Esta with a shoe right near the front door as she told Randy to get the belt, and then ordered Esta to go to her bedroom, as she continued beating her in the hallway and in the bedroom. Alexandra and Odessa pleaded with the Abba Zabba woman to stop but she told Alexandra and Odessa to get out of her way or they would get worse than they got earlier. Both sisters got out of the way and looked at Esta with sad faces as their eyes began to tear. She beat Esta for a long time while yelling at her and calling her a whore, bitch, and a mistake that she should have aborted.

Esta cried out, "I was just trying to enjoy time with my friends that I won't be seeing after graduation, can't you understand that?"

"You dare talk back to me?" she asked. "I'll beat you senseless." Esta cried and begged the Abba Zabba woman to stop hitting her. "I'll stop beating your good for nothing ass when I've had enough." *Whhhaap! Whhhaap! Whhhaap!* And the beating went on and on. Twice in the same day, Lacy heard screams and cries from the beatings. He thought he would be next on the list of people to get beatings because he felt that the Abba Zabba woman didn't like him. He believed if she would beat Esta then she would surely beat him, so he began to cry. Alexandra noticed Lacy crying and went to him to comfort him but it didn't work. He knew that somehow, his turn was coming. Odessa told Lacy to try to stop crying because if he got caught crying without a reason then he would get a beating for sure. When Lacy heard that, he snorted a couple of times to stop the flow of waterworks from his nose and eyes. He began wiping the tears away as fast as he could and tried to regain composure and act like everything was okay. He had no idea what a beating felt like but he knew it caused screaming and crying and he didn't want that. The sisters sat near him and whispered to each other about how horrible the Abba Zabba woman was and how she had lost her mind and how they could not wait to leave one day. When Lacy heard them talking about leaving one day he thought about what Esta told him about him leaving with her soon. He so badly wanted to tell Odessa and Alexandra about him and Esta leaving soon but he promised Esta he would not tell anyone. He thought Odessa and Alexandra could come along with him and Esta. He wanted to tell them so badly that he was fighting his urge and his eyes were quickly darting around the room.

"Lacy? What are you doing?" Odessa asked. "This is not the time to be playing or bringing attention to yourself. Stop fidgeting." Lacy stopped fidgeting and opened his mouth to tell the sisters about him and Esta leaving, but as quickly as he opened his mouth he closed it.

"What do you want to say?" Alexandra asked. Lacy was trying to think of something to say and Alexandra questioned him again.

He said, "I just want Esta to come out."

"She will," Odessa said. "She will, but when she does, try not to bother her. Let her come out and do what she needs to do and she will spend time with you later. After a beating, it's not easy to speak with anyone so leave her alone, okay?"

Lacy said, "Okay." The sound of the beating stopped and the Abba Zabba woman came out of the bedroom, stomping her feet across the floor as she entered the living room staring at Odessa, Alexandra, and Lacy while shaking the belt at them.

She yelled, "Does anybody else want a beating today because I'm in the mood to give them and I'm in no mood to take shit from any of you!" She kept her eyes focused on Odessa, Alexandra, and Lacy, and the three of them said no. Then, the Abba Zabba woman threw the belt across the room and it landed right in front of them. Lacy flinched because he thought it would hit him. The Abba Zabba woman stomped across the floor down the hallway to her room and slammed the door shut. Alexandra and Odessa got up to go see Esta and told Lacy not to move and that they would come back.

Lacy asked, "Where are you going?"

"To see Esta," they said.

"You said we should leave Esta alone," he said.

"No, we told *you* to leave her alone. She will need us to be with her right now. Now stay here and be quiet," Alexandra said, as they hurried to Esta. Lacy didn't understand why Esta would be okay seeing the sisters and not him after the beating. As he was thinking about that, he looked down at the belt and noticed that it was like what Gus wore around his pants when he went to the Boy Scouts but it was a caramel color. He remembered when the Abba Zabba woman came out from beating Esta, she had the belt wrapped around her hand with the skinny end hanging down. He thought she wrapped the belt around her hand and punched Esta with the part that was wrapped around her hand. As he looked at the belt lying on the floor, he saw images of himself being beat with the same belt repeatedly for things he had not done. It scared him, so he stopped looking at it. Randy stood over him smiling.

He leaned down, grinning in Lacy's face as he grabbed the belt and said, "Do you want sumaaa this?" Lacy wasn't afraid of Randy at that point. He was afraid of Randy making noise and bringing attention to him. He was afraid that the Abba Zabba woman would come out and see Randy with the belt thinking that he and Randy were playing with it, causing him to get a beating for something he didn't do. Lacy began to panic and Randy thought Lacy's panicking was due to him waving the belt around. "Aahhh! You're scared of the belt, aren't you?" Randy asked. "I should beat you like Alexandra beat me, you little pest. I hate you, and one day I'm going to knock your teeth out and Esta won't do a thing because she will get beat again." Randy hung the belt over his shoulder and gave Lacy a dirty look as he slowly walked away and sat in the rocking chair. Lacy wouldn't look at Randy because he was too concerned that the Abba Zabba woman would storm out of her room and head straight for the belt and beat his little black ass like she once said she would. Like a squirrel, Lacy stayed still and didn't move. He thought the more he moved the more Randy would see him. He realized his movements seemed to trigger Randy but his stillness somehow kept Randy calmer and made him less aggressive. Lacy just sat and sat and sat until Odessa came out of the room and got him.

"Come on Lacy, Esta wants you." Lacy jumped up and ran toward her but she quickly told him to stop running as she put her finger over her mouth and told Lacy to 'shh'. She told Lacy that they did not want to make too much noise and get in more trouble. They walked down the hall to the bedroom and Lacy saw Esta with tears running down her face, marks on her arms, and messy hair. Esta's hair was never messy. She would get up in the morning and make sure her hair looked nice before she went anywhere. She wanted to speak with Lacy alone so Alexandra and Odessa left the room and softly closed the door. Esta grabbed Lacy and hugged him tightly and Lacy hugged her just as tight.

"Are you okay Esta?" Lacy asked. She said yes, as she was still trying to gain her composure by making the same snorting sounds Lacy made earlier when he was crying.

"I'm alright," she said.

Lacy asked, "Are we going to be leaving here soon because I don't like it here and I don't want to get beat."

Esta said, "Not yet, and I can't say exactly when because it's not as easy as I thought. I don't have enough money to pay for everything that we need like a place to live, heating, lights, food, and clothes." Lacy's face tensed a little because he thought they were going to leave soon and live somewhere else. Esta said, "I'm sorry Lacy, it's just going to take more time but I'll figure something out because I can't take much more of this either," then she hugged Lacy.

Lacy said, "It's okay Esta, as long as I'm with you I'll be happy."

Esta grinned at Lacy and said, "And as long as I'm with you I'll be happy," then they both grinned at each other and hugged again.

The door burst open as the Abba Zabba woman said, "What are you two doing cooped up in here? Is Lacy asking you why I beat your ass?"

"No," Esta said. "He just wanted to be in here with me."

"Well, you need to be in here by yourself since you're grounded, so Lacy get up and get to the living room or somewhere else and don't bother anybody."

"Okay," Lacy said. As he left the room, he was nervous to walk by the Abba Zabba woman since she looked upset. Lacy went to the living room and didn't see Alexandra and Odessa but he heard their voices in the kitchen and smelled cookies. They were making peanut butter cookies, which was one of Lacy's favorites. Lacy walked into the kitchen and said, "Well, well, well, don't mind if I do," as he reached for a cookie, pretending they were for him. He stopped just before he grabbed the cookie and said, "Just kidding," then laughed, and the sisters laughed too.

"Didn't I tell you not to bother anybody?" the Abba Zabba woman said to Lacy as she entered the kitchen.

"Yes," Lacy said.

"Then why are you in here bothering Alexandra and Odessa?"

The sisters quickly said, "He's not bothering us."

Odessa said, "Yeah, we want him here to keep us company." The Abba Zabba woman looked at Lacy with her hands on her hips, top lip protruding over her bottom lip, eyes slightly squinted, and made a "huh" sound and walked away.

The sisters both looked at each other then looked at Lacy, motioning their heads to say, "that was a close one." Lacy looked terrified and moved closer to the sisters and asked them why she didn't like him and didn't talk to the other boys like she talked to him.

"Lacy, I wish I knew," Alexandra said.

"She doesn't like that you are so close to Esta," Odessa said.

"But I love Esta," Lacy said.

Alexandra said, "We all know that, but maybe others are jealous of how close you and Esta are with each other." Lacy just looked at the sisters and thought they must know why the Abba Zabba woman didn't like him and it must be more than his closeness with Esta. "Let's not think about that right now Lacy, we have some cookies to make."

Lacy said, "Yeeeees. What can I do to help?"

Odessa said, "You're helping just by being here with us but if you want to sing "Row, Row, Row Your Boat" to us we like that."

"Yees! Okay," Lacy said. "Row, Row, row, your boat gently down the stream, merrily, merrily, merrily, merrily, life is but a dream. Row, row, row, your boat gently down the stream, merrily, merrily, merrily, merrily, life is but a dream. Row, row..."

"Who's making all that racket?" The Abba Zabba woman shouted as she entered the kitchen again.

"I was just singing," Lacy said.

"Well stop it. I want some peace and quiet around here and you singing that dern row, row, row your boat isn't quiet or peaceful, so be quiet!"

"Okay," Lacy said.

"If I have to come in here just one more time because of you I'll tan your hide. You hear me?"

"Yes," Lacy said. When the Abba Zabba woman stormed out of the kitchen, Lacy started crying and both sisters rushed toward him and told him to stop crying as they were concerned he was going to get into a world of trouble if he made another sound. Lacy said, "See, she does not like me and she does not want me here. She never talks to the others like that. Never. I don't like her."

"Lacy," Alexandra said. "Please don't ever say that again, and please make sure you never think it or say it around Randy, Horace, or Marcel because they will tell and you will get into very big trouble. Here, have a cookie and just be here with us but keep quiet okay?"

"Okay," Lacy said. Tears began to fall from Odessa's eyes because she knew Lacy was right. She knew the Abba Zabba woman didn't like him for some reason and treated him much different than the others and liked to see him sad and upset. "You know I'm right about her, don't you Odessa?" Lacy asked. Odessa nodded her head yes. Lacy whispered, "If I were blind I couldn't see that." Both Odessa and Alexandra covered their mouths and giggled then huddled with Lacy as they all hugged, and that was when Randy walked in.

"What are you all doing?" he asked. "Give me a cookie or I'll tell that you were all in here telling secrets." Alexandra picked up a cookie and walked over to Randy. She raised the cookie up to his face, then raised her other hand near his face and made a fist with it.

She said, "Here's your cookie. If you say anything next time I'll beat you and I'll make sure you hurt for weeks, you understand me moron?"

"Just give me the cookie," he said, "and I'll think about not telling."

She said, "Try me Randy. You just try me and you will regret it." Randy bit into the cookie and walked about like a kingpin that felt in control of the situation. Alexandra looked at Odessa and said, "If I get a couple of friends at school to fix his wagon I won't get in trouble and he will learn his lesson." Lacy kept eating his cookie and acted as if he didn't hear that, but his face showed that he liked the idea.

Odessa said, "I don't know if that would teach him a lesson because he is so bad, and we will get in real trouble if he tells."

Alexandra said, "He won't tell. He knows better. He acts stupid but he ain't stupid enough to cross me."

"That's true," Odessa said, "but we have to stay close to Lacy tonight because Randy is up to something and he may try to get Lacy in trouble."

"I agree," Alexandra said. When all of the cookies were made, the sisters took them into the living room and told Lacy to sit on the floor by the coffee table. When he sat down, Randy immediately headed over toward him and Alexandra stepped in Randy's path, blocking him, and told him to go back where he was and not to cause trouble. Randy looked at her and just smiled. Alexandra smiled back at him with her fist in his face. Randy leaned to look past her at Lacy with a dirty look and Alexandra leaned over to block his view of Lacy, then Randy went back and sat down. They all watched TV until it was time for Horace and Marcel to get ready for bed. During that time, Alexandra and Odessa took Lacy into their room and took turns staying with him so they could each get their work done for the night before they went to bed. Lacy slept in Odessa and Alexandra's room that night since Esta was grounded and was not to see anyone, even those in the house.

THE TROUBLE CHILD
AND THE ARMY KING

The next day, when everyone was getting ready for school, Lacy was following Odessa and Alexandra around trying to avoid trouble. Esta's door was open. She had left already and it didn't look as if she had breakfast. "Okay, everyone in the car so we can go," the Abba Zabba woman said. Alexandra and Odessa pulled Lacy aside and told him to be good and that they would see him in a little while. Odessa turned on the TV for him and they both told him to be quiet and try to avoid any trouble and do exactly what he was told, right when he was told.

"I will," Lacy said. He looked concerned and fearful because he knew the Abba Zabba woman would be right back after dropping everyone off at school. As everyone left and closed the door, Lacy got in the rocking chair and began thinking about Esta and why she kept leaving without saying goodbye. He wondered if Esta was as afraid of the Abba Zabba woman as he was and if she left to avoid trouble or if he did something that upset Esta.

He wanted to see Jasper and hoped Jasper would come over and play Army men with him, but he did not want to ask the Abba Zabba woman about Jasper. In fact, he didn't want to ask the Abba Zabba woman anything because he thought she would just get upset with him and want to beat him. Cartoons were on, but Lacy wasn't focused on the cartoons because his focus was on staying out of trouble and how to do that, since everything he did lately seemed to get him into trouble. He thought of Shirley and wished he still went to her house because she was nice and no one bothered him there. *Click click.* The door was being unlocked and Lacy acted as if he was really into the cartoon and kept his eyes glued to the TV. The Abba Zabba woman came in and walked quickly through the hallway and went to the bathroom. When Lacy heard her finish peeing, he braced himself for whatever was to come. She came out of the bathroom, went to her room, and closed her door. He thought she would come out at any moment and start in on him. *She must be on her way out to get me,* he thought. Cartoons went off and "I Love Lucy" came on and still no Abba Zabba woman. Lacy didn't know what she was up to but he was less fearful the longer she stayed in her room. Much time had passed but he didn't want to make a sound so he stayed in the rocking chair. His eyes were getting heavy since it was near his nap time. He had not had lunch but that didn't matter to him because not getting a beating was better than eating. His head began to bob and his eyes were closing, closing, closed, and he was out like a light. "Wake up Lacy," the Abba Zabba woman said, as she stood over him. Lacy woke up and sat up looking like he saw a ghost. She said, "You shouldn't sleep in that chair because it's a very old chair and it's worth a lot. If you're sleepy you can lay on the sofa but don't let me catch you sleeping in the chair again." Lacy said okay, and quickly got onto the sofa and sat still. *Knock, knock, knock, knock. Who's that at the door?* Lacy wondered as he sat up a bit. The Abba Zabba woman came out from the kitchen and Lacy acted calmly and avoided connecting his gaze with her.

She raced to the front door and opened it. "HEY BEATRICE! HOW YOU DOIN'?" Lacy leaned back against the sofa back and sighed softly, thinking to himself, *it's only Lilly from next door.*

"Hey Lilly. Come on in," the Abba Zabba woman said. "I made some tea and drop dough biscuits for us to snack on while we watch Jack LaLanne sweat."

"Hahahaha," Lilly laughed and said, "Beatrice you do no howda burn in a kitchen. But, bein' from the South you musta been taught by da bes?"

"You know that's right," the Abba Zabba woman said. "Grits with cheese, greens with ham hocks and extra bits of bacon, Sock It to Me Cakes, dirty eggs, pancakes the size of a plate one half-inch thick, caramel cake, gizzards, and fried chicken to make you wanna slap ya granmama."

"Hahahahahaha." They both laughed and made their way to the kitchen and continued sharing southern stories about food, reunions, dances, and what you can and cannot do in the South and who they knew that died in the South due to racism. The word racism was a real buzz word for Lacy because he enjoyed running fast and racing whoever would race him. He ran so fast by the age of four that the neighbors kept saying he could be the next Jessie Owens. *I have to ask Esta to explain what racism is so I can be a part of it*, Lacy thought to himself. He also wondered why people died from racism. He wondered if they got hit by a car while they were racing or if someone didn't want them to win and did something to make them die. *I don't want to die from running,* he thought to himself, *but Esta will explain what it is and I'll learn how to do it without dying*. As Lacy sat listening to the ladies talk and had thoughts running through his mind about his future and what he would be and what he would do, there was another knock at the door.

The Abba Zabba woman looked concerned as she walked to the door that time and asked who it was. The voice said, "It's the police ma'am, please open the door."

Then Randy said, "It's me, Randy."

The Abba Zabba woman quickly opened the door and saw Randy standing with the police officer, crying. "Randy," she said, "what happened? Is everything alright? Officer, what happened?"

The officer asked, "Does this boy belong to you?"

"Yes," she said.

"Well, I saw him wandering the streets and thought he was too young to be out of school so I asked why he wasn't in school and he told me he didn't have to be in school because they let him leave early. So, I asked where he lived. He wouldn't tell me where he lived so I told him if he didn't tell me I would have to take him to the station until someone came to get him, so he told me. Are you sure he belongs to you?" asked the officer.

"Yes, why would you ask that a second time?" she asked the officer.

He said, "Well, ma'am, he's so dark and you're so light, so I want to make sure he lives here so I can put all of the facts in my report. I need for you to step outside so I can make note of all of this."

"Randy, go in the house and sit with Lilly in the kitchen," she said, then she went outside to speak with the officer. Randy went inside and quickly headed for the kitchen. He didn't say a word to Lacy but Lacy knew Randy was very upset. When Randy got to the kitchen, Lilly asked why he was crying and why he was home. Randy broke down crying and said that he wasn't doing anything wrong but the officer arrested him and brought him home.

"Arrested?" Lilly asked. "Boy, if you were arrested the officer wouldn't brang you home. Now, tell me what happened."

Just then, the Abba Zabba woman came back in the house and slammed the door shut, stomped her feet as she headed for the kitchen, and when she got there she said, "Alright! Now tell me everything, and I mean everything damnit! What happened today? You were supposed to go to school, listen to your teacher, and be good. WHAT HAPPENED?" Randy, started speaking as if he had been beaten because he was crying loudly while trying to speak. "I don't want to hear crying, I want answers damnit! They're trying to tell me that you're retarded, that you have a learning disability, that you steal, that you don't do what you're told and if I don't do something about it that you will get worse and end up in jail. You are not retarded, you just don't like to listen and do what you're told but you're going to listen to me. DO YOU UN-DERSTAND?"

"Yes," Randy said.

"Now, I'm going to drive you back to school and you are going to stay there and not give anyone a problem and you will learn. Are we clear?"

"Yes," he said, as he made crying sounds.

"Good!" she said. "Now go clean your face and don't you let me see you crying when no one has touched you. You ain't no sissy. Straighten up and stand tall and proud."

"Okay." Randy hurried up and went to the bathroom to clean himself up. He didn't say anything to Lacy or even look his way. The Abba Zabba woman was pacing in the kitchen and part of the dining room. Lacy could see her with her hands on her hips while she told Lilly that the school was trying to hold her boy back because they think he has a learning problem.

"He doesn't have a learning problem and is one of the smartest in that class," she said. They're just jealous and trying to intimidate him but I refuse to let that happen, that boy is smart."

"Lazy, but smart," Lilly said. "Beatrice, na I know he's yo son and you la dat boy. Do you think dat shcool might have a point?" she asked.

"Lilly, how dare you," the Abba Zabba woman said. "You think Randy is stupid?"

"No," Lilly said. "I never said dat. I just know dat Randy is different and does thangs that ain't right. Like that time he put a firecracker in that cat's ass and ripped dat cat to pieces and laughed about it."

"That's just bad judgment on his part but that doesn't mean he's re-tarded," the Abba Zabba woman said. "Many children have done things like that."

Lilly said, "But when he got caught he didn't see anything wrong wit it and still laughs about it today. He likes to see people hurt and git hurt, and from what you told me he does bad in school and fights with the teachers when they tell him to be respectful in class."

"Whose side are you on Lilly?" she asked.

"Na Beatrice, ya know I'm own yo' side but I want you to thank about dis and do the right thang for dat boy. If he needs help den get dat boy da help he needs is all I'm sayin'"

The Abba Zabba woman said, "If I thought he needed help I would get it but he doesn't need help, he just needs a teacher that isn't trying to intimidate him."

Lilly said, "Alright Beatrice. I'm wit you. I'm wit you."

"RANDY! LET'S GO!" Randy walked quickly back to the kitchen.

Lilly said, "I'll wait here until you get back."

"Okay," the Abba Zabba woman said. She and Randy made their way to the front door and neither of them looked Lacy's way. The Abba Zabba woman had an angry look on her face and Randy looked nervous and scared, probably because he didn't know what the Abba Zabba woman was going to say or do when she took him to school. When they left, Lilly came out of the kitchen and sat with Lacy.

"So, how you bin Lacy?" she asked.

"I've been okay," Lacy said.

"Ain't you gonna play wit you Aumy min?" she asked.

Lacy said, "Maybe later. It's more fun when I play with Jasper but he hasn't been here."

"No, I guess I haven't seen his car around here lately," Lilly said. "C'mon Lacy," she said, as she got down on the floor near the table and started pulling Army men out, "I'll play Aumy min with you. Show me how you setem' up." Lacy got on the floor with Lilly but it was easy to see that he didn't want to play Army men with her. "How do you play?" Lilly asked. Lacy began telling Lilly how to set the Army men up for the best strategies and Lilly interrupted and said, "Don't you jus shoot each otha making shootn' sounds?"

Lacy looked at Lilly and said, "No, the game would be over quickly if they all shot each other. Jasper taught me to set the Army men up in ways that make it more difficult for one army man to shoot another one."

"Oh, hell, dat ain't no game thas just a waste a ma time. You go ahead and play yo game an aum gone wait in da kitchen for Beatrice." As Lilly walked away, Lacy watched her sashay away in her peacock outfit as she dragged her feet in the open toe slippers with the fur ball on top puffing on her cigarette. Once she was in the kitchen, Lacy put his Army men back in the bag because he didn't want to get caught playing when the Abba Zabba woman got home. He knew she was upset already and didn't want to give her any reason to be more upset since it seemed like she didn't have a problem with giving him a beating. He just sat on the sofa and kept quiet while Lilly was in the kitchen smacking away on whatever she was chewing. He began thinking about Jasper and how he hadn't been around lately but hoped to see him soon. He also thought about what he would be like when he was big like Jasper and how he would be good to children like himself. Lacy wondered who taught Jasper how to play Army men and who taught him to be the person that he was because he thought Jasper was super 'neeato' and everyone loved him. Lacy liked the way Jasper spoke and pronounced his words and the way he walked, standing tall and happy. Jasper knew a lot about things and it seemed to Lacy that Jasper was a genius and could do anything. Lacy thought of being a fireman like Jasper but he liked watching the men in the old movies that ran and owned businesses and thought that would be much more fun. He thought owning a business would be more fun because the movies showed people working together and building companies that offered people something. He knew that firemen put out fires but fires didn't happen all the time so the firemen didn't have a lot to do most of the time. With a business, you could create and create and create and Lacy's mind was always creating stories and plans, so anything that allowed him to be creative gave him great joy. *Click! Click!* The door opened and in came the Abba Zabba woman.

"Lilly, I'm back," she said.

"I'm here in da kitchen enjuyin' deez drop dough biscuits. You better harry up before dey gooone," Lilly said.

"Hahaha, you better save me some," the Abba Zabba woman said.

"Lacy, do you want some biscuits?" she asked.

Lacy's eyes lit up and he said, "Yes please."

She said, "Well come on and join us in the kitchen." Lacy hopped off the sofa and wasted no time to get to those biscuits. He wanted to keep the peace between him and the Abba Zabba woman and was happy that she invited him. He thought, *maybe she saw that I wasn't so bad, especially after Randy got into trouble.*

When he got to the kitchen, Lilly said, "UUUUUUHH! THE AUMY MIN KING! Hahahaha. Ya know Beatrice, I got down own dat flo to play Aumy min wit Lacy and he told me I was doin' it wrong. Ain't dat right Lacy?"

The Abba Zabba woman looked at Lacy with an inquisitive but displeased look on her face. Lacy said, "I was showing how Jasper taught me to play."

"Lacy," the Abba Zabba woman said, "you should never tell an adult they're doing something wrong. It's disrespectful. Do you understand?"

"Yes," Lacy said.

"Now, go ahead and have a biscuit," she said. Lacy got the biscuit and put it on the plate but he sat there and didn't eat it. He felt that Lilly was trying to get him into trouble and lost his appetite. He didn't want to sit at the table with Lilly. *She's the adult and I'm the child,* he thought to himself. *Why is she acting like a child and trying to get the Abba Zabba woman to make her feel good just like Randy does?* Lacy thought to himself. "Aren't you going to eat your biscuit Lacy?" the Abba Zabba woman asked. "You wanted it, so make sure you don't let it get cold and go to waste," she said.

"Okay," Lacy said, as he looked at Lilly. She grinned at him and took a puff off of her cigarette looking like Rock Bottom from Felix the Cat. Lacy smiled back at her but he definitely didn't feel like the smile he gave her. He just wanted to make sure Lilly didn't tell the Abba Zabba woman that he didn't smile back. Lacy was quickly learning how to avoid trouble but didn't like it one bit. He wanted so badly to tell Lilly how she was acting like a child and should go home but there was no way he could pull that off without serious consequences. He began to pull pieces off of the biscuit and eat them when Lilly asked if he wanted some jam on his biscuit.

"No thank you," Lacy said.

"Oh, sho ya do boy, you don't know hodda eat dat buscuit." She said, "Here," as she grabbed his biscuit and slathered some jam on it then put it back on his plate. "Whatcha gooone say?"

"Thank you," he said, as he tried not to connect eyes with the Abba Zabba woman since he could tell she was looking right at him.

"Dat boy don't won dat biscuit," Lilly said. "Look atem. He thinks he too gooood fa suthen food after you took time ta make it." When Lacy heard Lilly speaking in a way that he knew would upset the Abba Zabba woman, he grabbed the biscuit and bit into it and started chewing like he couldn't wait to eat it. He looked at the Abba Zabba woman and smiled as he was chewing and she grew a partial smile back at him, then looked down at her plate and grabbed her biscuit and began eating. Lacy looked at Lilly and kept smiling but Lilly cocked her head back as she took a drag off of her cigarette, then put her cigarette in the ashtray and looked dead into Lacy's eyes as she grabbed her biscuit and took a big bite out of it. She chewed it slowly as she made a 'hmmph' sound and bucked her eyes at Lacy. As Lacy sat there eating in the lion's den, he thought about the people he had to watch out for. The Abba Zabba woman, Lilly, Randy, Horace, and Marcel. He knew that Horace and Marcel weren't his biggest worry, but the Abba Zabba woman, Randy, and Lilly were the main people to watch out for. He was thinking he could work harder at not making them upset and avoid problems as long as Esta tried to save enough money for him and her to leave and be away from the people that didn't seem to like him.

"Okay. Okay. Here's Jack!" the Abba Zabba woman said.

"OOOH YEEEAAH," Lilly said. "C'mon ova here Jack. Lilly got sumthin' fo ya. AHA AHA AHA HAHAHAHA! Beatrice, ya know that man got a good body and that Elaine wife a his don't know what she doin'. He need a woman like me."

"Hahahahaha," the Abba Zabba woman said. "Lilly, you oughta stop, you know that man is stuck on his wife and wouldn't give anyone else the time of day."

"Speak fo yoself," Lilly said. "She ain't got what I got and he would neva wont anyone else afta me. Tell you dat much. Hahahaha." Lacy didn't know what they were talking about but he was sure whatever Lilly had, Jack LaLanne would not want and would probably run for his life to get away from her and her nasty cigarettes. As they kept watching Jack, Lacy sat there quietly waiting for Jack to go off because Lilly always left when Jack went off and the Abba Zabba woman would take a nap about that time. This meant that Lacy could be alone with his thoughts and would not be in fear of making a mistake around the Abba Zabba woman or Lilly.

"We at da end uh da show a'ready," Lilly said.

"I guess so," the Abba Zabba woman said. Lacy was thinking GREAT! but he made sure he didn't show his excitement.

"Well, I better get going," Lilly said.

The Abba Zabba woman said, "Yes, and I better get some rest before Jasper gets here." Lacy perked up when he heard Jasper was coming.

"Oh, he comin' today?" Lilly asked. "I ain't seen him fo a few days."

"Yes," the Abba Zabba woman said. "He's been busy handling personal things but he's coming today and I can't wait to see him."

Lacy thought, *neither can I, we're going to play Army men. YEEEEEES!* "Well, let me get outcho hair an I'll see you lata."

"Okay," the Abba Zabba woman said. "I'll see you." As Lilly was walking out of the door, Jasper was walking up to the door.

"Heeeeeyy Jaspaaaa," Lilly said. "Ain't chu earlay today?"

"Hi Lilly. Yes." Jasper said. "I got out of work earlier today so I decided to come by earlier."

"OOH, I know why you came earlay," Lilly said. "You don't havta make up storess fa me. Hahahaha. Have fun Jaspaaaa! Hahaha."

Lacy was instantly excited. When Jasper got to the door the Abba Zabba woman was holding the screen door open for him and they hugged each other as he entered the door. "Hey Lacy," he said.

"HI JASPER," Lacy said.

"You're early. Is everything okay?" the Abba Zabba woman asked.

"Yes," he said, "I got out early today so I wanted to come early because I can't stay long today."

"Why can't you stay long?" she asked.

"I have a lot of things to do later," he said. She asked why he didn't call to tell her that so she would have known. He told her that it wasn't planned for him to finish early and to have things to do later but that was just the way it turned out. She turned and went to the kitchen, not looking happy. Jasper closed the door and went to Lacy. "How are you doing Lacy?" Jasper asked.

"Great," Lacy said. "I've missed you Jasper. Where have you been?"

"You've missed me?" he asked Lacy. "Really?"

"Yes, really," Lacy said. "Where have you been?"

Jasper said, "I've had a lot of things I had to do at home."

"Like what?" Lacy asked.

"Well," Jasper said. "I've had to move out old things I don't need anymore and I had to buy new things that I needed."

"Like what?" Lacy asked.

"Like what, like what, like what?" Jasper said as he began tickling Lacy while Lacy laughed hysterically.

"Jasper!" the Abba Zabba woman shouted, and he and Lacy stopped laughing and looked at each other like two children that just got caught doing something they should not have been doing.

"Yes?" Jasper said to the Abba Zabba woman.

"Could you come in here," she asked.

"Yes, I'll be right there," he said. "Lacy, I'll speak with you later." Lacy asked if they could play Army men later and Jasper said he wasn't sure. He told Lacy to let him finish his conversation with Beatrice then he would let Lacy know if they could play Army men. He said, "Lacy, always know that I love you and you are a good boy and will be a good man no matter what, okay?" Lacy looked at Jasper wondering why he said that. "Did you hear me Lacy?" Jasper asked.

"Yes," Lacy said.

"Then tell me what I just said," Jasper said.

Lacy said, "You love me and I'm a good boy and I will be a good man no matter what."

"That's right Lacy. Promise me you will never forget that."

"I promise," Lacy said.

"Good boy," Jasper said as he got up to go into the kitchen. Lacy grabbed Jasper by his arm and asked Jasper if he was leaving and not coming back. Jasper looked into Lacy's eyes and asked why Lacy said that.

Lacy said, "Because I saw that a day was coming when I wouldn't see you anymore."

Jasper looked sick to his stomach as he was looking at Lacy and said, "I'll see you Lacy, but right now I have to speak with Beatrice, okay?"

"Okay," Lacy said.

"Now, set up those Army men so we can play when she and I finish talking."

Lacy got excited and said, "Okay!" Lacy set up the Army men faster than he ever had before. Since he and Jasper had not played in such a long time he decided to pull out the entire Army men stash to have a big strategy session. When he was halfway through setting up the Army men he heard Jasper and the Abba Zabba woman's voices growing louder, so he began to listen to them.

"You haven't been here with me as much as before, or staying with the children through the night," the Abba Zabba woman said.

"Beatrice," Jasper said, "I have things to do too. I can't be here every morning and every night. Sometimes my schedule changes."

She said, "Jasper! You don't think my schedule changes? You don't think I have plenty of things to do? What's really the problem Jasper? No. I'll tell YOU what the problem is here and you know damn well what it is too! You got somebody else. You don't have time to be here because you're spending time someplace else. I should have known better than to be with somebody so much younger than me because you're always going to be looking for somebody else." Lacy's little ears were getting full and he stopped putting the Army men on the table because he knew when the Abba Zabba woman started raising her voice, things weren't going to end well. He also knew when Jasper got quiet during discussions with the Abba Zabba woman it meant he wasn't going to say much more.

"Look Beatrice, our schedules are just hectic and different and that makes it difficult to see each other as often and I'm tired."

"You're tired?" she asked. "You don't have any children and your job allows you a lot of time off and you're tired? Huh!"

"No. I meant I'm tired of the routine we are on because it's too difficult to keep up this schedule of being here in the morning, going home to take care of my house and needs, coming back at night to be with the children, then getting up early for work the next morning," he said.

"Jasper, then why don't you just move in and you won't have to run back and forth each day?"

The kitchen was quiet and Lacy's eyes widened, hoping Jasper would say yes. "I... just... don't think you understand Beatrice. Let's take a few days to think about this and talk then because I'm very tired and just want to rest. I told Lacy I'd play Army men with him and I want to do that before I leave so let me..."

"LET YOU WHAT?" she asked. "ARMY MEN? ARMY MEN? WE'RE HAVING A DISCUSSION AND YOU'RE GOING TO PLAY ARMY MEN?"

"Beatrice. Please lower your voice. Lacy doesn't need to hear all of the yelling."

"THIS IS MY HOUSE," she said. "IF I WANT TO YELL, I'LL YELL ANYTIME I'M DAMN GOOD AND READY! DO YOU HEAR ME? IS THAT CLEAR?"

Jasper said, "This is part of what I find tiring, your yelling and how you treat Lacy and the girls. It's just not right, especially how you act toward Lacy." When Lacy heard Jasper say what he said about him, he knew the Abba Zabba woman would not like that and would want to tan his hide or beat his little black ass. He felt that Jasper should not have mentioned his name and hoped they could change the subject.

"Lacy? Lacy?" she asked. "What the fuck does Lacy have to do with this? LACY GET IN HERE NOW!"

"Beatrice, no," Jasper said.

"Don't you tell me no," she said. "LACY!"

"Yes?" Lacy said, as he came around the corner.

"DO I TREAT YOU BAD? ANSWER ME GOT DAMNIT! DID YOU TELL JASPER I TREAT YOU BAD?"

Jasper jumped in and said, "Beatrice, I didn't tell you Lacy said you treat him bad."

"JASPER! SHUT UP! I WASN'T ASKING YOU, I WAS ASK-ING HIM. LACY! ANSWER THE QUESTION! DO I TREAT YOU BAD?"

"No, you don't treat me bad," Lacy said with a trembling voice.

"Listen to how scared he is right now," Jasper said. *Why doesn't he be quiet and stop getting me into this*, Lacy thought to himself.

"Are you scared Lacy?" she asked.

"No," Lacy said.

"Then why are you shaking and why do you look scared?" she asked.

"I wa- I wa- I was in the living room and an- and I thought I did something wrong and when you called me I thought I was in trouble."

"You see Jasper," she said, "he doesn't think I treat him bad, he was just startled by our conversation." Jasper looked down at Lacy and Lacy looked at him while his body shook and he kept fidgeting, trying to crack a smile. Lacy could see that Jasper wasn't happy with him for lying but Lacy would rather have Jasper upset with him than get his little black ass beat, so he had only one question at that moment.

He asked, "May I go back into the living room?"

"Yes," she said. "I just wanted to make sure Jasper knew how you felt. Thank you, Lacy," she said as he left the room without looking at Jasper. He went back to the sofa and sat there wondering what was going to happen next. The Abba Zabba woman kept talking and talking but

Jasper said nothing at all, and moments later he walked out of the kitchen and headed for the front door, passed Lacy without a word, opened the door, closed it, and left. The Abba Zabba woman stayed in the kitchen and began clearing dishes and running water and *CRASH!* The Abba Zabba woman ran from the kitchen to the front door and ran outside. "Jasper!" she yelled. Lacy jumped off the sofa and went to look. Jasper's car was in the middle of the street with another car nearby. The Abba Zabba woman kept asking if he was alright and he kept saying yes as he paced back and forth while talking with the other man that must have been driving the other car. Jasper kept looking at his car and putting his hands behind his head like people do when they lie back to relax but clearly, he wasn't relaxed. As Jasper and the man exchanged information, the Abba Zabba woman stood nearby and many neighbors came out of their homes to see what happened.

Of course, Lilly sashayed her way over with her cigarette in hand as she walked around Jasper's car saying, "Oh ma gad, OOOH maaa gaaaad. You ar'ight Jaspa?"

"Yes, Lilly," he said. Then she just kept sashaying around his car and the other car saying 'ooooh maaa gaaad'. Later, the Abba Zabba woman and Jasper went back into the house. They went back to the kitchen because Jasper needed to make a phone call. He spoke to someone on the phone and kept saying he had a fender bender but it wasn't bad. He was explaining that he had just begun to drive away from the curb and didn't see the car behind him and that was when the car behind him hit the back of his car. When Jasper finished his call, he and the Abba Zabba woman spoke for a little while then they went into the bedroom to finish their conversation. On their way to the bedroom, Jasper told Lacy they would play Army men after he and Beatrice finished speaking. Lacy said okay and perked up, then pulled out the Army men again and began setting them up. Much time had passed so Lacy fell asleep on the sofa.

"Lacy, time to get up so we can go pick up the others from school," the Abba Zabba woman said. Lacy sat up and looked around the room.

"Where's Jasper?" he asked.

"Jasper left a while ago. He saw you sleeping and didn't want to wake you and said you two can play Army men another time, so go ahead and put your Army men away so we can go."

"Okay," Lacy said. Lacy didn't quite understand what really happened because Jasper would wake Lacy up every time Lacy was sleeping if they had a plan to play Army men. *Why would Jasper leave and not tell me?* Lacy wondered. *Esta leaves now without saying anything, now Jasper is starting to do it. That's not very polite,* Lacy thought, because Esta taught Lacy to say goodbye before leaving even if you had to wake someone up. If the person wished not to be disturbed while sleeping, she said to leave them a note. Of course, Lacy could not write yet, but Esta wanted to make sure he knew what to do once he began writing. The Abba Zabba woman and Lacy got into the car and left to pick everyone up.

"Don't look so sad Lacy. You and Jasper can play another time. Right?" she said.

"Right," Lacy said. He thought it was easy for her to say that because she got to spend time with him, and she wouldn't be so happy if she didn't get to spend time with him. Lacy felt he had a good reason for not being happy about this, but knew it was best to hide his feelings and not risk getting into trouble for what he felt. As the school bell rang, all of the children ran toward the car and hopped in. Lacy wanted to sit next to Gus and ask about his day at school and what neeato things they did. Gus would explain what Arts and Crafts was and how they made different things in class with glue, paper, colored pencils, and fabrics. He also told Lacy about Math and Science since Lacy liked to hear about math and science questions and solutions or findings. Once they all got home, as usual, all of the children went in many directions to do whatever they felt like doing at the time.

PATCHING UP HOLES

The Abba Zabba woman went to her bedroom to rest because she planned to work later that night. Lacy would follow Gus, asking question after question after question, and when Gus got tired of answering questions Lacy would go to Odessa and do the same thing, then to Alexandra. By the time he tired those three out with his questions, it was nearly time for dinner and for Esta to come home. "Okay everybody, dinner's ready," Alexandra said. The boys stopped what they were doing and all went to the dining table to eat. As everyone was eating, Lacy asked Alexandra when Esta was coming home. Esta would normally tell Lacy what time she was coming home but she left that morning without saying goodbye so he had no clue as to when she would arrive. Alexandra didn't know either since the two hadn't spoken. Odessa said she wasn't even awake when Esta left but thinks Esta will be walking in soon. After dinner, the boys watched TV and Odessa and Alexandra went to their room to do homework or some type of crafting. As it got later, Lacy went to Odessa and Alexandra and asked if they could call Esta at work like they had done before to see when she was coming home. Alexandra said if she wasn't home by the time Horace and Marcel had to get cleaned up for bed she would call. Lacy said okay and asked if he could stay with them and watch what they were doing. "Yes," Alexandra said. "I can teach you to sew. Just watch what I do." Lacy said okay. As Alexandra sewed, she explained to Lacy how many people bought new clothes whenever they had a small hole or tear in their clothes and it was a waste of money to do that. She told him if he knew how to sew then he could save money by sewing his clothes when there was a hole or tear in the clothing. He asked her to show him how to get the string to stay on the pin. She explained that it wasn't called a string but a thread and not a pin but a needle, then she showed him how to thread the needle and told him to do it. Within minutes, Alexandra taught Lacy how to sew and how to patch up holes in clothing with patches that matched the color of the clothing. Lacy found this to be very exciting because he wanted to learn all he could about whatever people spoke about.

"Odessa! I know how to sew now!"

Odessa said, "I know, I was watching Alexandra teach you. Now you can sew all of my clothes from now on and patch any holes I have."

"REALLY?" Lacy said. "Where are your clothes?"

"Hahahahaha. I'm just playing, silly," she said. "You're not ready to sew clothes yet. You need to practice." He asked how he could practice, so Odessa asked Alexandra to give him some fabric to practice sewing. Alexandra gave Lacy some fabric scraps lying around for him to practice, and practice he did with a smile on his face. Odessa told Alexandra it was time for Horace and Marcel to get cleaned up.

Lacy stopped sewing and reminded Alexandra that she was going to call Esta when it was time for Horace and Marcel to get cleaned up. Alexandra had just pulled a new piece of thread from between her lips to moisten the thread to thread the needle.

"Huuh. Okay," she said. As she got up to go to the kitchen to call Esta, Lacy followed close by her, looking forward to Alexandra making that phone call. "Marcel and Horace, it's time for you to get cleaned up and ready for bed," she said.

"Already?" Marcel asked.

"Yes," she said. "C'mon Horace. You too. Get moving."

"Okay," Horace said. Alexandra began dialing the phone number and Lacy was standing by her side with anticipation, waiting to speak with Esta just to say hi and hear her voice.

"Hello," Alexandra said. "May I speak with Esta? She isn't? Okay. Thank you." Alexandra hung up the phone and said they said Esta wasn't working today. That was when the Abba Zabba woman came around the corner and asked Alexandra if she just said Esta wasn't working today. "Yes," Alexandra said.

"Then where is she?" the Abba Zabba woman asked.

"I don't know. I thought she had work today," Alexandra said. "She left so early this morning so I couldn't ask her if she was working or not."

"Hmmm? She's probably out running the streets with those friends of hers again," the Abba Zabba woman said, as she began fixing herself a plate of food the sisters made earlier. Lacy was nervous because he thought Alexandra and Odessa would get another beating and Esta would get one too when she got home. "If she's not home by the time I leave for work you make sure you tell her to call me at work."

"Okay," Alexandra said. "I'm going to make sure Marcel and Horace are getting cleaned up and ready for bed."

"Okay," the Abba Zabba woman said.

Alexandra said, "C'mon Lacy, so I can help you get cleaned up too." Lacy said okay and was very happy to leave the room with her without making eye contact with the Abba Zabba woman. He knew she was very upset with Esta and he wanted no trouble. When Alexandra got back to her room she closed the door halfway and told Odessa that Esta didn't work today and said Mom walked in and heard her telling Lacy. Odessa got off of her bed and asked Alexandra if Mom was upset and if Alexandra thought they would get in trouble again for Esta. Alexandra said she didn't think so because Mom told her to have Esta call her at work if Esta wasn't home before Mom went to work.

"I wonder where she is?" Odessa said.

"Me too," Alexandra said.

"Maybe she is doing a lot for graduation," Lacy said. "She keeps telling me she has a lot to do for graduation and it's been keeping her really busy." Both sisters looked at each other in a way that said graduation had nothing to do with Esta not being home. Lacy didn't exactly understand that look on their faces but he realized something was not right and couldn't wait to get to the bottom of it and speak with Esta about it when she got home.

After all, Esta never kept secrets from Lacy and he never kept secrets from her, so he knew she would explain everything that was going on and where she was. Alexandra whispered to Odessa that she would call some of Esta's friends once Mom left for work. Odessa said that was a good idea and Lacy said, "Yeah, that's a good idea."

"You need to stop listening to everything, nosey," Odessa said to Lacy.

Alexandra laughed and said, "Yeah Lacy Dick Tracy. You don't need to always figure things out like a detective and snoop around," she said as she continued to laugh.

"Why did you call me Lacy Dick Tracy?" Lacy asked.

Odessa looked at Alexandra and said, "You know he doesn't know who Dick Tracy is."

"Hahaha, but he sure acts like him."

"Who is he?" Lacy asked.

Alexandra said, "He's a famous comic book detective that discovers and finds things, people or places, and truth."

"Detective. I like that word. Detective. His name is Dick Tracy?" Lacy asked.

"Yes," Alexandra said.

"And he's in comic books?" he asked.

"Yes," Alexandra said.

"Then he's like a cartoon."

"Yes, right!" Alexandra said.

"How can I be like a cartoon? Shirley told me cartoons are made on paper and aren't real people."

"Right," Alexandra said, "but you act like that character in the comic book."

"How does he act?" Lacy asked.

"Lacy," Alexandra said, "he snoops and creeps around listening to people like you do to figure things out. Now, I don't want to talk about this anymore and have a long and drawn out conversation with you every time I say something. You've got a million questions about everything. Why do you have to ask so many questions? Can't you just listen and be quiet?"

Lacy said, "I can be quiet, but when I'm quiet you ask me why I'm so quiet. I ask questions because that's where the answers are. I want to know what you and everybody else knows."

"UUUGGGH! We're not talking about this anymore. I'm going to get back to my sewing, so if you want to sew with me you can but I don't want to hear any more about Dick Tracy or any questions about him. Okay?" Alexandra said. Lacy looked at Alexandra completely confused as to why she was so upset but he said okay. He didn't want to sew with her because she was upset, and Odessa saw this.

"Alexandra," Odessa said, "he is just trying to learn and he can't learn if he doesn't ask."

"Yeah, well, let him ask you and pester the heck out of you with his endless questions that nobody on earth would be asking at his age. What the heck is the matter with you Lacy that you have to ask so many questions? You're like a martian or creature from another planet and soon you'll be saying 'take me to your leader'. Hahahahaha." Alexandra went from being upset to cracking herself up.

Lacy just stared at her and didn't think anything she was saying was funny at all. But, he knew Alexandra was nothing like the Abba Zabba woman, Randy, Horace, or Marcel, and didn't try to get him into trouble like the others. Lacy also knew that Alexandra liked to be left alone and not be pushed or bothered too much. At age four it was difficult for Lacy to know how far was far with Alexandra, but he sure found out when she would go on the verbal attack.

Lacy said, "If you think I'm from another planet and then you should be nice to me because you don't know what I can do. Hahahha," Lacy laughed back at her.

"HAHAHAHAHAHAHAHAHAHA!" Odessa laughed hysterically. "Hahahahahaha. I guess he told you," Odessa said, "Hahahaahha."

"Uh, hahahaha," Alexandra laughed sarcastically. "You think you're so funny," she said to Lacy. "Boy, get over here so I can finish teaching you how to sew," she said with a smile. Lacy climbed onto her bed and continued his sewing lesson.

"Okay, I'm leaving for work," the Abba Zabba woman said as she peeked into the sisters' room.

"Okay," the sisters said.

The Abba Zabba woman said, "Remember, when Esta gets home you have her call me right away, you hear?" The sisters said yes. As the Abba Zabba woman walked toward the front of the house to leave, the other boys said goodbye to her, then she left. As soon as the front door closed, Alexandra and Odessa ran to the kitchen and began calling Esta's friends, and Lacy stood right there with them. After many phone calls and short conversations with as many of Esta's friends they could think of, they wound up with no clues to Esta's whereabouts. Lacy looked concerned and the sisters noticed the concerned look on his face.

Odessa said, "Don't worry Lacy, Esta is probably on her way home now."

Lacy said, "Maybe she doesn't want to come home because she got beat."

"Nooooo," Odessa said. "She'll be here. You watch. She will come back and you will see. You should probably go to bed so you can get your sleep and we will wait up for her."

"Yeah, c'mon Lacy, let's get you ready for bed," Alexandra said.

"Will one of you stay in the room with me until I fall asleep?" Lacy said.

"Yes," Odessa said. "We will take turns being with you until you fall asleep. Just don't start the million questions or I'll have to leave the room." Lacy said okay. After getting Lacy ready for bed, the sisters did as they said and took turns watching Lacy until he fell asleep but still no Esta. It must have gotten pretty late because both sisters were sleeping when the phone rang. Lacy was sleeping next to Alexandra and was woken up when she called out to Odessa to wake her because the phone was ringing. As they ran to the kitchen to answer the phone, Alexandra peeked into Esta's room but she was not there. Since Lacy was awake, he hopped out of bed and followed right behind them.

"Hello?" Alexandra said. "Hi. Yes. I know you did. But she's not here. I don't know if she came home and left again because we fell asleep and just woke up when the phone was ringing. Okay. Okay. I will. Goodnight."

"Was that Mom?" Odessa asked.

"Yeah," Alexandra said. "Mom said to put the chair in front of the door so that Esta can't get in and has to sleep outside."

"Are you really going to do that?" Odessa asked.

"Do I have a choice?" Alexandra asked. "If I don't do it and Mom comes home and finds Esta in her bed I will be in trouble, and Esta should have been here a long time ago. This makes no sense and I'm not taking the blame for her this time. She should have told us something and didn't, so that's on her."

"Why does she want you to put the chair in front of the door?" Lacy asked.

"Lacy, go back to bed," Alexandra said.

Lacy said, "But…"

"No buts Lacy," she said, "go to bed now."

"Odessa, will you take me to bed?" Lacy asked.

"Yeeeaahh. Come on. We can both go back to bed. I'll be there after I put the chair in front of the door, okay?" Odessa said. Minutes later, they were all back in bed, and Odessa and Alexandra exchanged small talk for a while about Esta and where she could be. Lacy tried to interject but they told him to go to sleep and stop talking. After a while, they were all asleep. When morning came, the sisters were up getting ready for school and talking, and that woke Lacy up. Lacy hopped out of bed and went to Esta's room but she wasn't there. He went to look at the front door and saw that the chair was still in front of the door. He went back to the sisters and told them that the chair was still in front of the door.

"Did Esta sleep outside?" Lacy asked.

Alexandra said, "We don't know because we didn't check, but if she came home she would have knocked on our window to let us know she was here and she didn't so she must have not come home at all last night." Now Lacy was really concerned and thought something must have happened because Esta would never miss seeing him or talking to him. There was a *knock, knock, knock* at the front door. Lacy ran quickly, thinking it was Esta and that she couldn't get in because the chair was in front of the door. The boys stood in the living room wondering who was at the door. Odessa and Alexandra told the boys to keep getting ready for school as they moved the chair to open the front door.

"Who is it?" Odessa asked.

"HEEEYY! IS ME! LILLY! YO MAMA ASS ME TA DRAV YAULL TA SCHOO! OPEN UP DA DOUGH."

"Ugh," Alexandra said.

Odessa said, "It's too early for her so I'm going back to getting ready."

Lacy moved quickly behind her.

After Alexandra let Lilly in, she said, "Harry up yaull. You cain't be late fa schoo."

"Okay," everyone said. Alexandra went to the back to finish getting ready.

By the time everyone was ready to leave, Esta came in the front door and Lilly said, "You jus get'n home? OOOOOO, yo mama gooone tear da assss up. Where you bin au night giiirrr?"

Esta said, "I was at work then I went with my friends to graduation parties."

"UHHH HUUUUHH," Lilly replied. "Weeeell, I don't thank you mama goooone like dat too much and if Shirley tried some shit like dat I'd tear her asssss up two taames and maybe a third taame fer crossin' me da wrong way. You thank you grown butcho mama goooone fix that. Uhahahahahaha. Yeeeep. Tear dat assss up fa sho. C'mon yau'll. Get'n da ca so we can go."

Lacy heard Esta's voice and ran to the front door. "ESTA!" Lacy said. She grabbed Lacy and picked him up and he hugged her tightly. "Where have you been Esta?" he asked.

"OOH, I had a long night. I worked then met some friends after."

"But you never came home and you didn't tell me I wouldn't see you last night."

"I know, and I'm very sorry Lacy. I didn't mean to stay out so late and not speak to you." Esta said. "Do you forgive me?" she asked.

Lacy said, "Yes, I forgive you Esta."

Odessa and Alexandra went to the front and saw Esta. "Where have you beeeen all this time?" Odessa asked.

"Yeah, Esta, where have you been? You didn't call or let us know anything," Alexandra said.

"I'm sorry," Esta said. She told them the same thing she told Lacy, that she was at work then met friends.

"Well, last night Mom told us to have you call her at work but now she is on her way home so you'll just have to speak with her in person and I don't want to be here for that," Alexandra said.

"Me either," Odessa said. "You remember what happened last time we tried to protect you? We got beat and I don't want that again."

"I won't be here when she comes home because I have to get ready for school," Esta said.

"School? How can you go to school after being up all night?" Alexandra asked.

"Oh, don't worry about me, I can do it," Esta said.

"Well, we have to get going," Odessa said. "Will you be home tonight?" she asked Esta.

"Yes, I should be."

"Should be? You have to watch Lacy, Esta, so there is no should be. You need to be here, so be here tonight," Odessa said.

Esta said, "Okay, I'll work it out, but I have to hurry up and get ready for school."

"Okay, see you later," Odessa said, and Alexandra said the same.

"Bye," Esta said, as she rushed to get ready. After the others left, Lacy asked Esta if he could go with her to school like he did before and she said no. She told him again that the teacher let her take him a couple of times because it was just for a short while since there was no one to watch him. He asked if he could stand somewhere outside the classroom and wait for her to get out. "No, Lacy. You can't." She said she could get into trouble if someone saw him standing around alone.

"Okay," Lacy said. "I don't like being here without you Esta." Esta stopped what she was doing and looked at Lacy. Then she bent down and hugged him and told him it was just a little longer before they leave and don't have to go back. Lacy's eyes lit up and he grew a big smile and said "NEEEEEATOOOOO!" Esta laughed and turned back to the mirror to finish getting ready to leave for school. Esta asked Lacy if he had eaten and he said no.

"What?" she said. "I'll get you a bowl of cereal and toast so you can eat when I leave."

"Is it okay if I eat in the living room so I can watch TV?" he asked.

"Yes, but don't spill anything or make a mess and put your dishes on the kitchen table after you eat. Don't forget."

"I won't forget." *Click Click!* "That's the front door," Lacy said. Esta looked nervous and Lacy said, "It's probably Jasper because he comes early sometimes."

They went to the front and were met with "WHERE IN THE HELL HAVE YOU BEEN? YOU THINK YOU CAN WHORE AROUND ALL NIGHT AND COME IN WHEN YOU WANT TO LIKE THIS IS YOUR HOUSE AND YOU'RE IN CHARGE?"

"I wasn't whoring around, I worked last night then I went..."

"STOP THAT LYING YOU LYING BITCH! ALEXANDRA CALLED YOUR WORK AND THEY SAID YOU WERE OFF YESTERDAY. NOW TELL ME ANOTHER LIE AND SEE IF I DON'T KNOCK HELL OUT OF YOU!"

"I'm telling the truth," Esta said. "I was supposed to be off work yesterday but I got called in for a few hours then left. My coworkers probably gave Alexandra my schedule and forgot to tell her that I came in for a few hours." *SLAP!* Right across Esta's face.

"YOU KEEP THE LIES COMING AND I'LL KEEP SLAPPING YOU SILLY!"

Esta held her face and said, "You never believe me!"

The Abba Zabba woman said, "That's because I'm sick of your lies. LIES, LIES, LIES!"

"I'M NOT LYING!" Esta said. *SLAP! SLAP! SLAP!* Right across both sides of Esta's face. The tears began to fall from Esta's face and Lacy backed away and squatted down near a wall hoping to not be seen, yelled at, or beaten.

"Now tell me. Where have you been and who have you been with all night you damn heffa! And don't you dare lie to me. I can spot a lie a mile away and you're just two feet away so don't try me. Now spill your guts you little bitch. Women ain't nothing but lyin' cheatin' bitches and whores. Lacy, you remember that. You hear me?"

"Yes!" Lacy said.

"Now Esta, talk." Esta was crying her eyes out and couldn't get her words out so the Abba Zabba woman grabbed her by her arm and pushed her to the floor near Lacy.

Lacy grabbed Esta's hand and said, "Tell her Esta, tell her."

Esta yelled at Lacy and said, "I DID TELL HER! CAN'T YOU SEE SHE DOESN'T BELIEVE ME!?"

"YOU HAVEN'T TOLD ME SHIT!" the Abba Zabba woman said. "But, I'm gonna get the truth from you one way or another." She left the room for a moment and came back with the belt. When she came back she said, "You can talk or you can bleed but I'm gettin' the truth today. I know those boys you've been hanging around with and those are some fast boys."

"I didn't do anything wrong," Esta said.

"LACY, GET AWAY FROM HER!" the Abba Zabba woman said. Lacy looked at Esta and didn't move, so the Abba Zabba woman pushed Lacy away from Esta and started beating Esta all over her body with the belt while calling her a whore, bitch, liar, and cheap slut. Then, there was a knock at the door. "Lacy, go see who that is. Esta, get your ass to your room and don't come out until I tell you, and if you sneak out the window I'll find you and finish beating your ass. I brought you into this world and I'll take you out GOT DAMNIT!" When Lacy opened the door, he saw it was Lilly.

"Beatrice," she said. "I heard all da yellin' and carryin' owwn, so I thought I betta come ova and make sure you weren't killin' nobody."

"Not yet," the Abba Zabba woman said, "but I'm working on it."

"Was dat Esta?" Lilly asked.

"Who else is coming in all times of the night around here?" she asked Lilly.

Lilly said, "Done be maaaaad a'me. I jus came over to tra to calm thangs down because you done need ta be goooin' ta jail ova no buuuuullshiiiiieet. You dun gat yoself all worked up and gooone give yoself da heard attack."

"You're right Lilly, but you know how these girls are. Just no good and always need to be watched."

"You ain't neva lied," Lilly said. "Das some hardco truth. A bitch is a bitch until she dead then da devil gat ta deal witta afta dat. Uhahahaha! You hear me Beatrice, you hear me ova hear crackin' ma ooowwn self up. Uahahaha. Look. You dun gat Lacy all up in da cona scare out his mand. Come oowwn ova here Lacy and…"

"NO," the Abba Zabba woman said, "you go right on in the room with Esta and don't come out until I tell you to come out."

"Okay," Lacy said as he walked quickly to Esta's room.

Lacy knocked on Esta's door and the Abba Zabba woman said, "I didn't tell you to knock, I told you to go in, so open that door and go in."

"Okay," Lacy said, as he opened the door and went in and closed the door. He saw Esta sitting on her bed crying and asked if she was okay.

"NO," she said. "She's an evil witch and one day God is going to punish her for all that she does to people." Because Esta was so upset, Lacy didn't want to ask her too many questions. "Lacy," she said, "one day you will be a grown man and live your life the way you want to, but as long as you are in this house you have to do everything she says or you'll get what you saw me get today." Lacy just listened as Esta told him that he had to use his brain and make a better life for himself. She told him that he was very smart and saw things other people didn't see and would be teased for that and not to let that stop him from living in a way that made him happy. She told him to stay near the people that understood him and believed in him and to do all he could to pull away from anyone that did not understand him and wanted to hurt him in any way.

"You mean like Randy and Horace and Marcel."

"Yes Lacy," she said, "but I also mean people outside that you will meet in your life as you get older. You have to keep yourself safe Lacy because people will try to take from you."

"Take what?" Lacy asked.

"Whatever makes you happy Lacy, that's what people will try to take so they can have it for themselves. People will be jealous of you and want to have what makes you, you. Your mind, your love, your happiness, do you understand?"

"I think so," Lacy said. "On Felix the Cat they always want his bag of tricks so they can have everything that comes out of the bag."

"Exactly," she said. "They are jealous of Felix and they want what has been given to Felix, which is a bag that helps him through life."

"Esta, I understand what you mean," he said.

"Then promise me you will be careful with the people you let into your life."

"I promise," he said. She hugged him and wouldn't let go and he hugged her tightly too. "I promise," he said again. She kept shedding tears, telling Lacy that she loved him and wished she could give him a better life. He told her that she takes good care of him and is glad he is with her. She continued to shed tears as she pulled him close and hugged him tighter. They could hear Lilly and the Abba Zabba woman talking in the living room and that was when Lacy asked Esta if she thought they would get a beating when Lilly left.

Esta said, "I don't know what that she'll do. No one knows what she'll do Lacy. Just make sure you don't get in her way and don't give her any reason to bother you, okay?"

"Okay," Lacy said. Both Lacy and Esta were in that bedroom so long they fell asleep and slept for some time until the Abba Zabba woman walked in and told Esta she wanted to talk to her. Esta got up and told Lacy to stay there. Esta and the Abba Zabba woman went to the living room to talk and Lacy stood by the bedroom door trying to listen to their conversation. The Abba Zabba woman told Esta that she had been living it up and doing whatever she wanted to do for a long time and wasn't handling her responsibilities. She told Esta that Alexandra and Odessa had been doing all of her work and handling her responsibilities.

"You know exactly what I'm talking about, don't you?"

Esta said, "Yes. I do." She said, "Alexandra and Odessa know I'm graduating soon and offered to help me as much as they can until I graduate."

"I don't care what they offered you. I told you what you had to do around this house and not to skip out on your responsibilities, didn't I?"

"Yes, you did," Esta said.

The Abba Zabba woman said, "So, from this point forward you will come straight home after school or work and if you don't, the beating you were going to get today will be given tenfold. Do you understand me?"

"Yes," Esta said.

"Good," the Abba Zabba woman said, "because I don't want to have to tell you this again. I don't think Lacy ate so you need to get in that kitchen and get him something to eat."

"Okay," Esta said. The Abba Zabba woman said she was going to take a nap and that Esta better be there when she woke up. She also told Esta to make her some food so she could eat after her nap. Esta said okay, then went to get Lacy to make him something to eat. When Esta went to get Lacy, she saw him standing by the door inside the room and told him to go with her to the kitchen. When they got in the kitchen, Esta asked Lacy if he was listening and Lacy said yes. "You better be careful Lacy, because one day she's going to catch you listening and beat you good." Lacy said he just wanted to know what they were talking about and if they were going to get a beating. Esta said, "It doesn't matter. You have to stop listening to conversations that have nothing to do with you."

Lacy said, "Esta, you're the one that spends the most time with me and teaches me things. When you are not here I listen a lot to try to learn."

"Lacy, I know you think it's okay to listen to others' conversations but it isn't, so please stop, okay?"

"Okay," Lacy said.

Esta made Lacy something to eat as he asked her about the word racism. She asked him where he heard that and he told her about the conversation he heard the day before. Before he said another word she said, "Again Lacy, you were listening to someone else's conversation. You just have to stop that."

Lacy said, "But I'm here all the time and hear the things everyone says but I don't understand all that I hear so I ask you Esta." She just shook her head and sighed. "Will you tell me?" Lacy asked.

"Tell you what?" she asked.

"Will you tell me what racism means?" he asked. She told him that was a word that she wished didn't exist. She told him racism was when a group of people or a person from that group believe they are better than other groups because of the race of people they come from. "I don't understand," Lacy said.

Esta said, "Lacy, some people won't like you because of your color because they believe their color is better than yours. They also believe all of the people that are the same color as them are better than you and people with your color."

"Why would they not like me because of my color?" Lacy asked.

"Lacy, I don't want to explain all of this to you right now, okay?"

"Okay Esta," Lacy said. "I thought racism was about racing like running a race."

"Well in a way it is, but you don't run with your feet you run with your color and the color most liked wins."

"OOH," Lacy said. "The color that people like most, wins. Do you think I can win?" Lacy asked.

"That would make you a racist and you would be part of the racism. You don't want people liking you because of your color and you don't want to like others because of their color Lacy. You want to like them because they are a person who is good to other people. Now, can you remember that?"

"Yes. But Randy calls Odessa names because of her color and Odessa calls Randy names because of his color. Is that why they don't like each other? Because they think they have the best color?"

"Lacy, please eat your food. We'll discuss this some other time."

"Okay," Lacy said.

The word racism was never discussed again between Lacy and Esta because he thought it upset her too much, so he just didn't ask her about it anymore. From that day forward, Esta didn't leave the house for school without saying goodbye to Lacy and she came home right after school or work on time each night and spent time with Lacy. As Esta's graduation got closer, she would sometimes stop home after school to pick up Lacy to go with her during after school functions with some of the students, then go right back home. One day, Odessa went with them to the school and Esta went away for a little while to speak with someone, so Odessa and Lacy went to the school gym so Odessa could talk to a boy. As Odessa spoke to the boy, Lacy saw some weights on the floor. It was a small dumbbell bar with no weight on it, so Lacy put a 2 and a ½ pound weight on each end and tried to lift it like Jack LaLanne. As he lifted the dumbbell, a weight fell off the bar right onto his toes.

"Ouch!" Lacy yelled. The boy Odessa was talking to ran over to Lacy right away and asked if he was okay. Lacy said, "It fell on my toes and it hurts."

Odessa asked, "Why were you touching those things? Nobody told you to touch those things."

The boy said, "It's my fault. I should have been watching since that's my job here."

"No," she said, "he knows better."

"It's okay," the boy said. "Your name is Lacy?"

"Yes," Lacy said.

"Take your shoe off Lacy, and let me see your toes." He wiggled Lacy's toes, making Lacy laugh. "This little piggy went to the market and this little piggy went home, this little piggy had roast beef and this little piggy had none."

"Hahahahahahaha," Lacy laughed out loud and said, "do it again, do it again."

"No, don't do it again. Lacy, he and I were talking."

"It's okay Odessa," the boy said, "I like children and Lacy is my new friend." Lacy's eyes lit up because he made a new friend. Odessa didn't look very happy, probably because she wanted the boy's attention that Lacy was getting. At one point the boy realized this and told Lacy he could lift the dumbbell bar by itself but to be careful, so that was what Lacy did. Odessa and the boy started talking again and Odessa fidgeted and looked around the room. The boy had a grin on his face as he rested his hand on a piece of equipment while leaning against it. When Esta was finished meeting whomever she met, she met Lacy and Odessa in the gym and said it was time to go, so they all walked home and Lacy listened to Odessa telling Esta about the boy she liked. Odessa asked where Esta went to speak with him but Esta told Odessa she would tell her later.

"She just doesn't want me to hear," Lacy said.

"I thought I told you to stop listening to people's conversations Lacy," Esta said.

"I wasn't listening Esta, you two were talking loud and I heard. I'm right here."

"Walk ahead of us Lacy and you won't hear what we're talking about." Lacy thought the two were not being fair so he started walking far ahead of them, and then he started running so they ran after him to catch him. They couldn't catch him because he was too fast, and when they got out of breath he stopped and laughed at them and said they should watch Jack LaLanne. When Esta caught up with him she slapped him on his butt and told him that was not funny.

Odessa started laughing and said, "It is funny when you think about it. How can he run so fast?"

"Odessa, don't encourage him. He should not do that," Esta said as she burst out laughing. Odessa asked Lacy why he wasn't laughing and he said he wanted them to laugh and chase him but he got spanked and now they think what he did was funny.

He said, "That's not funny to me." Then, Odessa and Esta laughed even harder and Lacy kept a straight face as he looked at them.

Esta said, "You can look at us like that all you want Lacy but you should not have run away and we should not be laughing but we are, so let's just go home now."

"Are you upset with us?" Odessa asked Lacy. Lacy just walked and didn't say anything. "Boy, I'm talking to you," Odessa said.

"I'm not upset," Lacy said, "but you two are not being fair. How would you like to get spanked then laughed at?"

Esta said, "Lacy. You made your point. It's over now so no more talking about it."

"I wasn't talking about it. Odessa asked me a question."

"Alright! Enough, and no one will ask you another question about it."

"Bahahaaha! Ooops! I'm sorry," Odessa said. "I didn't mean to laugh. Lacy just looks and sounds like a little man walking in front of us."

"Are you going to call me a forty-year-old midget like Shirley did?" he asked Odessa.

"Bahahahahahahaha!" Odessa laughed even harder. "She called you that? Bahahahahaha."

"Odessa," Esta said. "Control yourself."

"Yes Odessa, try to control yourself like you did with the boy at school." Odessa stopped laughing and she caught up to Lacy and asked what he said.

"Nothing," he said.

"Oh yes you did. Open your mouth one more time and see if I don't close it for you." Lacy didn't say a word.

Esta said, "This is what happens when you listen to other people's conversations and repeat their business Lacy. You better learn not to repeat other people's business because one day it just might not be Odessa that wants to close your mouth for you. You hear me?"

"Yes," Lacy said.

"Now turn around and keep walking home," Esta said. Lacy said okay and started walking, but he could still hear the sisters talking as they all walked home. He heard Esta telling Odessa that she spoke to someone but Lacy couldn't hear so he slowed down a little, hoping they would catch up so he could hear what they were saying.

"Stop slowing down," Odessa said, "you're not fooling anybody…still trying to listen." Lacy sped up and didn't say anything and kept his walking distance far enough ahead of Odessa and Esta to not hear what they were saying all the way home. When they got home, Esta, Alexandra, and Odessa thought it would be a good idea to cook together and make dinner and cookies and Lacy got to watch and learn from them as he often did. Lacy enjoyed this time greatly because Esta was spending much more time with him like before but she was also spending time and cooking more with Alexandra and Odessa. When the three sisters cooked together there was a lot of laughter and storytelling going on and Lacy looked forward to it - stories about June Bug and how he got into trouble with his parents and how he talks about going into the Army one day, stories about Michael Myers and how all of the girls like him and want to marry him one day, how Lilly beat Ari on the back of his neck with a cake cutter (steel forked comb for afros) until his neck bled because he forgot to take out the trash, how Leo across the street got jumped into a gang and is using drugs, stories about a girl who got pregnant and had twins while she was still in high school, the time one of the neighbors was siphoning gas from his mother's car to put it into his truck and accidentally swallowed some gas and had to vomit to get it out of his stomach and drink milk to dilute the residue. Of course, many of the stories were not ideal for a four-year-old but it was the way Lacy learned, and more importantly, he got to see the three young women working together and making conversation. Lacy thought when he and Esta left that house it would be great to have Gus, Alexandra, and Odessa with them because they all got along well. Sometimes Esta would ask Lacy to go into the living room and watch TV with the others so she and Alexandra and Odessa could speak in private. Lacy told Esta he thought they were *all* speaking in private and asked if he could stay.

"No," she said. "Now, please go into the living room." Lacy would look at Odessa and Alexandra hoping they would change Esta's mind, but they just kept doing what they were doing and remained silent. "Did you hear what I said?" Esta said to Lacy.

"Yes," he said, as he went into the living room. Of course, Randy noticed Lacy entering the living room and had to comment.

"Soooo, they kicked you and your four eyes out of the kitchen, huh?" Lacy got better at ignoring Randy's comments, and sometimes Randy would go back to watching TV or he would get up and go near Lacy to comment and heckle him more. Either way, Lacy would continue to ignore him and do his best not to react to Randy, especially when Lacy knew Esta, Alexandra, and Odessa were close by.

Lacy would say, "Leave me alone Randy." Randy would never listen the first time and would push or comment to Lacy again and that was when Lacy would tell Randy he was going to call for Alexandra. When Randy heard Alexandra's name he would give Lacy a dirty look and a make a 'pcchh' sound and walk away, but not before slapping the back of Lacy's head in an upward motion to catch his hand on the hook of Lacy's skull. Lacy would just keep doing what he was doing and Randy would go back and sit down. Lacy sat on the floor and watched TV with the others but he had one ear listening to the TV and one ear trying to listen to the sisters' conversation. He could not hear a word they were saying because they were whispering as they often did when he would leave the kitchen.

He learned about their whispering routine when he once snuck up on them to listen, and couldn't quite make out what they were saying but got caught when Horace yelled, "Lacy's eavesdropping by the kitchen!"

Alexandra was right near where Lacy was standing, behind the wall that separated the kitchen and the living room, so she jumped out and grabbed his arm and pulled him to the kitchen and asked what he was doing and what he heard. Lacy said he was trying to listen to what they were saying but couldn't because they were whispering.

"Yes. We were whispering to keep ears like yours from hearing things you shouldn't be hearing." Esta said, "Lacy, we've talked about this before, haven't we?"

"Yes," Lacy said.

"No cookies or snacks for you tonight, and you need to apologize to all of us for eavesdropping." Lacy apologized and was sent back to the living room. Since then, Lacy knew better than to sneak up and listen in on the sisters whispering, so on this night he just sat and watched TV and tried to listen to their whispers from the living room but couldn't hear a word. Part of Lacy's need to hear what the sisters spoke about had to do with how often he heard his name in their conversations. He could not understand why his name was mentioned in their conversations so much and why when he asked what they were saying they would get upset and tell him to mind his own business. He thought if his name was mentioned that the conversation was his business too. He would also hear Lilly and the Abba Zabba woman mention his name a lot. Even Jasper and the Abba Zabba woman mentioned Lacy's name a lot in their kitchen conversations but Lacy just couldn't listen in on the conversations good enough to know what was being said about him. So, he kept trying, hence the name Lacy Dick Tracy. The other part of Lacy's eavesdropping habit, however, was just childish curiosity. After they all had dinner that night, Esta spent time with Lacy watching old black and white movies that they both enjoyed until Lacy would fall asleep.

This was pretty much the routine each day leading up to Esta's high school graduation, with new adventures on the weekends. Like the time a guy named Benny, who was said to be a relative, took Lacy and Esta to the circus where Lacy ate so much cotton candy he got a tummy ache. Another weekend, Esta, Odessa, and Alexandra took Lacy to a school baseball game, but Lacy wasn't interested in the baseball as much as he was the shoelace red licorice. Each weekend before Esta's graduation, she would make sure she and Lacy had a lot of fun, including a weekend when she took him to school to watch an old matinee movie with all the popcorn you could eat. Lacy thought that was the life. He was with Esta and she was with him and the snacks kept coming. *OOOHHH YEEEES!* he thought to himself. *Things can only get better because the summer is coming and Esta, Odessa, Alexandra, and Gus will be out of school.* The Abba Zabba woman would still do or say things to make Esta cry, like the time she told Esta that she looked like a baboon in heat because of the way she walked..

Of course, Lacy had to ask Esta what a baboon was, but she was too upset to answer him at that time. Another time Esta was told that no man would ever want her because she was too homely and plain. Yes, Lacy was nearby and heard that too and needed to know what those words meant, but Esta was too upset to talk to him about it, so Lacy just sat with her while she sulked and cried. It seemed like time flew by and Esta's graduation was here. As she got ready, she explained to Lacy that he would be with Odessa and Alexandra and the boys while she was graduating because there wasn't enough seating for everyone. She explained to him that he would get to play on the big grass hill at the school that children enjoyed sliding down while sitting on flattened cardboard boxes. "Yeeeees!" Lacy said. He liked speed, and sliding down that hill on flattened cardboard boxes was more than enough speed for him. He and the others slid down that grass hill during the entire graduation and went through several flattened boxes since they fell apart after several uses. "There she is," Lacy said. "Esta!" he yelled her name as he ran to her.

She ran to Lacy with a few friends with her and picked Lacy up and gave him a big kiss on the cheek and said, "I'm done with high school and ready for college."

"Yes," Lacy said, "so you can get a good job and money to pay for things."

"YEEEESSS!" Esta said with lots of laughter. "Come on. Let's go eat," she said.

"Don't you want to slide down the hill Esta?" Lacy asked.

"No, not today Lacy, because I don't want to ruin my clothes and I'm hungry, so let's go," she said.

"Okay," Lacy said. When everyone got home they ate and had many snacks, including various cookies the sisters made the night before. Many of Esta's friends stopped by, congratulating her as she did them, since they had just graduated too. Her friends invited her to meet up with other friends for get-togethers and the Abba Zabba woman said she could go but had to be home early. Esta was so excited to go with her friends that she didn't finish eating and told Lacy she would see him later and to eat all of his food and enjoy the cookies.

Lacy was sad she was leaving but happy at the same time because he knew she was out of high school and would be around more in the summer, so he said, "Okay Esta. See you later."

"See you later alligator," she said.

"See you later alligator," he said back to her, then laughed as she left and continued eating his food. Lacy watched the clock for a while. Even though he couldn't tell time, he would watch the arms move because Esta used to tell him they leave for school when the little hand is on the eight and the big hand is on the ten. She told him everyone would be home when the little hand was on the three and the big hand was on the three or four. That night he kept seeing the little hand move from number to number and kept asking Odessa and Alexandra if Esta was coming home soon, but they told him the same thing every time he asked.

"I don't know when she's coming home because she didn't say."

"Okay," Lacy would say.

"Just relax Lacy, and enjoy the cookies and watch TV," Odessa said. "You will probably be sleeping when she comes home so have fun with us and look forward to seeing her when you wake up."

Lacy said okay and grabbed another peanut butter cookie, bit into it, and smiled at Odessa and Alexandra and said, "MMMMMM MMMM," then they all laughed and enjoyed the night. The next morning, Lacy woke up and Esta was right next to him sleeping, so he cuddled up next to her with a big smile as he put his arm over her to hug her. She woke up for a moment and said hi to Lacy and told him she was very tired, so he should ask Alexandra or Odessa to fix breakfast for him. Lacy did just that. He went to Odessa and Alexandra's room to ask them to make something for him to eat but they were not in their room, so he ran to the living room where they were watching TV. He told them that Esta was very tired and told him to ask them to make something for him to eat. Odessa asked Alexandra if she would do it because Odessa was more into the TV program than Alexandra was.

Alexandra said, "Okay, let's go Lacy." As Alexandra and Lacy were walking to the kitchen, the Abba Zabba woman walked into the living room, quickly stomping her feet as she walked.

"Alexandra! What are you doing?" she asked.

Alexandra said, "I'm about to make something for Lacy to eat."

"No, you're not," she said. "Where is Esta?"

"Oh, she's still sleeping," Alexandra said.

"Still sleeping, huh? You sit down," she said, "and Lacy you too, sit down." She stomped her feet across the floor and went into Esta's room and yelled, "IF YOU DON'T GET YOUR ASS OUT OF THAT BED AND GET THAT BOY SOME FOOD I'LL DRAG YOU OUTTA THAT BED! GET UP NOW. YOU DON'T HAVE ANY SERVANTS AROUND HERE!" then the Abba Zabba woman stomped back to her room and slammed the door shut.

Horace danced around Lacy saying, "You don't have any servants around here either," as he laughed.

Then Randy said, "Yeah four-eyes." Lacy had no idea why Horace was parading around like that. Lacy felt like he got Esta into trouble that morning. He was so happy to see that Esta was home that he spoke with excitement when he asked the sisters what Esta told him to ask. When he heard the Abba Zabba woman's feet stomping across the floor and her yelling at Esta he immediately thought he should have whispered to the sisters instead. When Esta came out of her room she was clearly upset and hurried herself to the kitchen, shaking her head left and right in a way that showed her dislike for what just happened. Alexandra and Odessa joined her in the kitchen and Lacy followed. Lacy quickly told Esta he was sorry for getting her into trouble and for speaking too loud.

Esta looked at Lacy and said, "Go into the living room and I'll tell you when your food is ready," then she looked away and continued preparing something for him to eat. Alexandra quickly told Lacy it wasn't his fault, then Odessa chimed in and said the same thing and that Esta would have gotten yelled at that day anyway just because she went out and had a good time. Lacy asked Odessa why Esta would have gotten yelled at for having a good time and that was when Esta said, "Lacy, I told you to go to the living room, now go!"

The Abba Zabba woman stomped across the floor again, entered the kitchen, and marched right up to Esta. "Who do you think you are raising your voice to in this house?" she asked Esta. Esta said she wasn't raising her voice, she just wanted Lacy to listen to what she said. "You calling me a liar?" the Abba Zabba woman asked.

"No," Esta said. "I was telling you what happened."

The Abba Zabba woman said, "I know what happened. We both know what happened, don't we? If I needed you to tell me what happened then I'd ask you, but since we know what happened you don't need to tell me a got damn thing." Then she stomped her feet all the way back to her room and left the door open. Lacy couldn't figure out what was going on that morning but he apologized to Esta again and that was when Odessa took Lacy to the living room and whispered to him to just sit and watch TV. Horace and Marcel were approaching Lacy but Odessa pointed at them and waved her arm to them in a motion that told them to get away. They ignored her motion and began making faces at Lacy and covering their mouths with one hand as if they heard something hilarious, then pointed at him with their other hand. Odessa stood up and gave the boys a stern look, then motioned her arm again as if to say, "get away", and that was when they ran to the Abba Zabba woman's room and told her that Odessa was pointing at them and giving them a mean look. The Abba Zabba woman called Odessa to her room and questioned her, then sent her to her room, and that was when Horace and Marcel laughed out loud. When Horace and Marcel went back to the living room, they headed for Lacy.

"Hey four-eyes," Horace said, as he pushed Lacy. Alexandra heard this and walked near Lacy and the two boys went back and sat down to watch TV. They knew that the Abba Zabba woman could send Alexandra to her room too, but Alexandra would get even with them at one point and it would be painful.

"Come back into the kitchen," she said to Lacy. She told Lacy to sit at the kitchen table and not to say a word.

GONE, GONE, GONE

Esta and Alexandra were whispering but Lacy could not hear many of their words and didn't try to. He knew Esta was upset and didn't want to make things worse, but he kept hearing his name mentioned by both sisters. Esta gave Lacy his food then she and Alexandra sat at the dining table where Lacy could still see them, and they continued whispering until Lacy was finished eating. Esta washed Lacy's dishes then she told him to come with her as she and Alexandra went to see Odessa. They entered the room where Odessa was to fetch her, and then to the Abba Zabba woman's room to tell her that the sisters and Lacy were in Odessa and Alexandra's room. Soon after, the Abba Zabba woman stomped her feet again across the floor, entered the bedroom where the sisters and Lacy were, and told Esta to get to her room and clean it up, and when she finished, to clean the kitchen and dining room spic and span. The relationship between the Abba Zabba woman and Esta only got worse when Esta was out of school and around the house more often. Since the Abba Zabba woman worked nights more than days, it seemed like the fun began after she left for work at approximately six-thirty in the evening. Music was played, games were played, it was cookies galore, and there was a lot of laughter. One night, the boys were in the living room playing games or with their cars while Odessa and Alexandra were in their room crafting. Lacy and Esta were watching an old black and white movie in the bedroom. The aroma of sugar cookies, caramel candy, and peanut butter cookies pervaded the house. The song "Cloud Nine" by The Temptations was playing from Odessa and Alexandra's room, which was one of Lacy's favorite songs. As he and Esta watched their movie, he was sort of bouncing his body to the song and eating cookies. Esta left the room several times saying she would be right back. She would either go to the kitchen with the other sisters to check on what they were baking and cooking or she would just go to their room and giggle with them there, then go back to join Lacy. As it got later that night and the snacks were all eaten and everyone's bellies were stuffed, Lacy was totally engrossed in the movie he and Esta were watching. His eyes were glued to the TV until he saw something move to the right of him, so he looked to see what it was. What he saw made no sense to him, so he kept staring. He saw an image of Esta running with a suitcase with things falling out of it, not looking back. "What are you doing Lacy?" she asked him.

"Nothing," he said, as he quickly looked back at the TV, puzzled by what he had just seen. Moments later, his eyes were drawn to the right of the room as Esta sat to his left on the bed. Again, he saw the same images of Esta running with a suitcase and some belongings falling out of it as she ran quickly, not looking back. She kept running until he could barely see her.

"LACY! What are you doing?" she asked.

"Esta, why are you leaving me tonight?" he asked.

"What?" she asked. "I'm not leaving you."

"Yes," he said. "You're leaving me tonight and not coming back. Why?" he asked.

"Stop saying that Lacy. I'm not going anywhere."

"Yes, you are. You're leaving tonight and you're not coming back, I just saw it."

"Stop it," she said, as she ran out from the room covering her face. Moments later, Odessa and Alexandra walked into the room where Lacy was and asked him what was going on.

Lacy told them what he told Esta and said, "She's not coming back,

I just know it." He asked why she left the room and why she was crying if she wasn't leaving. Odessa and Alexandra sat next to him and tried to comfort him and told him she wasn't crying. He said, "Yes she was, I saw her."

Odessa said, "Shhh shhh. She'll be back. She just needed to check something in the kitchen so we'll sit with you until she comes back okay?" Lacy said okay, but he knew they were all up to something because Odessa and Alexandra took turns rocking him as they sat next to him watching TV. Lacy knew when Esta, Alexandra, or Odessa rocked him they were trying to get him to go to sleep, so he was trying very hard to stay awake. He believed if he fell asleep and woke up, Esta would not be there. He was fighting sleep with everything he had in him, but the rocking motion got to him eventually. Lacy woke up sometime later, sat up in the bed, and noticed the window and curtains were open. He began to scream because he never liked sitting or sleeping with the curtains open at night because he felt like spirits were watching him through the window.

As he screamed for Esta, Alexandra and Odessa ran into the room and asked what happened and Lacy yelled, "The window and the curtains are open, please close them! Please close them. Hurry!" Alexandra quickly closed the window and curtains and told Lacy everything was okay.

He asked where Esta was, and Alexandra said, "We're in the living room but you should go back to sleep." Lacy asked to see Esta, but Odessa said he could see her in the morning and needed to go to sleep. "Yes," Alexandra agreed. Lacy said okay. They sat with him and rocked him again until he fell asleep. Lacy woke up hours later when the sun was up and didn't see Esta in the bed with him, so he got up and ran to the living room and kitchen to see if Esta was there but she wasn't.

He ran back down the hallway to Alexandra and Odessa's room and woke them up saying, "Esta's gone, Esta's gone. I knew she was leaving and wouldn't come back. She's gone, she's gone."

"Lacy be quiet, everyone else is sleeping," Odessa said. Gus entered their room and asked what was going on.

Lacy said, "Esta is not here and she's not coming back." Alexandra told Lacy to stop saying that just because he didn't know where Esta was. Randy, Horace, and Marcel came in and asked what was going on.

"Calm down everyone," Alexandra said. "She's probably in the back-yard."

"Let's go see," Lacy said, as he ran to the back door of the house and ran outside.

"Wait, Lacy," Alexandra said. "Come back here."

Lacy stopped where he was, waited for Alexandra, and said, "She's not here."

When Alexandra caught up with Lacy she said, "Let's look on the side of the house," so they walked over there and Lacy saw that Esta dropped a bottle of nail polish, a makeup kit, a brush, and bobby pins along the side of the house.

"She's probably in front of the house," Lacy said, as he was picking up Esta's belongings and quickly moved to the front of the house.

When they all got to the front of the house, Esta was not there. Lacy looked confused. He wondered if what he saw last night of Esta run-ning with a suitcase and her belongings falling out came true. "She's not coming back," he said to the others. "SHE'S NOT COMING BACK," he said, as he looked down the street and held her belongings tightly in his hands.

"Lacy, Lacy, come here," Odessa said. "We don't know where she is so don't think she's not coming back."

"I told you last night," Lacy said. "I told you I saw that she was leav-ing and not coming back and you and Alexandra didn't believe me. You and Alexandra kept rocking and rocking to make me go to sleep and If I didn't fall asleep I could have made her stay."

"Lacy," Alexandra said, "let's go back into the house and have break-fast and just wait for her to call or come home." She said, "I'm sure everything is alright and she will be home soon."

Lacy looked at Alexandra and Odessa and said, "We have to find her."

"We will," Odessa said, "but let's do like Alexandra said and go in the house and have breakfast and just wait for Esta to call or come home, and then she can tell us where she's been."

"Right," Alexandra said. "We know she's left early before, so this is no surprise."

Lacy said, "But this time is different because she's out of school and doesn't have to go to school to meet anyone early in the morning." Lacy noticed that Odessa and Alexandra looked at each other and didn't say a word, which was the look they got when they were caught or not telling the full story. Lacy felt and believed Esta, Odessa, and Alexandra were not being honest with him but he couldn't understand or figure out what was going on. He decided he would find out no matter how long it took. He began to walk toward the backyard to go into the house.

"What do you want for breakfast Lacy?" Odessa asked in a cheery voice.

"Nothing," Lacy said.

"Are you sure?" she asked. "You should be hungry." Lacy didn't say anything as he continued walking toward the back door. As he entered the back door he began crying and went to Esta's room and jumped onto her bed and lay there with tears running down his face. Alexandra and Odessa heard him and went to Esta's room and sat near him. They told him everything would be okay and that they were with him and for him not to worry. He didn't say anything to them.

They tried to comfort him for a while then Alexandra said, "Come on Odessa, let's make breakfast. Lacy, if you get hungry your food will be in the kitchen." Lacy did not respond. Both sisters left Esta's room and stood outside the door whispering to each other. Lacy could hear them out there whispering, but didn't care or try to listen to what they were saying. He felt that someone was lying and was very upset about it. Moments later, both sisters entered Esta's room and stood near the bed where Lacy was lying down and looked at him for a moment.

Lacy lifted his head and stared at them, wondering why they were just standing there looking at him and at each other. He believed they knew something and maybe they were about to tell him. Alexandra said, "Lacy, we don't want you to be sad because it's so much fun when you are happy and showing that big smile of yours. Will you show us your smile?"

"Yes Lacy, show us your smile," Odessa said. Lacy looked at the sisters and thought to himself that maybe they didn't know what was going on. They were still there with him and always had been, so he tried to crack a smile that looked like a smile you have when you've tasted something you don't like but try to smile through it.

"C'mon Lacy. Come to the kitchen with us and help us make breakfast," Alexandra said. Lacy got off the bed and wiped his eyes and walked to the kitchen with the sisters as they pat him on the head and held his hands. The other boys asked Odessa and Alexandra where they thought Esta went, and Alexandra said, "We don't know, so let's all just wait until she calls or comes home, okay? Breakfast will be ready so why don't you guys go and watch TV or go back to bed until breakfast is ready?"

"Why does Lacy get to stay in the kitchen and we can't?" Horace asked.

"If you want to stay in the kitchen you can but you have to help out too," Alexandra said.

"Okay," Horace said. Odessa told Lacy to stir the pancake mix as she made the bacon and Alexandra whisked and seasoned the eggs. She told Horace he could put butter on the biscuits when she took them out of the oven. As they were all in the kitchen making breakfast, the sisters were whispering here and there to each other. Lacy wasn't interested in what they were talking about, but Horace was. Horace said, "You're talking about Esta and Lacy, aren't you? When do you think she's coming back?" he asked.

Alexandra stopped what she was doing and turned to Horace and said, "I thought I said we should wait until she calls or comes home to find out where she was. Didn't I? I said it a few times now and I don't want to say it again."

"Okay," Horace said. Lacy looked at Horace and Horace looked at Lacy then whispered in his ear that Esta was going to get beat for leaving again.

"Be quiet!" Lacy said.

"What's going on over there?" Alexandra said. Lacy told her what Horace said and Alexandra told Horace to leave the kitchen because she didn't need any more drama that morning from anyone. When Alexandra had enough of foolishness or things that caused her frustration, she'd call it drama.

Horace started to leave the kitchen and said, "I didn't want to be in here with you guys anyway, I just wanted to tell Lacy that Esta's going to get beat."

"I'll beat you if you don't get out of here," Alexandra said to Horace as he ran to the living room.

"Lacy, don't listen to him," Odessa said, "just keep stirring that pancake mix so we can have some gooooood pancakes, okay?"

"Okay," Lacy said as he looked at her with the same awkward smile as before.

When breakfast was ready, everyone gathered at the dining table to eat, and boy did they eat. Everyone jumped in and grabbed what they wanted as if they hadn't eaten in days. Lacy was moving slowly and didn't really feel that hungry. He was already the slowest eater in the family and usually took more than thirty minutes to finish, but on that day, he sat there well after the others finished eating and even after Odessa and Alexandra washed the dishes and cleaned the kitchen. Odessa told him she would wrap his food up for him and he could have it later since there was no wasting of food in the house. He said okay. She told him to go with her so she could help him get dressed and he could do crafts with them or watch TV. After he was dressed, he just wanted to sit on the living room floor with Esta's belongings that she dropped. He sat on the floor and spread her belongings out in front of him and moved them around like he was playing checkers. As he did this, he thought about the night before when he and Esta were sitting and eating cookies and caramel candy. He kept replaying in his mind what he saw the night before - Esta running with a suitcase and her belongings falling out. He wondered why she was running with a suitcase and why he wasn't with her in that vision he saw. He began thinking about the time when he and Esta went to the circus with Benny and he ate all of that cotton candy and got a tummy ache. And when he and Esta went to that school to watch the matinee movie and ate all the popcorn they wanted. And stuffing his mouth with shoelace licorice at the ball game they went to together. As Lacy was thinking and playing with Esta's belongings, Horace and Marcel tried to take Esta's things from Lacy but Lacy chased and tackled Marcel and began hitting him and telling him to give those things back to him. Marcel threw the belongings across the room and Lacy ran and got them, then he went after Horace. The sisters ran into the living room and asked what was going on and Lacy told them what happened, so Alexandra yanked the belongings from Horace's hand and told him not to bother Lacy again or else. "That goes for you too Marcel. Here Lacy," she said, as she gave Esta's belongings back to him. "We're going back to our room, and if I have to come out here again for you two knuckleheads I'll sock you silly. Just try me," she said as she walked off, looking at both boys over her shoulder. "Lacy," she said. "You call me right away if either of them try anything else."

"Okay," Lacy said.

After the sisters left the room, Marcel said, "That's okay Lacy, we'll get you later when Alexandra and Odessa aren't here." Lacy gave Marcel a mean look and was in no mood to put up with anything from Marcel or Horace since he was already upset about Esta being gone and not knowing if she was coming back. Randy was too engrossed in a TV program to care about any of this, and Gus was in his room tinkering with things as always like taking a watch apart that he found so he could try to put it back together. Lacy went back to thinking about Esta and playing with her belongings that he was convinced she left for him to have. *Otherwise, why would she leave her things there on the ground?* he thought to himself. There was a sound from the kitchen so Horace and Marcel ran to see what it was. It was the Abba Zabba woman. She came in through the garage door that led into the kitchen. *Someone must have left the garage door open when we were looking for Esta,* he thought.

"Esta is gone, Esta is gone!" both Marcel and Horace shouted at the Abba Zabba woman.

"What do you mean she's gone? ODESSA AND ALEXANDRA! COME IN HERE," she shouted.

Horace and Marcel ran to the living room, and when they saw Odessa and Alexandra moving quickly to the kitchen, Marcel said, "OOOOOOO. YOU'RE GONNA GET IT NOW. BOTH OF YOU! AND I'M TELLING YOU'RE PUSHING ME AND HORACE AROUND!" Alexandra stomped her foot near Marcel as she was walking and he ran off, as did Horace.

The Abba Zabba woman was at the dining room table removing her purse from her shoulder just as the sisters simultaneously said, "Esta ran away."

"WHAT?" the Abba Zabba woman said. "When did this happen?"

"We don't know," Alexandra said. "She's just gone and a lot of her things are missing." The Abba Zabba woman plopped her purse on the dining room table and looked at Lacy with squinted eyes as if to say, *she left you, why?* She continued staring at Lacy and it made Lacy very uncomfortable, so he stopped moving Esta's belongings around and sat as still as possible.

"What's Lacy playing with?" she asked.

Odessa said, "Those are some of Esta's things that must have fallen out of her suitcase when she left. Lacy found them and has been playing with them all morning."

"Take those things away from him and throw them in the garbage! I don't want to hear her name ever again. DO YOU HEAR ME? GET THOSE THINGS OUT OF HIS GOT DAMN HANDS NOW, I SAID," she said, as she marched over toward Lacy, stomping her feet hard. She pulled the belongings from Lacy's hands and grabbed the other belongings from the floor.

"NO!" Lacy said. "Those are mine. Esta left them for me."

SLAP! Right across Lacy's face. "I said I don't want to hear her name ever again and I mean ever, do you understand me?" she asked Lacy, as she squeezed his face hard and pushed it away from her quickly.

"Yes," Lacy said, as he began crying and looking around the room.

Without missing a beat, Horace and Marcel ran over to him and Marcel said, "Poor Lacy. Too bad Esta ran away and she's not coming back ever and you can't say her name or you'll be beat and beat good."

"Yeah, beat real good," Horace said.

Alexandra rushed over to stop the boys from bothering Lacy and the Abba Zabba woman said, "Alexandra! I'm not done talking to you."

"But they're picking on Lacy," she said.

"I don't give a good got damn who they're picking on. From now on, you and Odessa will have to split Esta's chores between yourselves and take care of him," she said as she looked at Lacy.

"We will," Odessa said. "Can we go now?" Odessa asked.

"Yeah," the Abba Zabba woman said, "and get him oughta my sight," she said as she looked at Lacy again.

The sisters moved quickly toward Lacy, and Alexandra pushed Horace and Marcel aside and grabbed Lacy's hand and said, "Come with me."

The sisters took Lacy into their bedroom and before the door was closed, Lacy said, "So Esta did run away. She did just like I said. She's never coming back I just know it. She lied to me and we promised not to lie to each other. She lied."

"SHHHHH! SSSH! Shut your mouth and don't say her name again.

Didn't you hear? We were told not to mention her name again. Do you want to get beat, Lacy?" Alexandra asked.

"No," he said.

"Then you listen to me and you listen good. From now on if you want to say anything about Esta you wait until we are alone so no one else hears, do you understand?"

"Yes," Lacy said.

"I'm so sorry Lacy but it's going to get rough around here for you so please be careful and don't upset anyone."

"Please don't Lacy," Odessa said, as tears ran down her face and she looked up to the ceiling.

"Okay," Lacy said. "Esta told me that I need to be careful of people because many people will not like me and try to take from me."

"When did she tell you that?" Alexandra asked.

"Not long ago," Lacy said. "She was crying when she told me that." Both sisters looked at each other then had a three-way hug between them and Lacy.

"We have to stick together, as they say. Alexandra, you stay with Lacy whenever you can and when you can't I'll stay with him, and when we both can't we can ask Gus to be with Lacy."

"I really like Gus a whole lot," Lacy said.

"We know that," Odessa said. "You two are a lot alike, and he looks out for you but we don't want to get him into trouble, so we will only ask him to be with you if either one of us can't do it, okay?"

"Okay," Lacy said.

"Lacy, we know Esta loves you," Alexandra said.

"She was supposed to take me with her," Lacy said.

"What?" Odessa asked.

"Esta told me a long time ago that she would work and save a lot of money so she could leave here and take me with her," Lacy said. "But she lied to me. She lied, she lied, she lied."

"Stop it Lacy," Alexandra said. "She loves you and probably has her reasons why she didn't take you with her but she will be back, so just stop saying she lied. She loves you and you remember that always."

"Yes Lacy, remember that always," Odessa said. He said okay but he didn't believe it because she lied and didn't tell him she was leaving. She lied to him when he asked why she was leaving him the night before when she said she wasn't going anywhere.

"What are you thinking right now?" Alexandra asked Lacy.

"Nothing," Lacy said.

"Yes you are," she said. "I know when you're thinking and right now you're thinking a lot."

"I don't like her right now," Lacy said.

"Who?" Alexandra asked.

"Esta. I don't like her right now."

Odessa said, "Lacy, right now you are upset and that's why you feel like you do but you will feel better when you see her."

Lacy said, "I won't see her because she's gone and not coming back. I saw that last night and I think God was telling me that she was leaving and was not coming back."

"Okay Lacy. Enough. We are not talking about this anymore," Alexandra said. "We can do crafts or play games but no more talk about Esta right now."

"Okay," Lacy said. Several days went by and not a word from Esta, but Lacy would ask the sisters each day if they heard from her or if they could look for her. They would tell him they had not heard from her, and if they knew where she was they would take him there but they just didn't know. Each evening, Lacy would sit in the bedroom with Odessa and Alexandra crafting, playing games, or just listening to them talk about boys or other topics. Odessa and Alexandra really enjoyed listening to The Temptations. Since Esta left, the sisters took the record player from her room and put it into their room, and that night Odessa put on "I Wish It Would Rain". Lacy stopped listening to the sisters talking and listened to the words of the song, and just like "My Cherie Amour", he realized that other songs told stories too and thought that song was telling a story about a guy that lost someone. Lacy realized that the song's words were exactly how he felt. As he listened to the song, he kept asking Odessa to play it again and again and again. Lacy wanted to hear that song every day until the Abba Zabba woman walked in one day and scratched the record when she pulled the record player arm from the record.

She took the record from the record player and broke it into many pieces and said, "There's your rain now, I don't want to hear that song in this house again. If you get another record of that song I'll take away the record player, do you hear me?" The sisters said yes. Then the Abba Zabba woman left the room. The sisters told Lacy maybe they should all go watch TV, so they did. A little while later, the Abba Zabba woman called Lacy's name and told him to go to her room. Lacy looked terrified and looked at Odessa and Alexandra.

They pulled him off the floor by his arms and said, "Let's go." They went with him to the Abba Zabba woman's room and she told both sisters to go back to the living room. They said "Okay," as they pat Lacy on the head.

"Go," she said to the sisters. Both sisters moved away from the door but Lacy could see that they were still in the hallway because he was standing in the bedroom doorway. "Come over here Lacy," the Abba Zabba woman said.

"Yeeeah. Come over here," Horace said as he giggled, which caused Marcel and the Abba Zabba woman to giggle too.

Lacy walked over to her but kept some distance. "I said come over here now," she said. Lacy got closer. He felt very uncomfortable because she had her shirt off and her breasts were out as she sat in a somewhat reclined chair. "Watch this," she said to Lacy. "Horace, show Lacy what you used to do as a baby." Horace put his mouth on her breast and started sucking her nipple. For some reason that made Lacy even more frightened because he didn't know what was going on. "Now, you come do it Lacy," she said. Lacy shook his head 'no' nonstop. "I told you IF I WERE BLIND I COULDN'T SEE THAT! Now come over here and do it."

Odessa and Alexandra raced to the bedroom door and Alexandra said, "He's just scared, may we talk to him?"

"NO! Now get away from the door like I told you before I get out of this chair and pull rank on your asses."

Both sisters went back down the hall saying, "We love you Lacy, it's okay."

"Shut up!" the Abba Zabba woman said. "Now Lacy," she said, "get over here." Lacy made his way over to her and stood before her. He closed his eyes and thought of Esta and hoped she would pop through the front door at any moment. "Open...Your...Damn...EYES!" she said. Horace and Marcel began laughing and Horace called Lacy a four-eyed freak. The Abba Zabba woman said, "Okay boys that's enough. Don't make fun of him. He's not like you two so don't be hard on him." In Lacy's mind, he thought, *she's right, I'm better than those two and always will be. Esta told me about people like you.* "Boy, you better fix your eyes and stop looking at me with that anger before I beat the tar outta you," she said.

"Yeah, yeah, beat the tar outta him," Marcel said as he and Horace laughed hysterically. Lacy looked at the Abba Zabba woman and believed something was very wrong with her.

"Call me Mom," she said. In his four years of life, Lacy had never called anyone Mom, so he looked at her trying to figure out why he should call her by her name when he never had before. "CALL ME MOM, I SAID!"

"Yeah, call her Mom, four-eyes. Call her Mom," Horace said, laughing like a hyena. Marcel did the same as he looked at Lacy, waiting to see if he would call her Mom.

Slap! Right across his face, then she pinched his cheeks between her fingers and thumb and asked, "Do you want me to beat you until you call me Mom or can you do it on your own?"

"Call her Mom, call her Mom, call her Mom," Marcel and Horace chanted. Lacy began to cry and felt terrible inside because he felt calling her the word 'Mom' would somehow not be good.

Slap! "Call me Mom," she said.

"ALEXANDRA, ODESSA, PLEASE HELP ME!" Lacy cried and begged the sisters to come but they didn't say a word.

"OH, so you want Odessa and Alexandra. OKAY. GIRLS! GET IN HERE."

"Yes," they said as they walked into the room.

"Lacy wants you," the Abba Zabba woman said. "Go ahead Lacy, tell them what you want." Lacy cried and looked at them and asked for them to take him to their room. "If they take you to their room I will beat them then I will beat you for not doing what I told you to do. I'm the captain of the ship GOT DAMNIT! And you're nothing but a member of the crew. Now, call me Mom or I will string you up and beat your little black ass in front of everyone."

"Hahahahaha. Do it. Do it," Horace said as he laughed.

"Shut up Horace," Alexandra said.

"GO TO YOUR ROOM ALEXANDRA AND I'LL DEAL WITH YOU LATER!" the Abba Zabba woman said.

As Alexandra left the room upset, Marcel said, "Bye-bye Alexandra," in a mean voice.

"You're not leaving this room until you call me Mom, and you will call me Mom."

Odessa said, "Lacy, please call her Mom."

Lacy looked at Odessa, and that was when the Abba Zabba woman grabbed Lacy by his cheeks again and said, "She's the smart one so you better listen to her." Lacy tried to look at Odessa again but he couldn't turn his head while the Abba Zabba woman held his cheeks. She squeezed his cheeks tighter and tighter and said, "Say it."

"M...M...mo...m," he said.

"What?" she said. "I couldn't hear you. Horace and Marcel, could you two hear him?"

"No. I didn't hear what he said," Horace said.

"Make him say it again," Marcel said as he sat bouncing on the bed laughing.

She squeezed Lacy's cheeks very hard and said, "You have something to say, so say it."

"MOOOMM," he said.

She said, "Say it again."

"MOOOM..."

"Again," she said.

"MOOOOMMM."

She let go of his face and said, "Say...it...again."

He looked at Marcel and Horace then looked back at her and said, "MOM."

She said, "That's what I wanted to hear. You can go with Odessa now, and from now on you call me Mom. Do you understand?"

"Yes," he said.

"Yes what?" she said.

"Yes Mom."

"See, that wasn't so bad," she said. "Now you can go." Lacy turned and walked out of her room and went toward Esta's room.

Odessa said, "Come with me Lacy," but he didn't want to go with her. He wanted to be alone in Esta's room. He climbed in Esta's bed, but once the lights were out he decided to go with Odessa to her room since he was afraid of the dark. The sisters wanted to comfort him but he just wanted to be left alone. He remembered the dream where he was being chased by many men and dove into the bushes to get away from them. He was so confused and didn't understand why he was being treated the way he was and how he got into that house in the first place. *Who put him there and why did they put him there? How long will all of this last?* he thought to himself. *I'll be an adult one day and I won't have to be around these people.* Lacy thought these thoughts for a long time until he got tired and went to sleep. As the days, weeks, and months passed, the summer finally came to an end and Lacy began nursery school.

Stitches and Beatings

When Lacy began nursery school, the other children started going to another school across town. Randy and Gus became friends with the Stueve boys. Their parents owned Steuve Cattle Farms and Alta Dena Dairy and would invite Gus and Randy to the farm regularly. Gus, Randy, and the Stueve boys would try to ride the cows or ride motorcycles up small mountains of manure and came home smelling just like it. Since both families lived within a couple of miles of each other, everyone began carpooling to school to make it easier on the parents to take the children to school. This was a very good change for Lacy because he no longer sat at home by himself for thirty to forty minutes each morning. When the Abba Zabba woman picked him up from nursery school, she would take him with her to grocery shop, pay bills, or to a dance class that she took a couple of times a week. Since Lacy still wasn't comfortable being around Mom, yet alone with her, it was a relief to go with her to run errands and to her dance classes. He thought being busy would keep her from thinking about what she might not like about him or from possibly beating his black ass. Lacy liked going to watch the one-on-one dance class because Amando, her dance teacher, was very nice to Lacy. After Amando gave Mom her dance lesson he would put a song on and dance solo and it reminded Lacy of the movies he watched with Esta. The way Amando's feet moved reminded Lacy of Sammy Davis Jr., Fred Astaire, Ginger Rodgers, and Cholly Atkins dancing in the old movies.

When Amando danced he looked happy, free, and on top of the world, and that inspired Lacy to strive for the feeling Amando exuded. After Amando did his solo dance, it was nearly time for Lacy and Mom to leave, but Amando and Mom had to go into his office and close the door to have a conversation like she and Jasper used to have. Lacy didn't mind because he would walk around the dance floor and try to dance like Amando until Mom would come out of the office just in time for them to pick up everyone else from school. When they picked everyone up from school, Lacy liked seeing all of the children coming out of school because he looked forward to being in a big school like that and making friends like the others did. Lacy remembered the fun he had in Gus' class and how friendly the teacher and students were and couldn't wait to be part of the higher grades. Once they got home, Mom would get cleaned up and leave for work since her hours had changed. This way, she could help with the carpool on certain days since Jasper didn't seem to come around anymore. Odessa and Alexandra would get their homework done then start getting dinner ready. Randy would play with his yoyo, watch TV, or interrupt Gus, and Gus would do his homework or tinker with something. Marcel would practice on his kazoo, flute, accordion, or whatever instrument he saw on TV and asked Mom to get for him. Horace would ask Lacy to go outside so they could play, but Lacy rarely wanted to play with Horace because Horace usually found a way to try to hurt Lacy then say it was an accident. One day, Horace kept calling Lacy chicken and teased Lacy for not wanting to go outside with him. Horace must have teased Lacy for a whole half an hour. Horace decided to stop teasing Lacy and said he was sorry for all the teasing and really just wanted to play. He told Lacy if he went outside to play with him he would be fair and not do anything to hurt him.

Lacy said, "Okay. Let's play." Horace went outside first and held the screen door open for Lacy. Lacy said thank you and thought that was nice of Horace considering Horace's earlier behavior. Once they got outside, they just tossed a ball back and forth. After a few minutes, Horace started in on Lacy, telling him that he didn't know how to catch the ball. Lacy told Horace he had been catching the ball the whole time and Horace was the one that kept dropping it.

"Try to tackle me Lacy," Horace said.

"I don't want to," Lacy said. "Let's just keep tossing the ball."

"No, I want you to try and tackle me," Horace said.

"NO, let's just toss the ball or go in the house."

Horace said, "You can't tackle me anyway because you're too slow and can't catch me."

"I can catch you if I want to," Lacy said.

"Prove it," Horace said. Lacy just stared at Horace and Horace kept chanting, "Prove it, prove it, prove it you four-eyed freak, prove it." Lacy leaned down a bit then took off running at Horace. Horace began to move but Lacy got him and knocked him over. Horace got up and pushed Lacy down and Lacy got up and pushed Horace, then the fight was on.

Then came Lilly. "Boaz, Boaz, stop it na. I saw da whole thang. Horace, you don't gat ta be rough houzin' wit Lacy, he's smaller den you. Na play nice." Lilly stood nearby as the boys began playing toss the ball again, but the moment she went inside, Horace ran to tackle Lacy as Lacy was retrieving the ball from the plantern. Lacy's body smashed into the plantern and he cried out. Alexandra came outside and asked what happened and Lacy told her. She grabbed Horace by the arm and told him he better stop acting stupid and play properly or go into the house. He said he wanted to play so she let him go and told him not to tackle Lacy again. The boys played tops for a few minutes before Horace ran at Lacy again, but this time Lacy saw him coming and moved. Horace didn't like losing to Lacy so he kept trying to tackle him and Lacy began to get into the challenge. Horace's face showed that he was getting quite angry and he began swinging his arms to hit Lacy as he tried to tackle him. Lacy thought Horace would never stop trying to hurt him. Esta was gone and Odessa and Alexandra were not always there to protect him, so he had to do something to get Horace to leave him alone. He remembered what it felt like to smash into the plantern and thought Horace needed to feel that and maybe then he would leave

Lacy alone. Lacy began taunting Horace back as Horace taunted him.

"Hey chicken, you can't tackle me," Lacy said. Horace went off and running but Lacy moved and Horace stopped and ran back and tried again as Lacy taunted him. Horace missed when Lacy moved. He didn't notice that Lacy kept getting closer and closer to the plantern so the next time he charged Lacy and Lacy moved, Horace lost his footing and ran right into the plantern headfirst and gashed his forehead quite badly. His scream was louder than Odessa's screams when Mom beat her for not telling her where Esta had gone. Lilly ran over immediately as the sisters and boys came outside. Lilly told the sisters to get some ice and towels so she could take Horace to the hospital. *HOSPITAL?* Lacy thought to himself. *What did I do to Horace?* he thought. *Is he going to die? I only wanted to scare him and make him hurt like I did but I don't want him to die.* "Horace, I'm sorry," Lacy said. "I'm sorry. Please don't die."

"Ain't nobady gooonna daa boy. Na, outda way. Shirlaaaay. Shirlaaaay. Come out here giiirr. Gatta go to da hospidal. Odessa, you come wit me and Alexandra you stay here wit deez boaz. We be back." They left, and Randy told Lacy that Mom would beat him and beat him good for hurting Horace, and Lacy knew that was more than truth from Randy. Lacy was terrified and thought running away might be a good idea, or even hiding out at Gus' old school. Alexandra told Lacy not to worry because it was an accident. Lacy asked Alexandra if he could talk to her alone, so she took him into her room and he whispered to her it wasn't an accident. He told her he wanted Horace to feel the pain that he had been feeling from Horace picking on him. Alexandra broke out laughing hysterically. Lacy looked at her and thought maybe she didn't understand what he whispered.

"No, No. Let me tell you again what happened," he said.

She said, "I heard you, I heard you. Hahahahahaha."

"Alexandra, then why are you laughing?" Lacy asked.

She calmed herself down and whispered to Lacy saying, "It's about time you stood up for yourself and taught that bully a lesson. Mom might be mad at you but Horace will think twice about trying to hurt you."

"Alexandra, I don't feel good about Horace getting hurt," Lacy said.

"I don't feel good about him getting hurt either Lacy, but I feel good about *you* not getting hurt and Horace learning that he can't just push you around without him getting hurt somehow. Hurting people for no reason isn't right but standing up for yourself and protecting yourself is right and that's what you did Lacy. Do you understand?" Alexandra said.

"Yes," Lacy said.

"There's nothing wrong with standing up for yourself Lacy. It's up to you to decide how you will protect yourself and stand up for yourself whenever something happens that makes you feel like you need to. Understood?" Alexandra said.

Lacy said, "Yes, I understand," with a smile. Alexandra made sure the boys ate dinner and told them to watch TV for a while. They heard Lilly's car pull in and the car doors close, so Alexandra went over to Lilly's to check on Horace. Lilly told Alexandra that Mom was called at work so she went to meet Lilly at the hospital to see what happened to Horace but was on her way home since they gave Horace stitches.

"Stitches?" Alexandra asked.

"Yeeah, stitches," Lilly said. "Ya mama ain't ta happy wit Lacy so I hope she don't beat him too bad. I gotsta get dinna ready so aah see you later Alesandra."

"Okay," Alexandra said as she hurried home. When she got back in the house, Marcel asked what Lilly said. "Horace had to get stitches."

"Stitches?" Randy asked.

"Yeah," Alexandra said.

"OOOOHHHHH! Yo butt is gonna be so tanned when mama get done. MMMMmph," Randy said, "you really did it this time Lacy, she's gonna put the whoop on your tail toooooonight!"

"Stop it Randy," Alexandra said. Randy said he was just telling Lacy what was going to happen, and Alexandra told Randy if he kept up with trying to scare Lacy she would show *him* what was going to happen. Randy stormed off and grabbed his yoyo and began playing with it while looking at Lacy with a smile. Lacy looked at Randy and smiled back at him.

Randy stopped smiling and walked away and said, "You won't be smiling for long." Lacy stopped smiling and started thinking of hiding or running away again, and that was when he heard Mom's car pull up and the car door close. As Mom, Odessa, and Horace walked up the walkway, Lacy could see them through the screen door. Once that screen door opened, he heard his name.

"LACY!"

"Yes," he said.

"Get over here," Mom said. Lacy hurried over to her. "What happened to Horace?" she asked.

"We were playing and…"

Slap! "Don't lie to me. You weren't playing, you did this on purpose, didn't you? You're jealous of Horace and want to be just like him so you hurt him because you can't be him." The look on Lacy's face when he heard that said, *that's the silliest thing I've ever heard*, and Mom recognized what his look said and- *slap!* "You think you're too good for a beating? I'll show you how slaves used to get beat and I know exactly how to because my grandfather owned slaves and my father told me all about it. You little black son of a bitch. I oughtta string you up by your thumbs and whoop the shit out your ass." Lacy shook and tried to stay as still as possible in order to not upset Mom further. He didn't want to look into her eyes because it seemed that upset her more, even though she told him to look at her when she was talking. "Randy, get me the belt."

"Right away! OOOHH, this is gonna be good." Randy said as he laughed. "Mama gooone whooop dat booty," Randy said as he ran past Lacy. Lacy wasn't told to go to a particular room. She wanted to make sure everyone saw him get beat.

She went to work on him right in the living room and as she promised, she tore his little black ass up as he jumped around like a Mexican jumping bean screaming, "Esta, Esta, Esta!!"

"Lacy stop saying that," Alexandra said. "It'll just make things worse."

"Listen to Alexandra you little bastard," Mom said. "I told you I did not want to hear that name around here again and since you chose to ignore what I said I'm gonna beat your silly ass longer." Lacy screamed and tried to keep his mouth shut but the pain was too much, so he kept jumping around and looking around the room at the others wondering why no one said or did anything. Randy was looking at Lacy with a shocked look on his face because he had never seen someone jump around and scream like that before. Marcel and Horace grinned as Gus dropped his head and looked away with a look of discomfort on his face. Alexandra and Odessa were pleading with Mom, saying they thought he learned his lesson. "I say when a lesson is learned, not you two. I should beat your asses too for letting Horace get hurt," she said, then she threw the belt across the room and told Randy to pick it up and put it away. She looked at Lacy and said, "Now you know what a beating feels like. As long as you're in this house you do what I say when I say it or I'll beat the tar out of you. DO YOU HEAR ME?"

"Y, y, y, ye, ye, ye, ye, yeeeess," Lacy said.

"Good! Now get out of my sight. I don't want to see you for the rest of the night, but first, you get your ass over there and apologize to Horace." Lacy moved quickly over to Horace and apologized.

Horace said, "You better apologize."

"C'mon Lacy," Odessa said. Lacy went with Odessa and Alexandra to their bedroom. They got some cold towels to put on the areas of Lacy's body that were exposed and got hit with the belt to calm the stinging since it was his first time. As the sisters were helping Lacy, he kept thinking about that dream where he was being chased by many men and how they wanted to hurt him. He thought the people in the house that wanted to hurt him were like the people in the dream that chased him, and Odessa, Alexandra, and Gus were like the bushes that he jumped into for safety. The sisters saw that he was staring into space and asked what he was thinking about, but he just said nothing.

"Lacy, I know when you're thinking about something," Alexandra said. "Please tell us what you're thinking."

"I don't want to be here," he said.

Both sisters looked at each other, then Alexandra said, "Lacy, I'm sorry. If I could take you away from here to a better and safer place I would, but I just can't and neither can Odessa, but maybe one day."

"Esta said one day," he said. "One day I will take myself out of here and never come back. Everyone that hurt me will have a life of hurt and everyone that protected me will have a good life."

"Did we hurt you Lacy?" Odessa asked.

"No," Lacy said. Odessa started crying and looked at Alexandra.

"Keep your voice down Odessa," Alexandra said. "We don't want Mom coming in here starting up a mess so she can pick one of us to beat to get out her anger."

"You're right," Odessa said.

"Is the pain still bad Lacy?" Alexandra asked.

"Yes. It feels like when I burned my finger on the stove but it's all over my body."

"Somebody needs to beat her like she beat you," Alexandra said. "Don't make no sense for her to treat a child like that."

"Why doesn't she ever beat Horace, Marcel, or Randy?" Lacy asked.

"Because she treats them special and lets them do what they want," Alexandra said.

"Why?" Lacy asked.

"I don't know why," Alexandra said, "but it will hurt them when they are older because other people will not let them get away with being spoiled brats. They will learn the hard way."

"The hard way?" Lacy asked.

Alexandra said, "I mean they will meet people in their lives that will not let them get away with acting like that. If they tease others like they tease you those other people may punch them in the mouth or beat them up bad."

"They are older than me but act younger than me," Lacy said.

"Hahaha," Alexandra and Odessa both laughed softly when they heard what Lacy said.

"Yes, they act much younger than you Lacy," Odessa said. "You are very mature for your age."

"What does that mean?" Lacy asked.

Odessa said, "Mature means ahead or grown-up. You're ahead of them with your thinking and how you behave. You act more responsible and respectful than they do, which makes you seem like an adult at times."

"I can't wait to be an adult," Lacy said. "I will not act like Marcel, Horace, or Randy and I will treat children good and not spank them."

"I have a good feeling you will be a good father Lacy," Odessa said.

Alexandra said, "You will be a good father Lacy. A really good father." Lacy smiled happily as he looked at both sisters.

"You look sleepy Lacy," Odessa said. "Are you sleepy?" she asked.

"Yes," Lacy said.

"Okay. Time for bed," Odessa said, "so let's get your teeth brushed and pajamas on. You can have a bath in the morning, okay?"

"Okay," Lacy said.

TRUTHS, LIES, AND PREJUDICE

The next morning as everyone got ready for school, the sisters were in their bedroom speaking about which one would pretend they were sick so they could stay home with Lacy that day. They knew Horace was not able to go to school that day due to his injury and thought Lacy would probably get another beating if he was cornered between Mom and Horace's personalities. As they were having that discussion, Mom called Odessa to her room and told her that she needed to stay home that day to care for Horace since he was supposed to rest and take it easy. It turned out that Mom got called into work and wouldn't be able to stay home that day. Odessa told Alexandra the news and they both giggled. Alexandra placed her hand on Lacy's head and told him the angels must have been looking out for him because it was a blessing that Mom got called into work.

She said she needed to get ready for school and told Lacy to relax because it was going to be a really good day. Odessa gave Lacy a hug and told him she was with him and not to worry at all since Horace would stay in his room or on the sofa to rest. Lacy hugged Odessa and said he was glad she was staying with him. After everyone left for school and Mom went to work, Odessa made breakfast for Horace and Lacy.

Horace ate while lying on the sofa watching TV, and Odessa and Lacy ate at the dining room table. After everyone ate, Horace took a nap and Odessa and Lacy played games, listened to music, and she taught him a little bit about addition and subtraction. Lilly picked everyone up from school that day since Mom was supposed to drive the carpool that day but couldn't. By the time they got home, Odessa had already cleaned the house and made dinner. Odessa liked cleanliness and Lacy would follow her around, watching how she cleaned so he could learn how to do it. After the others finished homework, had dinner, and started watching TV, Mom came home. She went straight to Horace to check on him and asked him if Odessa took good care of him and fed him well. He said yes even though she and Lacy were in her room all day playing while he laid on the sofa. Odessa quickly jumped in and said Horace wanted to watch TV so she let him watch whatever he wanted and she and Lacy didn't use the TV at all.

Mom kissed Horace's head and said, "You just rest, Mama's home," as she gave a half-smile to Odessa. She said she had a long tiring day at work because she didn't plan on working that day so she didn't eat before she went to work. She said she just snacked throughout the day, so she was very hungry. After she ate dinner, she went to her room, closed the door, and slept for the rest of the night because she had work the next morning. Mom told Alexandra to stay home to care for Horace the next day, and that day was similar to the day before. The following day, Horace was able to go to school, and as days and months passed, Lacy had stopped thinking about Esta and much more about how Odessa and Alexandra cared for him and how Gus always treated him fairly. He also thought about being an adult and wanting to learn all he could at nursery school by watching and listening to the other children, but more importantly, listening to and watching the teacher and the other teachers and adults he would interact with each day. He got along fine with the other children and had great fun with them, but he saw adult life as a fascinating thing and liked speaking with all of the adults. One day when Mom picked him up from nursery school, the teacher told her that Lacy interacted well with others but he wanted to spend more time with adults than the children. Of course, the idea was thought to be that he liked speaking to adults because he got along with Odessa and Alexandra and related to older people better.

When asked why he liked speaking to adults and spending so much time with them, he said there was so much to learn, and adults were the best people to go to if he wanted to learn about being an adult and having a good life. The teacher told Mom that she told Lacy to spend more time with the children playing and talking, but Lacy wanted to stay with her and hear about the work she did at her desk and what she did to get that job. When Lacy and Mom left, she told him there would be no more questioning of teachers and other adults at the school and he was to only speak with other children. He said okay. Since he knew he could get in trouble if he continued speaking with the teacher and other adults and that he would get punished, he played with the children and watched the adults' interactions as best he could. One day, Lacy was climbing up the ladder of a slide at school and saw Mom walking toward his teacher and wondered why she was there. She told him if he got into trouble at school she would string him up by his thumbs and beat his little black ass in front of everyone, so he was a little scared. He hadn't gotten into trouble but still, he was concerned. A boy climbed up the slide from the sliding end and was at the top when he saw Lacy on the ladder of the slide.

"You're in my way, now get off the slide," he said to Lacy.

Lacy looked up and said, "You went the wrong way. You're supposed to slide down not climb up."

The boy said, "If you don't get off you'll be sorry."

Lacy said, "You're going the wrong way and the teacher said not to climb up the slide and to use the ladder." *BLAM!* The boy kicked Lacy in the face with his cowboy boots, knocking Lacy's glasses clear off his face, and Lacy flew off the ladder and onto the ground. The boy started laughing and calling Lacy four-eyes. Lacy found his glasses and put them on, then looked over his shoulder to see if Mom was watching but she wasn't, so Lacy sped up the slide ladder and grabbed the boys leg and yanked him off the slide. The boy went sailing to the ground. As the boy hit the ground, Lacy asked him how that felt and if he liked it. As Lacy was telling the boy to never kick him again, he noticed Mom and the teacher running toward him. His heart started racing and he began to shake a little as he thought about being strung up by his thumbs and getting his little black ass beaten in front of the class.

"What's going on here?" the teacher asked.

"I, see, he, I was on the slide and he kicked me off and…"

"NO, we just saw you pull him off the slide Lacy, so don't make up stories," the teacher said.

"Yes, but that was after he kicked me off," Lacy said.

The teacher said, "You should have told me what he did and I would have spoken with him, but you handled it your way and got caught so you cannot use the slide for the rest of week." Lacy's eyes widened because he realized he was being punished but the boy was not.

"What's that cut over your eye Lacy?" Mom asked. Lacy said it was from the boy kicking him in the face.

The teacher said, "I didn't see anyone kick you but I saw you pull him."

Mom said, "He didn't do that to himself so both boys should be punished, not just one." *WOW!* Lacy could not believe what he was hearing. She actually believed him and stood up for him. Lacy stood a little taller and appeared more confident knowing he wasn't on his own in this.

The teacher asked the boy if he kicked Lacy and the boy said, "No, Lacy's lying."

"I am not lying," Lacy said, "and you better tell the truth."

"Or what Lacy?" asked the teacher.

Lacy looked at Mom and the teacher and said, "He's lying, just ask the other children." The teacher called the children over and right away many children said it was Lacy's fault and that the other boy did nothing to Lacy. Then, a little black girl who kept to herself that no one played with except Lacy said Lacy wasn't lying, and the boy started it by going up the slide the wrong way and kicked Lacy in the face. The teacher put her hands on her hips and looked very upset.

She said, "That's just one child that says Lacy is telling the truth but many other children say the other boy is telling the truth. So, I must believe most of the children that say the other boy is telling the truth."

Mom said, "Come on Lacy. Get your lunch pail and let's get out of this prejudiced place. You do not need to be in a filthy place like this." As Lacy walked with Mom he looked over his shoulder and waved at the girl that said he was telling the truth. He felt sorry for her because she would be alone without anyone to play with since he was leaving. The other children went back to playing and she just stood there waving back at Lacy. "You should have knocked the hell out of that boy Lacy. Next time someone does something like that to you, you better make sure they learn not to do it again or I'll tear into you. Do you hear me?" she asked.

"Yes," Lacy said. Lacy was confused and had a question but wasn't sure if he should ask now or wait. He was bursting and couldn't wait. "Do you mean if Marcel or Horace do something to me I should fight them?"

"NO! That's not what I said got damnit! I'm talking about these racist sons a' bitches we got runnin' around here. I dealt with that shit all my life and you will too if you don't knock hell out of one of em' when they pull shit like that boy did. That teacher knew that boy was lying and he chose you to kick because his parents raised him not to like black people. You could see it in his face as he looked at you," she said. She went on and on and on about how she grew up in the South and black people were treated like dogs - spit on, beaten, stabbed, hung, shot, dragged behind cars, and thrown in jail all because they had dark skin. "I'm sick and tired of it. Just sick. Do you hear me?"

"Yes," Lacy said. They got into the car, and as they drove she kept talking about how wrong people like that were and how it needed to stop.

"That's how Martin and Malcolm died," she said. Lacy had no idea who those people were but he was not going to ask. "JFK too, he liked black people so they killed him." Lacy wondered how someone could name their child JFK.

Nursery School

"Even Jesus," she said. "They hated him so they killed him. What's this world coming to?" she asked. Lacy didn't have an answer to that question, but she kept talking so he thought maybe she forgot that she asked him a question. That suited him just fine because he didn't want to get in trouble for not having an answer. She drove all the way to the dance studio, upset and mentioning the words racism, slavery, Hitler, immigrants, rich people, poor people and how the world judges people. When they got to the dance studio, she raced out of the car so Lacy raced out too because he thought she was late, but once they got inside she told Amando the whole story. They didn't even dance that day. They sat in his office talking about what happened and she shared stories with him about the South and he shared stories with her about Cuba. They both spoke about that word racism and poor and rich people. When they finished talking about the racism word, Mom asked Lacy to go into the dance area of the studio and wait there while she and Amando talked privately.

"Okay," Lacy said. After their private conversation, they came out and danced for a few minutes, then Mom and Lacy had to leave to shop for groceries and pick everyone up from school. When they left the dance studio, it was as if Mom and Lacy had a different type of connection that seemed better than before. After grocery shopping and after all of the children were picked up from school, Mom explained to everyone what happened at nursery school as they drove home. She said Lacy would not be going back there and would not continue nursery school at all and just start kindergarten when the time came. Lacy liked the connection he and Mom had that day, but the thought of not being at nursery school meant being with her in the mornings and he thought she might get upset with him like before and he would get into big trouble.

Marcel said, "You're so lucky Lacy. I wish I didn't have to go to school."

"Don't speak that way Marcel," Mom said. "You are good in school and you are going to be great in life so keep practicing."

"If a boy kicked me in the face I'd stomp his lights out," Randy said. "Boys at school call me names like darky, tar baby, and burnt crisp. When I chase them, they stop teasing because they know I'll break their face."

"Really?" Alexandra asked.

"Okay, now Alexandra, let him talk," Mom said.

"Yeeahh. Let me talk Alexandra. You're not as dark as me so you don't know how much worse it is for me since you are so much lighter. And Odessa, you are so light no one even knows you're black so you really don't know what it's like."

"How do you know what I go through?" Odessa asked. "When people see me with any of you they call me tar baby lover, nigger lover, jiggaboo lover, and white trash, so I get it too."

Mom said, "Listen, we all get it, and if any of you haven't gotten it yet you will, and when you do you will never forget what it feels like." Gus was quiet as he usually was and just listened.

Once they got home, Mom went to the bathroom and then stayed in her room to rest while Odessa and Alexandra put the groceries away and the boys started their homework. Lacy couldn't wait to ask the sisters what the word racism meant and when he did, Alexandra asked where he heard that word. He said he heard Mom and Lilly say it a long time ago and he heard Mom say it again today as they left the nursery school. He told her that he tried asking Esta a long time ago too but he didn't understand it back then. "Alexandra, I think you should explain that to Lacy and I'll keep putting the groceries away," Odessa said.

"Racism," Alexandra said. "All of the people in the world belong to a tribe or group of people but over time we stopped calling those groups, tribes. There is the African tribe or group, Asian tribe or group, Hispanic tribe or group, Anglo tribe or group and so on. There are many African tribes or groups and we came from one of those African tribes. Today we don't say tribes, we say race. You are originally from people of the African race. Now, I don't like the word race when speaking about groups because the word race means competition and you only compete or get into a competition to see who is better, you or the other person. Racism is when a person or tribe, group, or race of people believe they are better than another race of people because they believe their race of people is more valuable and superior or above the other race of people. That's racism. When people believe their race is above or better than any other race they might do many things to prove themselves like hurt people of the race they believe is beneath theirs or that they feel is less valuable than theirs."

"Wow!" Lacy said. "Now I know why Mom said people died and got hurt in the South because of racism. Is there a race that we believe is not as valuable as us?"

"What's us?" Alexandra asked.

"What do you mean?" Lacy asked. Alexandra asked Lacy what his race was to see if he remembered what she said earlier. Lacy said, "You said I originally came from one of the African tribes."

"Correct," Alexandra said. "So, what race of people did you come from originally?" she asked.

"African people," Lacy said.

"But you were born in America so that now makes you American but you have African blood in your veins so you are American with African descent. Or, you are American but come from Africa. Don't ever forget that because each tribe, group, or race of people in America came from somewhere else except the Indians who were already here. You will learn more about the Indians in school but make sure you don't forget that you are American with African descent or origin. All other races of people in this country are proud of where their people came from and their origins so there is no reason why you should not be proud of yours."

"Okay. I'm American with African blood in my veins and I come from African people."

"Right! You got it Lacy."

FIFTH BIRTHDAY

"I'm sure glad you explained that Alexandra, because I would have just said it's when one race of people believe they are better than another race of people."

Lacy said, "That's a good answer too Odessa. Right Alexandra?"

"Hahahahaha," Alexandra laughed. "Right, I'm glad you didn't explain it. Yeah Lacy, her answer is good too, but we better get our homework started," Alexandra said as she turned to Odessa, "so we have time to play with Lacy outside before we make dinner."

"Good idea," Odessa said. As the day continued, the sisters got their homework done, played with Lacy, made dinner, and prepped for the next day. The house remained pretty calm. Mom woke up from resting and had dinner and enjoyed some TV after everyone else went to bed. Some months passed and it was Lacy's fifth birthday. Esta usually bought Lacy's birthday gifts but with her out of the picture, the sisters decided to make peanut butter and sugar cookies for Lacy and let him try to ride Alexandra's bike since he wanted a bike. Mom bought Lacy a yellow outfit with short pants and a jacket for him to wear to church. He was excited about all of the surprises but he could not wait to try and ride Alexandra's bike. However, when it came time, the bike was much too big for him. He couldn't sit on the seat but he was able to hold the handlebars and put his feet on the pedals. He took to riding a bike like a fish to water. On his first try, he rode clear down the street with the sisters following close behind, but he didn't know how much to turn the wheel and didn't turn it enough and crashed into someone's car. The sisters quickly grabbed the bike and told Lacy to run so they wouldn't get caught. When they got back near their house, Lacy said he wanted to try again but Alexandra said if he continued to ride the bike that way she wouldn't have a bike by night time.

"I won't," Lacy said. "Let me try again. I've watched you and many people ride bikes and I can do it. Please, let me try again."

"Odessa, what do you think?" Alexandra asked.

"Hahahaha, I thought it was funny the way he bounced off the bike after he hit that car and looked sillier than silly with his big eyes. Hahahaha."

"But what do you think? Should I let him go again or wait until next time?" Alexandra asked.

"Hahaha, let him go again so I can see his little legs pushing the pedals," Odessa said, as she laughed.

"Okay. C'mon Lacy," Alexandra said.

"Neeeeatooooo! Make way for the professor for I cometh to rideth my chariotteth."

"Bahahahahahahahahaa!" both sisters laughed hysterically.

"Where in the world did you get that kind of talk from Lacy?" Odessa asked.

"The Ten Commandments. The bald-headed guy put his hands on his hips and spoke like that."

"Yeah, but he didn't say chariotteth," Alexandra said.

"No," Lacy said, "I just said that because I'm going to ride the bike which is like a chariot because it has two wheels and will take me where I want to go."

Both sisters stopped laughing and Alexandra said, "C'mon here boy and get this ride over with."

"And who shall be getting this ride over with?" he asked both sisters.

"What?" Odessa asked.

"Who shall be riding this bike right now?"

"You knucklehead, now hurry up," Alexandra said.

"No," Lacy said. "The professor. That's who. Now, part the way so I can ride off into the sunset like in the cowboy movies." Neither Odessa or Alexandra were laughing anymore and seemed irritated. Lacy must have noticed the sisters' irritation because he stopped his antics. He put his foot on the pedals and held the handlebars and began to kick and push himself forward as he looked at them, wondering why they looked so serious. He was off and riding, and this time he was able to steer and handle the bike with more ease. The sisters couldn't believe it, and Marcel and Horace ran outside to watch.

"I want to try, I want to try," both boys said to Alexandra. Odessa told Alexandra she would watch them ride if Alexandra gave Lacy his bath later.

"Deal," Alexandra said. After Lacy rode with a huge smile on his face it was time for him to give the bike to Horace and Marcel. He watched both boys try to ride and both fell off and just couldn't get the hang of it. Alexandra had enough of watching her bike crash to the ground and said, "Okay. No more rides today."

Horace said, "But Lacy got to ride a lot."

"No he didn't," Alexandra said. "He rode a couple of times because it's his birthday but you and Marcel rode many more times than he did so don't complain."

"I'm not complaining, and I'm telling Mom you won't let me ride your bike," Horace said.

Marcel said, "Yeah me too." Moments later, Mom came out and asked why the boys couldn't ride the bike and Alexandra said it was Lacy's birthday and that was why she let him ride. She said she also let Marcel and Horace ride but they kept crashing so she told them to stop before they damaged her bike.

"Didn't Lacy crash?" Mom asked.

"Just once," Odessa said. "He is really good and can stay on the bike."

"What? That bike is too big for him, there is no way he can stay on it," she said.

"No Mom. He can ride," Odessa said.

"Lacy, get on that bike and show me what you did," Mom said. Lacy was excited to get on the bike again and once he got his foot on the pedal and kicked and pushed himself, he took off and rode like he'd done it many times before. He went up and back on the street and turned without an issue. He heard a car speeding up the street so panicked and steered the bike into Lilly's driveway and turned onto the grassy area, and when the bike slowed down he put his foot down while holding the bike upright with a big smile on his face. Mom wasn't smiling and told Lacy to bring to the bike over so Horace and Marcel could ride it.

Lacy gave the bike to Horace and Horace snatched it out of Lacy's hands and said, "I can ride better than you four-eyes." Lacy said nothing because Mom was looking at him with the look she gave him when she found out that Esta ran away. Lacy looked at Horace as he tried to get the bike going, and didn't want to look at Mom because he thought he was about to get into trouble.

As Horace and Marcel took several turns trying to ride Alexandra's bike and crashed it on the street or into curbs, Alexandra asked Mom if she could have her bike back before it got destroyed. *Slap!* Mom slapped Alexandra across the face and said, "You selfish bitch. You let Lacy ride but Horace and Marcel can't ride? Get in the house!"

"But it's my bike," Alexandra said as she cried, walking toward the house.

"Get in that house before I crack you again," Mom said. Odessa walked after her but Mom said, "Odessa, get over here and watch these boys ride that bike. Lacy can't ride again until Horace and Marcel get better since he's obviously been practicing trying to show them up." Lacy wanted to tell her he had not been practicing, but after he watched Alexandra take a hit to the face he thought it was best to keep quiet. "You think you're cute don't you," Mom said to Lacy. Lacy didn't know how to respond to that. She said, "You want to be better than Horace and Marcel but they are smarter and better at things because they are older and you need to learn from them. Do you understand?" she asked.

"Yes," Lacy said. But Lacy remembered what Esta said about people wanting to hurt him and take things from him. He knew he was good on the bike and liked riding it because it made him feel free. Marcel and Horace rode because they wanted to prove they were better and Mom wanted to prove that too. He remembered Esta and Mom arguing about that a long time ago but now he saw it for himself. As he stood there watching the two boys crash, he looked over his shoulder and saw Alexandra watching from the window as she cried. Lacy felt sorry for her and didn't like how Horace and Marcel laughed as they wrecked Alexandra's bike over and over.

At one point the handlebars went crooked and that was when Mom said to put the bike away and said, "Let's all go inside." Lacy and Odessa went to Alexandra. She was very upset and said Mom was a witch and evil as sin. She said God didn't like evil and Mom would have to answer to God one day for her evil ways. Lacy just listened and Odessa told Alexandra she was so sorry that her bike got damaged and offered to help her fix it. Alexandra said she didn't want the bike anymore, but that was her frustration talking. The next day, she and Odessa were in the garage trying to straighten the handlebars and called June Bug over to help fix it. Once the bike was fixed, Alexandra said she didn't want anyone to ride it again, but when Mom got home and pulled the car into the garage she saw it was fixed and told Marcel and Horace they could ride it anytime they wanted to. This made Alexandra very upset but she couldn't do anything about it. Since Mom said Horace and Marcel could ride anytime they wanted, Alexandra told Lacy he could ride it too, so one day Lacy was out riding while the sisters were watching him, and Mom drove up and saw him.

She pulled in the driveway and quickly got out of the car and yelled for Lacy to bring the bike over immediately. He rode over to her and she told him to get his little black ass in the house. He did as she said. "Randy!" she yelled. "Get me the belt." Lacy wondered if the belt was for him.

Once Randy got the belt he said, "Someone got a beatin' coming and it ain't me. Right Mom?"

"Hush Randy," she said. "Lacy, get over here. You think you're cute and like to show off on that bike so everyone can see you, don't you?"

"No," Lacy said. "I just like to ride because it's fun and it's a new thing I learned and I like learning."

"Well," she said, "you're about to learn what happens to show-offs in this house!" *Whap, whap, whap.* Lacy was doing the Mexican Jumping Bean dance again as she tore his little black ass up, and this time she moved too fast for him to block the belt with his hands and arms. As he was being beaten he looked at the others to see who would stop this from happening. He called to Alexandra because he felt Alexandra was the bravest and could help. Then he called to Odessa but she just cried and said she was sorry. He wanted to call to Gus but Mom yanked Lacy by his shirt and yelled, "LOOK AT ME!" Lacy looked at her, then she continued. His eyes fell upon Marcel and Horace as they sat on the sofa giggling, while Randy just stood off to the side with his eyes wide, mouth open, and his head moving up and down as Lacy jumped up and squatted down trying to dodge the belt. Then he looked back at Gus and saw that Gus' eyes showed that he was very unhappy with what was going on.

"Look at Mom!" Randy yelled.

"That's right!" Mom said. "I DON'T GIVE A GOOD GOT

DAMN WHO'S HERE. YOU LOOK AT ME OR I'LL BEAT HELL OUT OF YOU, YOU LITTLE BLACK SON OF A BITCH!" Lacy tried to keep his eyes on her as he jumped up and squatted down and ran to the left and right as she held his arm, beating him with the belt aimlessly. "NOW GET OUT OF MY SIGHT AND DON'T LET ME CATCH YOU ON THAT BIKE AGAIN UNLESS YOU ASK ME FIRST! DO YOU UNDERSTAND ME?"

"Ye, ye, ye, ye, yes, ye, yes, yes."

"GOOD!" she said. "RANDY!"

"YES MOM!" he said.

She said, "PUT THIS BELT AWAY." Then tossed it on the floor near him and headed for the kitchen. Randy grabbed the belt and hurried to put it away. She must have worn herself out a bit while giving out the beating because she went to the kitchen for a glass of water afterward.

"How does it feel four-eyes?" Horace asked.

"Want to ride the bike Lacy?" Marcel asked, then laughed like a hyena. Lacy just looked at them crying and wondering what was wrong with them and what he did to make them act that way toward him. It was as if they'd rather see him get beat than to go outside and play or watch something funny on TV. He couldn't understand what they got out of watching him getting beat and enjoying it so much. Was it the belt slapping against his skin? Or him jumping up and squatting down? Or his screaming and him begging Mom to stop? Lacy couldn't figure it out, but he remembered what Esta said about people being jealous and wanting to hurt him and take things from him. As much as he wanted to understand why those two acted the way they did and why they enjoyed watching his beatings, he felt sorry for them because he didn't see anything good for them as they got older. Lacy was getting beatings now but knew that he would also get them later when he was older too. Alexandra and Odessa told Lacy to come with them as they went to their room and closed the door.

Alexandra looked Lacy in his eyes and said, "That wasn't right, that wasn't right, Lacy, that wasn't right. She had no reason to beat you like that and Marcel and Horace need to shut their mouths. I'm so sick of her treating them like favorites around here. Are you okay Lacy?"

"Yes," he said. "My legs and my back and my arms hurt. My arm hurts a lot because she was squeezing it hard and yanking it when she was hitting me with the belt. She's nothing but a mean witch and knows she needs to beat Marcel and Horace for all that they do and Randy for stealing and carrying on." Lacy said, "I feel sorry for Gus because he doesn't do anything to anybody and he looks so unhappy when he sees me getting beat by Mom."

"Gus has a good heart," Alexandra said, "and as long as he minds his own business she might not bother him too much."

"I hope she leaves him alone because I like him a lot and he's nice to me," Lacy said.

"You should be worrying about yourself Lacy," Odessa said. "Every time Marcel and Horace can't do something as good as you, Mom will take it out on you."

"Why?" Lacy asked.

"We don't know," Odessa said. "It makes no sense because she should be happy and proud of you being able to do what you do at your age."

"Lacy, I have a question for you," Alexandra said.

"Okay," Lacy said.

"Where do you think Esta went?"

"I thought we weren't supposed to say her name," Lacy said.

"We're not," Alexandra said, "but it's just us and Mom won't know. Where do you think she went?"

Lacy said, "That night when she and I were watching TV I kept seeing her running with her suitcase..."

"We know that part Lacy," Alexandra said, "but where do you think she went?"

"Well, I was getting to that," Lacy said, "but I wanted to remind you."

"We're reminded," she said. "Just tell us what you think about where she went." Lacy looked at both sisters and wondered why Alexandra asked that question. They were the last to see her and knew that she ran away since they told Mom when she got home from work.

Lacy said, "She was supposed to take me with her but she went with someone else and will not come back for me. She was never going to take me with her but she felt sorry for me and told me she would but her plan was with someone else. She will not be happy. She will never forget that she lied to me and she will be sad about it." Both sisters kept looking at each other then looked at him as if they had something to say but didn't.

"Do you wish you could see Esta?" Odessa asked.

"I don't know, she lied to me and left. She told me that people will want to hurt me but she didn't say that she was one of those people."

Alexandra said, "Lacy, I don't think Esta meant to hurt you."

Lacy said, "She is an adult and adults should know if they are hurting a child. If they don't know, they should not be around a child."

"Are you upset with Esta then?" Alexandra asked.

"No," Lacy said. "She did what she thought was best for her and when I am older I will do what is best for me. One day she will want to talk to me but it won't be the same."

Odessa asked, "One day when Lacy?"

He said, "One day when I'm older like Randy's age. She will be very unhappy in her life and will want to see me so her life will be better but it won't." Tears fell from Odessa's eyes. "Why are you crying Odessa?" Lacy asked.

She said, "Because everything you say sounds so true as if you see what's going to happen...and I believe you."

"I believe you too," Alexandra said, "but I hope you don't hate Esta."

Lacy said, "Jasper told me not to hate. He said for me to use the word dislike because it means I don't like something or someone. He said to hate someone is like wanting them to be dead, so I don't hate her but I dislike her lying to me and leaving the way she left. She didn't even say goodbye."

"You're right Lacy," Alexandra said, "you're right."

"Do you want to play a game Lacy?" Odessa asked.

"No," Lacy said. "I just want to sit and think."

"Think about what?" Odessa asked.

"I want to think about my future when I'm an adult and how my life will be."

"How will it be?" Alexandra asked.

"It will be good and I will be happy and Horace, Marcel, Randy, and Mom will not be able to hurt me."

"Will we be in your future Lacy?" Odessa asked.

"Yes," Lacy said. "You, Alexandra, and Gus will be there and I will always be there for you. I will be there for Marcel, Horace, Randy, and Mom if they get better but they won't. Randy will get worse and worse, then I won't see him anymore." The sisters looked puzzled and concerned at the same time.

"Heeeey. Do you want some cookies Lacy? There are cookies left over from your birthday," Alexandra said.

"No thank you," Lacy said. "I just want to sit and think. I wish I could sit in the rocking chair to think but I don't want to get in any more trouble today."

"I heeear that," Alexandra said. "You go ahead and think, and I'm going to warm up some cookies in case you change your mind."

"Okay," Lacy said. As she left the room, Odessa told Lacy he had a very powerful imagination and imagined many things. Lacy told Odessa that sometimes it was his imagination and other times it was what was shown to him.

"Shown to you by who?" Odessa asked.

"By God," Lacy said.

"Why doesn't God show me or Alexandra what you see?" she asked.

Lacy said, "Odessa, God does what God wants so I can't answer that or I would be God."

"Right! Hahahahaha," she laughed and said, "I'm a dunce. You're right Lacy. What was I thinking? But, how do you know if it's your imagination or not your imagination showing you something?"

"That's easy," Lacy said. "When something is from my imagination it's from me thinking it up. When it's not from my imagination it comes out of nowhere as a message or answer just like me telling you something you didn't know."

"You can really tell the difference?" Odessa asked.

"Yes," Lacy said. "I didn't imagine Esta was going to leave that night when she and I watched TV together, it was shown to me but none of you believed me. She left just as I was shown and she dropped her things just as I was shown."

Odessa said, "How you knew she was going to leave confused me and Alexandra."

Lacy said, "Are you still confused? You don't believe I was shown she was going to leave?"

Odessa said, "I just don't know how you saw that or knew that."

"Why do people say they believe in God and talk about all of the things God can do but don't believe God shows us things?"

She said, "Lacy, because you're a child and children always say things they think or believe."

"Do they say things like I said about Esta then it happens?" Lacy asked.

"I don't know," Odessa said.

Lacy said, "Then maybe you should listen to me until you do know." Odessa told Lacy that was no way for him to talk to her or adults. Lacy said he was sorry. He said he didn't mean to be disrespectful, he just didn't know another way to say what he said so that she would understand. Lacy said, "It's not easy trying to tell you or the others what I see then hear you tell me you don't believe me, or not do something about what I saw."

Odessa smiled at Lacy and softly pinched his cheeks and said, "That must be really hard for you to deal with Lacy, but it's hard for me and others that hear what you say you saw. Maybe as you get older we will believe and listen to what you say about what you saw or see. Is that fair Lacy?"

Lacy said, "I don't know if it's fair but if I see things that can help you and you don't listen or believe me, promise you won't tell me I was not fair."

"Okay Lacy I promise," Odessa said. "Do you see anything now Lacy?"

"Yes," he said. "I see that Alexandra is taking a long time to bring the cookies."

"I thought you didn't want any," Odessa said.

"I didn't before but I do now," Lacy said, as he rubbed his hands together. "Talking about what I see and how I see must have made me hungry."

"It must have," Odessa said. "Let me see what's taking Alexandra so long."

"Okay," Lacy said. When Odessa went to the kitchen to check on Alexandra, Randy went to the sisters' room and asked Lacy if he enjoyed the beating he got. Lacy just looked at Randy.

"Answer me four-eyes," Randy said. "Did you enjoy the beating you got?" Alexandra walked up behind Randy and grabbed his shirt and twisted it, causing the shirt to tighten around his neck. Randy grabbed the front of his shirt, trying to release the tension around his neck as Alexandra asked him if he would enjoy getting a beating by her. "Nnnoo. No. Let me go," he said. Alexandra yanked him out of the room into the hallway just outside the door and said a few words to him in his ear that Lacy couldn't hear, but the look on Randy's face was total fear. When she let Randy go, he ran down the hall saying, "You don't scare me none." He said, "C'mon, I'll fight chu anytime, anywhere." Alexandra gave the plate of cookies to Odessa to hold and hurried down the hall, and all Lacy heard was Randy saying, "I was just kidding, I was just kidding! I don't want to fight chu because boys shouldn't be fighting girls."

"Yeah, especially this girl because I'll knock you silly. Now stay out of my room and leave Lacy alone."

"What's going on here?" Mom asked, as she came out of her room.

Randy said, "Oh Mom, just in time. Alexandra's been threatening me and she twisted my shirt around my neck then whispered into my ear that she was going to beat me so bad that she was going to beat the black off of me."

"ALEXANDRA! Did you say that?" Mom asked.

"Randy's making up stories," Alexandra said. "He was picking on

Lacy again and I told him to stop."

Mom asked, "But did you say you would beat the black off of him?"

"Yes," Alexandra said.

"Go to your room and don't you come out until it's time for you to cook dinner, do you hear me?"

"Yes Mom," she said.

"Yeah, see. She wanted to fight me and I told her anytime and anywhere but she doesn't want to fight me because I knock her silly," Randy said. Mom told Randy to go and watch TV and Alexandra walked to her room as she looked over her shoulder at Randy with a look that said, "one day Randy, one day."

"Alexandra! Get to your room and stop throwing hard stares at Randy." When Alexandra got to her room she closed the door and told Odessa and Lacy that Randy needed to get his ass whooped good, and that witch needed to stop protecting him so he could learn his lesson.

"I'd like to pop him in his mouth one time so he'd shut up."

"Nothing will make him shut up," Lacy said. "He needs a doctor or someone that can help him because something is wrong with him and he doesn't know how to stop acting the way he does."

Alexandra said, "He needs a doctor alright, and the medicine he needs is my hand smacking him in the face."

Odessa said, "Lacy's right, something is not right with him and he does need someone to look at him or find out what's going on with him. Mom refuses to listen to teachers when they tell her that. She gets so upset and blames the teachers and that makes Randy think that they are wrong and he is right so he continues acting the way he does and it gets worse."

"I mean, to put a firecracker in a cat's butt and laugh when it explodes is horrible. Then he swings his yoyo and hits a boy at school in the back of the head and laughs at that too but later says it was an accident. C'mon, really? He needs help because one day someone is really going to get hurt or someone could hurt him," Alexandra said.

"That's true," Odessa said. "Lacy what do you think?" she asked.

"I think the cookies are getting cold, may I have one?"

"LACY! This is serious!" Odessa said.

"I'm sorry," Lacy said. "But the cookies are getting cold and Randy isn't going to change today, so can we eat the cookies and talk about Randy after?"

"Boy, go ahead and eat the cookies," Alexandra said.

"Hahahaha, ain't nuttin' but a dern fool boy," Odessa said. "Sometimes you really crack me up. One minute you're like an adult and the next minute you're a child again."

As Lacy was chewing on the cookie he said, "Wrong. I'm the professor. How many times do I have to tell you that?"

Neither sister laughed, and Alexandra grabbed a cookie and bit it and said, "You know Lacy, one of these days I might have to teach you a lesson with that smart mouth of yours."

"I wasn't trying to be a smart mouth Alexandra, it's just the way it comes out after I hear what you say," Lacy said.

"Ummhhhmmmm. Well, you better practice saying what you need to say so that it comes out much nicer."

"Okay," Lacy said. "May I have another cookie?" he asked.

"Hahahaha," Odessa laughed and said, "yeeeeeess you little cookie monster, yes. Have another cookie."

"Yuuum!" Lacy said.

GOOD TIMES AHEAD

The months rolled by and the older children were excited to see the last day of school since it was summer break again. Lacy looked forward to the summer because Alexandra, Odessa, and Gus would be home more so he could spend time with them. He was also excited and looking forward to starting kindergarten after the summer so he only saw good times ahead. When everyone got home from school, they noticed a long yellow material on the front lawn that looked like a banner without words written on it. "What's that on the lawn?" Randy asked.

"You'll have to go and see," Alexandra said. Everyone got out of the car to go and see what the yellow material was. The box that it came in was on the ground near it.

"IT'S A SLIP N' SLIDE!" Randy yelled. "I'm going first," he said.

Marcel said, "No me."

Horace said, "No me, I'm going first." Gus, Odessa, Alexandra, and Lacy just looked at it, then Gus ran inside to put on shorts. Alexandra and Odessa told Lacy to come with them so they could all change into different clothes to get wet in. After everyone got changed and ran outside to play on the Slip N' Slide, they stopped cold in their tracks when they saw a man standing near the Slip N' Slide.

"Mr. Stache!" Alexandra said.

"Who's Mr. Stache?" Lacy asked.

Alexandra said, "He's Mom's friend, but be careful of him because he has a temper."

"What's a temper?" Lacy asked.

"Shhh," Alexandra said.

"Hello Alexandra, Odessa, and you boys."

"Hi Mr. Stache," they all said except Lacy, because he didn't know who the man was and was too concerned with the word 'temper'.

"Now, your mother bought you all this Slip N' Slide and I've connected the water hose and got it all slick and ready for you, but I don't want any fighting over it or anyone acting silly on it. Everybody gets a turn and no one is to hog turns or stop others from using it. Do you all understand?"

Everyone but Lacy said, "Yes Mr. Stache."

"Alright, who wants to go first?" he asked.

"Me," Randy said. "Because I saw it first and nobody can Slip N' Slide better than me." Odessa and Alexandra rolled their eyes at each other when they heard Randy say that.

"Okay Randy," Mr. Stache said. "Walk away from the Slip N' Slide then run as fast as you can, then slide and show us what you can do."

Randy said, "Piece a cake. PIECE A CAAAAKKE! LOOK OUT! School's in session."

"Bahahahahaha!" Alexandra laughed and said, "If you're the teacher then the school would close down immediately."

"Alright now Alexandra," Mr. Stache said. "That's enough. Get going Randy."

"Here I go," Randy said. He worked up some pretty good speed and jumped in the air and landed on the Slip N' Slide. When his feet hit the Slip N' Slide, they slid so fast that he lost control and fell right on his butt and yelled, "AAAAHHHHHH!" His legs flew into the air as he banged his back on the ground and flopped around until he came to a stop.

"Neeeeeatoooooo!" Lacy said. Mr. Stache asked Randy if he was okay. Randy got up and limped around and said no. He said he felt like he broke his butt bone and should go to the hospital. Mr. Stache told him to walk around so he could see if Randy was okay. He told Randy he was fine, but that he should go into the house and rest a while. Randy said okay, and when he was walking away to go inside, Odessa told him to put some ice on his butt so he wouldn't walk around with a big butt bump later, then she and Alexandra laughed. Mr. Stache told them to knock it off, then he asked Lacy why he thought Randy falling down was "neeeeatooo". Lacy said he didn't think Randy falling down was neeeatoo. He told Mr. Stache he thought the way Randy slid and flopped around was neeeatoo just like in the cartoons or in the cowboy movies when the stuntmen fell off the rooftops after getting shot. He said Randy looked like a stuntman.

"I see," Mr. Stache said. "Do you plan on being a stuntman Lacy?"

Lacy said, "No, but it would be fun."

Mr. Stache said, "Well, why don't you walk over there by the plantern and show us how fun it would be to be a stuntman?"

"Neeeeatooooo," Lacy said.

"Do you have to say neeeeatoooo Lacy?" Mr. Stache asked.

"Yes," Lacy said, "because it means GROOVY!"

Mr. Stache said, "Groovy? HMM? Okay. We're ready when you are." Lacy took off running with a big smile on his face and dove onto the Slip N' Slide just like he had seen a baseball player slide into the home plate at the baseball game Esta took him to long ago.

"NeeeetoooooooooOOOOUUUUCCHHH! AAAAAHHHHH. MY CHEST! AAAAAAAHHHHH!" Lacy got off the Slip N' Slide as fast as he could. "MY CHEST!" He screamed, "MY CHEST!" Odessa, Alexandra, and Gus ran over to see what happened since he was holding his chest and crying in pain.

Randy ran outside and asked what happened, and Horace and Marcel were rolling around on the ground laughing. Mr. Stache said, "This is what got him." There was a rock under the Slip N' Slide and he must have slid his chest right on it.

"Yes," Alexandra said. "His chest is red where he slid over the rock."

"Well, don't worry about it," Mr. Stache said, "he'll be okay. Hahaha, ain't nuthin' but a rock. He'll live. Now get back over there and try it again Lacy."

"I don't want to," Lacy said.

"Well, what kind of stuntman are you if you don't try again?"

Lacy said, "There could be more rocks under the Slip N' Slide so I don't want to try it again."

"I just took that rock from under the slide," Mr. Stache said. "So, go ahead and slide."

Alexandra said, "He doesn't want to so he doesn't have to."

"Was I talking to you?" Mr. Stache said.

"No," Alexandra said, "but I was talking to you."

"Oh, you were, were you?" Mr. Stache asked.

"Yeah, I was," Alexandra said.

"You know, I've got my belt on but I can take it off if you think you need me to take it off."

"No, she doesn't need for you to take it off," Lacy said. "I'll slide." Lacy got lined up to run and took off again, but this time he landed on his feet and slid all the way across the Slip N' Slide without falling down. He yelled, "Neeeeeeeatooooo!" After he slid, he ran over to Gus and the sisters and told them how much fun it was and how they should try. Alexandra wasn't exactly in the mood to slide since she didn't really like Mr. Stache or what he said to her. Alexandra told Odessa she was going into the house and Odessa said she would go with her. Odessa asked Gus to watch Lacy and he did. Gus and Lacy had a ball slipping and sliding. Horace and Marcel played too but they got tired and went inside. Gus and Lacy just kept sliding, and when Ari and Shirley saw how much fun they were having, they asked to join in and Gus said sure. Lilly was still upset about Shirley and Lacy's escapades but she was able to see them from her window and her son Ari was with them as well. Lacy stared at Shirley in her bikini but Gus told him to stop staring and slide, so he did and they slid and slid and slid until they were worn out. When they went inside, it was nearly time for dinner so they put on some dry clothes and prepared to eat. Once everyone was sitting at the dining table and started to eat, Mom told the children that Mr. Stache would be staying over a few nights a week to make sure the children were safe and doing all of the things they were supposed to do while she was at work. Alexandra and Odessa stopped eating.

Randy put his fork down and said, "I don't need him here watching me. I'm a big boy."

"You're a big boy?" Mr. Stache asked Randy.

"Yeah," Randy said. "I don't need you around here."

"Hush up," Mom said. "You don't talk to him that way Randy, now apologize."

"I ain't apologizin' to that turkey," Randy said. "He can jump in the lake for all I care." Mr. Stache jumped up from the table and yanked his belt off, then quickly walked over to Randy, grabbed him by the arm, yanked him out of his chair, and started swinging his belt. "You're not my father!" Randy yelled.

"No," Mr. Stache said, "but I'm the son of a bitch that's gonna beat your ass tonight."

"MOM HELP," Randy shouted.

"Donny, NO," Mom said. She called Mr. Stache by his first name, Donny. "He didn't mean it, did you Randy?" she asked.

"Yeah. I meant what I said about this turkey. He ain't nuthin' but a child molester that likes to beat kids that can't fight back, but one day I'll kill 'em."

"Oh, you gonna kill me you little bastard?" *Whap! Whap! Whap!*

"Okay Donny," Mom said. "That's enough!" Mr. Stache stopped and shook his belt at the rest of the children and said if anyone stepped out of line they would get the same thing.

"That goes for you too Lacy. You might be the baby but I'll beat your ass just like anybody else here. Do you understand me?"

"Yes," Lacy said as he dropped his chin and kept his eyes on Mr. Stache.

"Now, everybody eat your food so you can get ready for bed or whatever you do at this time," Mr. Stache said. Randy sat back down and started eating his food with tears in his eyes. Lacy looked at Randy and felt sorry for him and was glad he stood up to Mr. Stache. When everyone finished eating, the sisters took Lacy into their room and closed the door. Odessa asked why he looked at Mr. Stache the way he did. She told Lacy that he gave out beatings for less reason than Mom did so he shouldn't stare at him. Lacy said he stared at him because he could see that he has done some very bad things in his life and has hurt many people.

"What do you mean?" Odessa asked.

"I mean he is not a good person and I don't trust him. He's a very, very bad man."

"You're right Lacy, he's not a good person," Alexandra said. "He's a dirty buzzard and a nasty old man and I cannot stand him. I don't know where Mom found him but he belongs in a gutter somewhere." She said, "Lacy, you just make sure you stay out of his way." Lacy shrugged his shoulders and took a deep breath, and Alexandra asked why he did that. He said he had to watch out for Horace, Marcel, Randy, Lilly, Mom, and now Mr. Stache and he only had two eyes.

"Wrong," Odessa said. "You have four, hahahahahaha." Alexandra laughed too but Lacy just looked at the two of them and said that was not very funny. "I'm just teasing you Lacy," Odessa said.

"I know," Lacy said, "and I would laugh too but Mr. Stache seems really dangerous and doesn't know when to stop hurting people. If Mom didn't tell him to stop beating Randy he would probably still be beating Randy."

"Lacy's right," Alexandra said. "We better think of something or a way to protect ourselves if Mr. Stache loses control and goes crazy on us. We can talk to Randy because he will want our help against Mr. Stache and help us in return."

Odessa asked, "Do you really think Randy would jump in and help us? Because I think he'd run for the hills."

"Hahahaha," Alexandra laughed and said, "you are probably right, but the way he stood up to him makes me think that he would do it again, especially if he had help."

"If we do something to stop Mr. Stache, Mom will get upset and beat all of us," Lacy said.

Alexandra said, "You just saw the kind of beating Mr. Stache gives out, so who would you rather get beat by, Mom or Mr. Stache?"

"Are those the only choices?" Lacy asked.

"Don't be silly Lacy," Alexandra said. "You know those are the only choices and this is serious."

"I understand it's serious," Lacy said, "but I hoped there was a choice not to get beat."

"Lacy, sometimes in life the only choice you have is to step forward and stand up for yourself. It might hurt but you will be happy later that you did something to help yourself."

Lacy said, "I know you're right, but you and Odessa are older and don't have a lot more beatings to get but I have a lot more years to get beat, so I was hoping for a way to help me cut down on the beatings. Who came up with the idea of beatings anyway? It doesn't make sense to beat children when you can just talk to them instead."

Alexandra said, "I hear you."

"I'll never beat children," Lacy said.

Odessa asked, "What if you have a child like Randy?"

"I will still talk to him," Lacy said, "and if he needed help I would find help because beatings just make the child upset with the person doing the beating."

"You're right," Odessa said, "but if I had a child like Randy I don't know what I'd do."

"You will not have a child like Randy," Lacy said.

"How do you know that Lacy?" Odessa asked.

"I just know," Lacy said. "You won't have a child like Randy."

"Something you're seeing Lacy?" Alexandra asked.

"No," Lacy said. "I just know she will be fine and not have a child like Randy."

"Odessa and Alexandra, get in here," Mr. Stache ordered.

"Stay here Lacy," Alexandra said.

Lacy said, "Okay." The sisters went to the living room to see what Mr. Stache wanted.

"Aren't you two supposed to clean the kitchen after dinners?" he asked.

"Yes," both sisters answered. Mr. Stache looked at them and asked why it wasn't cleaned.

Alexandra said, "You told everyone to go to their room or do whatever it is that we do."

"Right," he said, "and you two are supposed to do the kitchen, right?"

"Right," the sisters said.

"Don't you let me tell you this again and make me have to take my belt off."

Alexandra looked him in his eyes and said, "If you have something to say you can just tell me or ask me but you don't have to threaten me."

Randy said, "Yeah, you don't have to come around here threatening everybody with your belt. Why don't you try that on someone your own size?"

Mr. Stache said, "I wasn't talking to you but I did tell you to get your ass out of that rocking chair, didn't I?"

Randy said, "This is where I sit and Mom is okay with it."

Mr. Stache said, "Well your mama left for work and she ain't here so I'M the head nigga in CHARGE! Or, didn't you know that?" he said as he pulled his belt off and walked over to Randy. He pulled Randy out of the chair and started beating him.

Lacy heard all of this and remembered what the sisters said about helping each other, so he ran into the living room, ready to jump in. He saw the sisters standing near the kitchen so he ran near them and said, "I'm ready."

"Ready for what?" Odessa asked.

"To help like we talked about."

"No Lacy, you stay here," Alexandra said. "C'mon Odessa." Both sisters jumped in and one sister grabbed his neck from behind and the other grabbed the arm he was beating Randy with. Once the sisters jumped in, Randy kicked Mr. Stache in the testicles but he must have missed because Mr. Stache didn't flinch one bit.

Randy kept kicking him wherever he could and kept saying, "Head nigga is now a beat nigga. Don't you ever lay your hands on me again."

Gus was sleeping but came out of his room running when he heard all of the noise, and when he saw the fight he jumped in to break it all up. He told Mr. Stache he shouldn't be fighting children and needed to leave. Mr. Stache was scratched up pretty bad on his face and neck and probably wouldn't be having children anytime soon if some of Randy's kicks landed in the right spot. When Mr. Stache saw that he was heavily outnumbered, he yelled, "You're all crazy and I'm not staying here with any of you badass kids. I will tell yo mama what happened here tonight."

"And we will tell her what happened too," Alexandra said, as she cried since she must have taken an elbow to the ribs or face in the fight. Odessa was worn too and crying. When Mr. Stache left with a loud door slam, Gus asked what happened and how the whole thing started. The sisters and Randy explained what happened, and Gus listened and said Mom was going to be very upset. Alexandra said, "Yeah, but Gus, if you tell Mom that you came out and saw us trying to help Randy she might not be as upset because she believes you."

"Will you?" Odessa asked.

"Please Gus," Lacy asked, "because she will beat us if you don't."

"I will tell her because he's not right and has a temper."

"Thank you," Odessa said.

"Let him at me again," Randy said.

"Oh, be quiet Randy," Alexandra said. "You always talk big after the fight."

"Hahaha," Randy laughed and said, "I know, I do, don't I. Hahaha. That nigga won't be around here anytime soon."

"Watch your mouth Randy," Alexandra said.

Randy said, "Okay, but you know what he is and what he does too."

"I hear you," Alexandra said, "but you don't have to say it." Lacy asked if someone would tell him what temper meant.

Gus said, "It means a person is calm or angry. You know which one they are because of how they act. Mr. Stache has an angry temper."

"OHHH! I get it," Lacy said.

"Good," Alexandra said, "but don't use that word around Mom or anyone you think gets angry quickly or for no reason."

"Okay," Lacy said.

The phone rang and Gus said, "That's going to be Mom. I'll get it." He answered the phone, and she asked Gus many questions but he just kept saying Mr. Stache was fighting Randy, Odessa, and Alexandra, and it started with Mr. Stache beating Randy for sitting in the rocking chair. He said, "We were trying to get him to stop and that's why we were involved." She asked to speak with Randy, Odessa, and Alexandra, and everyone said the same thing. Mom said she would be home in the morning and handle things then. After the phone call, Gus went back to bed, Odessa and Alexandra took Lacy to their room to go to bed, and Randy stayed in the living room a little longer to watch TV. The next day, Mom asked Horace and Marcel what happened but they had no idea since they were sleeping the whole time. Mr. Stache told her that Randy hit him and that's why he pulled his belt off to beat Randy. Mom made Gus, Randy, Odessa, and Alexandra apologize to Mr. Stache and said he was going to be there while she worked whether they liked it or not. He stayed there but thought twice about being so quick to pull his belt off. He still tossed out threats here and there but his biggest fight was with Randy. He would beat Randy often but the beatings lasted less than ten seconds because that's how long it took for Alexandra, Odessa, and Gus to appear. Mr. Stache was around that entire summer and any friends that would come by before weren't coming by with him there. Even Lilly didn't like Mr. Stache and thought he was an odd person and even told that to Mom one day when they were talking. Mom told Lilly that she didn't speak about people Lilly knew so Lilly shouldn't speak about people Mom knew.

Lilly said, "I know Beatrice, but dat main is a funny lil' sumthin' and he got da evil streak inem' don't he. I heard Randy scremin' up a storm many taaamms and I know you don't beat like dat."

Mom said, "Mind your own business Lilly."

"Okay Beatrice," Lilly said. "Isss yo pardie girl. You doin' you than and I get it. I get it."

Mom said, "Good," and that was the end of that discussion. It was about that time they stopped talking altogether, and Mom and the family moved from La Puente, California to West Covina, just before school started. They moved into a house with a pool but Mom didn't want the hassle of a pool, and since it was already filled with sand she decided to leave it that way. Moving into the new house meant a whole new neighborhood and new friends. When school started, Lacy met a lot of new children in kindergarten and was able to see Horace, Marcel, Gus, and Randy during recess. He would run over and say hello to Gus then go play with his friends in the sandbox or on the swings. He was really having a great time learning new things and working with the other children.

When snack time came with cheese crackers and punch, Lacy thought that was a party. And, when nap time came, man oh man it was just like the Jasper days all over again without the Army men. Lacy made a good friend named Ryan and they played with the puzzles and other toys and laughed at just about anything. One day, Lacy and Ryan were playing and laughing when the teacher Mrs. Johnson called Lacy up to her desk. Lacy got up from the floor where all the children were playing and ran up to Mrs. Johnson's desk to see what she wanted. Mrs. Johnson was a white woman with a bob cut and black-framed glasses. Lacy noticed her face didn't look happy. By that time in his life, he easily recognized an angry or upset look. "Yes Mrs. Johnson?" he said. She just looked at him and didn't say a word. He looked at her and wondered what was wrong with her. "Mrs. Johnson, did you want me?" Lacy asked.

"If I didn't want you then why would I call you up to my desk?" she asked.

"Right," Lacy said. "You weren't saying anything so I wanted to make sure you wanted me."

"You know, if I were your mother I'd whip the tar out of you."

"Why? What did I do?" Lacy asked.

"Go back and sit down," she said. Lacy left her desk with a puzzled look on his face and sat next to Ryan and didn't move an inch.

Ryan asked Lacy what Mrs. Johnson wanted and Lacy told him what she said. Ryan said, "She said that?"

"Yes," Lacy said. Ryan asked Lacy if he was going to tell on her. "Tell who?" Lacy asked.

"Tell your mom," Ryan said.

Lacy said, "No. Let's just forget about it."

"Forget about it?" Ryan said, "My mom wouldn't like Mrs. Johnson talking to me like that." Lacy didn't say anything because he didn't think Mom would believe he didn't do anything, and she already told him if he got into trouble at school she would tear his little black ass up and hang him by his thumbs in front of the class. "Lacy, you have to tell," Ryan said.

"Ryan, move to the other side of the room and play," Mrs. Johnson said.

"Why?" Ryan asked.

"Do what I told you," Mrs. Johnson said.

"I'm playing with Lacy," he said. Now Lacy was really getting nervous because he felt any trouble about to happen would be his fault, and Mom wouldn't believe him since the other children had no problems at that school except for Randy, but he had problems all the time so it was expected. Mrs. Johnson got up from her desk, went over to Ryan, and grabbed him by his arm and made him move to the other side of the room while he was twisting and kicking, telling her to take her hands off of him. When she let him go, he went right back over next to Lacy and sat down. Lacy couldn't believe what he was seeing because he'd never seen a child at school act that way toward a teacher. When Ryan sat by Lacy, Mrs. Johnson didn't make a sound and just sat back at her desk, staring at Lacy. When it was time for recess and everyone went outside, Lacy told Ryan he was going to get into trouble when his Mom found out what happened. Ryan said, "No way. When I tell my mom what Mrs. Johnson said to you and that she told me to move for no reason my mom will talk to her and want to know what's wrong with Mrs. Johnson." Lacy liked hearing how Ryan knew his mom would believe him and talk to Mrs. Johnson for him. Lacy wondered if he told Mom what happened if she would talk to Mrs. Johnson, but he didn't dare tell. He told Gus at recess and Gus couldn't believe what she said to Lacy. Gus told Odessa and Odessa spoke to Lacy to hear about what happened from him. By the time school ended that day, Ryan told his mom about everything that happened and his mom went to Mrs. Johnson and scolded her for her behavior. Ryan's mom told Mom what happened and Mom took Lacy home and tore his little black ass up for causing problems at school and told him to not speak to Ryan or play with him again. Ryan didn't understand why Lacy didn't want to play with him anymore, but it was clear that this made Mrs. Johnson happy. Lacy quickly realized that she might be one of the people that Esta spoke about who didn't want to see him happy. He did what the teacher requested during class and kept to himself most of the time. He looked forward to going home and spending time with Gus, Odessa, and Alexandra, and playing with the new neighbors, brothers Richard and Russell. Richard was Marcel's age and Russell was Lacy's but Richard liked playing with Lacy just as much as Russell did, so when everyone got out of school, Lacy would look forward to going to Richard and Russell's house when he was allowed. Since Lacy got out of kindergarten earlier than the other children finished school, he and Mom would still run errands and go to her dance class with Amando before picking up the others from school. During the errands and dance class, Lacy was pretty good at staying out of Mom's way and not making trouble for himself. When school was out and the others were home was when trouble seemed to erupt. When Randy would get into trouble at school, Mom would get upset with the teachers who she felt were picking on Randy and comparing him to the other children in the class that got better grades and were said to have behaved in class. This would make Mom furious, and those were the times she would press harder on Lacy, telling him to clean up or put things away that Marcel and Horace clearly left out, but Lacy would move quickly to avoid trouble. If the sisters got into trouble for talking to boys on the phone or not cleaning the kitchen right, Lacy got in trouble for it too. Somehow, when the sisters got into trouble it would open the door for Lacy to get a beating, put on restriction from going to Richard and Russell's house, or get yelled at because he should have either reminded the sisters to clean or because he distracted them from cleaning somehow. The sisters would tell Mom that Lacy had nothing to do with them not doing their work and that they either forgot or hadn't finished, but she was convinced it was Lacy's fault.

Mom would say, "You can tell me all you want that it's not his fault and I shouldn't blame him, just like Lilly told me that I shouldn't be upset and not blame Esta for stealing my two pairs of shoes." Lacy couldn't understand how Mom could be so upset for so long about Esta stealing two pairs of her shoes, especially when she had a lot of shoes and could buy more. *It's not right for someone to steal from anyone but being upset about it for a long time only hurts the person who's upset*, Lacy thought to himself. The beatings Lacy would get increased. He would usually get a couple of beatings a week and on good weeks he only got one. Often, they occurred when Mom got home from work or just before she went to work. To avoid beatings, Lacy developed a habit of staying in the sisters' room or somewhere in the backyard before Mom went to work or before she got home, hoping she would forget he was there. Many times, this worked, but other times Mom would call for Lacy or look around for him to give him chores. He didn't mind the chores and was happy to do them, but Mom would tell him later that the chores were either done incorrectly or not at all. To make sure his chores were done exactly as asked, Lacy began asking the sisters or Gus if he did the chores properly and they would tell Lacy yes, so Lacy had no reason to believe the chores were not completed properly. There were a couple of occasions where either sister got slapped across the face when they expressed to Mom that they believed the chores were complete. After seeing the sisters get slapped, Lacy didn't want to ask them to check his chores anymore and just did his best to get the job done. One day, Mom was just about to leave for work when she called Lacy into the bathroom to ask if he brushed his teeth that day. He said yes and that he did it at the same time Gus brushed his teeth. Mom called Gus to the bathroom and asked if Lacy brushed his teeth and Gus said yes, then Mom said Gus could leave. She looked at Lacy and told him to open his mouth so she could inspect his teeth. She told him to close his mouth and said that he was lying and that she was tired of his lying and all the liars in her life, so she was going to teach him how to brush his teeth and stop lying at the same time. She grabbed the Ajax cleanser and told him to wet his toothbrush. She poured the Ajax onto his toothbrush then told him to brush his teeth.

Lacy said, "But Gus told me Ajax is poisonous." *Slap!* Right across the face.

Mom said, "If I wanted to know what Gus told you I would have asked." She told him to wet his toothbrush again so he did. She poured more Ajax on his toothbrush and told him to brush. He looked at her and she yelled, "BRUSH!"

Marcel and Horace stood outside the bathroom and Horace said, "Brush four-eyes, before Mom beats your butt."

Randy saw what was happening and said, "Mom that's poisonous."

She said, "Everybody away from the door, and Lacy you brush or I'll take my shoe off and beat you senseless." Lacy had the shoe treatment before so he put the brush near his mouth and started crying as the brush met his mouth and teeth. "BRUSH!" she said. Lacy began brushing. "Harder!" she said. Lacy brushed harder. "I wouldn't swallow if I were you because it's poisonous," she said, "spit and rinse your mouth." Lacy spit and rinsed his mouth then she grabbed the brush out of his hand. "That is the way you're supposed to brush. Here," she said, as she handed him a bar of soap, "put this in your mouth and hold it between your teeth." Lacy looked at her as if he didn't know what she was asking him and *SLAP!* Right across the face. "Boy, don't you look at me as if you didn't hear what I said," she said. Lacy put the soap between his teeth like she said. "If that bar falls out of your mouth your black ass is mine." She handed Lacy a wet brillo pad with Ajax on it and told him to start scrubbing his knees because his knees were dark and she wanted them lighter. She said dark knees and elbows looked tacky like a runaway slave's, so he needed to brush that black off. She told Lacy about his dark knees before and he tried telling her that was his skin and the color didn't come off and she pushed him and he flung across the room, so he knew better than to tell her again. He began scrubbing with saliva dripping from his mouth since he was trying not to swallow the soap mixed with his saliva. "Look at you making a mess everywhere," she said. "I have to go to work so when I get back you better have this floor spotless and your teeth shining. Do you understand me?" she asked. Lacy nodded yes since that was the only way he could answer with the soap in his mouth. "I couldn't see that if I were blind." *Slap!*

She knocked the soap out of his mouth and he said, "Yes, I understand."

"Good," she said, then walked out of the room. As Lacy began cleaning up the mess, he could hear Mom saying goodbye to the others and told the sisters they'd better look out for Marcel and Horace and make sure they eat good. After she left, the sisters and Gus went to check on Lacy and helped him clean the bathroom. Alexandra put Merthiolate antiseptic on his knees since he broke the skin on them while rubbing them with the brillo pads. He screamed when the antiseptic hit his open skin but Alexandra told him it would hurt worse later if she didn't put the Methiolate on his knees. He asked why Mom treated him the way she does. Alexandra said she didn't know why and she was so sorry that she couldn't do anything about it.

"It's not your fault," Lacy said.

"It just isn't right," Gus said as he just stared at Lacy's knees.

"Lacy, if I could take you out of here I would in a heartbeat," Odessa said.

Lacy said, "That's what Esta said. I think Esta did something that made Mom very upset so she beats me because she can't beat Esta since Esta isn't here."

Both sisters looked at each other, then Odessa said, "Let's get you cleaned up, then you can just watch TV or do what makes you happy."

"Okay," Lacy said. "One day I will be an adult and take myself away from here."

"You will," Alexandra said, "you will and I will help you if you need it."

"Thank you," Lacy said.

"Me too," Odessa said.

"Thank you Odessa," Lacy said.

"You've got me too," Gus said.

Lacy smiled and said, "Thank you Gus!" When bedtime came, Lacy either slept with Alexandra, Odessa, or with Gus and Randy in the bed they shared. Since the sisters were getting older they stayed up later, and Lacy's bedtime became much earlier than theirs. On that night, Lacy slept with Gus and Randy, and as he lay in bed he wished he was an adult so he could skip the beatings and yelling from Mom. In Lacy's mind, he believed Mom wasn't upset with him nor hated him. He believed she was upset that she had to take care of so many children and only wanted to take care of Randy, Marcel, and Horace. Lacy wondered why she was taking care of so many children if she only wanted Randy, Marcel, and Horace. As Lacy thought about this, he fell asleep and woke up a while later screaming at the top of his lungs. "ESTA! ESTA! ESTA! ESTA!"

"Lacy, what is it, what is it?" Gus asked.

"Yeah bonehead," Randy said, "what's with you?"

"He's after me! The guy in the black hat and black coat wants to hurt me," Lacy said.

"What guy?" Gus asked.

"Hahahaha." Randy laughed and said, "This boy has lost his mind. Hahaha. I'm going back to sleep." Gus called Randy a jerk and asked Lacy to tell him the dream. Randy pulled the covers off his face, looked over at Gus and said, "Don't call me a jerk."

Gus said, "Then don't act like one. Now Lacy, tell me what happened." Lacy said the whole family was on the front lawn doing yard work—cutting grass, pulling weeds, and making the yard look nice when a black 1957 Chevy drove up. "How did you know it was a '57 Chevy?" Gus asked.

Lacy said, "Because you've shown me that car many times and said that's what you want to have."

"OOOHHH yeah. That's right," Gus said. "Keep going Lacy. What else happened?"

"There was a guy driving the car that looked as white as Casper the Ghost. He sped up the street and stopped right in front of our house then he got out of the car. He was wearing a black hat, black coat, black pants, and black shoes. He walked over to me without looking at me at all and grabbed me and carried me to the street and lay my body down on the grass just before the curb with my head hanging over the curb."

"Then what?" Gus asked.

Lacy said, "Then he got back into his car and backed the car up very far, then started revving the engine really loud. Then he sped with smoke coming from the tires and he raced toward me. I was crying and screaming for help but none of you listened to me and just kept pulling weeds and cutting the grass. No matter how loud I screamed none of you could hear me or see me. As the man raced his car toward me, at one point he stepped on the brakes and the car skidded all the way to me and stopped right next to my head. Then the man got out of the car without looking at me at all and picked me up and put me back on the lawn near all of you and none of you looked at me or noticed him. He walked back to his car and got in it then he slowly drove away as he looked at me with a scary face."

"WOW!" Gus said. "Are you okay?"

"I'm really scared," Lacy said.

"Hahahahaha." Randy laughed and said, "A white man in a black suit in a '57 Chevy wants to drive over your head then changes his mind. Hahahaha."

"Don't listen to him Lacy," Gus said. "Try to relax Lacy, and maybe you can go back to sleep."

"I don't want to sleep," Lacy said, "because I think he's waiting for me to fall back asleep to get me."

"Hahahaha. Boo!" Randy said.

"Knock it off Randy," Gus said. "If you keep it up it's going to be you and me and I mean it."

Randy said, "I ain't afraid of you."

Gus said, "You don't have to be afraid to feel pain and you're going to feel pain if you keep it up."

Randy said, "Psshhhhh."

"Pssshhhh yourself," Gus said. "Try to sleep Lacy."

"Okay," Lacy said. He went back to sleep and stayed asleep until it was time to get up. He thanked Gus for not making fun of him and listening to his dream.

"You're welcome," Gus said. "You can always tell me about your dreams or anything you want to talk about, okay Lacy?"

"Okay Gus! Thank you. I'm so glad you're here."

"What about me?" Randy asked. "You glad I'm here too?" Lacy looked at Randy and didn't know what to say.

Gus said, "Leave him alone Randy, he's doing fine."

"Yeeeeah, whatever," Randy said. As they got up and had breakfast and got ready for school, Randy told Lacy's dream to all of the children. The sisters asked Lacy to tell them the dream and when he did, Marcel said he was going to tell Mom, and Horace laughed and asked if the man had four eyes too. Lacy told Horace that if he saw the man again in his dreams that he would tell the man to grab Horace instead.

Horace got upset and said he was going to tell Mom.

"What?" Lacy said. "I don't care. You and Marcel always make fun of me and one day you will be sorry."

"Hush Lacy," Alexandra said. "You don't want to get into trouble."

"I know Alexandra, but they are being dumb and can't be fair and nice to me. They just can't."

"They can Lacy," Alexandra said, "but they choose not to be fair and nice."

"We don't have to be nice to him but he better be nice to us or we'll tell," Horace said.

"Tell, tell go to hell and hang your booty on a rusty nail," Lacy said. Both Odessa and Alexandra burst out laughing and Marcel and Horace said they were going to tell Mom what Lacy said as soon as she got home and that she was due home any minute.

"Lacy, don't say anything else," Gus said, "and you two clowns mind your own business."

Horace and Marcel kept quiet while Randy just laughed and repeated "hang your booty on a rusty nail." "Hahahahaha. Mama's gooone tear your booty up fa dat one Lacy. Hahahaha."

"You just said it too Randy," Lacy said.

"Yeah," Randy said, "but she ain't gooone touch me because I'm older and you're just a little squirt."

"Don't worry Lacy," Odessa said. "You're leaving for school soon and this will all be forgotten by the time everyone gets home."

"I won't forget," Marcel said. "I have a good memory and…" *Click click.* "Mom's home," Marcel said.

"Hahahahaha. YEAH! Booty beatin' time," Horace said.

"Hi Mom, hi Mom," both Marcel and Horace said as they stood on opposite sides, hugging her.

She said, "Hi boys. Did you eat this morning?"

"Yes Mom. But Mom," Marcel said as he looked at Lacy. "You should hear what Lacy said to Horace."

"It's my story Marcel," Horace said, "so let me tell it."

"Okay, you tell me Horace," Mom said as she looked at Lacy. "What did Lacy say?"

Horace said, "I told Lacy I was going to tell you about his dream about a bad man. Lacy said next time he had that dream he was going to tell the man to get me and I told Lacy I was going to tell you he said that. Guess what he said to me when I told him I was going to tell you."

"What?" Mom asked.

He said, "Tell, tell go to hell and hang your booty on a rusty nail."

"WHAT! Odessa and Alexandra! You let Lacy talk to Horace like that? RANDY! GET ME THE BELT!"

"But Mom, Horace isn't telling you the whole story," Alexandra said.

"I don't need a whole story. GET ME THAT BELT NOW!"

"But they have to leave for school," Odessa said.

"Shut your mouth Odessa," Mom said. "I'm about to beat some natural ass. Lacy get over here."

"Here's the belt Mom," Randy said.

Alexandra said, "But Mom, Randy said the same thing Lacy said."

"Don't you dare try to lie on Randy, Alexandra," Mom said. *Whap, whap, whap, whap.* Lacy was doing the Mexican Jumping Bean again and bumped into the kitchen cabinet since it was a tight space in the kitchen. "Ruining my cabinets jumping around like a dern fool," Mom said. "Now I need to beat your black ass for that too. When I get done beating your behind you won't know what day of the week it is you little black son of a bitch!" In an instant, she stopped beating Lacy and said she smelled bacon. She looked toward the stove then at the table and saw the bacon, and grabbed a piece and said she was hungry as she bit into the bacon. Lacy was crying and looked at Odessa and Alexandra wondering what was going on. As Mom ate the bacon, she asked Lacy to tell her the dream. He told her and she smirked as she ate the bacon and said, "That sounds like you were visited by Mr. Death. Some people call him the Grim Reaper but that was death visiting you and he let you go. HUH! You're not that lucky," she said, "I didn't forget about your black ass." *Whap, whap, whap, whap.* She continued the beating.

When she finished, she told Lacy to get his ass in the bathroom and clean himself up before he made the others late for school. The sisters and Gus helped him get cleaned up quickly, then he and the boys walked to school since Mom was expecting company. The boys usually left for school before the sisters did. On the way to school, Horace and Marcel started to tease Lacy but Gus put an end to that right away. Randy asked Lacy why he didn't tell Mom that he repeated what Lacy said. Lacy told Randy that he wasn't a tattletale and Mom wouldn't care anyway because he and Marcel and Horace got to say and do whatever they wanted without trouble.

"Keep quiet Lacy, and just walk," Gus said.

Lacy looked up at Gus and said, "Okay."

Randy kept asking Lacy questions but Lacy kept quiet and said nothing. As they walked to school there were a few children on the other side of the street walking in the opposite direction. "LOOK! It's the Jackson 5!" a boy shouted. "It's five of them and they look like the Jackson 5."

Randy said, "We are not the Jackson 5."

Lacy said, "If we were the Jackson 5 I would be Michael, right?"

"No," Randy said. "You have no talent so you couldn't be Michael."

Gus asked Randy if he could ever say anything nice or if his brain was broken. This caused a pushing match between the two boys but it ended quickly. Randy would talk a big talk but didn't want to tangle with Gus because Gus took no prisoners. He would give out a warning then strike the next time someone purposely crossed him the wrong way. Randy heard the warnings but often pretended he didn't hear them and paid the price for it. When the boys got to school, Horace and Marcel ran to their classes, Randy meandered around the hallways before going to class, and Gus walked with Lacy all the way to his classroom and told Lacy he would see him later. Lacy would say see you later, then watch Gus as he walked away to go to his class. Gus would tell Lacy he needed to go inside the classroom and Lacy would say, "I will after you turn the corner." Lacy admired Gus and it meant a lot to Lacy to have Gus walk him to his class and care for him the way he did. When Lacy went into the classroom he would say hello to many of the students he knew, then he would keep to himself to avoid issues with Mrs. Johnson. He figured if he was quiet that she would have no reason to bother him. Well, that didn't work at home and it didn't work with Mrs. Johnson either. She asked the students to stand up and say what they wanted to be when they grew up. Some students said astronauts, some said nurses or doctors, and others said lawyers or the president. When Mrs. Johnson asked Lacy what he wanted to be, he said he wanted to be a fireman then later a doctor so he could help people feel better.

Mrs. Johnson's face looked like she got slapped by Mom and didn't know what to do about it. She said, "Well, not everybody can be firemen or doctors. Lacy, maybe you should think of something else."

Lacy asked, "Like what Mrs. Johnson?"

She said, "You would make a good janitor because you're good at picking up after yourself and the other students when we do arts and crafts. You could even be a busboy or waiter but a fireman or doctor probably isn't for you." Lacy told Mrs. Johnson his friend Jasper the fireman told him he could be a fireman or a doctor because he was very smart and had a great memory which was needed to be a doctor. Mrs. Johnson told the other students to play amongst themselves in the play area and told Lacy to meet her at her desk. Lacy knew that wasn't a good sign and walked up to her desk knowing she was going to scold him or be upset with him.

"Yes Mrs. Johnson," he said.

"Listen to me you little nigra. Ain't no little black boys like you gonna grow up to be a fireman or a doctor or have any respectable jobs like that because that's for white folk. Do you understand me?" Right then, Lacy's mind drifted for a moment because Mom would ask the same thing after scolding him. Mom would scold him then ask, "Do you understand me?" Lacy wondered if Mrs. Johnson and Mom weren't sure he heard what they said or if they didn't think they spoke clearly. *Why did they ask that question after clearly stating their thought?* he wondered. "Are you listening to me?" Mrs. Johnson asked.

"Yes," Lacy said.

"So, let me hear you say that you want to be a janitor or a waiter or a busboy."

"But I don't want to be any of those things Mrs. Johnson."

Mrs. Johnson stood up and asked, "Am I going to have to call your mother?"

"Why would you call her?" Lacy asked.

"Because you are being DIFFICULT!" she yelled. Lacy knew the other students heard her yell at him. "Now, are you going to tell me what you are going to be or do I call your mom?" Lacy kept quiet and stared at her. He knew he would get his little black ass beat but that day he chose to get another beating rather than to be bullied by another person for something that he did not agree with. He also knew the students saw that he did nothing and hoped, really hoped, that Mom would talk to Mrs. Johnson since she talked to the lady at nursery school. At break time, Mrs. Johnson called Mom and Mom went to the school. Lacy was pulled out of class and Principal Holtz spoke with Mom, Mrs. Johnson, and Lacy. Lacy was questioned about the situation and when he told the story, Mrs. Johnson denied saying all the things she said. She told the principal to ask the students, but Lacy said that she told him to go to her desk so the only thing the students would have heard was when she yelled the word "difficult."

Mr. Holtz asked Lacy if he was being difficult and said, "Mrs. Johnson is a good teacher and she wouldn't say you were being difficult if you weren't. She loves her classroom and all of her students, black, white, and everything in between. Now, don't you want to apologize to Mrs. Johnson?" he said. Lacy looked at Mr. Holtz for a moment, then he looked at Mom. Mom sat with her purse in her lap and had that same look on her face when she sped to the dance studio to talk to Amando about racism.

Lacy looked back at Mr. Holtz and said, "No Mr. Holtz. Mrs. Johnson owes me an apology."

Mrs. Johnson jumped out of her chair and said, "What did you just say to me?"

"I said you owe me an apology for telling me if you were my mother you would beat the tar out of me. I'm a child so I don't have tar in me. Today you told me that no little black boy is going to grow up to have a job like a fireman or a doctor. You said those jobs are for white folk."

"Mr. Holtz he's lying," she said. "I would never say such things and the other students will tell you I didn't say those things."

"Did you call me up to your desk today Mrs. Johnson?" Lacy asked.

Mrs. Johnson looked at him, then Mom, then Mr. Holtz and said, "You're not here to ask questions, you're here to answer them."

Mom said, "Answer the question please Mrs. Johnson." Mr. Holtz said nothing as he leaned back in his chair looking at Mrs. Johnson. "We're waiting," Mom said.

Mrs. Johnson looked down her nose at Mom then she looked at Lacy and said, "Yes, I did call you up to my desk."

"Why?" Lacy asked.

"Mr. Holtz," she said, "are you really going to allow this?"

"Answer the question Mrs. Johnson, or we will never get out of here," Mr. Holtz said.

"I told Lacy to come up to my desk because he was not behaving in class."

"That's not true," Lacy said, "I always behave in class. It's the other students that don't behave and you don't do anything about it." Lacy turned to Mr. Holtz. "Mr. Holtz," Lacy said, "if you asked all of the students they will tell you that I behave in class and do what I'm supposed to do." Mr. Holtz said that wasn't necessary and he thought it was a good idea for Mrs. Johnson and Lacy to apologize to each other and put the situation behind them.

"No," Mom said. "Lacy wouldn't make up a story like this. If he was in the wrong he would have apologized long ago and no one would have to have called me up here wasting my time. So, here's what's going to happen," she said, "Mrs. Johnson, you're going to apologize to Lacy for your behavior and it's not going to happen anymore or I will report you to the school authorities." Mrs. Johnson stood there with her mouth open, looking at Mr. Holtz for help.

Mr. Holtz said, "I'm okay with that decision."

"You better be," Mom said, "because if she doesn't apologize I'll be reporting you too for allowing her behavior and you don't need that since you're already in trouble for having young girls in your office after school. Mrs. Johnson, you wanna hurry up with that apology?"

"I'm sorry. There I said it. Satisfied?"

"No," Mom said. "I'm never satisfied when someone is forced to give an apology. Would you be satisfied to eat shit? I didn't think so. Lacy won't be going back to class today so the students won't ask a lot of questions and you would have had a reason to call him to your desk. Hopefully, you can organize your classroom and speak with the students today to avoid a scene in your classroom tomorrow. It might be best to say that Lacy didn't feel well and he will be back tomorrow."

"I like that," Mr. Holtz said. He looked at Mom and asked, "Have you ever given thought to being a teacher or working with us here at the school?"

She looked at Mr. Holtz and smiled then got up and said, "Come on Lacy." Lacy got up and walked with her to the car. He thought it went pretty good in Mr. Holtz office but he would know what the situation was for sure once he and Mom got into the car. She would hold in her temper until she was behind closed doors, either at home or in the car. The car doors closed and Mom said, "Who in the hell do those people think they're trying to fool? I knew she was lying before she spoke because she kept fidgeting since she was nervous and knew she got caught. She really didn't know what to think when she was being questioned by Lacy Dick Tracy, hahahaha." Mom laughed hysterically at what she said. Lacy was thrilled that she called him one of his nicknames. "You cornered her in her own web of lies. Where did you learn to do that?" she asked Lacy. Lacy thought she would get angry if he told her the truth, which was that he heard her do that with Randy's teacher, people in stores, and people on the telephone. So, he gave credit to the TV show detective Perry Mason. "Yeeeees. Perry Mason," she said. "That is a great show. He corners people just like you did. You surprised me today Lacy. Let's go get some ice cream at Thrifty's."

Lacy's eyes lit up and he said, "NEEEEATTTOOO! OOOOOPS! I'm sorry. I'm not supposed to say that. I'm sorry."

Mom looked at Lacy as she drove and said, "We can forget it this time but don't say that again or people will think you're retarded."

"Okay. I won't." They got the ice cream cones and finished them as they walked toward the dance studio for her to have her lesson with Amando. As Lacy watched Mom in her dance class he thought about what she was saying to Lilly about the South and racism and how she reacted at the nursery school and how she spoke to Mrs. Johnson and Mr. Holtz. He thought maybe some people here were like the people in the South and she didn't like it. He thought maybe racism was present where they lived too or at least Mom thought so from what she would say. After the class, they picked up some things from the grocery store then picked everyone up from school. Randy said he heard that Mom went to the school and spoke with Mr. Holtz and asked what happened.

She told everyone what happened and Randy said, "Yeah, Mrs. Johnson is a bigot and I have seen her giving Lacy mean stares."

"Why didn't you tell me that Randy?" Mom asked.

"Because I didn't think it would be a big deal but I guess it is."

"Yes," she said. "If any of those teachers treat any of you different than the other students you should all tell me right away. I will not tolerate any teacher treating any one of you like you are less than any other student because they might not like the color of your skin. You just make sure you are always in the right and that you do everything you were supposed to do and I'll do the rest."

"Okay," everyone said.

"You should have heard Lacy Dick Tracy today. He cornered Mrs. Johnson in her web of lies, and that weak good for nothing principal with no nuts at all that was accused of touching underage girls didn't know what to do."

"Yeah," Randy said, "he always has the eighth-grade girls meet him in his office and they both come out later giggling and looking at each other like boys and girls in love do."

"MMMMHHHMM! The dirty buzzard."

"So Lacy isn't going to get a beating for making you come up to the school to talk to Mr. Holtz Mom?" Horace asked. Mom was quiet for a few moments so Lacy got nervous and just looked straight ahead and sat as if he was frozen to avoid bringing attention to himself.

"No," she said. "I'd like to beat that Mrs. Johnson's ass though and make her lick the bottom of my shoe afterward. The heffa. I'll smack those glasses right off of her face. Who does she think she is to tell anyone that they can't be a fireman or a doctor because they're not white. Don't get me started," Mom said. "That skinny bitch better be glad the principal was there or I would have grabbed her by her raggedy ass hair and flung her around the room and made her tell me she is a horrible teacher just like she told Lacy to tell her that he wanted to be a janitor."

Randy said, "Yeah. If we're not singing, dancing, or running on a field throwing or catching a ball we might as well be invisible. That's why I won't play sports because that's all we are known for."

"What?" Mom said. "NO. Black people built and made just as much of this country as anyone and if you look through history everybody helped. Everybody. All of you have to choose what you want to do with your life and do it but you have to be happy with your choice and not care what others think of your choice. Unless someone is paying your bills, you don't give a shit what they think. You hear me? Don't give a shit unless they pay your bills and kiss your ass at the same time. Tell them to go straight to hell if they don't like what you do for a living. You hear me?"

"Yes," everyone said.

"Shiiiieeet. I've worked for many years and been treated like dirt many times but I handle my business and let people say what they want, but you all eat don't you?"

"Yes," everyone said.

"You have a roof over your head, don't you?"

"Yes," everyone said.

"You have heat and clothing, right?"

"Yes," everyone said.

"Then I'm doing my job, and anyone that doesn't like what I do and how I pay for all of you can kiss my natural ass and smile afterward. Shiiiiiet." Lacy tried not to laugh as Mom spoke because he thought it was funny when she cursed, especially when she wasn't cursing at him. When they got home, the older children helped get the groceries out of the car and Marcel and Horace raced inside the house to watch TV, as they were especially looking forward to the children's show "H.R. PufnStuf." Lacy was looking forward to playing with Gus' Hot Wheel Sizzlers and race track, and he would play with those cars as long as Gus allowed or until dinner was ready. After Marcel and Horace finished watching the shows they liked they would go to Gus and Randy's room where Lacy was having fun with the racing set. Often, they would stand near the entryway of the room and whisper into each other's ear then make their way over to Lacy. Even though they could see what Lacy was doing they would ask him what he was doing, then giggle to each other as they walked away from each other, approaching Lacy from each side.

"I'm racing the cars," Lacy said.

"Oh really," either boy would say, then they would lift the car off the track as it came around near them.

"Put it back," Lacy said.

"Make me," Marcel said.

"Yeah, make us," Horace said. Lacy stood up and tried to get the car back from Marcel and he would toss the car to Horace, creating a game of pickle with Lacy in the middle. Gus heard the noise and entered the room and shouted to put his car down. The boys didn't listen and kept tossing the car back and forth. Gus stepped between both boys and caught his car when it was tossed and told the boys to get out of his room. The boys headed out of the room and Horace said, "We're telling Mom that Lacy is being a game hog and not letting us race with him."

"Get out of here," Gus said. "Go ahead and keep playing Lacy, since the trouble makers are gone." Gus decided to stay in the room with Lacy and turned on the TV set and sat down. Since the channel knob was stripped, channel five could be channel seven or nine, so Gus realized the channel he selected wasn't right and asked Lacy to change the channel and that he would tell him when to stop.

"Okay Gus," Lacy said. As Lacy was changing the channels the knob would skip channels, making a flicking sound as it usually did.

"Wow, that channel changer is getting worse," Gus said.

"I know," Lacy said. "Soon it's going to not work at all and…"

"What the hell do you think you're doing?" Mom asked as she grabbed Lacy by the neck and threw him to the floor. "That's no way to turn that knob flicking the channels like that," she said.

"But Mom, it's broken," Gus said.

"It's probably broken because of the way Lacy's changing the channels. Who do you think you are to break things that I paid for?" she asked. "You don't pay for shit in this house and think you can tell people what they can and can't do, huh? If Marcel and Horace want to play in here with you GOT DAMNIT YOU'D BETTER LETTEM'. I'm going to teach you some manners today so help me God!" She reached down and yanked the orange flexible track apart and began beating Lacy with a track piece. Gus tried to tell Mom that Marcel and Horace weren't telling the truth and were bullying Lacy.

"Gus, you stay out of this unless you want some too," Mom said. Lacy shook left to right, telling Gus not to get involved because he didn't want Mom to beat Gus too. Gus watched Mom beat Lacy and the look on Gus' face was one of disgust and sorrow. Somehow the sense of decency that Gus showed in that moment seemed to have minimized the pain Lacy was going through as he saw Gus' face. At that moment, Lacy was reminded once again how wonderful a person Gus was and Lacy's trust and admiration for Gus grew tenfold from that point forward. Of course, the pain was real and the welts on Lacy's arms and legs were too, but the desperation to have someone believe in you and care about you was what Lacy needed and he saw that in Gus. He saw it with the sisters too, but the sisters were getting older and spending more time with boys and their friends and less time with Lacy just like Esta did before she left. As these thoughts were running through Lacy's mind during the beating, Mom saw that Lacy was zoning out mentally and didn't have his full attention on her so she grabbed him by the arm and yanked him around the room. "Do you hear me talking to you, you little black son of a bitch? I'm the captain of this ship and you're nothing but a member of the crew, I can throw your ass off the ship at any time. If I throw your behind into foster care you'll wish you were back here with me," she said. "Now clean up this room, and don't you let me catch you touching that TV anymore dure I'LL WHOOP THE BLACK OFF YOUR ASS," she yelled, as she threw the race track piece onto the floor. When she was flustered she would use the word "dure" instead of saying the word "or." When she left the room, Horace and Marcel ran in and told Gus that they get to play with the race track anytime they wanted to, so they got on the floor and started playing and laughing.

Gus stood by Lacy, pulled Lacy into him from the side, and placed his hand on his shoulder and said, "It's okay Lacy. It wasn't your fault."

"Th, th, tha, tha, thank yo, yo, yo you Gus," Lacy said as he cried. Gus just looked at Marcel and Horace and his race track and cars, and from that day forward Gus didn't really play with that track or the cars again. Over time, Marcel and Horace even destroyed the cars. When Lacy calmed down, he asked Gus what foster care was and when Gus explained what it was Lacy got scared and told Gus he didn't want to go there. He asked Gus if he could help him do what he needed to do to not go there. Gus told Lacy he was doing all the right things and did nothing for him to be sent to foster care. He told Lacy he thought Mom was just trying to scare him in order for Lacy not to fight with Marcel and Horace. "Okay," Lacy said, "but one day those two will feel like I feel because of all they are doing to me."

"How do you know that?" Gus asked.

Lacy said, "I just know. I won't be happy when it happens but I just know."

"Well, don't say that to them because they will tell Mom and you'll get another stupid beating for no reason, okay?"

"Okay," Lacy said. As much as Lacy tried to avoid problems with Marcel, Horace, and Mom, the accusations from Marcel and Horace and beatings from Mom just kept coming that year. Of course, he had good days of fun with Richard and Russell from across the street and the sisters and Gus, but the concept of being an adult was heavy on Lacy's mind as he wanted to avoid the beatings. When he started the first grade, Lacy found a piece of paradise. Mrs. Smith was his first-grade teacher. She was an older white woman with salt and pepper hair and she wore dresses and short heels. She reminded Lacy of the women he saw in the old black and white movies he and Esta watched together. Mrs. Smith walked with a smile that could make anyone feel great and she didn't put up with nonsense from Mr. Holtz. If Mr. Holtz came to their class to speak with her about how she was running things, she would speak to him in a low voice, but not low enough to keep Lacy from eavesdropping. She told Mr. Holtz he was welcome to her class anytime to observe but it was her classroom and she would run her class the way she wanted to, and if he didn't like it to report her and they would handle it then. Mr. Holtz would tell her that everything was fine and there was no need for her to take action and to keep doing a fine job.

"Good day Mr. Holtz," she would say, and he would leave. She knew Lacy was listening so she would smile at him and Lacy would smile back. On the first day of school, she pulled Lacy aside and told him she heard what happened with Mrs. Johnson and that he would not experience anything like that with her and if he needed help with anything to tell her. She also told Lacy her door was always open to him so if he wanted to speak with her during recess he was always welcome. This made Lacy very happy and he did end up speaking with her a couple of times at recess and asked how she liked being an adult and she told him she loved it. He asked her if she thought he could be a fireman or a doctor and she told him she believed he could be anything he wanted to be and that she believed he would be a great man one day. She told Lacy not to let anyone stop him from using his brilliant mind because his mind would help many people one day who were waiting for him.

"You see that too, Mrs. Smith?" Lacy asked.

"I do Lacy," she said. "When I was a little girl people didn't understand me and the things I saw but as I got older life got easier for me and it will for you too and you will see. Please don't worry Lacy, you will be fine if you believe in yourself and all that you will do for others in the future."

"WOOOOW!!! Thank you Mrs. Smith," Lacy said, as he jumped toward her and hugged her arm and shoulder as they sat near each other.

She hugged Lacy and said, "It's all going to work out for you Lacy. Now go have fun and play before the bell rings and recess is over."

"Okay," Lacy said. He ran to play while shouting, "THANK YOU MRS. SMITH!"

Even though Lacy was getting plenty of beatings at home, his days at school with Mrs. Smith made up for the pain. He was doing well in her class and raised his hand whenever she asked the students questions. Some people called Lacy teacher's pet but he didn't care because he saw Mrs. Smith as his friend and she understood him and he understood her as best he could at a child's age. Mrs. Smith would smile at Mom when they saw each other, but Mom wouldn't give the best smile back and would question Lacy about her. Lacy didn't tell Mom how he and Mrs. Smith spoke a lot because he didn't think Mom would like that and would find a reason to beat him, so he just said she was better than Mrs. Johnson because she was nicer to the students and told stories.

Mom asked if she ever asked about how things were at home and Lacy said, "No. She just asks us students if we need help with our work and that's it." Mom looked at Lacy as if she didn't believe him so Lacy tried to change the subject and asked if she had her dance class with

Amando. Mom would talk about her dance class and forget about Mrs. Smith. When that school year was done, Mrs. Smith told Lacy she would miss having him in her class and said that he would be having Mrs. Redfox for the second grade. She told Lacy that Mrs. Redfox was friends with Mrs. Johnson and to be careful in her class. She told Lacy to be a good student in Mrs. Redfox's class just as he was in her class, but if he had any problems he could go to her class anytime and talk to her. Lacy gave her a big hug and thanked her and said he wished she could be his teacher for all the grades until he finished school.

She laughed and said, "Me too Lacy, me too. You better go and not keep your mom waiting and always remember, my classroom is open to you."

"Thank you Mrs. Smith," he said, then he dashed off and met up with Gus and the others to go home.

MR. DEATH HIMSELF

Everyone was happy it was summer again, and as they got into the car they noticed Mr. Henry was in the front seat behind the wheel and Mom was in the passenger seat. Everyone said hi to Mom and gave a softer hello to Mr. Henry. He was a guy that Mom would meet for dates and stayed at the house from time to time. When they got home, Mom told Lacy to go into Gus and Randy's room and wait there. Lacy said okay with a very concerned look on his face because Mr. Henry gave beatings like Mr. Stache, but Mr. Henry closed his eyes and swung the belt in every direction, missing the target many times. But when he hit the target, he got the proper screams he wanted. He was much taller and bigger than Mr. Stache and he had superhuman strength based upon what Randy said since Randy was the only one beaten by Mr. Henry. Lacy sat waiting to see what was going to happen and wondered what he was in trouble for because he had no clue as usual. He began thinking about Mrs. Smith and wondered what life would be like if he lived with her. He thought if he, the sisters, and Gus could live with Mrs. Smith they would have a wonderful time. "LACY! GET IN HERE!" Mom shouted. Lacy jumped up and quickly went to the kitchen where everyone was sitting and standing.

"Yes?" Lacy said.

"Lacy," she said, "we've all been in here making decisions and now it's your turn to make a decision." Lacy stood quietly. "Mr. Henry is going to drive me to Peoria, Illinois to see friends and family and the boys are going with me but the girls are staying here. Do you want to go with us or stay with the girls?" she asked. Lacy looked at Gus then he looked at the sisters.

Odessa said, "Stay with us Lacy."

"Yes," Alexandra said, "stay with us and we will have a great time."

"Yes," Odessa said, "we can go to the park and have cotton candy and teach you to swim and have a great time." Lacy looked at Gus as he really wanted to be with both Gus and the sisters.

"Hurry up Lacy, we haven't got all day," Mom said. "Make up your mind."

Lacy said, "I want to be with Gus *and* Odessa and Alexandra."

"That's not a choice, and since you can't make up your mind you can stay with Odessa and Alexandra," Mom said.

Lacy looked at Gus as if he betrayed Gus but Gus said, "Lacy, you will have a good time and I'll see you when we get back. It's okay."

Lacy smiled at Gus and said, "Thank you Gus."

The sisters said, "Come here Lacy and give us a hug."

"We will all have a good time together," Odessa said.

"Good," Mom said. "It's all worked out. Randy, Gus, Marcel, and Horace will go with us and the three of you will stay with Mr. Stache." Lacy's eyes widened and he felt the room begin to spin.

He looked at the sisters and Odessa looked at him and said, "Lacy, we will have a good time, don't you worry."

He looked at Mom and she just smiled at him and said, "Yes, you will all have a good time and we will too." Lacy looked at Mr. Henry and Mr. Henry looked away from him like many people looked away from beggars in the street.

"How long will you all be gone?" Lacy asked.

"Well, it will take many days to get there since we'll make stops along the way," Mr. Henry said, "but we'll be back in six weeks."

"Six weeks?" Lacy said.

"Yes, six weeks," Mom said. "Do you have a problem with that Lacy that you and I need to fix?"

"NO," Lacy said.

"Good," she said, "now go with your sisters and pack because you're leaving tonight." Lacy looked like he just got kicked in the stomach and was told to brush with Ajax again.

"C'mon Lacy," Alexandra said. When the sisters took Lacy to pack, Lacy told them they should just stay home and there was no need to go to Mr. Stache's. They said they asked Mom if they could stay home but she said they were too young to be alone and staying with Mr. Stache was the best idea.

"It's the worst idea," Lacy said. "That guy needs help and might hurt us."

"Lacy, don't worry. My boyfriend Mealo will stop by from time to time since he's older and has his driver's license," Alexandra said.

"I don't like this," Lacy said, "I don't see anything good with Mr. Stache."

"Lacy, we have to hurry before Mom gets upset," Alexandra said.

"I'm upset," Lacy said.

"We know, and so are we," Odessa said, "but let's hurry and ask Mom to stop at the store so we can get some goodies for tonight."

"Okay," Lacy said. After they were all packed, they piled into the car and were on their way. Mr. Henry stopped by the store for the sisters and Lacy to get some goodies, then they were off to Mr. Stache's. As they got closer to his house, Lacy told Gus he would miss him and think about him and Gus told Lacy the same.

"Are you going to miss me four-eyes?" Horace asked Lacy.

"Who are you calling four-eyes?" Mr. Henry asked Horace since Mr. Henry wore glasses too. "Speak up boy," Mr. Henry said. "Who are you calling four-eyes?"

"Mom, do I have to answer him?" Horace asked.

Mr. Henry pulled the car over, stopped, and looked at the back seat at Horace and said, "Yes you have to answer, and if you don't I'll get out of this car and snatch your ass out of that seat and enlighten your ass, compliments of four-eyes. You dig?" Lacy looked at Horace with a smile on his face, waiting for him to answer.

Horace said, "I was talking to Lacy."

"Then call him by his name from now on or you'll be hearing from me."

"Okay," Horace said. Then Mr. Henry started driving again.

Horace looked at Lacy with a dirty look and Lacy looked at Horace and just kept smiling with his teeth showing as Randy said, "Horace almost got enlightened with the leather strap. Hahahahaha."

"Alright Randy," Mr. Henry said. "You'll be next if you keep it up. Now quiet back there!"   As he drove, the sisters whispered to each other the whole ride and Lacy was trying to listen but couldn't hear what they were saying. He started thinking about Mrs. Smith and how much fun he had in her class and how much he learned as he noticed Mr. Henry exiting the freeway. That was when Lacy's heart began to race because he was concerned with Mr. Stache and his temper. When they arrived at Mr. Stache's apartment building somewhere in Los Angeles, all of the children looked around at the area and the building. The looks on their faces were of concern and fear. Everyone was happy it was summer again, and as they got into the car they noticed Mr. Henry was in the front seat behind the wheel and Mom was in the passenger seat. Everyone said hi to Mom and gave a softer hello to Mr. Henry. He was a guy that Mom would meet for dates and stayed at the house from time to time. When they got home, Mom told Lacy to go into Gus and Randy's room and wait there. Lacy said okay with a very concerned look on his face because Mr. Henry gave beatings like Mr. Stache, but Mr. Henry closed his eyes and swung the belt in every direction, missing the target many times. But when he hit the target, he got the proper screams he wanted. He was much taller and bigger than Mr. Stache and he had superhuman strength based upon what Randy said since Randy was the only one beaten by Mr. Henry. Lacy sat waiting to see what was going to happen and wondered what he was in trouble for because he had no clue as usual. He began thinking about Mrs. Smith and wondered what life would be like if he lived with her. He thought if he, the sisters, and Gus could live with Mrs. Smith they would have a wonderful time. "LACY! GET IN HERE!" Mom shouted. Lacy jumped up and quickly went to the kitchen where everyone was sitting and standing.

"Yes?" Lacy said.

"Lacy," she said, "we've all been in here making decisions and now it's your turn to make a decision." Lacy stood quietly. "Mr. Henry is going to drive me to Peoria, Illinois to see friends and family and the boys are going with me but the girls are staying here. Do you want to go with us or stay with the girls?" she asked. Lacy looked at Gus then he looked at the sisters.

Odessa said, "Stay with us Lacy."

"Yes," Alexandra said, "stay with us and we will have a great time."

"Yes," Odessa said, "we can go to the park and have cotton candy and teach you to swim and have a great time." Lacy looked at Gus as he really wanted to be with both Gus and the sisters.

"Hurry up Lacy, we haven't got all day," Mom said. "Make up your mind."

Lacy said, "I want to be with Gus *and* Odessa and Alexandra."

"That's not a choice, and since you can't make up your mind you can stay with Odessa and Alexandra," Mom said.

Lacy looked at Gus as if he betrayed Gus but Gus said, "Lacy, you will have a good time and I'll see you when we get back. It's okay."

Lacy smiled at Gus and said, "Thank you Gus."

The sisters said, "Come here Lacy and give us a hug."

"We will all have a good time together," Odessa said.

"Good," Mom said. "It's all worked out. Randy, Gus, Marcel, and Horace will go with us and the three of you will stay with Mr. Stache." Lacy's eyes widened and he felt the room begin to spin.

He looked at the sisters and Odessa looked at him and said, "Lacy, we will have a good time, don't you worry."

He looked at Mom and she just smiled at him and said, "Yes, you will all have a good time and we will too." Lacy looked at Mr. Henry and Mr. Henry looked away from him like many people looked away from beggars in the street.

"How long will you all be gone?" Lacy asked.

"Well, it will take many days to get there since we'll make stops along the way," Mr. Henry said, "but we'll be back in six weeks."

"Six weeks?" Lacy said.

"Yes, six weeks," Mom said. "Do you have a problem with that Lacy that you and I need to fix?"

"NO," Lacy said.

"Good," she said, "now go with your sisters and pack because you're leaving tonight." Lacy looked like he just got kicked in the stomach and was told to brush with Ajax again.

"C'mon Lacy," Alexandra said. When the sisters took Lacy to pack, Lacy told them they should just stay home and there was no need to go to Mr. Stache's. They said they asked Mom if they could stay home but she said they were too young to be alone and staying with Mr. Stache was the best idea.

"It's the worst idea," Lacy said. "That guy needs help and might hurt us."

"Lacy, don't worry. My boyfriend Mealo will stop by from time to time since he's older and has his driver's license," Alexandra said.

"I don't like this," Lacy said, "I don't see anything good with Mr. Stache."

"Lacy, we have to hurry before Mom gets upset," Alexandra said.

"I'm upset," Lacy said.

"We know, and so are we," Odessa said, "but let's hurry and ask Mom to stop at the store so we can get some goodies for tonight."

"Okay," Lacy said. After they were all packed, they piled into the car and were on their way. Mr. Henry stopped by the store for the sisters and Lacy to get some goodies, then they were off to Mr. Stache's. As they got closer to his house, Lacy told Gus he would miss him and think about him and Gus told Lacy the same.

"Are you going to miss me four-eyes?" Horace asked Lacy.

"Who are you calling four-eyes?" Mr. Henry asked Horace since Mr. Henry wore glasses too. "Speak up boy," Mr. Henry said. "Who are you calling four-eyes?"

"Mom, do I have to answer him?" Horace asked.

Mr. Henry pulled the car over, stopped, and looked at the back seat at Horace and said, "Yes you have to answer, and if you don't I'll get out of this car and snatch your ass out of that seat and enlighten your ass, compliments of four-eyes. You dig?" Lacy looked at Horace with a smile on his face, waiting for him to answer.

Horace said, "I was talking to Lacy."

"Then call him by his name from now on or you'll be hearing from me."

"Okay," Horace said. Then Mr. Henry started driving again.

Horace looked at Lacy with a dirty look and Lacy looked at Horace and just kept smiling with his teeth showing as Randy said, "Horace almost got enlightened with the leather strap. Hahahahaha."

"Alright Randy," Mr. Henry said. "You'll be next if you keep it up. Now quiet back there!" As he drove, the sisters whispered to each other the whole ride and Lacy was trying to listen but couldn't hear what they were saying. He started thinking about Mrs. Smith and how much fun he had in her class and how much he learned as he noticed Mr. Henry exiting the freeway. That was when Lacy's heart began to race because he was concerned with Mr. Stache and his temper. When they arrived at Mr. Stache's apartment building somewhere in Los Angeles, all of the children looked around at the area and the building. The looks on their faces were of concern and fear.

Of course, children would be concerned about being in a new environment, but this environment didn't seem safe and as clean as Mom wanted her house. There was nothing clean about the area as far as the eye could see. "Is this where we're supposed to stay?" Odessa asked Mom.

"Yes! Do you have a problem with it Odessa?" she asked.

With a trembling voice, Odessa said, "No, I was just asking." Alexandra didn't say anything and Lacy looked at both sisters wondering if the three of them were going to be left there forever while Mom and the others lived by themselves. After all, the sisters and Lacy were the ones that Mom cracked down on the most, so he thought she was tired of them and decided to send them to live with Mr. Stache. Mom told the sisters and Lacy to get out of the car and she took them into a building with people standing around that looked like they had no idea who they were or if they were about to topple over.

"Stop looking Lacy, he's drunk," Alexandra said. Lacy stopped looking and just walked.

"Hey yawl," another man said to them. Mom gave the man a very mean look and told Lacy and the sisters to go up the stairway as she continued giving that man a mean look until he looked the other way.

When they got upstairs, Mom told them to knock on the door, and moments later Mr. Stache opened the door and said, "Alexandra, Odessa, and Lacy, come on in."

The sisters looked at each other and Mom said, "Stop gazing at each other and get inside. Lacy you too, and say hi to Mr. Stache." They all said hello then stood around not knowing what to do. Mom stood in the doorway and told Mr. Stache she had the others in the car waiting so she had to go, and handed him some money. Odessa started crying and asked Mom to take them with her. Mom said to hush up and stop the crying. She told Odessa that there wasn't enough room in the car for everyone to sit comfortably on such a long drive. When Lacy saw Odessa crying he thought Odessa knew something bad was going to happen to them. "Now, get yourselves comfortable here. Don't give Mr. Stache a hard time and do exactly as he tells you and there will be no trouble."

"That's right," Mr. Stache said. "I have rules in my house and as long as you follow them we will all get along just fine, ain't that right Lacy?" Lacy was too busy looking at Odessa crying that he heard his name but not Mr. Stache's question.

"HUH?" Lacy said.

Mr. Stache said, "Boy if we're gonna get along you better learn to listen."

"Okay," Lacy said.

"Well, I have to go," Mom said as she turned to walk away, and Odessa ran toward the door as Mr. Stache was closing it.

He blocked Odessa from the door and told her to go and sit down. She said she wanted Mom, and he said, "She's gone, now go and sit down. ALL OF YOU! And that means you too Alexandra."

It was clear to Mr. Stache that if he was going to have a problem, out of the three of them it would be with Alexandra. She despised him and thought living with maggots was better than being within five feet of Mr. Stache, as Lacy overheard her saying that some time ago. After they sat down, Mr. Stache took his belt off and draped it on the arm of a chair as he stood near it. He told them he was not a babysitter or there to listen to their complaints. He said he was asked to do a favor and that favor was to let the three of them stay there until Mom got back from her trip. Mr. Stache told them there would always be food in the house but to only eat at breakfast, lunch, and dinner and nothing in between because his home wasn't an All You Can Eat buffet and he wasn't going broke feeding mouths that didn't belong to him. He told the sisters they would be responsible for cleaning up around the apartment so that they wouldn't just be lounging around like lazy bums. He told Lacy he was responsible for cleaning the toilet bowl and sweeping the floor, making sure there were no crumbs or lint on the floor at all. Lacy looked at the floor and thought it was the nastiest floor he'd seen in his entire life. After Mr. Stache lay down a few more rules, he told the sisters to get up and follow him so he could speak with them in private. Lacy got up and followed, but Mr. Stache told Lacy if he didn't want to see his belt up close he'd better go back and sit down. Lacy sat down, but he didn't feel as if the sisters were safe because they kept looking at each other. Once the three were in a room with the door closed, Lacy heard Odessa crying and a tussle between Mr. Stache and Alexandra as Alexandra was yelling at him. Lacy jumped up and ran toward the door and tried to open it but it was locked. "Get away from that door now!" Mr. Stache yelled to Lacy. Lacy let go of the doorknob then peeked in the skeleton keyhole. Since those old doors had such large openings for the key, he was able to see right into the room and saw the sisters sitting on a bed facing Mr. Stache as he stood and faced them.

"GET AWAY FROM MY SISTERS!" Lacy yelled. Mr. Stache backed up toward the door as he told the sisters not to move, then he turned and opened the door as Lacy ran toward the living room and around furniture, trying to avoid being caught until Mr. Stache gave up the chase and told Lacy to sit his ass down and to stay away from the door. Once the door was closed, Lacy ran back, looked in the keyhole and shouted, "GET AWAY FROM MY SISTERS!"

"Lacy, go back and sit down," Odessa shouted.

"Yeah you little pissant, go sit down," Mr. Stache said.

"No," Lacy said, "I want my sisters. Odessa and Alexandra open the door and come out." Mr. Stache opened the door and caught Lacy and smacked him in the mouth. He then carried him to the sofa and dropped him on it and told him to stay there or he would get worse.

Lacy remembered how Randy and the sisters beat up Mr. Stache before and couldn't figure out why the sisters weren't fighting. Lacy got off the sofa and ran to the door again and right when he was about to yell to them the door opened, and the sisters came out crying and pushed Lacy to the living room as they moved quickly. The sisters sat and held each other and Lacy while they cried. Mr. Stache came out and put his belt on slowly with a sneaky rat-like grin on his face and said, "Like I said, you all follow my rules and we'll all get along just fine." Lacy looked at Mr. Stache and thought he was not a man but a destroyed human being. "You have something to say, Lacy?" Mr. Stache asked.

"No," Odessa said, "he doesn't." Alexandra grabbed Lacy's chin and turned it toward her so that he would stop looking at Mr. Stache.

She said, "Look at me."

"Yes, look at her Lacy, before you get yourself in trouble the first night at Casa de Stache." Lacy's chin was facing Alexandra but he moved his eyes to look at Mr. Stache. Alexandra shook his chin and gave him a look that said to stop it, so Lacy dropped his eyes and started tearing up. "Hahahaha. That's right," Mr. Stache said as he laughed. "Cry them tears because I'm the head nigga 'round here and Lacy when you think you're man enough to handle me you come try." Then he walked away laughing as he went into his room, closed the door, and locked it. Lacy told the sisters if that was the way Mr. Stache wanted it to be then Lacy would return when he was a man and beat Mr. Stache with his belt until he begged Lacy to stop.

"I would love to see that Lacy," Alexandra said. "Somebody needs to kick his ass good."

"We can't stay here," Odessa said.

"We have no choice," Alexandra said. "We don't have keys to our house so we can't go there, and Mom said she would put Lacy in foster care if we ran away from here."

"When did she say that?" Lacy asked.

"She told us that right before she called you into the kitchen and asked if you wanted to go with them or us," Alexandra said. Lacy's whole body slumped because he realized they were stuck there for six weeks with Mr. Death himself, just like that dream he had of the man in the black suit that pulled up and grabbed him from the front lawn. Alexandra said they should go to the room where they were supposed to sleep and once they got there they locked the door. They made a plan not to go to the bathroom at night unless they all went together, so that made for many sleepless nights. As the days rolled by, the sisters and Lacy developed a routine. Mr. Stache wanted everyone up before he left for work because he didn't think anyone should sleep past six in the morning. He left for work by eight and didn't get home until three or four o'clock in the afternoon, but the sisters and Lacy would wait until eight-fifteen or eight-thirty to make sure Mr. Stache didn't return as he sometimes did as he often forgot things at home.

The sisters and Lacy would go back to bed for a couple of hours to rest since they were up at night looking out for each other when they went to the bathroom. Then, they would get their chores done, go to the park, to the skating rink, or to the public pool to teach Lacy how to swim in his cut-off shorts that the sisters always laughed at. They told Lacy he looked like Buckwheat from the Little Rascals in those cut-off shorts. Thankfully, the sisters began saving money in their piggy banks and in other safe places years earlier because that money allowed the three of them to eat and do the things they did. Older boys were always coming up to the sisters and asking for their phone numbers but the sisters would say no, especially Alexandra because she was sweet on Mealo. They always made sure they were home before Mr. Stache. One day when they were at the park trying to teach Lacy to swim unsuccessfully, Odessa had an idea. She told Alexandra if the older boys that wanted their number stopped by Mr. Stache's house, Mr. Stache might leave them alone because Mr. Stache was nothing more than a coward and a bully. Alexandra thought that was a good idea so she started having Mealo stop by. Mr. Stache didn't like having any of those older boys stop by and told the sisters if it wasn't a boy that they had known for a long time that the boy couldn't stop by. Odessa began dating one of the older boys so he started coming around but not as much as Mealo did. Mealo came over as often as he could and really liked Alexandra but didn't care much for Mr. Stache. Mr. Stache didn't care for him either but didn't seem to have the guts to tell Mealo not to come over. Even though Mr. Stache was part of a motorcycle group and wore a member's jacket from the motorcycle group, he didn't want to have any issues with Mealo because Mealo had many friends and some weren't so nice. Lacy liked when Mealo came over because Mr. Stache acted nicer then, but Lacy didn't think Mealo was a good choice for Alexandra. Lacy would tell the sisters which guys were good and which were not and the sisters would laugh later as they agreed Lacy was right every time. Alexandra was completely sprung on Mealo so Lacy's words about Mealo fell upon deaf ears. One day, Mealo was visiting Alexandra. Alexandra went to the bathroom and Mealo asked Lacy if he wanted to see a match burn twice. Lacy told Mealo a match couldn't burn twice. Mealo told Lacy he was just a kid and had a lot to learn about what was possible in life and what wasn't possible. Lacy told Mealo he wasn't a kid but a child and that he did like to learn and wanted to see the match burn twice.

Mealo said, "OOHH OOOH OOOH Kaaaaaayy." He lit a match and told Lacy to count to five and blow it out. Lacy counted to five and blew out the match, and Mealo quickly pressed the match to Lacy's cheek and Lacy screamed to high heaven.

"THAT HURTS! OUUUUUUU! WHAT'S WRONG WITH YOU YOU YOU BIG STUPID!" Mealo laughed so hysterically that he fell off the chair onto the floor laughing. Lacy began kicking Mealo's body and Mealo kept laughing. "YOU ARE A BROKEN HUMAN BEING AND NEED HELP YOU BIG STUPID!" Lacy said. "WHY WOULD YOU DO THAT?" Mealo started blocking Lacy's kicks while laughing and told Lacy that he asked for it. Immediately, Lacy remembered when Mom said he sucked Randy's penis only because Randy asked him to do it, which meant Randy wasn't wrong for that situation. Esta told Lacy that Randy was wrong and even if he didn't force Lacy to do it he knew better than to tell him to do it. Lacy knew Mealo should have known better and had intentions of hurting him. "YOU KNEW THAT WOULD HURT AND DID IT ANY-WAY AND NOW YOU'RE LAUGHING LIKE A HYENA YOU DUMB DOORNAIL!"

"What is going on in here?" Alexandra asked as she raced into the room. "THAT BROKEN HUMAN I TOLD YOU TO STAY AWAY FROM BURNED MY FACE WITH A MATCH," Lacy said as he held his face.

Alexandra asked to see Lacy's face and saw it had been burned. "Mealo, why did you do that?" Alexandra asked.

"BECAUSE HE'S A BIG STUPID," Lacy said. Mealo was no longer laughing and was getting upset that Lacy was calling him a big stupid. Just then, Mr. Stache entered the living room and asked what all of the noise was in his house.

Lacy told him what happened and Mr. Stache looked at Mealo and said, "Good one," giggled, then went back to his room laughing. Mealo told Alexandra that he asked Lacy if he wanted to see a match burn twice and Lacy said yes, then he explained how it worked. Alexandra burst out laughing and Lacy looked at her and Mealo while he held the cold towel that Alexandra gave him to his face.

"What he did to me will only be worse for you if you keep him around Alexandra," Lacy said. "Something is wrong with him." Mealo told Lacy to shut up. "You want me to shut up because I'm telling the truth about you and you know it. Listen to me Alexandra, please!"

"Okay Lacy, calm down," Alexandra said. "You're upset with Mealo for what he did and Mealo is going to apologize, right Mealo?"

"I don't want his stupid apology because it means nothing. He's a big stupid and he will hurt you too and you will see if you don't listen to me Alexandra. He's sneaky and no good." Mealo got up and moved toward Lacy and Lacy said, "See Alexandra. He wants to hit a child and that's what he will do to you when he gets upset. Come on you big stupid," Lacy said, "I'll fight you and burn your face good you dumb dumb dumb human." Mr. Stache came out of nowhere and grabbed Lacy from behind and spun him around and told him if he didn't shut his mouth that he would shut it for him. Mealo began laughing hysterically again and Lacy looked over his shoulder at Mealo with eyes that could slice a brick wall.

Mr. Stache shook Lacy and said, "One more time, ya hear?"

Lacy said, "I hear." Mr. Stache let Lacy go and Lacy went to the room where they slept and sat on the bed and didn't want to speak to anyone. He thought he was surrounded by dummies and just wanted to be alone. Odessa was down the stairwell talking to the boy she liked and found out what happened later and felt sorry for Lacy. She later told Alexandra that Mealo was very wrong and she needed to be careful with him. Alexandra told Odessa to mind her own business. That was when the bond between the two sisters began to break and when Lacy overcame part of his fear of being alone since he was feeling more and more alone at Mr. Stache's house.

RUNNING FAST

Over the next few weeks, the sisters still took Lacy to the park and they still spent time together, but things were different since the sisters were spending more and more time with their boyfriends. During those last few weeks, Mr. Stache had a woman he liked come by from time to time which seemed to make him happy and friendlier, so Lacy's fear of Mr. Stache decreased a lot. Mom and the others came home a few days earlier than expected but that was fine by Lacy because he wanted to see Gus and get back home. When Lacy and the sisters got back home, Gus and Lacy shared stories. Gus had many stories about the people he met during the trip. Lacy told Gus about the days at the park, the skating rink, and seeing how a match burned twice. Gus was glad Lacy had a good time but he wasn't happy about the match burning twice situation and said he would tell Mom.

"NO," Lacy said. "It's okay. Please don't tell Mom, I don't want trouble." Gus said okay and that he wouldn't tell, but he knew it was wrong. Even though Marcel, Horace, and Lacy didn't see eye to eye they all seemed happy to see each other. That emotional connection lasted for just a week before Horace and Marcel began picking on Lacy again. During their stay at Mr. Stache's house, Lacy learned more about patience and how not to talk so much and to listen. When Marcel and Horace picked on Lacy, it didn't bother him as it did before because he'd seen and experienced more than those two pushed his way. When they couldn't upset Lacy as they did before that made Marcel and

Horace upset, so they would try to heckle Lacy even more. Randy was happy to be home and play with the yoyos he got while he was away. Mom seemed very happy and seemed closer to Mr. Henry. Mom pulled Lacy aside and asked him a lot of questions about his stay with Mr. Stache. She asked him where the sisters slept and where Mr. Stache slept. She asked if Mr. Stache beat the sisters or him and Lacy said yes. Lacy wondered why she was asking him those questions instead of asking Mr. Stache since they were friends. As the questioning continued, it was as if Lacy grew up a great deal during those weeks at Mr. Stache's house because he was not afraid to look her in her eyes that day as he answered her questions. When the questioning was over, Mom called Odessa and Alexandra to her room and spoke with them in private. On their way to her room, they asked Lacy what she wanted with him and he told the sisters that Mom asked about Mr. Stache and where they slept and if he beat any of them. Lacy said he told her they slept in the spare room and that he did beat them in the beginning but not so much later on. He said he also told Mom that he would take the sisters into his room and lock the door. The sisters asked Lacy why he told Mom Mr. Stache took them into his room, and Lacy said because he thought if he didn't that she might find out anyway and he would get a beating for it. The sisters looked concerned as they went to speak with Mom. They were in the room with Mom for quite some time and when they came out they didn't say much to Lacy and wanted to be left alone. Randy asked Lacy what Mom wanted with him but Lacy said it was private. Randy slapped Lacy in the back of the head and said he didn't want to hear what stupid things Lacy had to say anyway. After a few days, the sisters didn't seem as upset with Lacy but they didn't spend as much time together as they used to because the sisters were spending even more time with their boyfriends. The other children were with their friends or were involved in outside activities.

For the duration of the summer, Lacy spent time playing games and going in the pool, and also made sandcastles with Russell from across the street. When school began, Lacy was excited to be in the second grade, and once again Mom told him if he caused any trouble he should expect to be beaten and hung by his thumbs. When Lacy got to class, he met Mrs. Redfox. He remembered that Mrs. Smith said Mrs. Johnson and Mrs. Redfox were friends, so he did his best to behave and show her as much respect as possible. Many of the students in the classroom were the same ones from first grade but there were some new students and some students went to another school. One of the new friends Lacy met was a girl from Yugoslavia named Frances. Lacy wanted to know all about her because she was from another part of the world, and learning about the world was what Lacy wanted. She was very friendly to Lacy but her parents saw them talking after school one day and didn't seem happy about it, so the next day at school Frances told him that her parents said she could not be friends with him or talk to him. Lacy asked why, but she said they just said to do what they told her, so that friendship ended well before it started. At recess, Lacy played with his other friends. Two of those friends were Billy, who looked like the comedian Eddie Griffin, and Mark, who looked like a young Dennis Quaid. Billy liked to run fast like Lacy so they were always running through the school. Mark always came to school with new stories about taking karate lessons, guitar lessons, going surfing with his older brother, and going to car races. Gus would walk over to Lacy and Lacy's friends to say hi and play with them for a few minutes before getting back to whatever games he was playing, and that made Lacy's day each time. All of Lacy's friends liked Gus and never wanted him to leave. One day, as Lacy was playing with his friends, Mrs. Redfox called him and Billy over to speak with her. She told the boys that they had to slow down when playing with the other children. She said it wasn't fair that Billy and Lacy could run faster than the other children, making it difficult for the other children to catch them. The boys said okay, but they walked away from Mrs. Redfox wondering and asking each other why she didn't call Mark and the other boys over because they were quite fast too.

Mark asked the boys what the teacher wanted so they told him what she said. "NOOO WAAAY!" Mark said. "You shouldn't have to slow down for those slowpokes," he said, "they have to learn to keep up or play another game."

"Yeah, but I don't want to get into trouble with Mrs. Redfox," Billy said. Lacy said, "I don't either."

"You guys are wimps," Mark said. "If I told my dad a teacher told me to slow down because other kids couldn't catch me during games he'd tell the teacher to jump into a lake." Billy and Lacy looked at each other and simultaneously laughed out loud because they didn't believe a word Mark said. "No kidding," Mark said. "Wait until my dad picks me up today and let's ask him."

"Yeah, let's ask him," Billy said. Lacy didn't say anything because he thought asking Mark's dad about that would somehow get back to Mom and it could end with him getting into trouble. After school, Mark called to Lacy and Billy as he stood near his dad's car. Billy ran over to Mark's car but Lacy saw Mom and waved goodbye to Mark and pretended that he had to leave right away. Lacy sat in the car with Mom waiting for the others. She asked Lacy what he did in class and while he was explaining what he did in class, he noticed that Mark's dad got out of his car and was walking toward Mom's car and Billy and Mark were with him. Lacy looked straight at Mom as he spoke and hoped they wouldn't come up to the car, but they did. Mark's dad greeted Mom and told her that his son Mark and Lacy were friends and asked to speak with her. Mom agreed and got out of the car. Billy and Mark went to Lacy's side of the car and told him to get out of the car so he did. They told Lacy that Mark's dad was not happy with Mrs. Redfox and what she told Billy and Lacy.

Lacy looked to see Mom's expression as she spoke with Mark's dad because her expressions usually told him if a beating was coming or just harsh words. She had a neutral expression that gave no clue as to what to expect. "My dad's so cool," Mark said. "He wants your mom to go with him to speak to Mrs. Redfox right now about this."

"What?" Lacy said.

"Yeah," Billy said.

"Lacy, come here," Mom said.

"See you later guys," Lacy said as he went to Mom. She asked Lacy to tell her what the teacher said and Lacy did. The look on Mom's face went from neutral to "someone's going to be sorry" twisted.

"Let's go," she said to Mark's dad. "Boys, you stay here."

"OOOHHH YYYYEEAAH! Mrs. Redfox is going to get it now," Mark said.

"That's only going to make her mean to us in class," Lacy said.

"Right," Billy said. "If I get into trouble in class I'll get a whoopin'."

"Me too," Lacy said.

"You guys worry too much," Mark said. "My dad's cool, so don't worry." Mom and Mark's dad were gone for a while. Gus and the others were waiting near the car with Lacy wondering where Mom was, so Lacy told them what was going on.

"You in trouble again?" Horace asked, laughing. "Mama's gonna tear her up some little black booty toniiiiight. Hahahaha." Mark and Billy started laughing.

Lacy forced out a nervous laugh because he didn't want Billy and Mark to know about the beatings and said, "Horace is such a kidder," then continued his nervous laugh.

"Here comes Mom," Randy said.

"Lacy, come over here," she said.

"You too Mark and Billy," Mark's father said. The boys went with Mom and Mark's dad into the classroom. Mom told Lacy to tell her again what Mrs. Redfox said. Lacy explained what the teacher said and she denied it.

Mark's dad asked Billy if what Lacy said was true and he said, "Yes, that's what she told us." Mrs. Redfox got upset and said the boys misunderstood what she said. She said she called the boys over to ask if they were having a good time playing, then told them to be careful running. Billy and Lacy looked at each other shaking their heads no at each other.

"Lacy, if I was blind I couldn't see that. Does that mean no?" Mom asked.

"Yes. It means no. That's not what Mrs. Redfox said." Mrs. Redfox's face turned a few different shades of red as she denied telling the boys to slow down their running so other boys could catch them. Mark's dad told her that she didn't tell off his son or a few other boys that were much faster than the rest of the students. He told Mrs. Redfox that he sees the children playing after school and knows who is fast and who isn't. He told her he believed that she singled out Billy and Lacy because she was a bigot and needed to teach and not divide.

He said, "All of the boys are friends but your actions can destroy their friendship and you know it."

"That's right," Mom said. Mrs. Redfox stuck to her story and said the boys misunderstood and that she wasn't a bigot. Mark's dad told her that her bigotry has been evident for a long time but it better not affect any of the boys or he would take action.

Mrs. Redfox said, "If that is all, this meeting is over." Mom thanked Mark's father and wanted to speak with Mrs. Redfox privately, so the boys and Mark's father left the room and Mom closed the door. Mark and his dad left, Billy went to lie on the playground to wait for his parents, and Lacy went to the car to wait for Mom. Mom was gone for a while but when she came out she walked quickly in her low heels, making a loud stomping sound with each step. When Mom got into the car, she didn't say a word. She started the car and drove off.

"What happened?" Horace asked. Mom didn't answer, so he asked again.

"Sit back Horace," she said. After picking up the older children from school, Randy asked why everyone was so quiet and Horace said Lacy got into trouble again.

"Lacy," Mom said. "When we get home, I want you to strip naked and wait for me in Gus and Randy's room."

"OOOOOOO! I KNEW IT. GONNA BE A BEATIN'

TONIIIIIGHT!" Randy said. There were giggles from Marcel and Horace but everyone else was quiet including Lacy.

"What did you do Lacy?" Gus asked.

"I don't know," Lacy said in a low voice as he looked up at Gus with tears in his eyes.

"I don't want to see any tears now," Mom said. "You can save those for later when I tear that black ass up…Sitting back there acting like you don't know what you did. You know dern well what you did."

"Yeah Lacy," Horace said. "You know what you did, so fess up four-eyes."

"Be quiet," Gus said to Horace. On their way home, Gus and the sisters would try to keep Lacy's spirits up by smiling at him or whispering to him that he'd be okay. When they got home, Lacy did as he was told and went to Gus and Randy's room, stripped, and waited for Mom. Marcel and Horace danced around Lacy pretending to be Indians doing a rain dance and told Lacy a serious beating was going to rain down on him, then they laughed and continued the dance. Moments later, Mom walked into the room and saw the antics of Marcel and Horace and laughed then told them to leave the room. As Mom closed the door, she told Lacy she was going to teach him a lesson for embarrassing her. She walked over to Lacy and started swinging the belt as if she were swatting flies.

"I'll kill your little black ass, do you hear me?" she asked, as she beat and beat and beat Lacy. He did the Mexican Jumping Bean dance at first but the beating lasted so long that he was exhausted and lay on the floor covering himself as best he could. "Now," she said as she stopped swinging the belt, "next time something happens at school I don't want another parent questioning me about what happened to you. YOU HEAR ME?" she said as she waved the belt in Lacy's face.

"I, I, I, I, I, I, I HE, HE, HE-AR YOU," Lacy said.

"If something happens with you at school you come to me and tell me instead of letting me get embarrassed by other parents knowing first. Now, put your clothes on and do any homework you have or just sit and be quiet." Lacy had no homework that day so he sat quietly. The sisters went to Lacy to comfort him but he asked them not to and to leave because he didn't want Mom to see that he wasn't being quiet. He did what he was told and sat and stayed quiet until Mom left for work, then he had dinner and went to bed shortly after. Each school year to follow involved similar experiences. After moving to a new house, Lacy started a new school, as did the other children. His third-grade teacher was Mrs. Strite. She was about sixty years old and looked like the old woman that lived in a shoe. Once she knew Mom would tear into Lacy for the simplest things, Mrs. Strite gave reports often and that was how often the beatings came. Mrs. Strite also had an issue with Lacy's ability to run faster than the other children so she would excuse Lacy for recess a couple of minutes after everyone else. She told Lacy that he always had first pick of the tetherball, kickball, football, or basketball courts because of his speed and it wasn't fair. When Lacy brought this to Mom's attention, Mom spoke with Mrs. Strite about it. Mrs. Strite denied what she said to Lacy and told Mom that Lacy was always the first one out of his seat when the recess bell rang because recess was more important to him than getting his work done. Lacy said he never left his seat until his work was turned in and his work was always turned in before the recess bell. What Mom heard was that Lacy was putting recess before learning and she didn't care if it was a lie or not. Since she left school after the eighth grade and worked as hard as she did, there was no way Lacy would not get a beating after what Mrs. Strite said. It was shortly after that beating that Mom recognized Mrs. Strite's dislike for Lacy. Lacy was good friends with a boy called Mike and they hit it off the very first day of school. After school, Lacy would walk to Horace and Marcel's school and wait for Mom to pick them all up. One day while walking, Lacy saw Luke and Eddie, two trouble-makers in Lacy's class, beating up Mike. Lacy dropped his books and ran over to help Mike. Luke and Eddie stopped and told Mike they would get him later. It got so bad with Luke and Eddie picking on Mike that it started happening at recess too. Mike and Lacy made a pact that they would help each other when trouble came, and it came a lot from Luke and Eddie. It turned out that Luke's older brother was in a gang, which, neither Mike or Lacy knew of. Luke's brother was trying to train Luke to fight and be tough, and Eddie was his sidekick. When Mrs. Strite told Mom Lacy was disruptive in school and started fights, she tore his little black ass up. Days later, Mrs. Strite fell sick so a substitute teacher stood in for her for a couple of weeks.

Mom had a talk with the substitute teacher to find out how Lacy was doing in class and the teacher said Lacy behaved very well during class and was probably the politest child she had ever met. The teacher told Mom that Lacy offered to help her carry things to and from her car and always said good morning and goodbye after school. Mom had a surprised look on her face and Lacy wasn't sure how that information would make Mom feel, but he was hoping the teacher would stop talking and felt like she might be stirring up trouble for him. The teacher told Mom about Mike and said that he was an only child and two boys picked on him every day, but Lacy played with him and helped keep those boys away. Now, Lacy was sure he'd see a belt before the day was over. Mom asked Lacy to leave the classroom so she could speak with the teacher. When Mom came out, she and Lacy walked to the car. "That substitute teacher really likes you Lacy," Mom said. "She told me Mrs. Strite picks on you in class and makes all the students laugh at you. She also said that you're protecting a little boy that can't protect himself."

"That's true," Lacy said.

"MMMHHHMM!" Mom said, then she went quiet. On that day, Marcel and Horace were sick and stayed home, so Mom and Lacy stopped by the grocery store to pick up some remedies for them. Once they got home, Mom told Lacy to go to Gus and Randy's room and strip and wait for her. He did as she said, and when she got there she told him he was getting beat for not telling her about Mrs. Strite making fun of him. After the beating, Mom told Lacy to leave Mike alone and let him defend himself and if he couldn't, it was too bad. Lacy did as she said. This caused Luke and Eddie to come after Lacy since he was by himself, but Lacy imagined Luke and Eddie were Horace and Marcel heckling him and fended them off well enough for them to never bother him ever again.

MR. BODYBUILDER

The next several years up to and including the seventh grade were some of the toughest years because Mom was getting older, her patience was lessening, and she lost her temper much quicker. She went through several boyfriends and lost two to death. Randy was getting arrested a lot, so police cars surrounding the house was a regular thing. The family car was constantly getting repossessed, preventing Mom from working those days, which added to her frustrations. Both sisters got married at seventeen and moved away and were pregnant within the year. One day, Mom drove the boys to visit someone she knew and hadn't seen in a long while. They arrived at an apartment building and went to the second floor to meet this person. Once they were all inside, this woman that looked like a young version of Mom said hello to everyone and gave Lacy a very firm hug and kiss on the cheek and said she missed him so much. Lacy didn't know what to say, so he walked over to Gus and asked who she was. "That's our sister Sandrine," Gus said.

Lacy looked at Sandrine then back at Gus and asked where she had been all these years. Gus said Mom put her in foster care because she fought with Mom.

"WAIT! I remember," Lacy said.

"I don't think so," Gus said, "because you were too young to remember her."

Lacy said, "We all went to visit a girl at a courthouse or a holding room and Mom told all of us to say exactly what she told us to say. Mom told me I better say everything she told me to say or she would beat me. The woman at that place asked if Mom beat us and I said no because that was what Mom told us to say. Sandrine cried and yelled that was not true."

"WOW! You do remember," Gus said.

"She's the one that Odessa and Alexandra called Sandy. She's my sister?" Lacy ran over to her and hugged her and let her know that he remembered her. Sandrine cried profusely and thanked Lacy for telling her that. All of the experiences Lacy was going through was overwhelming but the worst part was not being able to tell his friends at school. He did everything he could in order to not let any of his home life spill into conversations with his friends, like the times Randy would unleash fists of fury on Lacy due to his own life's frustrations. One day, Randy was smacking Lacy around a bit, so Lacy grabbed a BB gun that looked like a 45-caliber pistol and snuck up on Randy when he was sitting down. Lacy told Randy to turn around, and when Randy turned around the gun was inches away from his face. Randy was stunned and frozen. Lacy told him he only picked on people smaller and younger than him because he was a yellow-bellied sapsucker. Lacy told Randy to call himself the punk that he was. Gus heard Randy yelling for someone to get Lacy so Gus ran into the room and told Lacy to give him the gun. Lacy said, "This punk is twenty years old and eight years older than me and needs to be locked up somewhere."

Gus said, "I hear you Lacy, but give me the gun, okay?"

"Gus," Lacy said, "if I give you the gun he's going to jump out of that chair and attack me but right now he's scared shitless and needs to sit in that shit for a minute."

"Lacy," Gus said, "I know he's done a lot to you over the years but he'll get what he deserves from the type of people he hangs out with. Give me the gun, and Randy you better not do anything."

"Alright," Randy said. Lacy gave Gus the BB gun and Randy leaped at Lacy, connecting a fist to his face as Gus grabbed Randy then threw him across the room. Gus warned Randy if he took a step closer he'd knock the hell out of him as he should have long ago. Randy sat down and just smiled at Lacy with a look that said, "I'll get you later," and Lacy smiled back with a look that said, "You're a punk."

"Stop Lacy," Gus said. Lacy respected Gus greatly and knew when to stop. He followed his lead because Lacy could see that Gus' mind and lifestyle were working for him and getting him into the world properly.

After a couple of days, Lacy wanted to talk to his friends or someone about the incident but still couldn't chance things getting back to Mom, and Randy wasn't about to tell Mom exactly what happened because he'd appear weak to her. Instead, Randy told Mom that Lacy was playing with the BB gun in the house so he was restricted from using it anymore and beaten. Often, his friends told him that he acted differently around his family compared to when they were out as friends. Lacy pretended he didn't know what they were talking about because he knew if he tried to explain the situation to his friends they would ask Marcel and Horace about it, which was Lacy's fear to carry for quite some time. One of Lacy's favorite songs from 1971 was "Smiling Faces Sometimes" by The Undisputed Truth, and it played in his head whenever Randy, Marcel, or Horace were in the same room or vicinity as him and his friends. It was especially difficult for Lacy to convince his friends that he slept on the floor because he wanted to, and not because he didn't have a room or a bed. Lacy would get teased and told that he seemed more like a visitor instead of a family member. Lacy would laugh along with his friends but it hurt and he knew they had no idea how much it did because they didn't know what was going on. Gus was in the military at this point and Lacy felt more alone than ever before. His friends would ask about the man that was in the house all the time, ordering him around. "Tex. That's Mom's boyfriend," he said. "He wants me to call him Dad but that's not going to happen." What Lacy didn't tell his friends was that Tex liked to push him around when no one was there. Since it was Mom's boyfriend, Lacy didn't believe she would take his side so he just kept quiet until one day he had enough. Lacy was watching "The Little Rascals" and Tex told Lacy to get up so he could show him some fighting skills, which was code for "I want to slap you around a bit". Lacy told Tex to wait until Randy got home so he could teach some skills to someone his own size. Tex slapped Lacy in the back of the head and Lacy charged right for Tex and fisted him right in the testicles.

Tex grabbed Lacy and pinned him down on the ground with his arm over Lacy's throat, cutting off his airway. Lacy thought Tex would kill him and put the blame on him, and if he lived, the worst that could happen was a beating, so Lacy punched Tex in the throat but missed. The punch hit Tex under the chin, causing enough shock for Lacy to get away. He ran around, underneath, and over the dining room table to get away from Tex. At one point, Lacy tipped over a chair as he passed it and Tex tripped over it, so Lacy turned around and jumped on Tex's back and kicked him in the back of the head then ran back around the table. Tex got up yelling and that was when they heard a car door shut.

"Your ass is gonna get it now boy! Yo mama's home and I'm gonna tell her to skin your ass raw."

"NOT TODAY YOU MISERABLE COWARD! You and I know Mom despises weak men and the only thing she hates more is weak men that have no money. If she finds out that I got some licks in on you she will kick you out as fast as she walks through that door. If you tell I will get a beating for sure, but today will be your last day here and there will be no more late-night fun for you." Click click. Mom opened the door and walked in.

"What have you two been doing and what's all this mess?" Mom asked.

"Ohh, hehehe! Well, ya know me and Lacy. Hehehe. We was just horsin' round. We were just about to pick things up. Sorry for the mess Beatrice," Tex said.

Mom looked straight into Lacy's eyes without smiling and that was when Lacy said, "That was a lot of fun Tex. Let's clean up like you said then the watch "The Little Rascals.""

"Good idea Lacy," Tex said. Mom knew something happened that day between Tex and Lacy but she never heard about it from them. From that day forward, Tex and Lacy got along great, but Lacy kept having visions during the day and dreams at night of Mom bringing another man to the house to replace Tex. The visions and dreams showed him that the new man would be older, slower, and whenever he would visit Mom would not be nice to Lacy. Lacy had no reason not to trust the vision shown to him since earlier visions and dreams gave him a glimpse of truth coming his way. This was about the time Lacy began bodybuilding and training with Gus' equipment that he left behind. Mom didn't like Lacy working out because she said he would be a muscle-bound freak and she didn't want that in her house. Lacy found this odd because she used to watch Jack LaLanne religiously with Lilly and ogle and ogle and ogle over him.

"Football, baseball, and basketball are acceptable sports for men but bodybuilding is for idiots," she said. She asked Lacy how he planned to support himself and support her by being a bodybuilder. Lacy told her that he would become world champion and open his own fitness facility and work with people individually to help them with their health and bodies. "Hahahahahaha," she laughed and told Lacy that he would be a muscle-bound failure, needing to borrow money from Horace and Marcel his whole life and that he'd be better off opening a hamburger joint. Whenever she had guests over and they asked what the boys wanted to do with their lives, she sang praise for Horace and Marcel and said Lacy wanted to be a muscle-bound freak that would end up borrowing money from Marcel and Horace to survive. During those episodes, Tex visited less and less until one day he was gone, and days later when Lacy came home from school, an older, slower man named Mr. Lincoln was there.

He didn't talk much and didn't share any opinions unless asked. He and Lacy didn't say much more than hello to each other when they saw each other. It seemed that Mom strived to prove herself to Mr. Lincoln and show herself in the best light she could while in his presence. Just like the vision Lacy was shown, Mom ridiculed him and put him down in front of Mr. Lincoln as a regular routine. One night, Lacy was on his way to sleep and Mom called him to come to the living room where she was. She and Mr. Lincoln were drinking a fifth of Pinch Scotch. She told Lacy to take his top off and show his torso to Mr. Lincoln. Lacy did as he was told. "Now, do you think he can be world champion bodybuilder looking like that?" she asked Mr. Lincoln as she laughed. Mr. Lincoln asked Lacy if he wanted to be a bodybuilder and Lacy said yes.

Mr. Lincoln looked at Lacy then dropped his head for a moment, then looked at Lacy and said, "Well, if a man can walk on the moon I guess you can be world champion," then laughed.

"Fat chance," Mom said. "Mr. Bodybuilder. The dern fool will be lucky to get on a stage and not get laughed at because that's what's going to happen. You're not gonna be world champion, Mr. Body-builder, so put your shirt back on and go to bed and dream about being world champion because your dreams are the only place you'll be world champion." Lacy went to bed and cried and stayed awake for hours promising himself not to give up. That night, Randy was in the kitchen and heard everything Mom and Mr. Lincoln said. He heard Lacy crying and went to him.

"Don't fuck with me man! If you've come to add to the stupidity we can just go at it right now and I won't stop until one of us is in the hospital."

"Naaah man. Naaaah. I'm not here for that Lacy. Jussss cool it man. I heard everything and that shit ain't right. You've been through a lot maaaan and I'm sorry. I'm sorry. I know Mom didn't mean it."

"Randy," Lacy said. "Don't ever apologize to me for someone else, okay? Either it comes from them or the apology doesn't exist. I appreciate you saying you're sorry but, are you sorry for your part or her part?" Lacy asked. Randy was quiet.

"Does it matter?" Randy asked.

"It does," Lacy said.

"Why?" Randy asked. "Jusss be happy you heard the words," Randy said. Lacy asked Randy if he stuck a needle in his eye and said he was sorry while the needle was still in his eye, would Randy hear him? "See, that's your fuckin' problem," Randy said, "you always talk like a wise old man in a cave. You really need to stop that shit."

"Answer the question Randy," Lacy said. "Are you excusing yourself or Mom by saying you're sorry?"

"I was saying I'm sorry Mom embarrassed your ass and that's it, okay? I don't owe you anything."

"Randy, listen to me and listen good," Lacy said. "I'm not an adult so I'm not the one that should feel embarrassed and I don't. Anyone that has made life difficult for me, harmed me, and works to ruin my future will trade places with the life I started out with."

"Are you on drugs? You sound stupid as shit," Randy said.

"Randy," Lacy said, "remember when we lived in La Puente and I told you if you don't change life will not be good for you?"

"Yeah, I remember that shit. So what?"

Lacy said, "So, you've been arrested many times."

"So what! People get arrested all the time," Randy said.

"NO! People do not get arrested all the time Randy. You get arrested all the time because you do wrong and it will get worse. If you can't learn to apologize for the things you've done and stop doing the things you do, you will remember all that I'm saying while sitting behind bars and your life will end that way. If you want to laugh you go right ahead because I know you hear me and if you don't you will when those jail doors close."

"Nigga, I came in here to check on you but fuck you," Randy said.

"NO!" Lacy said. "You didn't come to check on me. You came because you feel guilty for all that you've done to me and your conscience is killing you. When you heard Mom and Mr. Lincoln it made you feel terrible for all that you've done. I don't need any more lies from any of you because I'm seeing things clearer and clearer each day. If you are willing to be right with me then we will get along and if not then we will not see each other in the future because I will raise my family differently."

"Huh, nigga you too stupid to have kids." Lacy said nothing and just smiled and gave Randy a stare that let him know that he couldn't push Lacy around without consequences anymore. "Later, stupid ass," Randy said as he walked out. His words had little effect on Lacy at that point, especially after the mean teachers, beatings, staying with Mr. Stache, and the Tex incident. Lacy began to look at those situations as if it was training for his adult life and what he may face. As Lacy got older, it became much clearer to him that the dreams and visions he would have were glimpses into what may happen or what he might expect. He realized the dreams and visions were not always exactly what life presented but the dreams and visions that manifested into his reality were clear enough for him to understand, or put those glimpses of knowledge to good use for himself and others. He also realized what Esta meant when she told him to be careful and protect himself because people would want things from him. He realized Esta knew that his dreams and visions told stories that people would want to hear and that was why Shirley asked Lacy about her future and the sisters would ask about boys they met. On good days, Horace, Randy, and Mom would ask him many questions regarding life, health, and people, and Lacy was happy to answer them with hopes of bridging the gaps of tension. No matter how many questions Lacy answered it didn't change how he was treated for long, but his physical strength was getting better due to weightlifting and his inner strength was growing rapidly too. One day when he was told to rearrange the living room furniture, he noticed a chair that was always too heavy to move suddenly felt as light as a feather. It was later that day that Horace chose to grab Lacy and rest his body weight on him until Lacy's legs gave out and Horace was on top of him on the floor pinning him down. Horace was about one foot taller and much heavier than Lacy, so towering over Lacy to pin him down was easy. On this particular day when Horace grabbed Lacy by the back of the head and pushed him down, Lacy reached down and grabbed Horace's legs as he put his neck and head between them, lifted him up, and tossed him over his shoulders. *BLAAAMMM!* Horace hit the ground hard and screamed out.

"WHAT'S GOTTEN INTO YO- YOU FOUR-EYED FREAK?" Horace said.

"Call me what you want," Lacy said, "but if you try that ever again, you'll hit the floor harder. I promise."

"Mom's gonna hear about this when she gets home," Horace said.

"Go ahead and tell, but whatever she does to me I will do to you, and if you tell her I said that, you'll get worse. You guys have pushed me around long enough and now that I'm older it will stop or you'll feel the pain I feel."

"You don't scare me," Horace said.

"I don't want to scare you but I'll kick the fuck out of you if you ever come at me the wrong way again. From this day forward we will get along or say nothing to each other but if you touch me I will touch you harder," Lacy said.

"Go to hell," Horace said.

"Where do you think I've been all this time?" Lacy said. "Now it's your turn if you cross me."

"Stay away from me," Horace said as he walked away. When Marcel got home, Horace told him what happened and Marcel told Lacy he got lucky and he better not try anything with him or they would gang up on Lacy. Later that evening, Mom called Lacy to her room and as he was walking toward her room, he passed the bathroom where

Marcel was. Marcel heard Lacy coming and kicked Lacy in the side of the knee, causing Lacy to go down immediately. Lacy screamed in pain and told Marcel that he did that on purpose because he had always been jealous of his bodybuilding.

Marcel just laughed and said, "You will never be world champion, especially if your knees don't work." Lacy leaped at Marcel and smacked him across the face, knocking Marcel into the wall.

Marcel didn't know how to respond to that but Mom said, "Lacy, get in here now." Lacy went to her and she asked what he thought he was doing. Lacy explained what just happened and asked if she heard him fall down after Marcel kicked him. After all, it was just outside her door. "No," she said. "I heard Marcel yell at you after you hit him. Now apologize to Marcel for hitting him."

"This is wrong," Lacy said. "He kicked me, and he and Horace get away with doing things like this all the time."

"Apologize or find a place to stay." Lacy was shocked that she said that because it was the first time that she had said that to him. Lacy looked at Marcel, waiting for him to find a slither of decency to correct the situation.

Marcel looked at Lacy and said, "I'm waiting for my apology." Lacy looked at Mom, then looked at Marcel and said he was sorry. Marcel told Lacy if he ever hit him again he would hurt him. Lacy had just started the eighth grade and knew he couldn't tackle the world just yet, so he kept quiet since Mom was just itching to put him out. From that day forward, Lacy and Marcel settled their differences after Mom went to work. After a while, Horace and Marcel realized Lacy had been beaten so many times that their hits just felt like gnats bumping into him, but Lacy's hits caused pain. When Mom would beat Lacy she made sure the marks could be covered by clothing and that was the same thing Lacy made sure to do with Horace and Marcel so Mom wouldn't see. He made sure to never hit them in the face. Randy was a different story as Randy was a foot taller and his hits knocked the wind out of people. He could have easily been a boxer. Actually, he could have been a number of things. He could play several instruments without training, his singing voice was similar to Michael Jackson's, and any sport he played he mastered. He chose not to do any of those things because he felt slaves provided entertainment for the masters and he refused to be on a field or stage to entertain like a slave. But, he had no problem getting locked up behind bars like a slave. He liked to coerce people and if he couldn't, he would bully them. One day, Lacy was in the backyard with his friend Sam when Randy tossed a couple of rolled-up dollars and told Lacy to go to the store to get him some Doritos. Lacy told Randy to get the Doritos himself. Randy ran up on Lacy, yelling that he should have let Mom put Lacy in a foster home years ago. Then he punched Lacy in the solar plexus, pushing Lacy through the air into a chain-link fence, causing Lacy's body to bang against the concrete.

"Oh shit," Sam said. "Randy, we'll go to the store, c'mon Lacy."

"No Sam, you don't understand what's going on," he said. "Is that all you got BITCH?" Lacy said to Randy.

"OH MY GOD!" Sam said. "Lacy don't get up and please be quiet."

"I've been quiet Sam," Lacy said, "and this bully doesn't scare me." As Lacy was getting up, he took another hit to the chest and flew into the chain-link fence again and hit the ground.

"Randy, please stop," Sam said. "I think he's had enough."

"No," Lacy said. "Randy's a punk and he will never have enough for me."

"Lacy, shut the fuck up man. Randy's gonna kill you."

"Let a punk like him stop me, NEVER!" Lacy said.

"Man, I can't watch this," Sam said, "I heard something crack." Lacy stood looking at Randy and Randy stood looking at Lacy.

"Maaaann. I'll hospitalize your ass," Randy said.

"That's today," Lacy said, "but one day I'll be your age then what?"

"You best shut yo mouth," Randy said as he walked back into the house.

"What THEEEEEEE FUCK was that about?" Sam asked.

"I don't want to talk about it if it's okay with you," Lacy said to Sam. Sam didn't know what to say, so he asked Lacy if he wanted to hang out at his house for a while so Randy could cool off.

Lacy said no. He told Sam he had to work out soon and stay on his training schedule. Sam asked Lacy if he was able to train because he got hit pretty hard. Lacy told Sam his chest hurt, but the future that he saw for himself depended on his training and discipline. Sam told Lacy he was sorry for what just happened and he would be at home if Lacy wanted to stop by later. Lacy said, "Cool," and thanked Sam. Lacy went into the house to get some water and rest up a bit before training. Regardless of what was going on or what may have just happened to Lacy, he would put on a song by The Isley Brothers called "Climbing Up the Ladder" to get into the right mental place before training. If for some reason he wasn't able to play the song, he would think about the words of the song as he trained. It was very important for Lacy to train his mind as well as his body. He would imagine that all those that opposed him in the house were the weights that he would push and pull. When he pushed or pulled heavy weight he would imagine his worst days, so he would push and pull the weights as long as he could to prove to himself he was stronger those days. One day, he was training and had a vision that he would not reach the potential of world champion until the year 2000. That would mean he would be thirty-five years old. Lacy shook his head in disbelief but as he was training the vision came back again, showing that he would win many titles but not the world title until the year 2000. Lacy tried his best not to think about that vision, but it kept coming, just like that dream he had at four years old of him being chased. He was sleeping one night and had a dream that he was on a stage winning a world title, and there was a man that would offer him success if he used drugs. The message in the dream was clear - Lacy should not get caught up in the drug scene or his hopes and dreams would be lost. The dreams and visions Lacy would experience came more and more often as Lacy began to get nervous and wonder where all of the messages were coming from. His belief in God was not shaken since the day Esta came to him about God. He thought he was betraying God somehow by using the dreams and visions to help direct his path, so he began ignoring the dreams and visions as best he could but that caused sleepless nights here and there. It was about that time that Mom placed a book on the side table by the sofa by Edgar Casey. Lacy didn't pay attention to the book at first, but when heard Marcel and Randy talking about the book and saying they wished they were clairvoyant like Edgar Casey, his ears perked up. One day when Lacy was home by himself, he began reading the book but felt very uncomfortable reading it as if that book was not meant for him. But, he was very curious as to why Mom placed that book in plain view. Lacy heard Mom over the years telling friends about dreams she had and what they meant, so Lacy knew Mom had to have known that he had similar experiences.

She was trying to find out how aware and comfortable he was of such an ability. He believed Mom wanted him to get better at his understanding of the dreams and visions, not for his life but to enrich her own. Mom realized Lacy was getting stronger, better at understanding the dreams and visions, and beginning to figure out some truths about himself, so Mom worked hard to prevent his knowledge of the truth. When Mom would ask Lacy questions about Horace and Marcel in regard to girls they were interested in, Lacy would say he had no clue about the girls. Mom told him to tell her what he felt about the girls when she gave Lacy their names. Lacy said he really didn't know. This made Mom furious because she said she put food on the table for all of them and they owed her. She told Lacy he was being very selfish and everyone owed her for all that she had done. Lacy said, "I thank you for putting food on the table and working as you have done but I don't know anything about the girls."

"Tell me what you see damnit! You take from me but you don't want to help me just like Esta. That bitch stole two pairs of my shoes and now you want to eat and sleep in my house for free. You better think twice about where your meals come from, you hear me?" she asked.

"Yes," Lacy said.

"God doesn't like ugly and He punishes those that are selfish and those that are all for themselves and are ungrateful. You need to go read the Bible and learn how to be thankful for what you have, you selfish bastard. I ought to whoop your black ass for ruining my day, now get out of my sight." Lacy went outside and went for a walk. He couldn't understand why Mom was asking him about the girls Marcel and Horace were involved with because they were with the exact type of girls she wanted them to be with – naïve and generous with their money. When Lacy was eleven, Mom wanted all the boys to meet her at the dining room table for a talk. She said she was going to teach them about women and what she expected from the boys. She said to remember that all women were nothing but bitches and that went for the sisters too, especially Esta, the lying bitch that stole two pairs of her shoes. Lacy couldn't figure out why Mom could not get over her two pairs of shoes being taken. *Unreal,* Lacy thought to himself. Mom also said that women were not to be trusted because they were like snakes with pussies and their pussy was the trap that ruined any man that was weak and stupid. She said to never let a woman drive because they would think they were in charge and never marry them because the boys would lose everything, including themselves and their soul. She said to never wash a woman's panties because that was her way of turning a man into her bitch permanently. She said to never let a woman get on top during sex because she would feel dominant and the man would be her bitch, then soon she'd stick something up his ass or bring a man into the bedroom to fuck him as her fantasy. She said, "It wouldn't be her fantasy, it would be her tricky slippery snake-like way to further turn you into her bitch and then she will take your money and find her next victim." As she spoke, Lacy began to think of the men she dated and how they arrived strong but left weak and complained about their money and how she took their money. As Lacy was thinking about what she was saying, Mom told Lacy to go get the Bible. Lacy got the Bible and sat back down. Mom said that Lacy's teacher Mr. McCafferty told her that Lacy daydreamed a lot in class. She asked Lacy if that was true. Lacy said yes. Mom told Lacy he was there on school time to learn, not to daydream. "What do you daydream about?" she asked. Lacy said that he would see a lot about the future and it took his attention away. Mom said, "Well you're going to read out of the Bible and explain to me what the passages mean without daydreaming, and if you can't explain the passages I will beat your ass each time you can't do it." Lacy looked at her and said that the Bible was difficult to understand and that was why the preacher in church had to explain it to adults. "You getting smart with me? I'll beat your narrow black ass, now open that book and read from a passage and you better tell me exactly what it means." Lacy's hands were shaking as he opened the Bible. He was searching for a passage, but his mind drifted to wondering how Mom could say all women were bitches just moments earlier and now demand he read from the Bible. "Hurry your ass up before I cash in your black ass and ask for change." Lacy found a passage and read it but he was confused by the biblical language and couldn't figure out the meaning of the passage, especially at age eleven without guidance. "Get your ass up and get over here," she said. She beat Lacy in front of the other boys including Gus as this was before he went to the military. After she beat Lacy, she told him to sit down and find another passage. Lacy turned the pages, crying, with his hands shaking and his eyes blurry from the tears.

"Take your time and think about it when you're ready," Gus said.

"You're not calling the shots here," Mom said to Gus. "Now start reading, or do I have to come over to you and beat you where you sit?" she asked. This went on for a few more beatings before Marcel told Mom that he would have trouble interpreting the Bible too and he was three years older than Lacy. Mom's face had a twisted expression on it as she looked at Marcel. She said, "That boy can interpret, he's just being lazy and you're not helping, so keep your mouth shut." All of the boys dropped their heads which signaled to Lacy that Mom was pressing him so much that they were all disgusted. After a few more attempts, Mom finally told Lacy to get out of her sight and for all the boys to remember to fuck as many women as possible but not to make it possible for them to fuck them. Lacy thought that was one of the most confusing and twisted days of his youth.

ESTA AND THE ANIMAL CRACKERS

The more Mom spoke negatively about women, the more Lacy paid respect to women and catered to them in every way he could. Opening doors, carrying bags and boxes, and doing whatever errands that would make their lives easier. Lacy remembered how the sisters took care of him and looked out for him when he was a boy, but felt that men should look out for women. But, that sense of chivalry was challenged a couple of years later when Lacy was thirteen. Mom woke up from a dream and told everyone to meet her in the dining room. Once everyone was seated, Mom told them she had a dream that their refrigerator had nothing in it except an eggplant, but moments after seeing the eggplant it began to wither quickly as if death grabbed it. Then, it moved from the back of the inside of the refrigerator to the front, then a phone rang in the dream and that was when she woke up. She said the feeling she got from the phone ringing in her dream meant bad news was coming and she wanted everyone to be ready for terrible news. She was concerned that someone in the family was sick or dying and that news would hit home soon. A few days later, Esta called and wanted to talk to Mom and see Lacy. Mom was convinced that Esta was the one with the terrible news. She told the boys that Esta was coming over on the weekend but Lacy had no reaction. Randy asked Lacy if he heard what Mom said.

"Yes," Lacy said.

"Well, aren't you excited to see Esta?" Randy asked.

"Why would I be?" Lacy asked Randy. Lacy said, "I haven't seen or heard from her since I was four and don't know her."

"That's a cold way to act Lacy," Randy said.

"Hahahahahaha!" Lacy laughed. "You of all people are going to preach to me about being cold," Lacy said to Randy.

"She's coming to see you Lacy," Randy said.

"No. She's coming because she needs something. Watch and see," Lacy said.

"You always think you know everything Lacy but you don't. She probably took a lot of time to think about how she left and now wants to make it up to everyone," Randy said.

Lacy smiled at Randy and said, "That's possible, but that dream Mom had was about Esta and she will want something. I don't wish her any harm or any ill will but a lot has happened since she left and my life has begun without her."

"You should tell Mom what you just said," Randy said.

"I'm pretty sure Mom already knows."

"You used to wait up all night to see Esta, Lacy, I can't believe you're not excited that she's coming."

"Randy, I'm thirteen, not four," Lacy said. "She lied about leaving then left in the middle of the night. Mom told us not to speak her name again and I got beat for it, so I had to move on without Esta giving any reason over the years to remember or think of her."

"Maaaann, she's gonna be hurt to hell if you don't show some excitement," Randy said.

"Then I won't be here when she gets here to avoid causing her pain."

"Lacy," Randy said, "that would be worse."

Lacy said, "Randy, how can you or anyone expect me to concern myself with her feelings? I would never leave any child without saying goodbye and lie about leaving in the first place. She's not coming for me. Mom's right, she's selfish and she stole two pairs of Mom's shoes, so she's a thief too and probably coming to ask for something she doesn't deserve."

"Well, she's not a saint and was promiscuous."

"What do you mean by promiscuous?" Lacy asked.

"You're thirteen," Randy said. "You don't know what promiscuous means?"

"I know what it means," Lacy said, "but I'm asking what you mean by that statement. I don't remember Esta that way."

"Of course not, you were just a child. Where do you think she was when she wasn't at TG&Y or when she left early for school before you woke up?"

"You're making this up," Lacy said.

"I ain't makin' up shit," Randy said. "Nobody is perfect, not even you Lacy, so give her a chance."

"I'll be cool," Lacy said, "but I'm just not in the mood for lies, tears, and long drawn out stories about why she left."

"I heeeeaaar that," Randy said, "but like you said Lacy, jus be cooooo man."

"I will," Lacy said. When Esta arrived that Saturday, Lacy was watching the World's Strongest Man competition in the back part of the house. Horace went to Mom's room to let her know a car pulled up outside and that he thought it was Esta. Lacy heard Horace but kept watching TV.

"Come on Lacy," Horace said. "I think Esta is here." Lacy didn't say anything.

Mom said, "Lacy if you don't want to come out you don't have to, but Esta and I need to talk."

"Okay," Lacy said. A few minutes later Lacy heard hellos and how are yous from the front of the house, but he refused to get out of the chair and kept watching the competition.

"Where's Lacy?" Esta asked.

"He's in the room watching TV."

"Oh," Esta said. "May I see him?" she asked Mom.

"Sure," Mom said. Horace took Esta back to where Lacy was.

"Hi Lacy," Esta said as she entered the room.

"Hi," Lacy said as he looked at her with a plain face.

She said, "Lacy, you have so many reasons to not like me or want to talk to me but I am happy to see you. I brought you something." She reached into a bag and pulled out a red box of Barnum Bailey Animal Crackers with the white string box handle. She had a huge smile on her face as if she expected Lacy to jump for the box like he did when he was four.

Lacy looked at Esta, wondering if she realized he wasn't a little boy anymore, then smiled and said, "Thank you," as he took the box.

"You don't want to see me do you," she asked. Lacy looked at her and didn't say anything. "It's okay," Esta said. "I understand. Maybe in time you will want to see me." Lacy just looked at her with a smile, trying to be nice. "I'll be out front talking to Mom so if you want to talk to me I won't be far."

"Okay," Lacy said.

"Were you surprised to see the cookies?" she asked.

"Esta," Lacy said, "I stopped eating those cookies after you left. I don't eat them anymore." Esta began shedding tears. "I'm not trying to hurt you," Lacy said, "I just don't know you anymore and you definitely don't know me. I do not like having to pretend and I hope you understand."

"I understand," Esta said. "I'll be up front talking to Mom."

"Okay," Lacy said.

Lacy could hear everyone talking at the front of the house when he heard a little voice say, "Hi Uncle Lacy." He looked to his left and saw a little boy.

Then he heard another voice say, "Hi Uncle Lacy," from a girl that looked like the little boy's sister. Lacy was in a state of shock because the little boy's face looked so familiar. The little girl looked just like a very young Esta but Lacy couldn't figure out why the boy looked so familiar.

He asked the little boy what his name was and the boy said, "My name is Jasper."

"WHAT?" Lacy said.

"Jasper. My name is Jasper and I'm named after my father." Lacy felt sick to his stomach. *The children are Jasper's children and Jasper was Mom's boyfriend*, he thought to himself. As Lacy got older, he realized all the sounds he heard from Mom's bedroom long ago was her and Jasper having sex. He quickly realized Esta ran off with Jasper. *Why isn't Mom in there kicking her ass up and down the street?* he wondered to himself. "C'mon Uncle Lacy, let's go play outside in the backyard," little Jasper said.

"N- not right now. Um, will you two go up front and I'll see you later? Because I was watching this important program and need to pay attention."

"Oh, may we watch too?" little Jasper asked. *He talks like me,* Lacy thought to himself.

"Uuh. Okay. You two can sit over there on the bed." The children watched the program and kept asking questions about the men lifting heavy weight and Lacy kept staring at the children with tons of questions running through his mind. "How old are you two?" Lacy asked. When they told him their ages, Lacy realized Esta got pregnant not long after she left. "Have you ever played Army men little Jasper?" Lacy asked.

"YEEEESS! All the time," he said. "How did you know that? Do you play?" little Jasper asked.

"I was just wondering since many children play that. No, I don't play," Lacy said, "but I used to play." All of the pain Lacy felt when Esta left grew around his neck and tightened like a noose. Lacy needed to be alone and asked the children if they would meet him up front and said that he would be there very soon.

"Okay Uncle Lacy," the little girl named Amara said. "Come on Jasper, let's go."

Little Jasper said, "Okay Amara."

"Uncle Lacy, those guys are neeeeatoooo," he said. "Maybe we can watch more later."

"Who taught you to say neeeatooo?" Lacy asked.

"Our mom did," Amara said.

"I used to say that word a lot too," Lacy said. "It's great to hear you say it because your face lights up when you say it." Lacy was working hard to hold back the tears.

"Are you okay Uncle Lacy?" little Jasper asked.

"Yes," Lacy said. "Just a hair in my eye but it's okay. Go ahead and go up front. I'll be there." When they left the room, Lacy stood up in a fit of frustration and began pacing the room, trying to put the puzzle pieces about Mom, Jasper, Esta, and what that three-ringed circus was all about, together. He wondered why Esta always took care of him and Mom didn't. The time when Esta left was the time Mom made him call her Mom when he never did before. Why did Randy mention countless times that Mom took Esta to Milwaukee because her stomach was bad and began to swell? Mom and Esta were gone for many months while the others stayed in Los Angeles with Mom's friends and surrogate family. Why would Randy tell Lacy he would be short and fat just like Dad? The photos of the man Lacy was told was everyone's dad was six feet and two inches tall and built, so how could Lacy be short and fat? After all, Horace, Randy, and Marcel were all over six feet already. Mom would tell Lacy that he was a late bloomer and he would grow more before he turned twenty. Lacy took her word for it, and he believed Randy was just spouting off words of frustration as usual. But Randy's words were starting to make sense and Mom's reasons for being upset with Esta also started making more sense. She ran off with Mom's boyfriend, had children with him, and stole her shoes. Lacy began to feel sorry for Mom and wondered how she could even allow Esta in her house. He began thinking that Mom was taking much of her frustration out on him because he and Esta were so close and her dislike for Esta spilled over to Lacy. But, now that Mom and Esta were talking, Lacy thought Mom would treat him better and the others just might too. Lacy turned the TV off and sat back down to try to think this through, because he was beginning to think that Esta might be his mother and that was why he never called anyone Mom until the age of four when Mom demanded it. He believed she demanded that from him because it would make life easier for her if she didn't have to explain that he was her daughter's son, and that her daughter ran off. *That was why Esta made my meals, dressed me, and why I slept with her in her bed*, he thought to himself. That was why she would clean the goop from his eyes in the mornings and clean him up if he wet his pants. As Lacy was thinking about all of that, he heard Esta crying and Mom asking her when she found out. *Found out what?* Lacy wondered. He leaned closer to the doorway to eavesdrop but he couldn't hear well enough, so he walked into the hallway, hid behind the wall, and listened.

"...Kidney transplant," Randy said.

"Yes," Esta said. She said her kidney was bad and she needed a transplant right away.

"Did you come to ask Lacy?" Mom asked Esta.

"Yes," Esta said. Lacy's eyes flew wide open, his mouth dropped, and he backed up slightly from the corner of the wall where he was standing. He knew he would be called to the dining room to talk to Esta, so he thought he better get out of there.

Just then, little Jasper said, "Uncle Lacy is going to come out soon to play with us but I can go get him if you want me to."

"Yes," Mom said, "please tell Lacy to come here." When Lacy heard Mom say that, he went into Mom's bathroom and snuck out of the door that led to the backyard. He closed the door quietly then ran down the street away from the house so that no one would see him through the window. He ran around the corner and further up that street, then around another corner, then ran a couple of miles to Sam's house. Lacy rang Sam's doorbell while panting like he ran a marathon.

Sam opened the door and Lacy said, "SAM, MAN, SHE WANTS MY KIDNEY."

"WHAT? WHO WANTS YOUR KIDNEY?" Sam asked.

"Esta does. Remember I told you about Esta and that she was coming over today?"

"Yeah," Sam said.

Lacy said, "Well, she's here and she needs a kidney because hers is bad and she wants me to give her one."

"WHAT," Sam asked. "That can't be right," he said. "How can she come to you after all this time and ask you for a kidney?"

"Man, I don't know," Lacy said, "but no one's cutting into me and that's why I ran over here. You gotta hide me and please don't tell your parents I'm here just in case someone calls looking for me."

Sam said, "COOL! But wait, I have a better idea. Let me get my bike and ride us to the mall so we can hang out there, then later we can hide down the street from your house and wait for her to leave."

"YEEEES," Lacy said. "Now you're talking. Can you believe this Sam?" Lacy asked. "I've just started my bodybuilding career and now she wants my kidney in exchange for a stupid box of animal crackers."

"HAHAHAHHA! What?" Sam laughed.

"No bull," Lacy said. "She used to bring me animal crackers when I was a little boy, so today she brought animal crackers trying to butter me up for my kidney. ANIMAL CRACKERS."

"HAHAHAHAHAHA." Sam just laughed, then he asked Lacy where the animal crackers were.

"Why?" Lacy asked.

"MAAAANN! Those are some good ass cookies."

Lacy laughed hysterically and said, "You better be careful Sam. I can imagine someone popping out of a corner offering you some animal crackers for your kidney, then later you're lying in a hospital bed with an IV in your arm saying, 'MAAAAAAN, these are some good ass cookies.'" Then they both laughed hysterically. The boys spent a few hours hanging around the mall and the surrounding areas, then they rode towards Lacy's house through the back streets.

Once they were a couple of blocks down from Lacy's house, they camped out around the block out of sight from anyone entering or leaving the house. They sat on the curb talking and laughing while eating snacks that Sam took from his house before they left. Periodically, they would peek to see if Esta's blue Toyota Corolla was still parked on the side of the house and if it was safe for Lacy to go home. They sat, camped, then rode around, then camped out more for at least two and a half hours before Esta finally left. "Hey Lacy," Sam said. "She left. You can go home now."

"Not yet," Lacy said. "She might come back to see if I returned. Let's play it safe and wait for thirty minutes to see if she comes back and if she doesn't, then the coast is clear."

"I like the way you think Lacy Dick Tracy the Funkiest…"

"Don't say it," Lacy said. "Reminds me of Alexandra's boyfriend who became her waste of a time husband who burned my face."

"Hahahahahaha." Sam laughed and asked Lacy why Mealo called him that in the first place.

Lacy said, "He heard the sisters calling me Lacy Dick Tracy so he added extra words and started calling me Lacy Dick Tracy the Funkiest Nigga in Town because I was afraid to take a bath in the bathroom by myself. Marcel would sneak in and turn the light off and close the door and hold it closed while I was trying to get out, so I avoided taking baths and would stink or smell funky."

"Hahahahahahaha." Sam fell over, laughing his tail off. "MAAAAAAAN! IS THAT WHY THEY CALL YOU THAT? HAHAHAHAHAHA! Wait 'til I tell the guys," Sam said.

Lacy said, "Naahh man. Don't tell anyone. It's bad enough I told you. Just keep it between us, okay?"

"Lacy," Sam said. "This is some good shit and the guys would dig it."

"SAAAMMM," Lacy said. "Don't. If you do that it will spread all over the place and before you know it people will get it confused. You know how people are. Some guy at school will pop up and say, 'Hey, aren't you the funkiest nigga in town?' People will completely forget the first part and only say the second part and you know Randy already does that."

"YEAHHH! HAHAHAHA," Sam laughed. "I've heard him do that. HAHAHAHAH."

"Okay, okay, okay. Let's get all the laughs out now but please keep it quiet, alright man?"

"You've got my word Lacy, Lacy DICK TRACY, or shall I call you

Mr. Funky? BAHAHAHAHA!" Lacy just looked at Sam with a straight face, wondering when Sam would finish laughing. "Alright man, I'll stop, I'll stop, but that's the funniest shit I've heard all week."

"Uh-huh," Lacy said.

"Look, Mr. Lincoln just got to your house," Sam said.

"Yes, we're supposed to have dinner with him. I better get out of here."

"Cool," Sam said.

"I'll catch you later."

"Okay."

"And Sam, maann, thank you for saving my butt today because I would have starved hiding out waiting for her to leave if you weren't home today."

"Don't mention it Lacy. You'd do the same for me."

"You know I would," Lacy said, then Sam rode off and Lacy went home.

When Lacy got home, Mom asked where Lacy had been and he said he was with Sam. She didn't seem upset. She told Lacy that Esta wanted to say goodbye and hoped to see him another time. Lacy said okay. Mom asked if he wanted to see Esta and Lacy said not really. Mom said she understood. Mom didn't mention anything about the "Esta needing a kidney" thing but Randy did later. Randy told Lacy that Esta needed a kidney and wanted to talk to him about it, but realized she shouldn't once she saw that he left the house. Randy told Lacy that Esta realized he would more than likely say no. Randy asked Lacy if he would do it and Lacy said no. Randy asked why. Lacy said Esta showed him how much she cared about him over the years with her absence, so if he were going to give up a body part for anyone it would be someone that showed they cared for him or a person that was dying and needed it right away. "Man Lacy, that's cold."

"What about you Randy?" Lacy asked. "Can you help Esta with your kidney?" Randy said Esta wasn't there for him so there was no point in answering the question. Of course, Lacy knew Randy would absolutely not even consider giving up a body part for anyone. Randy told Lacy that he should consider it and not be so selfish. Lacy told Randy being selfish wasn't part of his character and it wasn't fair that Randy tried to make it sound as if he was the selfish one. "Randy," Lacy said, "for years people have told me how I am and what I am and what I will be but I am the only one who can really answer that. Guilt trips don't work on me as much as they did before and I will only get better at identifying them. So, I will not consider giving up my kidney for her and if anyone feels like I'm being selfish then they can call Esta and meet her at the hospital, strap in, and get cut. Not I."

"Nigga, you always have to sound like Sherlock Holmes or some character out of 'The Ten Commandments,'" Randy said. "Sometimes I think you were abducted and came back with some alien shit in you. You look through people and talk to them like Spock from "Star Trek." Chill nigga, chill! Shiiiiet."

"I wish you wouldn't call me that Randy," Lacy said.

"What? Nigga?" Randy asked.

"Yes," Lacy said.

"Awe nigga please. You know I don't mean nuthin' by it. It's just me talkin'. Got those animal crackers nigga?" Randy asked, then laughed hysterically. Lacy just looked at Randy and Randy said he was just playing and said, "I'll try to stop calling you nigga." The talk about Lacy giving his kidney to Esta went no further than that day. Esta would visit every other weekend with her children for a couple of months then she was gone again. Lacy was growing more and more focused on his bodybuilding training and future, so Esta not coming around wasn't a problem for him because he made a deal with himself to connect with people that kept their word and respected other people's time.

JACKIE

Respecting others for being a human being rather than for any descriptions or possessions was important to Lacy, but that didn't always sit well with Mom, especially in the case of Jackie. Since Mom didn't like anything about Lacy working out, she made it clear that if he were going to work out that he had to take the equipment off of the patio and put it on the concrete outside. Having to put the equipment outside and put it all back after training would cut into Lacy's training time since he had other chores, but it wasn't going to discourage him from training. Hot sunny days, heavy rain, or wind didn't discourage Lacy's training. Those sessions taught him more about discipline and encouraged him to further his learning about nutrition because he got sick many times from training on those cold wet days. Lacy trained seven days a week, but Monday through Friday, Jackie would walk by after school on her way home. Lacy would be grunting away, doing heavy squats or biceps curls, and Jackie would walk by. At first, they just smiled at each other until one day she walked up to the chain-link fence and said hi to Lacy and told him her name. Lacy walked up to the fence and said hello and gave her his name. They spoke for a few moments about where she lived and went to school and where he went to school and why he trained so much, then Lacy told Jackie he had to get back to his training. Each day after that she would stop by for a few minutes so they could talk about each other's day, and that was how they became good friends. One day, Herman, pronounced "airrrrmaun," walked up to the chain-link fence and introduced him-self. He told Lacy that he was impressed with Lacy's discipline and intense training he saw each day on his way home from school. He told Lacy he was a soccer player and admired any athlete that took their sport seriously. As they spoke, Lacy found out that Herman was a year older than him and that he was Jackie's brother. With each passing day, Lacy, Jackie, and Herman grew closer as friends and one day Herman invited Lacy to his house to meet his parents, older sister, and to have dinner. His parents owned a food mart in El Monte, California, and worked very hard day and night to keep it going. One day, Horace saw Lacy and Jackie talking at the chain-link fence and later asked Lacy who she was. Lacy rarely told the others about any girls he would speak with because they would tease him and ask when he was going to pop their cherries. That would upset Lacy in the worst way because he didn't want to be like Horace, Marcel, and Randy. Marcel was bringing girls home all the time and had his way with them while Mom was in the next room. Afterward, he would come out wearing nothing but his tighty whities as he'd head to the kitchen to get a glass of cold water to cool off from the sixty seconds of hard work. Randy was playing the field and was juggling four to six girls at a time that would pay for mov-ies, food, trips, and hotel rooms. Horace was wining and dining girls left and right and would get a goodnight kiss or just a "goodnight," which made him furious. That would also cause Horace to try to get Lacy into trouble so that Horace would feel vindicated somehow. In grammar school, a girl Horace really liked told him to tell Lacy to look her up when he got to high school because he was such a stud muffin. That really infuriated Horace, but not as much as the Patti situation.

Once Lacy got to high school, Patti asked Lacy to the All Night Marathon Dance. Lacy said sure. When he got home, Mom called him to her room and asked why he agreed to go to an All Night Dance with a girl that was Horace's age and that Horace liked. Lacy looked shocked and told Mom he had no idea Horace even knew Patti. There were only a handful of Filipino students at the school but Patti stood out because of the way she carried herself and because of her wonderful smile and disposition, which were great qualities that got Lacy's interest. Mom wasn't having it. She believed Horace and said Lacy asked Patti to the dance to hurt Horace and must decline taking her to the dance. Lacy said he didn't know Horace was interested and would be happy to step down. He explained everything to Patti and Patti made it clear she had no interest in Horace. Still, Lacy told her he couldn't go with her. Later, Horace spoke with Patti and she was upset with him for interfering and didn't want to talk to him. Horace told Mom and surprisingly, Mom told Lacy to contact Patti and take her to the dance. Lacy told Mom he already told her no. Mom insisted that Lacy take Patti to the dance and if he didn't he would be punished. Mom felt that Patti was a tramp and wanted Lacy to get close to her then break Patti's heart for hurting Horace. Lacy didn't like that plan at all but pretended to go along with it until he got to the dance. Marcel was at the same dance and was able to keep his eyes on Lacy, but Lacy was able to speak with Patti and told her that he liked her but he was fully committed to his bodybuilding and couldn't date because he just didn't have the time. Patti wanted to kiss Lacy but Lacy had never kissed a girl and was so afraid of being like Marcel, Randy, and Horace that he kept turning his face away. Patti thought he just wasn't interested in her but Lacy told her he was interested but things were complicated for him so dating wasn't an option. She said she understood, but during school she avoided him and when they'd pass each other in the halls she would look the other way. Lacy felt sorry about the situation but he was glad it was over...the Patti situation anyway.

A few short months later, Horace met Tara. She looked like the actress Nia Long, and was already in college, working, and proud to be driving a new Mazda RX-7. She would park on the side of the house and sit in her car watching Lacy through the chain-link fence as he trained. Lacy thought she was waiting for Horace to come out but Horace was working at the grocery store during the times she would come by. One day, Tara got out of her car, walked up to the chain-link fence, and opened the gate as Lacy was training. Lacy asked what she wanted and she told Lacy she wanted him.

"WHAT? I'm not like that Tara," Lacy said. "You're with Horace."

Tara said, "He might be older, but you have it going on." The more she spoke the more irritated Lacy got with her because she thought she could just walk up and bat her eyes and he would disrupt the already chaotic homestead just for her. He told her he was training and needed to stay focused, then asked her to leave. She moved toward him and tried to touch him but Lacy stepped back and told her to leave. She told Lacy that she could buy him all the protein and food he needed to help him with his bodybuilding. Lacy went quiet for a moment, then he asked why she would do that. She said she liked a guy that was determined and focused on making himself better. Lacy told her he was definitely determined and focused but she was not for him and needed to leave, and if she left at that moment they could forget the whole thing. She told Lacy she would leave but she was not going to forget. Later that evening, Horace got home screaming and yelling at Lacy so Mom asked what was going on. Horace told Mom that Lacy went behind his back and asked Tara out, so Tara went to his job and broke up with him.

Mom looked at Lacy and said, "SPILL IT!" meaning "spill your guts and confess what you've done."

Lacy said, "That isn't what happened." He told her the real story and explained that he wasn't interested in her and she drove to their house and approached him. He told Mom that Tara was upset because he turned her down so she wanted to create a fight between Horace and himself because she didn't get her way. "Isn't that exactly what you told us to watch out for when it comes to women?" Lacy said to Mom. She slapped Lacy across the face and told him not to try and use her words against her, then she paused for a moment and told Horace that was exactly what was going on.

Mom told Lacy to go out with Tara and clean her out. She said, "If she's going to be a ho then treat her like a ho and leave her fancy pants ass with nothing." Lacy didn't say anything. "No, you won't do it will you," Mom said, "because you're too good for that. You'd rather see Horace get mistreated by that bitch than to help him get back at her."

Lacy asked, "Why do we have to get back at her? She's gone, so why not just leave her alone to fester in her own behavior."

"Fester…" Mom said, "in her own behavior…You will be used and taken by every woman you meet because you refuse to listen to me. You're gonna end up just like Joe Louis. He gave women all of his money and died broke. You lay down with dogs you'll get up with fleas. If a woman isn't helping you make money then she ain't shit. Now, get outta my sight Mr. Bodybuilder." Lacy walked away and went outside to go for a walk and was quite upset about what just happened. When Lacy was walking he ran into Jackie, so they walked together and talked. Jackie asked Lacy why he was quiet and seemed upset. Lacy didn't want to tell Jackie what happened and definitely not what Mom said. He asked if they could go to her house and hang out. She said sure. Lacy was at Jackie's house for about an hour and a half. When he was leaving, he and Jackie were walking toward the street from the front door and Horace turned the corner and saw them and gave Lacy a mean look. Jackie asked what that was about and Lacy said Horace was goofy and had many faces and not to pay any attention to him, then they said their goodbyes and Lacy went home. When he got home, he headed to the refrigerator to get some cold water and Mom asked where he was. Lacy looked at Horace because Horace had a huge grin on his face.

"Go ahead four-eyes," Horace said. "Tell Mom where you were."

With the refrigerator door open, Lacy kept his eyes on Horace and said, "I was over at my friend Jackie's house."

"Jackie? Who's Jackie?" Mom asked.

"She's a cute little chick down the street that Lacy's been talking to for a loooong time and hasn't even kissed yet," Horace said. Lacy kept his composure and kept looking at Horace, with the refrigerator still open.

"WHAT?" Mom said. "You've been talking to that girl for how long?"

Lacy said, "About six months."

"And you haven't kissed her?" Mom asked.

"No," Lacy said. His face was tensing up as he kept looking at Horace. Horace wasn't grinning as much and realized he crossed the line with Lacy.

"Close that refrigerator and get your ass over here," Mom said. Lacy walked over to her, still looking at Horace.

"Don't you have someplace to be?" Lacy asked Horace as he looked into Horace's eyes in a way that encouraged him to leave the room.

"Where are you going?" Mom asked Horace.

"I have homework," he said.

"You stay right here until I get to the bottom of this. Ain't no boy in this house gonna talk to a girl for six months and not get something in return. Are you gay?" Mom asked Lacy.

"No," Lacy said as he kept looking at Horace.

"Listen," Mom said, "you better stop looking at Horace and look at me before I knock the hell outta you. If you're not gay then why haven't you kissed this Jackie girl?"

Lacy said, "Because she's thirteen."

"What does that mean?" Mom asked.

"I'm sixteen," Lacy said. "She's too young for me and still has some growing to do."

"I don't care that she's thirteen," Mom said. "In some countries, they get married at thirteen. You need me to call someone to take you to a strip joint or somewhere to teach you how to screw?" she asked. Now Lacy was lit.

He looked at Horace and said, "Everything is fine. Horace over there likes to butt his nose in other people's business and make things seem worse than they are. Jackie and I are friends and that's it. She's not interested in me and neither am I."

"Then what good is the bitch?" Mom asked.

Lacy's eyes moved toward Mom and he said, "She's my friend."

"AAHHH HELLL! Friend," she said. "Okay, friend. When you're broke at the hands of a woman you'll need a friend to help wipe up your tears from being taken to the cleaners by a gold digger. Friend my ass.

You better keep your eyes open because she just might be training you to wash her panties like a little bitch." Lacy was trying to stay calm but his face told another story. "You better take that look off your face like you plan to do something to Horace because if I find out you did something to him I'll string your black ass up by your thumbs and beat you in front of your little friend...What's that bitch's name?"

"Jackie," Lacy said.

"Oh yeah, Jackie. Ain't nuthin' but a bitch." Lacy's eyes went to Horace again, then he smiled. Lacy and Horace had an understanding. Horace knew when Lacy smiled at him it meant they were going to fight. They once fought for two hours. They separated for a few minutes, then words flew and they started again. The day of the fight, they were home alone and they fought in every room in the house. It ended when they fell onto a bed and Horace rolled off while holding Lacy's arm and Lacy yelled loud enough for heaven to hear. He realized something must have torn or got strained, so he went buck wild and used his other arm and feet and stomped Horace into the floor until Horace begged him to stop. That was the last fight they ever had. Lacy couldn't train properly for a couple of months but his knowledge of joints helped him get around the shoulder issue. Mom never knew about that fight and Horace never told Mom any of Lacy's personal business again, and if he did, it didn't get back to Lacy. After that, Lacy started having much more fun with his friends because he didn't have to hide his emotions and sense of joy around the house as much. He still hid his emotions and joy when he was around Mom but not as much around the other boys in the family. He was careful with what he said and did but the situation was better. His friends recognized that he was more open but mentioned that he still seemed uncomfortable around his family. Sam was his oldest friend and only knew about five percent of what was going on while the others knew about three percent. The two brothers, Eric and Arthur, would ask questions, and Lacy would find a way to get off the subject but their father and mother knew something wasn't right. That was part of the reason why Eric and

Arthur would invite Lacy over after school before he trained. Their parents would feed Lacy. Lacy tried to be polite by only eating one helping but Eric and Arthur's parents knew Lacy was very hungry and told him to eat, eat, eat.

Their father would say, "Lacy, you gooon to be world shampiyoon! You must eat. So eaaaaaat."

Lacy would look at Eric and Arthur and they would say, "Listen to our mom and dad man. They believe in you, so eat man, eat. Don't worry man, you're with us. Just eat." So, Lacy ate and ate and ate. Then Eric, Arthur, and Lacy would listen to music while sitting around laughing about school stories, or play ping pong, then they would drop Lacy off at home so he could train. Lacy had already entered four teenage bodybuilding competitions and lost all of them, so he decided to take a year off from competing and train harder and get bigger and better. It worked. A year later he won third place in the Mr. Teenage Los Angeles competition then first place in his next two competitions. The more Lacy excelled the more Mom interrupted his training or restricted him from training, or she would find reasons to beat him. This caused Lacy to go back to his earlier practice of training at times when Mom wasn't around, but Randy would tell Mom of Lacy's training when Lacy would not run errands for Randy or put up with Randy's violent behavior. Mom and Randy realized that bodybuilding meant a great deal to Lacy and taking it away would be the only way to really hurt him because nothing else did anymore, not even the beatings. He was so used to the beatings that he wouldn't even cry or flinch anymore, until his final beating at age sixteen.

Although Lacy had never witnessed Mom drunk or out of control with alcohol, she had been drinking with some friends during a holiday and told Lacy to toss out some food that was left over. Lacy knew Mom's rule about wasting food. *If you waste food you would go to bed without dinner.* So, Lacy asked if she was sure she wanted it tossed out because it hadn't been touched. Mom yelled and told him to never question her and to move his ass and do what she said. One of her friends said, "Beatrice, that food is good and has not been touched. I don't think you want that thrown out." Mom thought her friend was protecting Lacy because many of her friends would. This made her more upset so she told Lacy if he didn't get that food out of her sight immediately she was going to beat his ass with a shovel. Since Mom had beaten his ass with everything but the kitchen sink, he had no reason not to believe her words, so he grabbed the food and took it outside to the trash then came back and finished washing the dishes and cleaning the kitchen. Then when he was watching TV, Mom wanted to know what happened to the food that was left over. He reminded her that she wanted it tossed out. She gave Lacy a backhanded slap across the face, knocking his glasses clean off his face and told him he was a damn lie. She told him to strip and meet her in Randy's room since Lacy still had no room or bed of his own. She returned with a wet, whip-like cord and went to work on him. Marcel and Randy were laughing hysterically until she finished and they saw his body. When Lacy turned to look in the mirror and saw his body, it was as if the life was knocked out of him. On that day, suicidal thoughts ran through his mind, not because he wanted to die but because he thought that would be the only way anyone including the police would see what had been going on. He thought the police would see a dead beaten body and make an arrest. But, many visions ran through his mind, including a little boy and two little girls that looked just like him. He saw himself running a business and speaking to people but he was much older. He stayed in the bathroom for two hours seeing visions and making promises to himself and God and did what he could to avoid and stay out of everyone's way in that house from that day forward.

ZOOM

The next day, Lacy saw his friend Sicilian Jimmy, known as SJ, and he asked Lacy why he was walking so oddly. Lacy took SJ to the school restroom, locked the door, and asked SJ to help him take his shirt off. SJ was shocked and thought a gang got to Lacy until Lacy explained. Lacy knew he could trust SJ to keep his secret because SJ saw his mom go through a similar situation with his father. SJ told Lacy he only had a little longer before he could leave home and be away from that hell and to remember his future that he shared with SJ. When Lacy was able to train again, instead of listening to the Isley Brothers' "Climbing Up the Ladder" before his workouts, he began listening to Lionel Ritchie and The Commodores' song "Zoom." It also became the song he would use to practice his bodybuilding poses as he got ready for competitions. That was when Lacy learned the meaning of choreography. He connected with Lionel Ritchie's words just as he connected with David Ruffin's words in the song, "I Wish It Would Rain" that he listened to when Esta left. He was able to connect his emotions with the singer's words and create poetry in motion with his body, and that was evident when he won the Best Poser award as well as the entire competition. Later, when Mom found out Lacy won the competition, she told him he got lucky because white people were not going to let him excel beyond a certain limit. She said the sooner he realized that the sooner he would stop his fantasies of being world champion and do something different like fashion photography, because it paid much more than the cost of a trophy. She also felt the promoters were using Lacy because he had become the guy to beat, as they put him on posters and wanted to feature him in two magazines and put him on the cover of a third magazine at age seventeen. Lacy looked at those trophies as confirmation that he was on the right track and knew the money would come later, but Mom didn't see it that way. She refused to let him do the magazines and that ruined his relationship with the promoters. It spread within the organization because they thought Lacy was someone who just pulled out at the last minute since he was afraid to tell them Mom said he couldn't do any publicity.

He was afraid they would contact her and ask for her permission and that would have pretty much gotten Lacy kicked out of the house for sure. Lacy accepted that Marcel and Horace could get Mom's support anytime they wanted. He believed she would get behind him when he started winning, but it seemed as if she became very jealous and bitter whenever Lacy would win, except when he won that race in the second grade. Back then, Lacy loved to run and run fast with friends, so Mom told him she signed him up for track. Lacy had no idea what track and field meant but quickly found out and didn't like it because he was running to compete with others and he just wanted to run with others for fun. Mom didn't care. She was selling a supplement called Shaklee Vitamins. She wanted to showcase Lacy's speed and sell the vitamins. Many could not keep up with Lacy, so he was racing the eighth-graders at school and various ages at local track meets. At that time, bigotry was alive and well, and Mom liked to expose it and slap it in the face any chance she got, but Lacy was too young to really understand his role and the bigger picture. One particular race was to be held in a part of town where some said a few KKK members lived. As Lacy and the family drove to the area, Randy kept telling Lacy to run fast and get the race over with so they could "get the heck outta dodge," which was slang for "get the heck out of there." There were so many boys on the starting line that it looked like it was going to be a marathon race, but it was the one-hundred-yard dash. "On your marks, get set, GO!" The boys immediately blocked Lacy and tried to trip him, but he elbowed his way through and pulled away from the pack and won the race by a long shot. "RESTART!" the announcer said. He thought Lacy must have started early because he was so far ahead, so the announcer called it a false start. "Ready, set, GO!" The boys crowded Lacy even more this time but he saw a gap and took it and ran the race by a long shot. "RESTART!" The announcer suggested taking a break for a few moments and trying again. Mom took Lacy to the car and pulled out his Buster Brown shoes with absolutely no traction and told him to remove his sneakers and put the Busters on. Lacy told her they weren't meant for running. *Slap!*

"You put those dern shoes on or I'll beat your little black ass right here in front of everyone. I want to make a point here today just like Jessie Owens did in Germany." She said, "Lacy put the shoes on," and was not smiling about it. When he went to the starting line almost everyone was laughing, including the runners. Lacy made up his mind that this was the last time he was going to run in that race no matter what happened, a beating or not. He kept his eyes on the finish line. The boys were teasing him horribly but he just focused on the finish line.

"Ready, set, GO!" Lacy left the starting line, slipping and sliding as if he were on ice, which caused more laughter in the stands.

Somehow, he caught traction and flew passed the boys, passed the finish line, and ran straight to the car. Randy ran after him and asked what he was doing. Lacy said, "I'm not running again, no matter what happens. This is wrong and stupid. All of it!"

"But you won," Randy said, "you have to get your ribbon."

"I don't want it," Lacy said. He stayed by the car and Randy went to get the ribbon. To avoid future races, Lacy said his leg hurt when he ran and thus, he never ran track again. Lacy learned to mask his happiness around Mom very well because showing his happiness made her angry and increased her desire to prevent his happiness. When he graduated the eighth grade, Gus asked Mom if Lacy could stay with him in Las Vegas for a few weeks that summer. Gus was still in the Air Force but he lived off base. Mom said yes and Lacy couldn't believe it. Gus drove out to pick Lacy up, and for three weeks he and Gus had a blast. Movies, go-karts, pinball arcades, eating out, car races, and Crash n' Smash Derbys with his friends and uninterrupted workouts. That was the first time in Lacy's life he felt free, but he certainly paid for that freedom. When Mom drove to pick Lacy up, she arrived with Mr. Lincoln. They got to Las Vegas a couple of days earlier to gamble and must not have done well. As Mom pulled the car away from Gus' apartment, Lacy could see the concern in Gus' face and the pit of Lacy's stomach was twisting and turning because Mom's face didn't look happy.

"So, you've been away for three whooooole weeks huh?" she said.

"Yes," Lacy said.

"Weeell, just to make sure you don't forget where you live I have your work all cut out for you." Lacy sat in the back seat wishing he was still at Gus' apartment. He wondered what Gus was doing while he was miserable in the back seat listening to Mom tell Mr. Lincoln how Lacy must think he was a big shot after staying in Las Vegas for three weeks. That went on for four hours all the way back home. They got home at about two o'clock in the afternoon. Mom told Lacy to put his things in the house and to meet her in the front yard. He met her in the front yard and she told him all of the things she wanted cut, mowed, and chopped, and when he finished the front he had to go to the backyard and do the same. By the time he finished all the work it was nearly eight o'clock that night and he had not had dinner yet. When he went into the house to get cleaned up, Marcel and Horace were watching TV.

Horace asked him if he had fun in the yard, then both Horace and Marcel laughed like hyenas. Mom heard their laughter but it was okay with her because Lacy was somehow feeding all of their cruel needs, but that need didn't seem as if it was quenched as Lacy got older. Lacy made a lot of friends and when they would visit his house, it wasn't easy for Mom, Randy, Horace, and Marcel to behave as they usually did. It was as if they knew they were being watched.

Sam, Eric, Arthur, and SJ were Lacy's longer-term friends, but Phil, Alex G, Frankie C, Speed, Johnny L, and many others became a good part of Lacy's life, and they had some great, great times at the dances, games, and just hanging out together, lying about who kissed who and who had sex with whom as teenagers do. Frankie and Speed weren't lying, but the others had to lie to keep up. Even though Lacy liked someone at school, he still was too fearful of his home life getting out. He spoke to different girls but just couldn't get himself to break past that fear. He ended up getting to know a girl called Stacy M. They spoke for quite some time but never dated. She went to one of his competitions and was supportive of his goals but she was focused on other things. Then, graduation came. Lacy had been speaking to friends about moving away from home and his friend Phil said he, his brother, and roommate were looking for a fourth person to move into the fourth room of a house they were renting. Eddie, their roommate, offered Lacy a job working with him in his construction and plumbing business. He told Lacy he would teach him as he worked. Lacy was excited and decided to move out immediately. Mom started a small side business selling clothes to a few customers, and she often took Lacy with her for safety since many of the customers lived in unsafe areas. After collections, Lacy told Mom he was moving out and to Lacy's surprise, Mom was disturbed by his decision. She pulled the car over with a very shocked look on her face and asked why. Lacy said it was time. She said that Randy, Marcel, and Horace hadn't even moved out yet. She asked if it was something she said or did. Lacy looked at her as if she had been in a daze for the last eighteen years.

He said, "It's just time." She teared up a bit and began driving and asked if there was something she could do to change his mind and he said no. She told Lacy she hoped he would change his mind because she wanted him to stay. Lacy just looked straight ahead at the road and thought to himself that this was the first time she had ever said anything like that to him. "No. I have to get out on my own and dance with the world," he said. "I believe I have a lot to do out there and it's time to start." Mom began driving the car and after about thirty seconds of silence, she told Lacy she hoped that he would find all that he was looking for and to remember that nothing was more important than family. She told him that he could pick his friends but he couldn't pick family and that was who would be there for him if he needed help. "Thank you," Lacy said. "I'll be fine."

"You don't like me, do you?" Mom asked.

Lacy looked at Mom and said, "This isn't about liking or not liking you. It's about loving myself and putting that love into my future."

"All for self," she said. "You think your bodybuilding will pay your bills and make you rich, then you won't have to be bothered by any of us, huh?"

"Mom," Lacy said. "I wanted to let you know I was moving out. I'm not sure what's going to happen but I need to figure it out, and Randy, Marcel, and Horace will have to do the same one day."

"Oh, you think once you move out Randy, Marcel, and Horace will see that you left then they will leave too. You just want to cause problems for me because you're upset with me."

"Not true," Lacy said. "Randy lived in Las Vegas with Gus but Gus had to kick him out since Randy made a move on his wife, remember? Gus made it clear if he saw Randy again, Randy was done and that was why Randy moved back home. We all have to stand as men and I've been ready for that for a long time."

"Oh, you have?" Mom said. "Well, Mr. Man, you do what you have to do but nobody gives handouts, so good luck."

"Thank you," Lacy said.

"You getting smart with me?" Mom asked.

"No. I mean it. Thank you for everything you said. I listened and I use all that I hear from you and everyone."

"Okay professor," she said sarcastically. It didn't matter to Lacy how she said it because her mentioning the word professor to him meant that she had not forgotten that he was the professor. He believed deep down she knew that he was very determined and wouldn't give up on his childhood dream of building a good future. When she called him the professor, he also had a flashback to the dream he had as a child where men were chasing him and he dove into the bushes to get away. He realized the power that Mom had over him along with the beatings and threats of being kicked out of the house was no more. What he was feeling at that moment was more than liberating. He felt very alive and ready for the world. When Mom and Lacy got home, he went to Horace's room to watch TV since Horace wasn't home. He turned on the television to watch VH-1, which was the premier music video channel at that time. They had very few new videos, so one of the artists they would constantly play was Prince. Lacy was a huge Prince fan because he once heard Prince say that he applauded people who brought originality to the table and had no interest in copycats. Lacy had spoken of originality since he was a child as he learned the word from Jasper. He admired Prince for his ability to be himself and for his mental flow and creativity. As Lacy was watching television, Mom walked in and told Lacy someone was on the phone that wanted to speak with him. When Mom told Lacy that someone wanted to speak with him on the phone, that usually meant there was someone on the phone that Lacy didn't know who was going to try to persuade him to do, or not to do something.

"Hello," Lacy said.

"Hi Lacy," an older male voice said, while sobbing a little.

Lacy had a real issue with men that he didn't know crying and carrying on without any explanation, especially after the numerous beatings he got and being told not to cry during them. "How may I help you?" Lacy asked.

"Help me, oohh, no I don't need no help. I want to congratulate you for graduating high school."

"Thank you," Lacy said. "That's very kind of you."

"Do you know who this is?" the man asked.

"Yes," Lacy said. "You're the guy on the other end of this phone line crying and congratulating me for graduating high school. Sound about right?" Lacy asked.

The man went quiet for a moment, then he broke out laughing and said, "Maaaaan, I like your spunk. You don't pull no punches and I like that. You gooone do aaaaarrrright. This is Joe."

Lacy said, "Hi Joe, thank you for sharing your name with me. Who are you?"

Joe sobbed a bit more and said, "Oooh, I'm a friend of yo mutha's. See, she and I go waaaaaay back. I've known your mutha since she was thirteen." As Joe kept talking, Lacy's mind started to drift, since he remembered long ago when he was eavesdropping on a conversation Mom was having with friends. She mentioned her parents dying early in her life and how she was in the streets at age thirteen and her aunts couldn't control her. Lacy wondered if she met Joe while she was in the streets. "Are you there?" Joe asked Lacy.

"Yes," Lacy said. "I'm here."

"I just wanted to tell you how proud I am of you and how different life will be for you. Yo mutha tells me you movin' out."

"I am," Lacy said.

"Weeeell, do you think that's a good idea?" he asked.

"I believe it's a great idea," Lacy said.

Joe said, "Weeell, I respect yo decision but just like Dorothy said in the "Wizard of Oz," ain't no place like home." Not only did Lacy find it irritating speaking with Mom's friends on the phone that spoke as if they knew him, but he was further irritated by those same people for not being around during difficult times and appearing much later and speaking so nonchalantly. Joe said, "You know it's a big world out there full of dangerous people and…" Lacy tossed the cordless phone onto Horace's bed and walked to Mom's room and told her they were done talking. Mom picked up the phone in her room and began talking, so Lacy went to hang up the other phone, then he went for a long walk just to get out of the apartment. Lacy didn't like being disrespectful, so if he was disrespectful to anyone it meant he had enough of whatever charade that was being presented to him. During Lacy's senior year of high school, the family house in West Covina, California was repossessed, so they moved into an apartment in Pasadena, California. Lacy missed West Covina, but he felt his journey and future would begin in Pasadena. As he walked the streets in Pasadena, he received many visions of his future. He must have been thinking about his past when all of a sudden, he got glimpses of the future. One glimpse was a vision of his own fitness business that would exist a few miles from the streets he frequented - Lake Avenue, Delmar, Colorado, and Green Street.

AEROBICS & NAUTILUS

As Lacy walked, he thought about his days growing up in La Puente before and after Esta left. He thought about West Covina and the barbecues in the backyard, riding bikes with Eric and Sam, being in Las Vegas with Gus for three weeks, going to high school football games with friends, and Marilyn's Backstreet night club for people under twenty-one. Lacy and Sam would go there all the time since it was a few blocks from where Lacy lived in Pasadena. As he thought about the fun times, he also thought about the tough times and told himself there was no room for that type of bullshit in his future, and anyone from the family that would try to engage in past drama would be avoided at all costs. Lacy worked at Aerobics and Nautilus Unlimited in Pasadena for a couple of months after graduation. He would open the club at six in the morning and leave at eight, just two hours later when the owner would arrive. He quit his job since he was moving back to La Puente to live with his roommates Phil, who was his friend from school, and Phil's brother Abe who was a teacher at the school. His third roommate was Ashraf, who everyone called Eddie. Eddie hired Lacy as his assistant in his plumbing and construction business and told Lacy he could work with him for as long as he wanted. Eddie was surprised at how fast Lacy learned and asked Lacy if he was sure he didn't want to go into the plumbing and construction business. Lacy said he really enjoyed learning how to build and fix things because it might come in handy in the future, but as a career, it wasn't for him.

Eddie laughed and said, "Yeah it's a lot of hours."

"Right," Lacy said. "It would be difficult to manage a bodybuilding career with a job like this." Eddie and Lacy were on the road by six in the morning and often wouldn't get back home until ten at night. Regardless of the time they got home, Lacy still got his workout in. He was still using Gus' equipment and the extra weights that Gus and his friends bought or gave to him, along with a bench press that Mom bought for Marcel and Horace that they never used and planned to throw away. Lacy's goal was to work with Eddie until he found a job with hours that would allow him to train and rest properly because the long days, as well as his workouts, were wearing him out. One day he was cutting a pipe for Eddie to install in someone's house and was so tired that he forgot to reach under the cutter and reached over it instead, slicing his arm right near his brachial artery. As soon as it happened, Lacy heard Eddie's voice in his head instructing him to never reach over the cutter because he could slice his arm.

"Where's that pipe Lacy?" Eddie asked.

"Coming up," Lacy said as he was bleeding and getting the pipe for Eddie. He gave the pipe to Eddie with his body turned at an angle so Eddie wouldn't see the blood, but Eddie was very sharp and asked Lacy if he was alright. Lacy didn't want to tell Eddie what happened because he thought Eddie might not want to work with him.

"Oh shit," Eddie said. "You're bleeding! Come here." He lifted Lacy's arm and said, "Hold on." He grabbed some supplies from the truck and cleaned up the wound and patched it up. He asked Lacy if he was alright and Lacy said yes, but he was embarrassed by the situation. Eddie said it was time for them to take a break anyway. They went to Old World Delicatessen on Amar and Azusa in La Puente. They went there a lot on breaks and Eddie would tell Lacy to eat to his heart's content because Eddie knew of Lacy's bodybuilding goals. During this time, Stacy from school would visit Lacy or he would visit her and her parents since he lived about five minutes away from them.

After working with Eddie for a couple of months, seven days a week, he received a call for an interview with Alpha Beta grocery store. Don the manager liked him right away and sent him to another store for training. After getting hired, Lacy was able to set a better training schedule, however, the store hours were too few, so Lacy needed a second job that would still allow for his training schedule. Lacy's friend Sam was attending Pasadena College and worked in the phone room at Aerobics and Nautilus Unlimited, and Lacy asked how he liked that job. Sam said it was fun and he made decent money. Lacy asked Sam if he would ask his boss if there were any openings. Sam said someone had just gotten fired so the manager needed someone as soon as possible, and gave Lacy the number for Mark the marketing manager. Lacy contacted Mark from upstairs and Mark told Lacy to come in for an interview. Lacy didn't have a car so he took the bus from La Puente to Pasadena, which took about one and a half hours one way. When Lacy arrived, Mark told Lacy he had a very good radio and television voice and wanted to see him in action. Lacy didn't know what that meant.

"Okay Lacy, watch me and do what I do." Mark opened the phone book to the white pages and looked for names and numbers in the Pasadena area. He said, "Here I go." He called a random person and when the person answered, Mark greeted the person with, "Hi. My name is Mark and I'm calling from Aerobics and Nautilus Unlimited. You've just won two free weeks to use our facility free of charge. When would you like to come in and get your two free weeks?" Mark hung up the phone and said that person clearly wasn't interested but some people would be and those were the ones you'd want to get in the club. Lacy asked how people won two free weeks. Mark asked why that was important to him.

Lacy said, "If a person asks how they won I must know what to say."

"Very good Lacy," Mark said. "That's not a question trainees tend to ask."

"Thank you," Lacy said. Mark said they put out lead boxes all throughout town that offer the chance to win a trip to Hawaii or passes to the club.

"Once we get enough entries in the lead boxes we do a draw to see who goes to Hawaii and who gets a free membership. But, all of the people that come in the front door give the sales team downstairs a chance to sell them a membership."

"What a great plan," Lacy said.

"Okay Lacy, let me see you in action." Lacy found a name and number and made the call, and the person Lacy called asked how they became a winner because they hadn't signed up for anything. Lacy told the person they entered a draw to win a trip to Hawaii or a free membership at the health club, and this was their first round of the draw and that they had won two free weeks. The person was so happy that they came in that same day and joined the club. Mark gave Lacy the job from three o'clock in the afternoon to six o'clock in the evening. That was just in time for Lacy to catch the bus back to La Puente. Things were looking up because Lacy would work in the mornings at Alpha Beta, train at the club in the afternoon before making phone calls, then return home. Although both jobs were going well, Lacy was getting some static from the assistant manager who was also named Don, like the manager. The assistant manager would tell Lacy much of what he was doing was wrong or that he was not cut out to work at a grocery store. Whenever Don the manager was nearby, he would praise Lacy for his eagerness to work and his willingness to help everyone even if it meant staying overtime. One day, Lacy was bagging groceries when a woman and her daughter told Lacy they recognized him from television. Lacy told them they may have seen him on "Eye on L.A." with Chuck Henry. He told them he won a competition and that it was aired on television.

"That's it! That's where I saw you," the woman said.

"Go put this away," Don the assistant manager said, as he threw his jean jacket at Lacy. The jacket landed on Lacy's head like an oversized hat.

Lacy pulled the jacket off his head and looked at the assistant manager and said, "That was not very nice," and he put the jacket on the counter.

"I told you to go put that away." The woman in line that Lacy was talking to suggested Lacy go put the jacket away so he wouldn't lose his job. Lacy thanked the woman for her concern and informed her that he was in the union and he wasn't hired to have things thrown at him or be humiliated in front of customers. The assistant manager went quiet and finished serving the customer, then he said, "Follow me," to Lacy. Lacy followed the assistant manager inside the cold storage area behind closed doors. The assistant manager stopped sharply, turned to Lacy with his hands on his hips and asked Lacy what his problem was. Lacy told him he had no problem and wanted to know why the assistant manager felt comfortable throwing his jacket at him. "I didn't throw it at you," the assistant manager said.

"The woman and her daughter both said it was rude of you to do what you did and I agree with them," Lacy said.

"You know, there was a time your ass would be dragging from the back of a truck for talking to me this way," the assistant manager said, as he moved closer to Lacy.

Lacy took his smock off and said, "It looks like you have something you want to say that doesn't require words." The assistant manager asked Lacy why he took his smock off. Lacy said, "You didn't bring me in this particular room to talk so let's do what you brought me here for or let's both get back to work."

"Why don't we just forget about this and get back to work," the assistant manager said.

"No," Lacy said. "I've been forgetting, overlooking, and giving people free passes for far too long. If you don't know how to behave yourself that's your shortcoming, not mine. I'm going to the manager's office right now to report you."

"Wait Lacy," he said. "I'm sorry, okay? I'm sorry."

"No, you aren't," Lacy said. "You're sorry you're in trouble but you're not sorry your bigotry slipped out." Lacy went to the manager's office and told Don the manager what happened. Don apologized for the assistant manager's behavior and said that the woman and her daughter also told him what happened. The following week, the assistant manager was transferred and working at the store was a much more pleasant experience for Lacy. Lacy wasn't seeing his roommates as often as before since he didn't get home until nearly nine o'clock in the evening. He had his sights on getting a car so he could cut down on travel time and see his roommates more. Just as he began to look for a car he found out Alpha Beta store number thirty-four, was closing. That was his store. He spoke with Don the manager about options and Don told him he could work at another store that was about an hour away since that was the only store that would have openings. Don also told Lacy that the entire company was having problems and they would close more stores over time. He told Lacy it was in his best interest to look for work outside the Alpha Beta store family. That was when Lacy asked Mark if he could get more hours in the marketing department at the fitness club. Mark told Lacy he didn't have more hours to give, so Lacy went downstairs and spoke with the owner about working with new trainees when they joined. Pat the owner told Lacy he would love having him downstairs since he was a great asset to the club as the marketing voice. But, he also told Lacy that as long as he worked upstairs he could not work downstairs unless he was fired from telemarketing. *LIGHTBULB MOMENT!* Lacy took a gamble and prayed it would work. He purposely pulled back on the number of calls he was making, allowing other telemarketers to pass his record in calls and arrivals for the sales department to talk to.

Mark didn't accept excuses or lack of progress so he fired Lacy within a couple of weeks. Lacy went downstairs and told Pat the owner he got fired from upstairs and Pat said, "Their loss. I'll have someone show you how to do tours, contracts, and sales." Lacy was very excited about getting the job downstairs because it would allow him to train people and inspire them as well as earn much more money for a car. When he got home that evening, his roommates told him that the owner of the house they were renting put it up for sale and they needed to be out within a couple of months. Phil and Abe were going to get their own place because Abe met a woman and wanted her to move in with them. Eddie told Lacy they could share a place together, but Lacy told him he couldn't afford the rent of a two-bedroom apartment and began looking for rooms for rent. He found a room for rent about two weeks before they were all supposed to be out of the house. Lacy was happy because the room for rent was within minutes of where he was currently living and the rent was lower than what he was currently paying. When he met the new guys, they were pleasant and kind but something told Lacy he would not live with them for very long. He wasn't sure what that vibe he got was about but moved in and hoped for the best. The first night he moved in he heard a knock at his bedroom window and pulled the curtain back. A guy spoke to him through the closed window, telling him that he was the old roommate and he knocked at the door but no one answered. Lacy said he would meet him at the front door. When Lacy opened the door, four guys rushed in past Lacy and the guy who was at the window walked in last and thanked Lacy for opening the door. Lacy's two roommates came out from the back of the apartment and exchanged some heated words with the old roommate and the guys who were with him.

The old roommate grabbed a few things, then left with his crew. One of Lacy's new roommates said, "Lacy, come with us." Lacy went with them and once they were outside in the dark of the night walking in the parking lot toward the old roommate, Lacy saw that his new roommate raised a gun and pointed it at the old roommate. The old roommate's crew raised their guns, and the old roommate grabbed a rifle out of the back of the truck and told Lacy's new roommate to lower his gun, and he did. The old roommate walked over to Lacy's new roommate while pointing the rifle at him and told him they were even. The old roommate told Lacy's new roommate he wasn't going to pay the final rent because of some altercation over a girl. Lacy quickly realized the girl that was inside the apartment when he moved in used to be the old roommate's girlfriend. The old roommate walked over to Lacy and cracked a smile while putting the gun right up near his chest, and thanked Lacy for opening the door. He told Lacy he looked like a bodybuilder.

Lacy said, "You're welcome, and I am a bodybuilder." The old roommate laughed hysterically and told Lacy most people would be shitting their pants if they had a gun at their chest. He was tickled that Lacy was able to hold a conversation as if there was no gun at all. Lacy wasn't sure what was going to happen but he remembered when he held the gun at Randy that the only thing that kept him from shooting Randy was the fact that he stayed very still. The old roommate was shocked to find out how old Lacy was, and a member of the old roommate's crew recognized Lacy from a bodybuilding show that was on TV. After making jokes about Lacy being bigger than all of them, the old roommate pointed the rifle back at Lacy's new roommate and told him Lacy seemed like a decent guy and that he should learn a thing or two from Lacy. The old roommate told Lacy good luck with all he did and to stay away from riff-raff if he wanted to be on top of the world. Lacy said, "Solid advice. Night to you all." The crew burned rubber, making a horribly loud screeching sound, and were gone.

"Solid advice?" Lacy's new roommate said. "They just robbed us."

"We could be dead but we're not," Lacy said. "I went with you guys because I thought someone wronged you but none of this is my business. I don't know what exactly happened with all of you and don't want to know." After that night, the roommates didn't spend any time together. Regardless, Lacy was too focused on work and training because he was getting ready for the Mr. America competition. Marcel would see Lacy walking toward the bus stop from the health club since Marcel worked minutes away. He told Lacy he should stop by the apartment and say hi to everyone. He told Lacy that Mom missed him. Lacy looked at Marcel and told him that Mom missed no one. Marcel told Lacy she told him that she missed Lacy. Lacy told Marcel he'd stop by. When Lacy stopped by for a visit, he, Mom, Randy, Horace, and Marcel all had dinner and spoke about what Lacy had been doing. Lacy talked about not living with Phil, Abe, and Eddie since the house got sold, and about having new roommates. He also spoke about his job and the Mr. America coming up. Randy told Lacy he should stay with them here and there to cut down on the bus travel.

Mom said, "Yes, that makes perfect sense so you don't run yourself ragged."

Lacy thought for a moment and said, "Okay. Thank you. That would help a lot right now." Randy patted Lacy on the back and told him to eat and relax. Of course, this meant Lacy would sleep on the floor again but that didn't bother him because he looked forward to the bigger picture and knew it was temporary.

Lacy would stay at the apartment with his roommates in La Puente two to three days a week and they would comment on his absence and how he must have met a girl or struck it rich. Lacy told them he was staying with his family from time to time. They asked when the competition was because they wanted to watch the show. He told them it was two weeks away. They also asked if he would be home days prior to the show so they could wish him luck in person. He told them that he would not be home that entire week before the show because he needed to keep his stress levels down because stress produced fat and caused water retention. They told him not to worry or get stressed because he would do fine and they would be there. He was now nineteen and was looking forward to competing in the Mr. America since it was to be held in Pasadena. When he got to the event, he quickly realized the other competitors were fifty to eighty pounds bigger than him. He placed very low and realized he had a lot more work to do. That night, Horace told Lacy that he'd come a very long way and shouldn't worry about the loss of the event. Lacy told Horace he wasn't worried but needed to get more serious. They decided to walk to Wichell's Donuts and bought a few, then went back to the house and spoke about what

Lacy had in mind for his future. Randy pulled up a chair and they all chatted about what Lacy had in mind. Lacy was careful with his words because he wasn't sure what the two may have been up to and why they had a sudden interest in Lacy's endeavors. The next day, Lacy went home to La Puente and knew his roommates were going to tease the heck out of him for placing so low. When he got home he was shocked to see that the new roommates had emptied out the apartment and had taken all of his things, including his training equipment. He went to the manager's office and asked if she knew what happened and she said his roommates moved out days earlier and that they moved in a big hurry without paying rent. She told Lacy that he wasn't responsible for their rent, just his. As they began walking away from each other she told him to wait a moment as she ran back to her office. When she came out of her office, she reached out and handed Lacy one of his competition photos and told him she found it on the floor of the apartment. He told her it was from his photo album. At that moment, he realized those roommates plotted to take his things long ago and that was why they wanted to know if he would be home prior to the competition. It made more sense to Lacy why that old roommate showed up with a crew and guns and how the earlier vibe he had of not living there long was right on point. He was beginning to trust his instincts more and remembered what Jasper told him when he was four years old: set up the Army men strategically to discourage a war rather than to engage in one. Since he couldn't afford the apartment by himself and had no time to find roommates, he stayed at Mom's house seven days a week.

It wasn't long before staying at Mom's house began to feel as it did before. Like the earlier days, Lacy did what he could to avoid spending too much time around Mom, so he would meet with Sam or two other friends he made at the health club, Frank and Wael. They would go to Marilyn's Backstreet under twenty-one club or just hang out at Conrad's Restaurant or a cafe and talk all night about their futures. It seemed that every day Mom wanted Lacy to help drive her during collections but he couldn't with his schedule. Lacy also knew Mom didn't just want him to help with collections, she wanted him to help her sell more clothes. Lacy always liked fashion and knew how to pick the right outfit for anyone, but he thought it was a very, very bad idea to work with Mom based on their past. Randy kept telling Lacy he would make more money if he worked with Mom and got into fashion photography. Horace, Marcel, and Randy were so much more available and didn't do much during the day, so Lacy couldn't figure out why Mom was pressing him so much about going with her. Randy told him that bodybuilding was a white man's game and that Lacy didn't fit into it and he knew nothing about business so he'd already lost. Lacy told Randy that he spent his entire life telling others what they couldn't do but he'd never shown the world or himself what he could do. Randy told Lacy he had a smart mouth.

"Where do you think I learned to talk like this?" Lacy asked Randy.

"Just watch yourself," Randy said.

"Yep, you do the same," Lacy said. At that moment, Randy's eyes and expression showed that he realized Lacy was now a lion and no longer a cub to push around. Mom heard that exchange between Randy and Lacy and told Lacy he was only a guest and needed to watch how he spoke to Randy. Deep down inside, Lacy always felt like a guest but hearing her say that helped keep him focused on moving out as soon as possible. He spoke to Frank and Wael and another friend Diego about becoming roommates since they all lived in Pasadena with their parents. They all wanted to move out, but they were in no position to live on their own. Each day, Lacy would try to find a roommate because he could sense that things at Mom's house were not going in a positive direction. When Lacy was walking to work early one morning, a man that looked like Morgan Freeman asked Lacy if he could spare some change for him to get something to eat. Lacy said sure, then gave the man some money.

The man said, "Thank you, and please don't ever lose that smile and the light that shines around you."

"You see a light?" Lacy asked the man.

"Anyone would have to be blind not to see it, but be careful because people will be envious, jealous, and want to use you and take from you." Lacy's eyes widened because that's what Esta told him long ago.

"Do I know you?" Lacy asked the man.

"No, I'm just a homeless man that needed some money to eat. But, you be careful," he said, "and be careful of family, friends, or anyone in your life that can't see your light and appreciate it. The people that need you or want to help you do what you are here to do will find you. Promise me you'll be careful with your light and that you will do your best young man."

"I promise," Lacy said. They went their separate ways and Lacy continued walking to work when he felt a presence around him that he felt many times in his life. It was that same invisible energy force that moved near him when he was four years old sitting in the rocking chair. He looked over his shoulder at the man he just spoke with, but the man was nowhere to be seen. As he continued walking, he saw himself in a small fitness studio that looked like the description he shared with Marcel years earlier. It felt as if that fitness studio was somewhere close. The video-like images he saw in his mind showed people coming and going with smiles on their faces and a mountain in the background. Then, in an instant, that vision and those images left as quickly as they came, and so did the energy or force he felt near him. When he got to work, he was on a natural high because he knew that vision he had was going to happen. He also thought about what the older man said about being careful. Each day after that, he hoped to see that man again but never did. Several days later, Lacy was walking to the fitness club to work out and a reporter from the Pasadena Weekly Newspaper named Ted Soqui saw Lacy walking and turned his car around, got out of his car, and walked up to Lacy and told him that he saw him walking around here almost every day. Ted asked Lacy if he was a football player because of his size. Lacy told Ted he was a natural drug-free bodybuilder.

"Really?" Ted said. Ted told Lacy that he always looked happy and walked as if he didn't have a care in the world. Lacy smiled and said thank you. Ted told Lacy he wanted to do a story on him. Lacy looked shocked and thrilled at the same time.

"What kind of story?" Lacy asked.

"The kind of story people need to read," Ted said. "You're a very positive person from what I've seen almost daily, and just speaking with you I can tell you're going places and are as sharp as a tack. You are an inspiration, and I want people to be inspired by you and the story I write."

When Ted said that he wanted people to be inspired he pressed the right button with Lacy because inspiring people was what he believed his future was all about. When Lacy and Ted met for the interview, they met at the gym where Lacy worked out. Lacy was excited to get started. Ted wanted to start by taking photos of Lacy training and interview him afterward. Ted told Lacy once he worked out he would probably be more relaxed for the interview.

"Good idea," Lacy said. He told Ted the only other interview he'd done was on the hit TV show "Eye on L.A." with Chuck Henry, after winning Mr. Teenage California.

"You interviewed with Chuck Henry?" Ted asked.

"Yes," Lacy said, "but it was backstage and very fast."

Ted looked at Lacy and said, "Man, you're definitely going places. Let's get started."

Ted asked Lacy where he grew up and Lacy said, "La Puente, West Covina, and Pasadena, California."

"Cool," Ted said. "Do you come from a big family?"

"Yes," Lacy said.

"Tell me about them," Ted asked. Lacy got quiet and froze.

"You okay Lacy?" Ted asked.

"Yes. I'm fine. I just thought you wanted to ask questions about me, so when you asked about my family it confused me."

"OOH! I see," Ted said. "Okay. Let me start the recorder again."

"Do we have to use a recorder?" Lacy asked.

"Yes, but it's just for me so that I don't lose or miss great material as I'm writing."

"Okay," Lacy said. "I'm the youngest of nine children."

"NINE CHILDREN!" Ted shouted.

"Yes," Lacy said. "Ted?"

"Yes," Ted replied.

"Is it ok if we don't get into family questions because I don't feel comfortable with that."

Ted put his pen and pad down, turned off the recorder, and looked Lacy right in his eyes and said, "I understand. We don't have to get into family. This will be a great article, I promise." Ted said, "Lacy, regardless of what may have happened back then, you, my friend, are a good man and it's easy to see that. Promise me one thing Lacy."

"What's that Ted?" Lacy asked.

"Promise me that you will inspire as many people as you possibly can with your presence and words just as you've inspired me."

Lacy grew a big grin and said, "That will be easy. I promise, so help me God!" They continued the interview and Ted printed it and titled it "Mr. Pasadena." That article raised the interest of local residents. When people joined the health club they recognized Lacy from the article and wanted to train with him. The owner of the club told Lacy that he was happy that Lacy got out of the telemarketing when he did, otherwise, he'd be hidden upstairs and no one would see him.

"I have a feeling you're going to have a place of your own in the not too distant future Lacy," the owner said. Lacy told him that was his goal and the owner told him he would reach it.

Some time had passed since Lacy saw that man on the street that asked him for some change. What that man shared with Lacy stayed on his mind as well as the vision he had that day of his own fitness studio. One day he was watching TV in Horace's room since Horace wasn't home. Usually, when Lacy would watch TV he wasn't really watching what was on because his mind rarely stopped going. He was always thinking of his next move and further goals.

Randy walked in and asked what Lacy was watching and Lacy said, "Nothing really, you can change the channel to whatever you want to watch."

"I know that nigga…uh, Lacy. I know that. I don't need your permission."

"Right," Lacy said. "I was letting you know I wasn't watching anything in particular or paying attention to the TV because I was thinking." Randy asked what Lacy was thinking about. Lacy told him that he planned to meet his friends at Pasadena City College soon since they had all spoken about taking classes. He said he was thinking about whether he should take classes or not.

"Is that why you looked so serious when I walked in?" Randy asked. Lacy said he was also thinking about the day he would have his own fitness studio and how good it would feel to help people feel and look like they want to.

"You really think you're going to have a fitness studio one day Lacy?" Randy asked.

"I will," Lacy said.

"Bahahahahahaha." Randy laughed and said, "Check it out maaaan, check it out. They'll be naming cars and planes after me before you have your own fitness studio. Bahahahaha. I don't mean to laugh, but you wouldn't know the first thing about opening and running a fitness studio."

"You do realize I'm currently working at a fitness club now and they are teaching me everything about running a club, right?" Lacy asked.

Randy stopped laughing and said, "They are only teaching you enough to be their slave for pennies and that's it."

"Randy," Lacy said.

"What maaan. Tell me something I don't know Lacy. Come on. I'm waiting."

"Okay," Lacy said. "You said they only pay me pennies."

"That's right," Randy said.

"Do you remember when I was thirteen I told you if I could make one penny at something I could make millions of pennies at that same thing?" Lacy asked Randy.

"I do remember that," Randy said.

"Well, this is the earlier stage of those pennies," Lacy said. "Do you remember many years ago when Marcel asked what my fitness studio would look like and I described it for him?"

"I remember that," Randy said.

"Do you remember that he drew it to scale and it was long and oddly shaped with a drinking fountain in the corner near the back?"

"Yeah man. I remember that whole thing, so what?" Randy said. "I also remember Marcel drawing a picture of you walking down a street with a rolled-up unemployed certificate in your hand. Hahahahaha."

"Yes," Lacy said, "but that was Marcel's mental perception of himself and he was trying to project his negativity onto me. I know you would rather laugh than believe in truth Randy, but you do remember that dream I had of John Brown?"

Randy said, "Yeah. The bodybuilder who came up to you backstage in your dream and told you that you were going to win that show in your dream, then a couple of weeks later that actually happened. How could I forget that Lacy? You wouldn't shut up about it."

"That's just it Randy, you and others think shutting up is best but I'm not supposed to shut up, especially if I am to help others."

"HELP OTHERS? Nobody needs your help. What you need to do is get after that nurse from the fitness club I saw you walking with."

"Debra?" Lacy asked.

"Yeah her. She's got legs for days and I heard that ass talking a mile away."

"She's ten years older than me and needs someone her speed."

"Man, if I was you I'd be tapping ass on all those girls I see you with, especially that model that hangs out with Magic and Arsenio."

"I know who you're talking about Randy but that's not what I need right now."

"No! That's exactly what you need Lacy. You need to be fucking your brains out on a regular basis but you're runnin' round here playing businessman. You know what your problem is Lacy?"

"What?" Lacy asked.

"You've watched so many of those old black and white movies and think just because you believe you can be a big businessman it will happen."

"No," Lacy said. "We are all here for a reason and sitting around doing nothing with my life is not the reason I was born. We all started out swimming to get to the uterus to be born into the outside world, but once we're born we should just sit in a corner and do nothing?" Lacy asked Randy.

"Fooo! The way you talk you *NEED* to be in school getting a degree as a teacher. You'd be good working with children and teens and teaching them a thing or two."

"I'll be helping them in the future with or without school."

"Sam and Eric are in college," Randy said.

"Yes, and that's great for them. There are so many people telling me to go including customers at the club. Frank, Wael, Diego, and I will meet in a few minutes to talk about maybe taking some helpful courses at Pasadena City College. I've considered night school because that's the only time I have now, but I really feel like I need to stay on the course of what I'm doing or I'll miss the timing and opportunities that are on the way."

"On the way?" Randy asked. "There are no guarantees in life and you could get hurt while training and your bodybuilding career would be over."

"Randy," Lacy said, "bodybuilding is just part of the equation and not the total sum of my goals."

"Then maybe you should consider taking some business courses so you can become a millionaire and buy me a daily supply of Fat Burgers."

"You and your Fat Burgers and Doritos," Lacy said.

"All day every day," Randy said. "Alright man, finish telling me what you were saying about the drawing Marcel did."

"The fitness studio I saw in my mind that I described to Marcel is the studio I believe I will have." Lacy said, "I was walking on Lake Avenue some time ago and I had a vision of my own studio that wasn't far from here. I saw many people with smiles on their faces and I was pretty happy too."

"A vision huh," Randy said.

"Yes," Lacy said. "I also saw a mountain in the background of the vision and the location felt close by."

"What do you mean it felt close by?" Randy asked.

"It's a feeling. Just like when you feel you have to go to the bathroom. You feel when you have to go to the bathroom and there is no confusion about that feeling so you go to the bathroom. I will have a fitness studio of my own and I believe the club where I am now is a stepping stone for me."

"Weeeeelll, weeee goooooone seeeee," Randy said.

"Randy, when I was nine years old you said one day we would pay to watch TV, pay for bottled water, and by the time I was of age to buy a house they would cost at least one million dollars. How could you have been so right about those things and not see me with a thriving fitness studio helping many people?"

"Because there are no black Jack LaLannes and you're too young to fill those shoes, but good luck and don't say I didn't warn you."

"Randy," Lacy said, "long ago you told me I'd never beat you in Monopoly but after one hundred and seventy games I beat you. You told me I'd never beat you on the pool table but we played over two hundred consecutive games and I finally beat you."

"Negro! What's your point?"

"I waited a long time to be an adult and now I'm here and it's time to perform," Lacy said. "If I was patient enough to beat you, you don't think I'll use that same patience to reach my goals?"

Randy said, "Patience or no patience, don't say I didn't warn your ass."

"Randy," Lacy said, "in the future, you will see me doing all that I've told you and I hope you'll be able to swallow your pride and say congratulations."

"Congratulations my ass. You ain't doin' shit that white folk don't let you do."

"Let's talk straight Randy. Have white people or white cops or white guards stopped you from getting into trouble? Because if they haven't then stopping me will be even harder. What I am to do in life has already been written, I just need to act out the lines in the script. We all have a purpose as I've said for years but that purpose has no legs if we have no desire to step up to our purpose one hundred percent."

"Dude, I'm outta here but don't say I didn't warn you."

"We'll both see soon enough," Lacy said. Randy went to the kitchen to get some Doritos and Lacy went to meet Frank, Wael, and Diego at Pasadena City College, which was just a few blocks away from Mom's apartment.

Once they all met up, they all agreed to take some courses. They had their transcripts sent to the college and were in class by next term. The others went to school during the day, so they spent less time together since Lacy had classes at night. During class, Lacy met Barbara, a girl who looked like Tisha Campbell. They sat near each other and ended up speaking before each class. One night she asked Lacy why he was studying English and he told her that he believed everyone should be good at speaking and understanding their own language. He said as a businessman he wanted to make sure he was crystal clear to his customers. Barbara asked what business he was in. He told her he was building his private one-on-one fitness training business. She told Lacy she admired his professional attitude then asked if he would come to watch her softball game the next day. He told her that tomorrow he would be busy with training, working, and working on his business plans. Right there on the spot, Barbara told Lacy that he was the type of guy she was interested in and wanted to get to know him. She asked if they could get a bite to eat after class. He was about to say yes, but when she said she wanted to get to know him, he told her that he already had plans. Since she was a very inquisitive person, Lacy figured that he was in for a ton of questioning that would eventually lead to questions about family. He was really not ready for that.

Barbara said, "Well maybe when you get some time you'll let me know."

"Barbara," Lacy said. "I can see you're a cool person and a lot of fun to spend time with but I'm not attracted to you that way. Please forgive me if we don't get together." Barbara looked at Lacy and told him he was the first guy to ever be upfront and honest with her.

"Most guys say "sure," or "I'll call you," then don't. Thank you Lacy for your honesty and not stringing this along."

"You're welcome," Lacy said, then they smiled at each other and said they would remain class friends. On that same night after class, Lacy was walking through the center of campus and saw a girl he'd seen several times after class. She looked like Clair Huxtable from the Cosby show. They connected eyes each time and usually only smiled at each other, but that night he said hello. She said hello and asked Lacy if he enrolled recently because she didn't see him last semester. He said yes and introduced himself and asked for her name.

"Gigi Williams," she said.

"Nice to meet you Gigi," Lacy said. "Now when we pass each other we don't have to keep looking over our shoulder wondering who the other person is."

"Hahahahaha." Gigi laughed and said she liked a sense of humor.

He said, "So do I. It will be your turn to say something funny next time we pass each other."

"You're on," she said, then they said goodnight. As Lacy began walking, Barbara walked up to Lacy and asked who the girl he was talking to was.

"What?" Lacy asked.

"Who were you talking to?" Barbara asked. "I just asked you out for a bite to eat and you said no and now you're out here chatting up some other girl."

"You are correct," Lacy said. "You asked me out for a bite and to watch your softball game but I told you I was not attracted to you and you thanked me for my honesty."

"Yeah, and now you're out here chatting up Miss Thang instead of me."

"Barbara, thank you for your interest but I don't need any of this right now. I'm really not the type of guy that you would be happy with because I would end up telling you to go straight to hell if you made a habit of talking to me this way and I really don't want to do that. So, please have a good night and any interactions we have in the future are only going to happen during class about classwork and it will only be casual conversation."

"No. You can just get fucked," she said as she hurried away. Girl must have been reading Mom's playbook, Lacy thought to himself. When he got home, he ate and thought about Barbara and was inspired to write some notes down about how to deal with dissatisfied or verbally hostile customers. Then, he went to bed. The very next day at the fitness club, Lacy was working with a woman, and her girlfriend walked in and slapped her, then asked why she had not called her. Lacy was stunned since much of the slapping he'd seen up to that moment was Mom slapping Esta or the sisters, or Alexandra slapping Randy. But this slap knocked the glasses off the woman's face, leaving a scratch.

"Don't you even think of interfering," the woman with the power slap said to Lacy.

"Who are you?" Lacy asked.

"I'm her other half," she said.

"Oh. Okay. Uh. Okay. Listen, slapping, fighting and losing control will not solve anything and I don't want to see anyone get hurt, so if you'd like I can take you both upstairs so you can speak in private if you promise not to wreck the joint and really talk."

"Why should we go upstairs?" the slapper asked.

Lacy said, "If you two don't leave I can promise you that your girlfriend will feel very embarrassed by what just happened and may happen, but if you go upstairs and leave later in a much better mindset you will both be happier."

"You must be that fitness instructor she told me about that helps people get through their shit while making their bodies look good."

"Fitness trainer, yes," Lacy said. The slappee asked if they could go upstairs, so Lacy took them upstairs and when he went back down he sat at one of the desks and thought about the time when he and Marcel got into a fight late at night in the backyard. Marcel kept swinging a baseball bat at Lacy, pretending to hit him, and Lacy told him to stop but he didn't and hit Lacy in the leg. Lacy dove at Marcel and got him on the ground and began punching him until Randy and Horace ran outside to stop the fight. Randy grabbed Lacy from behind and pulled him off of Marcel, and Marcel got up quickly to race toward Lacy. Horace grabbed Marcel from behind just as Marcel launched a kick toward Lacy. Lacy's arms were confined by Randy's bear hug so when Horace grabbed Marcel, Marcel fell back while his kick was in full launch and his foot hit Lacy in the face. The kick broke the lenses out of Lacy's wire-framed glasses and the wire frame tore into his eyelid and blood flew everywhere.

Lacy broke free of Randy's bear hug and went after Marcel again, knocking him to the ground, and Horace shouted, "LACY YOUR EYE!" Lacy didn't stop. He had enough of Marcel and it was time to make sure Marcel knew his bullying days were over.

"Lacy, it's dripping all over your face," Randy said.

"I feel the sweat dripping," Lacy said, "and I'm used to sweat, and if I have to sweat all night teaching this idiot to stop bullying people so be it."

"NO LACY! IT'S BLOOD," Randy shouted. Lacy looked at the ground and saw the blood then looked at Marcel and went at him again. "No, we have to get you to the hospital." After the hospital visit and several stitches later, Lacy was back home and Randy told Lacy to lie in his bed and just rest. Marcel entered the room and told Lacy they weren't finished.

Lacy sat up and said, "Wrong. I'm not finished. Cross me just one more time. Just one more and you will stay at the hospital for a few days, you poor excuse for a human being."

"Hey, hey, you two. Don't you think there's been enough fighting tonight?" Randy said.

"Stitches or no stitches, I'm never too tired to deal with him. He's a disgrace and has a very dark sense of humor and takes pleasure in other people's pain. Get out Marcel."

"Lacy, I hear you man but just relax before you damage your stitches. They said it was very close to your eye and you need to get that swelling down," Randy said. Lacy lay back down and focused on a time when all of that chaos would be over.

"Lacy!"

"Yes. What's up?" he asked the coworker.

"You must have been daydreaming because I called you like four times."

"Sorry, yes. That situation earlier with the two ladies got me thinking about something but I better go up and see how they are."

"Yep," the coworker said. "We don't want to be on the evening news for a domestic situation that became a club situation."

"Don't worry," Lacy said. "I can tell they really care for each other but someone is holding secrets that need to come out."

"How do you know that?" the coworker asked.

"I just know," Lacy said. Lacy went to get the ladies, and when they came down they both apologized for the display. The slapper thanked Lacy for having them go upstairs and they agreed with each other to talk and be more open and not to keep unnecessary secrets from each other. Lacy smiled and told them he was happy he could help and that he would see the slappee on her next visit and hoped her glasses weren't broken.

When Lacy walked to school after work he thought about what happened at the club with the two ladies, his recollection of the fight with Marcel, and the first time he got hit with a baseball bat and needed glasses. He was four years old. Lacy went to the garage to get the Big Wheel that Esta got for him. Odessa was in the kitchen swinging a baseball bat because she was practicing her swings for the softball team tryouts. When Lacy went to the garage, she told him to stay out of the kitchen. He told her that he was going to get his Big Wheel from the garage to sit in the living room to watch TV. Odessa told him to hurry up so he rushed to get his Big Wheel. When he was trying to pull the Big Wheel up a couple of steps and hold the kitchen door open at the same time, the door kept closing on him. The door had a spring or a hydraulic capsule at the top of the door, forcing it to close after it was opened. Lacy got the bright idea to push the door open with his back while holding the handlebars of the Big Wheel. As he made his way into the kitchen, the baseball bat hit him in the center of the back of his head, causing him to fly over the big wheel and into the garage, landing on the concrete floor head first. His head was ringing and he tried to stand but fell down and couldn't get out the yell that was somewhere in his throat. He was holding the back of his head and all of a sudden…"HAAAAAAAAAAAAAAAAAAAAA! EEEEEEEEEEEEEEEEE" sounds came out, simultaneous with inhalation, then, "HAAAAAAAAAAAAAAAAA!" He was crying so loudly that Alexandra ran to see what happened. When she asked what happened, Lacy pointed at Odessa because he was crying too much to get his words out. Odessa told Alexandra she accidentally hit Lacy with the bat.

Alexandra shouted, "ACCIDENT!?" She jumped on Odessa and wrestled her to the ground and told her that she shouldn't be playing with the bat in the house in the first place. Alexandra stopped fighting with Odessa and said they needed to check on Lacy to make sure he was okay. They got Lacy to calm down and offered him candy, cookies, and other goodies to make him feel better. They put ice to his head for the bumps. Both sisters agreed not to speak of this again or tell Mom. A few days later, Mom heard Lacy telling Gus that he could see three Gus' instead of one. Mom grew tired of Lacy saying this and shook him and told him to stop acting stupid. Gus told Mom that he thought something was wrong with Lacy's eyes because one was turned in near his nose. Mom looked at Lacy and realized Gus was right. That was when Alexandra told Odessa to tell Mom what happened. Odessa started crying and told Mom what happened. The next day, Lacy got his eyes checked and the doctor mentioned the abnormalities caused by the blow to the head and told Lacy he would need glasses from that day forward. He also told Lacy if he ate carrots until he was thirteen he would no longer need glasses. When Lacy turned thirteen he realized the doctor was just trying to get him to eat his vegetables, which was never an issue in the first place.

When Lacy got to his class at Pasadena City College, he thought one day he would write a book regarding these episodes of his life, hoping to inspire others to strive for their best regardless of their circumstances, their past, and where they came from. Barbara looked over to Lacy and said, "Hey you." Lacy said hello, then they listened to the teacher while Barbara looked at him a couple of times, but he ignored her. After his class as Lacy was walking toward the center of campus, he saw Gigi. She flashed a big bright smile and said she had not thought up a good joke and gave him her phone number and told him to call her so they could get together. She kept walking as if she were in a hurry to get somewhere.

Lacy turned in her direction, which was the direction he had just come from and said, "I'll call you later Gigi." Barbara was standing a few feet from where Gigi was walking. Barbara gave Gigi a mean stare but Gigi just kept walking and Lacy liked that because he saw Gigi as confident and proactive but not over-the-top arrogant as he saw Barbara. Barbara shouted to Lacy that he could do better and Lacy just smiled and headed home.

THE IMPORTANT THINGS

The next day, Lacy put out flyers offering his private training. He put them on car windshields, restaurant seats, inside the fitness club, and handed them out to people at the mall. He also put flyers out at the college for students to help him recruit customers. He offered to pay students for each new customer. Lacy began getting customers but didn't know what to charge people as he never thought about it. He put so much time and effort into his plan to help others and how he would help them that he forgot to set a price. Minimum wage then was three dollars and thirty-five cents so that was what he charged per hour. People loved that price and flocked to train with him. Many customers told him his price was too low for all the work he did with them. One person suggested raising the price to ten dollars and another person suggested fifteen dollars but another said five dollars. Lacy raised the price to seven dollars per session and everyone was happy. A few weeks later, the fitness club owner said that he sold the club and then introduced all of the workers to the new owner. The first owner introduced Lacy to the new owner and told him that he should make Lacy the manager of the entire club. The owner's eyes widened and he asked Lacy how old he was. Lacy said he was nineteen, and the new owner laughed.

The first owner said, "Laugh all you want but many of the people that are in here right now are here because of Lacy."

The new owner stopped laughing, grabbed Lacy's hand and said,

"Congratulations, you're my new manager." Lacy looked at both men and said thank you to both of them. Later, Lacy spoke with the first owner and asked what he should ask for in terms of salary. The first owner told Lacy that he should ask for five percent of all sales and a weekly salary of nothing less than two hundred dollars. Lacy shook the first owner's hand and thanked him, and went to the new owner to speak about terms. The new owner told Lacy that he would rather give him ten percent of sales and no salary. Lacy told the new owner that sounded like a good deal but if he got paid from sales alone he would want fifteen percent of sales to make up for no salary. The new owner agreed with the previous offer of five percent of sales and two hundred dollars as a weekly salary. Within three weeks, the new owner disappeared and wasn't responding to Lacy's phone messages. Lacy called the first owner to ask if he heard from the second owner and he said the second owner ran out of money and was closing the club. Lacy had collected cash and checks from people that had joined within that time, but he never saw the owner so he kept the funds in a locked desk drawer. The landlord put a notice on the front door that said to pay or quit and soon the phones were turned off. Lacy gathered all of the numbers of people that recently joined and called them. He went to a red English-style phone booth at the Burlington Arcade in Pasadena on Lake Avenue and called several people to meet with him to get their money back and told them he had no idea what was going on. A couple of people told him to keep the money they paid as a reward for his honesty and kindness. Others met with Lacy to get their money back, and a few became Lacy's clients because they trusted him. One day when Lacy was at the empty building waiting for people to arrive to get their money back, a guy walked in and asked what happened to the fitness club. Lacy told him he wasn't exactly sure. The guy told Lacy he was an accountant and financial planner and if he needed help to call him. Lacy told the man that he wanted to do what he could to keep the club open and asked the man if he had interested investors. The man gave Lacy his card and told Lacy to call him the next day. Lacy and the man met up the next day, along with the man's partner. After a lengthy discussion, it was clear that trying to keep the club was not in Lacy's best interest, but he now had connections with an accountant and financial planner. A few days later, Lacy arrived at the building and all of the equipment and furniture were gone. Lacy called the second owner and finally got him on the phone. He apologized to Lacy profusely and told Lacy he had good intentions but got in over his head. Lacy told the owner that he gave people their money back.

"Why did you do that Lacy?" the owner asked.

"Because it's theirs," Lacy said.

"No," the owner said, "technically it's mine."

"No," Lacy said. "They paid to join a health club and there is no health club."

The owner hung up on Lacy and that was the last time they spoke. At that moment, Lacy realized he didn't want to have a large fitness club but a small private studio instead, where people paid for the service weekly to avoid payment and service issues. Many of the people he was training joined Aerobics and Nautilus Plus just a few blocks away near the corner of Lake Avenue and Delmar Boulevard. Lacy joined that club and continued training his clients there. It seemed that more people were contacting Lacy for training, but it was difficult for many to maintain a schedule with their busy lives. Lacy didn't have the luxury of using the equipment whenever he wanted to like he did at the other club. At this new club, he was a member and not an employee or manager, so he had to wait for all of the equipment he wanted his clients to use, which interrupted sessions greatly. One night, he was in class but was more focused on how he was going to provide a better service for his customers than the schoolwork in front of him.

"Lacy," Barbara said.

"Hi," Lacy said.

"You seem spaced out," she said. "Are you okay?" He said he was just thinking some things through that needed to be taken care of and thanked her for asking. She told him he didn't have to thank her.

"I appreciate your concern," he said. The class ended and she asked if he wanted to walk with her. He said no because he wanted to speak with the teacher. She said okay and left. Once all of the students left the room, Lacy asked the teacher if he had a moment to speak with him.

"Sure Lacy. Come on up here. What's on your mind?" he asked. "By the way, I just wanted you to know that you are doing great in my class and I'm happy to have you here."

"Thank you for that," Lacy said. "I like your class but I've started a business and feel like I need to really invest my time there. I have a feeling if I don't take advantage of the opportunities in front of me that I may not get them again." The teacher asked Lacy what his business was. Lacy explained what he had been doing and the teacher was surprised Lacy was doing what he was doing at his age. He asked Lacy if there was anything he could do to get him to change his mind and stay. Lacy said no. The teacher told Lacy his class would be there for him if he changed his mind. Lacy said thank you to the teacher for all of his kindness but said he didn't think he would ever see him again.

The teacher said, "If that happens due to your success I would be more than pleased." They shook hands and Lacy left.

Lacy ran into Gigi and she asked why he had not called her. He explained everything that was going on and she understood. She invited him to a party that weekend and they had a good time. One of Lacy's clients was having a toga party the following weekend, so Lacy invited Gigi to that party. They had a good time there too, but it became a bit awkward after the party because they were both virgins yet they were interested in being together that night. They spoke about sex and Gigi said she wanted sex but wanted to wait. Lacy was very pleased to hear that because he didn't want to get that close to anyone just yet due to his business plans. They went out a few more times but Gigi wanted a lot of Lacy's time and he just didn't have any time to give, so they didn't see each other anymore. By that time, Lacy was also training a few clients at Aerobics and Nautilus Unlimited in La Crescenta. His old boss owned a few locations and allowed Lacy to train clients there. Since

Lacy still did not have a car, the clients that wanted to train in La Crescenta would pick him up then take him back to the Pasadena club. Because of all of the travel, he met many people and made many friends, including Brian and Howard. The three of them got together every weekend. He still saw Wael, Frank, and Diego, but they had jobs and school so they had even less free time than Lacy did. Brian, Howard, and Lacy enjoyed going out to Westwood to an under twenty-one night club much like Marilyn's Backstreet night club. The building had four floors and a dance floor on each floor. Every floor catered to a different crowd with music that suited them. One night, when they left the club, a girl named Janel walked up to the guys and said hi to Lacy.

"Hi," Lacy said.

"You have pretty eyes and a beautiful heart."

"Thank you," Lacy said. "You can see my eyes, but how do you know about my heart?" he asked.

"Any fool can see that."

"Check it out Lacy, she just called herself a fool," Brain said. "Not too bright. Watch out for that one," he said laughing. She looked at Brian and told him she liked his sense of humor and was sure his mother did too, then told him to run along. Lacy laughed out loud harder than he did in quite some time. Janel laughed hysterically at Lacy being so ticked at what she said. They exchanged numbers and went their separate ways. Howard suggested they crash the Beverly Hills Hotel, sit in the lounge, relax, and just talk. That was exactly what they did, and Lacy kept reminding Brian what Janel told him and he would laugh hysterically as if he heard it for the first time. As he was laughing, he heard someone say his name. He looked up and was shocked to see Georgiana. Georgiana looked like the actress Keiko Kitagawa. She was as friendly as could be and thought the world of Lacy. They met in high school during freshman year, as they sat a few rows away from each other in math class. When the teacher would read test grades out loud, Georgiana and Lacy both had high scores and that impressed Georgiana. She would strike up a conversation with Lacy when class was over, but he always had to leave so he kept the conversation short but was courteous. He really liked her but was just too afraid to get close to her because he was ashamed of his home life and didn't want anyone knowing about the beatings. He knew he could never take her to his house without facing serious embarrassment or ridicule from the family. After freshman year, she went to another school and they didn't see each other again until a few months before the Beverly Hills Hotel encounter. He was walking on Lake Avenue in Pasadena and heard his name being called. Georgiana was on the opposite side of the street and she walked quickly toward him in her heels. They hugged each other and commented on how long it had been since they saw each other. She asked what he had been doing and he mentioned bodybuilding and his fitness training business. She said she was very happy to hear about what he was doing and how enthusiastic he was about his plans. He asked what she had been doing and she said she was doing an internship that required her to be in Pasadena for that day. She was in a hurry but she gave Lacy her number and asked him to call her so they could get together. He took the number, then they hugged and said their goodbyes. She was smiling ear to ear and so was he, but as he continued walking to the fitness club, he knew he just wasn't ready to expose himself to her. She seemed as if she was doing quite well in life and he was still starting out. He thought about her for a few days and made attempts to call her in the red English phone booth at the Burlington Arcade, but hung up the phone each time without making the call. He was frustrated with himself for not being able to make the call and found a quiet place to cry it out, hoping she would forgive him one day. He told himself if he saw her again he would tell her everything to make up for not being honest with her in the first place. That opportunity came when she walked up to him at the Beverly Hills Hotel. When she said his name, he recognized her voice immediately. He stood up quickly and reached for her and said hello as he hugged her. Their embrace was like it had been each time, strong and endearing.

"We keep running into each other, my God," she said. "It's so great to see you Lacy."

"Georgiana, you have no idea how great it is to see you. I want to talk to you because I have so much to tell you," he said.

"Oh Lacy," she said. "I am in a huge hurry but let me give you my number in case you lost it."

Lacy said, "Yes, please do. I will call you tomorrow." She asked if he could call in a couple of days because she would be very busy before then. "Sure," Lacy said. Then they hugged and she walked away, looking back and smiling at him as he stood there smiling at her.

"Whoooooo iiiiiiiiisss SHE?" Howard asked.

"YEEEEAAAH! Daaaaaaaammmmnn boooooooy! Who the hell waaaaaas that?" Brian asked.

"Yo Brian, don't you have some jokes to share with yo mama?" Lacy said, then laughed hysterically.

"Awe fuck you man! Enough with that," Brian said. "Seriously, who the hell was that chick who looked at you as if you were her long-lost knight in shining armor?"

"Did she really look at me that way?" Lacy asked.

"YEEEESSS!" Howard said. "If you don't call her back, you, my friend, are not only an idiot but not deserving of a good woman."

"MMMHHMM," Brian said, "that girl be wantin' some Lacy stew with Chianti and hold the bullshit."

"Hahahahaha, you're crazy," Lacy said to Brian. "What do you mean hold the bullshit?" Lacy asked.

"Maaaan, I'm telling you Laaaace, she ain't about the bullshit and drama. You have to be square up with a chick like that and hold no secrets because she seems upfront, honest, and no bullshit and wants no bullshit. Keep Randy away from her for sure because he will purposely wreck your shit with her."

Lacy sat back down and said, "You're right. She's on the up and up and is solid as a rock."

"Look at us poor saps over here dreaming about finding a good girl and Lacy's been holding out on us," Howard said. "Laaaaace, maaaan, you gotta hook us up with her friends."

"I don't know her friends," Lacy said, "but let me contact her and take it from there." For the rest of the evening, they laughed and talked in the lounge. Each day after that night the guys kept asking Lacy if he contacted Georgiana, but he said he wanted to give her time. The truth was that he was still afraid. He was more afraid to contact her this time, especially after Brian telling him that she was not one for drama as Lacy's life was nothing but drama. One day, he pulled her number out to call her in the red English phone booth and just stood there. He imagined their lives together and how wonderful it could be, but he felt once she knew of his home life and him having no solid connection with his mother or father that she would change her mind about him. He believed that she came from a good family with good values and teachings and her parents would never allow such a union. He looked at the phone number on the piece of paper, tore it up, and leaned against the inside of that phone booth with tears streaming down his face like the time he leaned against the bathroom wall after his last beating from Mom. Someone walked up to the booth and asked to use it, so he walked out with his head down, wiped his eyes, and hurried away from the area. He went to a park where he frequently did chin-ups and just sat and thought. He believed he completely destroyed any chances with Georgiana and believed he would not run into her again. When the guys asked about her and if he called, he told them she must have accidentally given him the wrong number because the number was not good. Lacy knew the guys would never understand his reasoning because they had no idea what Lacy's life was like, and he was not about to tell them.

Months passed and Lacy was now twenty years old. His one-on-one training business was up and down because three people would start and two would quit due to job changes, life changes, or scheduling conflicts. Lacy got home early after working with just two clients and turned on the TV. Shortly after, Randy walked into the room and asked why he was home so early. He told Randy it was a slow day. Randy told him many days would be like that and that was why he should ditch the fitness business idea and get into fashion photography or another line of work. Lacy told Randy he really didn't want to discuss his career and just wanted to think. Randy laughed and asked what career Lacy was talking about. Lacy said nothing back and kept staring at the TV.

"Okay," Randy said, "I'll change the subject. Tell me about that fine ass named Tania. You know the one Lacy, that chick that brought you food a few days ago after a fashion show she did."

"She and I are just friends. Besides, every guy in town wants her and I think it means a lot to her that I'm not trying to get into her pants."

"Yoooouuuuzzzz a foooooo. Nothin' but a day dreamin' fooooo," Randy said. "If it were me, maaaaaaaannnn! I'd be all in dat booty. I ain't bullshittin'. Bitch be bringing me food EEEERR' DAY. YOU HERE ME POTNA! EEEERRR" DDDDDAAAAAMN DAY HOME BUAI!"

"I'm really trying to concentrate, would you stop please?" Lacy said.

"What?" Randy asked. "SSSSwrong witchu?"

"Tania is my friend, and when she came over the other day after her show she was excited to tell me all about it. The food she brought was leftovers from the show. Since I had no way of getting to her show, she and her girlfriend Karen brought food from the show to share with me and tell me about how it went."

"Karen?" Randy asked. "Where was that bitch?" he said. "I only saw Tania."

"She's not a bitch," Lacy said, "and she was parking the car and planned on coming inside but Mom ran Tania off."

"OOOH thaaas right. I forgot. Tania grabbed a piece of candy from the candy dish and Mom laid in on her," Randy said.

"No," Lacy said. "She didn't just lay into her. She told her to get her grubby little paws out of her candy dish and to get her nasty whore self out of her house." That day, Tania looked at Mom as if she was possibly not well, then told Lacy she would see him later. Lacy apologized for what happened and said he would walk her to her car.

Mom said, "That's right, walk that whore bitch out of my house and get my piece of candy back. Just what I thought, Lacy would be the one that saves the bitches and whores from themselves instead of treating them like the hoes that they are." Lacy looked back at Mom in disbelief that she said what she said in front of Tania. "Don't look at me like you haven't heard me talk before Lacy," Mom said. "Now, walk your little whore to her car and wash her panties while you're at it." Since Randy was just on his way out that day, he didn't see the whole situation, so when Lacy told him exactly what happened, Mom heard him telling Randy the story. They thought she was napping but she was lying in her bed in the next room listening to everything. "LACY," Mom yelled. "Get your black ass in here now." Lacy heard her yelling, wondering what in the world was she yelling for. He walked into her room and she sat up in her bed and yelled at the top of her lungs. "I took care of your black ass for years, fed you, clothed you, and kept a roof over your head and you have the gall to tell Randy what I did in my own house! You're just like that bitch Esta, who stole my two pairs of shoes!" Randy stepped in and told Mom Lacy wasn't bad-mouthing her but simply explaining what happened that day. "I don't give a good got damn," she said. "I could have put his ass in a foster home years ago or tossed his ass on the street and forgotten all about him. I'd have a hell of a lot more money in my pocket today if I kicked you out long ago." A single tear began to roll down Lacy's face because he could not understand what he did to Mom to cause her to hate him so much and speak to him as she did. He kept seeing her mouth move but no longer heard her words because they no longer had an effect on him. She was going on and on about how he cost her money over the years and even mentioned that sliding door he walked through one night where he ended up in the emergency room. He could never understand why she was so upset about that broken sliding door because she had a couple of friends take the sliding door from the house they just moved from and replace the broken one. Lacy could have been sliced to pieces by all of that glass and was spared with only a cut on the forehead and glass splinters resting in his ears and hair. As he was watching her mouth move, her head bobbing from side to side and her hands flailing, he heard words that she wanted to say to him for years. "GET YOUR BLACK ASS THE FUCK OUT OF MY HOUSE YOU BLACK SON OF A BIIIIIIITCH!" Lacy wasted no time. He turned and left her room, grabbed some bags, and gathered the clothes he had. She was still yelling and Randy tried to calm her down, but it didn't work. Randy told Lacy to wait a moment and Lacy said no. He said one of the worst things a person could do was to stay where they were not wanted and he wasn't about to do that anymore. "That's right," Mom said. "Mr. Professor, GET THE FUCK OUT OF MY HOUSE!"

Lacy finished gathering his things and headed for the front door. Randy put his hand on Lacy's shoulder and said, "Man I'm sorry for this."

Lacy said, "I'm not. I like knowing where I stand with people so that there are no misunderstandings or guesswork about how people really feel."

"Listen to him," Mom said. "...Like he knows shit. GET OUT!"

"Thank you for everything you've done for me. I was the one that asked for the least from you because I never felt I could ask. I promise you will never have to do anything for me again," he said to Mom. Then he turned to Randy and said "Take care of yourself Randy," then left. Lacy went to the red English phone booth and called David. David lived in a building across the street from the lot where Lacy would make his calls. Lacy had lived in that building before because that was the building Mom moved into in his senior year of high school. When Lacy was in the process of moving away from home, Mom moved a few blocks away into another building where Lacy stayed before she kicked him out. David answered his phone and Lacy explained his situation and asked if he could stay with David for a while to get himself situated. David told Lacy he was sorry to hear what happened and he could stay as long as he needed to. Lacy walked across the street and pressed the intercom for David, and David answered then buzzed Lacy in. As Lacy walked into the building toward David's condo, he thought back to the time he met David. Lacy and Sam walked into the game room to play a game of pool, and that was where they saw David playing pool with one of his friends.

HAWAIIAN PUNCH

At first glance, Lacy thought David and his friend were gangsters because they were dressed in slacks, collared shirts and ties, wore Fedoras, and smoked weed. At that time in Pasadena, that was a sure sign of a gangster and the gangster life. During that time, Pasadena was a hotbed for drugs, crime, and gangs that allowed for the rise of Ray Ray Browning. It was said that he was responsible for many deaths and drug trafficking in many states and was worth millions. Many teenagers back then would do anything to work with Ray Ray just to get a piece of the pie. When Lacy saw David he said, "Uh, excuse us. We'll come back."

"No, stay. We were just leaving," David said, as he put the cue away and grabbed his jacket, slid it on, and nodded at Sam and Lacy. Lacy and Sam nodded back, then they stopped walking and David asked, "Say, aren't you the guy that lives with that woman who's always yelling at you?"

Lacy looked at Sam then looked at David and said, "Yes," then asked if he heard yelling a lot.

David said, "Man she be trippin' a lot on you. What's your name?"

"My name's Lacy and this is my friend Sam."

"Lacy. Cool name. Hello Sam."

"Hey," Sam said.

"I'm David and this is Ronnie, my runnin' buddy."

"Good to meet you, David and Ronnie," Lacy said.

"Yeah, good to meet you guys," Sam said.

"Likewise," David said, then they left. Sam and Lacy thought they were gangsters for sure and spoke about their clothes and Stacy Adams shoes, which were very popular at that time and were made famous by Morris Day from the hit group "The Time". Lacy frequented that game room to play pool, and David was often there with a bunch of girls and guys and invited Lacy to join them. Many times, Lacy declined the invitation, until one time one of David's friends named Cheryl asked him to stay and play a game with her. Lacy said okay. David asked anyone smoking weed to put it out since Lacy was a bodybuilder and wasn't into the smoke, as David called it. Everyone was very respectful and put out their weed. Lacy and Cheryl began talking and Lacy asked how they got away with smoking weed in the building. Cheryl laughed and said the manager of the building liked weed too and lived near the game room, then both Cheryl and Lacy laughed. As Cheryl and Lacy spoke, she told him that David told her that he felt sorry for a guy in the building that got nothing but yelling from some white lady on a daily.

"Is that you?" she asked Lacy. Lacy looked embarrassed while his eyes darted around the room, wondering who else knew. She told Lacy it was okay, and not to feel uncomfortable because they all had stories of their own, so he wasn't alone. Lacy looked at her and smiled.

He said, "Yes, I'm the guy that gets yelled at."

"Who's the white lady?" Cheryl asked.

"Ohhh," Lacy laughed. "She's just very light-skinned. I thought she was white too when I was a child. That's my mom."

"Your mom?" she asked.

"Yes," Lacy said. David said that she looked like that Florida Orange Juice lady Annette something. "Annette Funicello," Lacy said, as he laughed hysterically. "I've never heard that one before, but yes that's her."

"How do you deal with her yelling at you like that without yelling back or slapping the shit out of her?" Cheryl asked. "You're a big guy and don't look like you need to take shit from anyone."

Lacy said, "I would never hit her or talk like that to her."

"Why not?" Cheryl asked.

"Because that's not the way I do things. It may be the way she does things but it's not my way," Lacy said.

"Hahahahaha." Cheryl laughed and said, "Booooooooooy. You've got a lot to learn about us women. Some men or many men must have done her wrong and she's taking her frustration out on you or she's not your real mother, which makes it easier for her to treat you like shit." *DING DING DING DONG!!!!* A bell rang in Lacy's head and woke him up. He remembered when he was thirteen, Esta visited him needing a kidney, then in his junior year of high school, the biology teacher talking about kidneys and the best donor matches. He also remembered how Esta was the only one who took care of him as a child and that Mom never spoke to him like Esta did. He never called anyone Mom until Esta left and Mom forced him to call her Mom. "Lacy, you okay?" Cheryl asked.

Lacy looked like he was in a daze. "Yes," he said. "You just said something that got my attention."

"What, that you should slap the shit outta her?"

"Hahahaha, no," Lacy said. "I don't think she's my mother."

"No shit Sherlock. Boy, you are rare and any woman that snags you has a real gem. You better watch yourself because women will entice you and get pregnant then take you for all they can." Lacy told her that Mom told him that. "She was telling you the truth so don't forget that shit. Any woman that's a taker will see you coming from miles away."

"Why are you telling me all this?" Lacy asked her.

Cheryl said, "Because I like you and would love to fuck your brains out but you're still a virgin and I can't go there."

"What? I'm not a virgin," Lacy said. He knew everyone in the room heard Cheryl say he was a virgin and he was very embarrassed among the older crowd.

Everyone laughed and one guy said, "If he's not a virgin then I'm not high as a kite, hahahahaha." Everyone laughed again, then Cheryl apologized for outing Lacy as a virgin. He told her it was okay. He told her he was saving himself for the right person.

"Bahahahahah," she laughed and told Lacy the right person may not be able to fuck, which would make them the wrong person.

Lacy looked at her and said, "That's a good point. I still want to wait, but that's a damn good point." Cheryl kept looking at Lacy and licked her lips slowly. Lacy looked away then back at her then away again because she was very attractive and had that witty mind that Lacy liked.

"Bahhahahaha," Cheryl laughed and told Lacy not to even think about it because she was just playing with him. "After you've been with a few other women and learned a few things then look me up and we'll have a great time together." Lacy just smiled.

Lacy thought about all of this as he walked through the building to David's condo. He rang David's doorbell and David opened the door and greeted Lacy with, "What's up Mr. Universe?" It was no secret that Lacy wanted to be Mr. Universe, so plenty of people called him that.

"Hey David, what's going on?" Lacy said.

"Man Lacy, what's going on with you and that mother of yours?"

"You know, I believe she feels I owe her for all that has happened in her life and the only way for me to repay her is to let her treat me like a verbal and non-verbal punching bag."

"She just kicked you out onto the street like that?" David asked.

"Yes." Lacy explained the conversation he and Randy were having and how Mom called him into her room and went off like a siren.

"She didn't have words for Randy too?" David asked.

"NO. She never has words for him," Lacy said.

"I'm surprised because that Randy is a baaaaaad muthafucka and everyone in town that I know knows of him and his dealings."

"Really?" Lacy said.

"OOOOHHH YEEES," David said. "He's rolling with some woman that had a huge nest egg left to her and he's playing behind her back with another woman who's a banker."

"Okay, I don't want to know any more," Lacy said. "The less I know the better."

"Word," David said. "I just can't understand why your Mom kicks your ass on a regular since you don't do shit to anyone and stay so focused on your goals. I'd think Horace would be on her shit list way before you."

"David, if it's okay, I don't really want to talk about any of them right now. My brother Gus is the coolest and he's always been square up with me, but the other guys have been under Mom's influence for so long that they don't know who they are and how to maneuver around in life with their own decisions. They've been sucking on her tits since birth and don't know how to stop and she loves that they don't know better. Gus saw the light many years ago and made his move and that really helped me see my way through."

"What about your sisters?" David asked.

"I speak with Odessa and Alexandra and love them, but I'm closer with Gus," Lacy said.

"Yeah, I've heard you speak about him a lot with Cheryl. He sounds like a really hip dude."

"He is," Lacy said.

"Well man," David said. "I was just about to go out but you can sleep on the sofa. Blankets are over there in the cabinet and you can find your way around I'm sure since you've lived in this building before."

"Cool," Lacy said. "Thank you David. This is a huge help and it's perfect timing too."

"Say no more. We can figure out a small weekly rent that fits your budget tomorrow but for now, relax and make yourself at home, and if you bring any honeys in here you let me know so I don't walk into anything."

"Hahahahaha." Lacy laughed and said, "That will be the day, but if Cheryl stops by when you're not here who knows what could happen."

David said, "What would happen is that she'll work you over and have you washing her panties by morning and have you begging her to give you another taste. Hahahahahahha."

"WHAT?" Lacy said.

"Yep," David said. "You don't want to play with Cheryl because she plays for keeps."

Lacy said, "Mom used to mention the thing about the panties."

"Well, she was right. For some women it's a sport just like it is for many men. Watch yourself man, don't get pussy whipped by the wrong woman because if you do you can kiss being Mr. Universe goodbye."

"Got it," Lacy said.

"Later Lace."

"Solid," Lacy said. All was going good with Lacy renting from David because he could really concentrate on his plans, clients, workouts, and save money. Lacy's friends visited often, as did David's friends, and they all met each other and got along well. After three months or so, David told Lacy he was gay and found him attractive. Lacy had met many gay men and lesbian women in the sport of bodybuilding and as always, he respected everyone for who they were unless they gave him a real reason not to respect them. Lacy told David he was surprised to find that out because he always had women around him, and also told David that he was not attracted to men at all. David asked Lacy if he ever thought about being with a guy and Lacy said, "Not at all."

"After everything your mom put you through Lacy, you still want to be with women?"

"My mom is not all women. Hell, I don't want a woman like my mom and there are plenty of women to choose from. You don't like being with women at all David?" Lacy asked.

"She would have to be drop-dead gorgeous," David said.

"So, then you do like women?" Lacy asked.

"Just the really beautiful ones," David said.

Then Lacy laughed and said, "Man that's all I've seen you with."

"You don't have a problem with me being gay Lacy?"

"Why should I?" Lacy asked. David said that many people looked at gay men and lesbian women like freaks. "Well, I've been treated like a freak for years in my own home so I understand how it feels to be on the outside looking in. Add that to being black in a world that sees black people as problematic misfits and everything just gets tougher."

"Who you tellin'? Try being a gay black man and see how those shoes fit."

"Naaah. I'll take my chances with the cards I've already been dealt," Lacy said, and they both laughed hysterically.

"Well, now you know," David said. Lacy told David he had previously wondered if there was a chance David was gay because he heard Cheryl mention something about a guy that wanted to show David where the goodies were. Lacy thought that was an odd statement for a man to say to a woman about another man unless the first man lost his bag of goodies from the grocery store. "BAHAHAHAHA. HOHOHOHOHOHO, SHHHIIIIEEETTT, HEHEHEHH-HEHE, OOOHHH DAAAAAMN! Now that's some funny shit Lacy," David said. "You ever thought of doing stand-up? Because you say some funny shit." Lacy said he just said whatever was in his head and that he thought the statement was odd but now it all made sense. "I'll bet it does," David said, as he kept laughing.

"So David," Lacy asked, "are we straight?"

"Bahahahahaha." David laughed and said, "You are but I'm not. Ba-hahaahahha."

Lacy said, "Nooooo man, I mean are we cool and do you understand that I am not interested in you or guys in general."

"OOOH YEEAAAH MAN," David said. "I respect your position and glad you accept me for me."

"Cool," Lacy said, then he went to work out. As days passed, David started walking around the house in his underwear and other times nothing at all. He asked Lacy if it made him uncomfortable and Lacy said no. He said he grew up with brothers walking around the same way so it was no big deal. David told Lacy that he appreciated Lacy's acceptance of him and Lacy told David people accepting people for who they were was what should be happening in the world and David agreed. David was a pretty good cook and was surprised that Lacy knew his way around a kitchen as well. David would cook dishes and get Lacy's opinion on the dishes that he would prepare for his dates. One late afternoon, David made an excellent fried chicken dish with mac n cheese that he was going to take to his friend's house. He asked Lacy to try it and he thought it was another excellent creation. David took the wrapped up food and left for his friend's house for their date. When David got back that night, Lacy was watching the music video channel and asked David how his date went. Clearly, David had a few drinks and said it went really well but his friend had to get up early the next morning so he couldn't stay the night. David told Lacy that they made some great tasting punch and that he had to try it. Lacy asked if there was alcohol in it and David said no and that he knew better than to offer Lacy alcohol since he didn't drink. "What did you make it with?" Lacy asked.

"Believe it or not we used Hawaiian Punch," David said, "along with other fruit juices for a strong fruity flavor."

"I used to love Hawaiian Punch back in the day," Lacy said, "let me get a glass. Fill 'er up." David did as Lacy said and filled his glass up. Lacy tipped the glass back and drank a bit. "MMMMMM! OOOOOOOOOWWWWWEEEEE! That's a bit tart but really good," Lacy said.

"I told you," David said. "Enjoy it."

"I will," Lacy said, then he sat back down and continued watching music videos.

"I'm going to be in my room reading," David said.

"Cool," Lacy said. Just minutes after Lacy drank the punch, he felt a bit sleepy and his body felt very heavy. He thought he was just sleepy, so he started to get up to put his glass in the kitchen but sat back down and put the glass on the floor. He woke up hours later and noticed his sweatpants were undone and his ass didn't feel right. He felt pressure as if he had to go so he went to the bathroom, stumbling a bit. As he sat on the toilet feeling like he had to go, he was trying to remember things and what time he went to bed that night. Then he heard, *click click*. He realized that was David locking his bedroom door. Lacy wondered why he'd be locking his bedroom door in the morning. As Lacy's brain became less foggy, he remembered drinking the punch and watching TV and an unusual sleepiness took over him and the heaviness of his body was very strange. He remembered he was not the least bit sleepy before drinking the punch. Lacy finished, pulled up his pants and began washing his hands, then stopped and looked in the mirror and thought to himself, *HE PUT SOMETHING IN THAT PUNCH TO KNOCK ME OUT THEN TOOK ADVANTAGE OF ME! THAT RAT BASTARD!* Lacy left the bathroom and knocked on David's door. David didn't answer so Lacy told him to open the door and David asked what Lacy wanted. Lacy told him to open the door again. David said he was afraid to open it. Lacy went to the kitchen and got a spatula, slid it between the crevice of the door near the lock, and unlocked the door as he saw Randy do many times in order to get into Mom's room to take money when she wasn't home. Lacy was going to knock hell out of David but when he got the door open, David had a gun pointed at him with his hands shaking. When he saw the gun and David's hands shaking he backed out of the room and stood on the other side of the wall. "WHY?" Lacy asked David.

"I'm sorry Lacy, I'm sorry. You're so wonderful and I just wanted you. I wanted to make that dinner last night for you but I couldn't tell you that. Please forgive me Lacy. Please."

"You're lucky you've got that gun," Lacy said. "I suggest you stay where you are and don't put it down for a second." Lacy went to the phone and called Howard and asked if he could ask his mom if he could stay there.

Howard said, "Man you know she's cool with that, you okay?"

"I am now. I'll be waiting at the phone booth," Lacy asked.

"On my way," Howard said. Lacy packed his things and headed for the front door while David was in his room repeatedly screaming he was sorry, but Lacy didn't respond and left. Lacy waited near the red English phone booth just two hundred yards from David's place and three blocks from Mom's place. He thought about how close he was to both places yet couldn't trust going to either.

He thought about Esta telling him they would leave together and how she left without him, Randy telling him his dick tasted like candy, and Horace breaking Mom's mirror and blaming Lacy for it which earned Lacy a terrible beating. He thought about Mom and her never-ending anger over two stupid pairs of shoes. He also thought about Mrs. Johnson telling him how she would beat the tar out of him and the kindergarten teacher who believed the child that kicked him in the face, making him fall off the stairs of the slide. He thought about getting suspended from school from laughing because a parent thought her child would be possessed by the devil, since Lacy's friend said it looked like the other boy was humping the ground during pushups. Suspended for laughing at nonsense, Lacy was thinking to himself, shaking his head. Then, he thought about the offer he got when he was seventeen and had just won Mr. Teenage California. The man told Lacy he was clearly the next Arnold since he was big for his age and the audience loved him, so he offered Lacy a sponsorship and backing only if Lacy would agree to do steroids. Lacy said no and the man told Lacy he would change his mind eventually. The man approached Lacy again at age nineteen and Lacy still said no, so the man told Lacy that he had a lot of pull in the sport and for Lacy to remember that. He remembered the fight with Tex because Tex was a coward and was mentally immature and needed to feel powerful. He remembered the countless times he was called a black son of a bitch at home and how many times he was called a black son of a bitch outside the home and couldn't figure out which number was higher. Then he remembered the assistant manager at Alpha Beta who let his bigotry get the best of him as did many people along the way. Lacy thought of the situation with the club he was so honored to manage, but later realized he was to play the fall guy because it was so easy to believe a black person fucked up and stole customers' money since that seemed to be the narrative in movies, news, and on so many lips. Yet, black had never started a world war or a large-scale war, built a Ponzi scheme that hurt generations of people then got off scot-free in a country club prison, or caused a stock market crash that hurt millions of people to reset the books, or squandered insurance market money leaving many destitute. Black wasn't responsible for the atrocities all around the world in so many degrees yet the war on drugs and massive incarceration looked black and brown and that got huge attention. How is this possible? Lacy thought to himself. How is it possible that so many black inventors helped shape America and the world greatly but people just swept that knowledge under the rug and acted as if blacks were just problematic people? If it wasn't against the law for blacks to have patents back in the day, more than half of the Fortune 500 companies would be black-owned and the industrial revolution would have looked very different, but people were stupidly blind to that and blind to the minds that existed in them. Just crack open a book and read about black history in America everyone. It's there in black and white, BLACK AND FUCKING WHITE!

That blindness, lack of concern, and bigotry was a disease that spread into black families, causing mental breakdowns and abuse within the families due to self-hatred. Motherfuckers!!! Mom is fucking blind to my mind and who I am. Fucking Esta was blind and fuck her too. Mr. Stache is a damn child molester, Mrs. Strite was a fucking bigoted jackass, Mr. McCafferty was a bigoted pig. Mrs. St Jermaine wanted to be white so badly. She was a horrible teacher and was just weak-minded and ashamed of her Spanish roots and spoke down to Blacks and Hispanics daily and kissed the white children's asses. How fucking stupid are people? If God created us in His image and breathed life into dirt, the fucking dirt was brown or black. Even science says the only non-white people on the planet that can make a white baby is black people. In fucking essence, we are all just different shades of each other you fucking narcissistic lunatics. There's not one person on this planet that could have things stolen from them repeatedly and still act right. Not one. Not one. Not one. Not...ONE? ONE? Jesus, I get it. I get it now.

Holy damn. God, why didn't you just say so instead of putting me through all this? I have to get fucked in the ass for you to wake me up. We could have come to some understanding well before that. God please, in the future, please tap me on the shoulder a little harder and I'll listen. Because I…

"Yo!!! Lacy, you look like you're collecting garbage man, hahaha-haha. Let's go dude," Howard said. Lacy grabbed his things and went to Howard's car. He thanked God for the epiphany. Before he got to Howard's car he made up his mind that no one would find out about what happened at David's house. "You been crying man?" Howard asked. "Jesus, your shirt is freaking wet from your tears. What's up man? What happened between you and David?"

Lacy tried to perk up as if it wasn't really that bad of a situation and said, "Ahh, he's just too much of a partier with friends over all the time and I can't get any sleep there."

"I told you man," Howard said. "That guy is like a rockstar and lives like one, but why are you crying?"

"Man," Lacy said. "The first part of my life has been bumpy and really hit me hard a few minutes ago but I'm okay. I think things will be better moving forward, I just have to listen to the signs."

"What signs?" Howard asked.

"Have you ever thought you should do something but put it off then realized putting it off caused your overall stress or pain?"

"OOOHHH DUUUUUDE! I do that all the time," Howard said.

"Exactly," Lacy said. "If you choose not to put that thing off when you're inspired to do it then you just respected and listened to the sign that told you to do that thing."

"HUH?" Howard said.

"Let me ask you this," Lacy said. "Before I called you and asked you to pick me up did you think of me at all today?"

"Actually, I did," Howard said.

"Okay," Lacy said. "How soon did I call you after you thought of me?"

"That's what's so funny, because you called right as I was thinking of you."

"EXACTLY," Lacy said. "You weren't thinking of me, you felt me thinking of you. We tend to believe when we think of someone then they call us soon after it was all by chance. Noooooo. We all feel each other's energy but many of us misunderstand the messages or signs we're receiving. Rather than asking ourselves for an answer as to why we feel that person's energy, or why we are suddenly thinking about that person, often times we just dismiss the thought or feeling altogether. Not asking ourselves why we feel that person's energy or why we suddenly thought of that person causes us to totally avoid our power and abilities to connect at a higher level without verbal contact."

"Dude, did David slip an outer space pill in your fruit smoothie or whaaaat?"

"Why did you say that?" Lacy asked with a confused look on his face, since David did slip something into a fruit drink.

"Because you're talking silly," Howard said.

"NO. Listen. You and your mom go to church all the time and you believe in the prophets and angels but you don't believe we have the ability to feel another person's emotions and state of being."

"I don't know man," Howard said.

"What if I told you I will have a son and two daughters and the daughters will come at the same time."

"Fucking hell Lacy, you knocked up two chicks at the same time?"

"Howard, dude, get off the pot. NO. I'm saying I have seen this in my future and I know it's coming. Just like I know I will have my own fitness studio before I'm twenty-five and that's when my life will really change."

"You know, it is interesting how you knew you my mother would lose her job months before it happened. And, I will never figure out how you knew her old boyfriend would contact her and move in with her. Sometimes Lacy, you really freak everybody out with that shit. If for any reason you're an alien please don't bite my head off or stick a tentacle in my rib cage and suck my brain out. Just level with me and I'll be cool," Howard said.

"Howard," Lacy said. "I'm not an alien and I'd probably get food poisoning if I ate your brain and end up high as a kite from all the pot you've done. The truth is that I get glimpses of different time frames and things that happen in time frames but most of the time it happens when I sleep. Really, yes. Like that time I told you I didn't want to go to Hollywood that night but you wanted to go so badly that we went. Then, when we walked around a corner those two guys pulled out shotguns just as I saw in my dream that I told you about."

"Yeah, and man I shit my pants on that one. I still don't know how you knew that," Howard said.

"I'm trying to tell you that we all have this ability but it's not meant to be abused or overused. We are all living a human existence with higher levels of sensing. Earlier men and women used their senses to feel the potential presence of danger or to find food but we have allowed technology to be our brains and senses. That's why you see me memorize things all the time like phone numbers and not use drugs or get drunk. I don't want to rely on technology so much that it makes me weak and desensitized as it has done to so many others. Just look around and notice the people that are irritable, constantly stressed, lack patience, or fight about everything. They have lost their way. You have to keep your brain clean and strong as well as your mind to tap into your higher senses and abilities."

"Lacy, you're the only person I know that speaks this way but when you speak I feel calmer and more at peace and I don't know if that's because I'm not thinking of other things in my life or if your words are calming," Howard said.

Lacy said, "It's both, but the bigger part is that your higher senses connect and relate to what I'm sharing with you and your higher senses are thirsting to be tapped into and used more often. Please practice sitting in peace and feeling the calmness you're feeling right now to see things as I sometimes do. I'm still learning and growing, but I had a breakthrough today that I thought was actually a breakdown and that's why I was crying. I was confused but I just didn't understand how

standing in clarity felt. Watch my life from this point forward Howard.
I will have my challenges but my past is about to be topped by serious
greatness."

"Just don't forget about us little people," Howard said.

"You know I don't walk through life pushing people aside like garbage, man."

"Hahahaha. I know Lacy. I was kidding, but there are some people
you should kick to the curb but I'll keep my mouth shut on that one."

"Cool," Lacy said. When they got to Howard's house, Lacy learned
that Howard's mom was out of town for the week. Howard told Lacy
he called his Mom and told her that Lacy was coming to stay for a while
and she was cool about it. Lacy told Howard he was exhausted and
would take a nap. Lacy locked his door and pressed his back to the wall
as a precaution based upon his experience the night before. He just
wasn't taking any chances. As Lacy lay in bed he thought about all the
things he thought about just before Howard picked him up. He
thought about what he said about not one person on this planet acting
right if they were stolen from repeatedly. He realized that how we deal
with adversity was what set us apart from each other. If one person
could deal with it in a way that showed humility and grace while attempting to forgive and not hate while maintaining a positive outlook,
then others would see that and maybe try to do the same. *I get it. I
GEEEEET IIIIT*, Lacy said in his head. At that moment, he felt so
proud to be a member of a group of people that were viewed as misfits
and problematic because those labels were just that, labels. Everyone
gets labeled for something but the label only stuck if it could be proved
and if it was accepted by the person that was labeled. He decided at
that moment, no labels for him, unless it expressed something the
world could grow from. Anything else was garbage. He thought of Mrs.
Smith from the first grade and how she was kind and caring and treated
him as if he were her son. He thought of his seventh-grade teacher Mr.
Kielty, who accepted no bigotry or bigoted comments in his class and
spoke to Lacy in private about striving for the best even if people

thought less of him or made fun of him because of his color. He also thought about Mr. Parsons, his tenth-grade teacher that told him that he was a former police officer. He told Lacy when he was in the force he and buddies would purposely harass blacks but he realized it was wrong and quit the force. He said that he became a teacher to right his wrongs and to help all people no matter what they looked like. He told Lacy if Lacy needed help with anything to let him know and he would move mountains to help. He prepped Lacy for his driving test by taking him out for driving lessons and supported Lacy's dreams of being a world champion bodybuilder. Lacy thought about how much good there was in so many people but how many people got suckered by the idea of what the color of wealth and prosperity should look like. *That false idea is believed by both sides of the fence and is mentally damaging to all that get suckered into the belief,* Lacy thought to himself as he fell asleep. Lacy slept a lot that day and all night too since his system was ridding itself of whatever David put in that punch.

Lacy had to work the next day. Since he no longer lived right across the street from the fitness club, Howard drove him to the club since Howard wasn't working. The club manager told Lacy several times that since he was not an employee of the club that he was not supposed to be getting calls at the club. Lacy told the manager that he never gave their number out and the people that called just knew he trained there and wanted training. When Lacy got to the club that day, the club manager told him that someone called for him and left a message, and that would be the very last message he would take for Lacy. He said that he also told all the employees not to take any more messages for Lacy. "I understand," Lacy said. He worked with his clients then went to the red English phone booth and called the person that left a message for him. It was a woman from the La Canada YMCA, and she told Lacy she had heard of him and his training and wanted to know if he would be interested in an interview for a job with them. Lacy said yes. The woman asked if he could stop by that day. "Yes, I can," Lacy said. After they finished speaking, Lacy called Howard and asked if he could drive him to the interview and Howard said yes and was excited for Lacy. Lacy did the interview and got the job. As Lacy was leaving, a guy approached him and told him he only got the job because he was black. "What do you mean?" Lacy asked.

"Affirmative action is what got you here," the man said.

"Why do you say that?" Lacy asked.

"Because that's what got me here. I'm the guy they fired to hire you. They need to have at least one black person working and you're now that person."

Lacy said, "I'm good at what I do. Many people get hired for their color, beauty, or connections each day. But, those that rely on those things alone will not last. I promise you I rely on my abilities. This is an opportunity and I'm supposed to take it. Why did you get fired?" Lacy asked.

"They didn't like me getting too friendly with the manager's daughter," he said.

"That was a very risky move regardless of your color," Lacy said.

"You sound like an Uncle Tom siding with them," he said.

"Actually, you're the Uncle Tom that was trying to get into Becky's pants. I'm here for a job to build my future. That's not Uncle Tom behavior, that's professional behavior. I'm sorry you lost your job but I'm not sorry for the behavior that got you fired," Lacy said.

"Maaan. You sound just like a politician because I didn't understand a word you said."

"My ride is here," Lacy said, "but I hope things get better for you." Weeks later that guy contacted Lacy and told him that he was just upset that day and felt Lacy did the right thing. He also asked if he could interview Lacy on his radio show on KPPC called "An Hour with Captain G." Lacy agreed and the interview regarding Lacy's bodybuilding career went very well and they stayed friends until Captain G moved away. Shortly after Lacy got the job at the YMCA as the main instructor in the private membership training room, Aerobics and Nautilus Plus informed him he could no longer train his clients there. The entire chain no longer welcomed outside trainers to use their equipment to train their clients even if the client and trainer were members. Lacy was so happy that he landed the YMCA (sometimes known as the 'Y') job but he lost some clients since they didn't want to drive seven miles on the freeway to La Canada as it was not a convenient process. Lacy gained great recognition at the Y but his boss was very jealous because he graduated with a degree in exercise physiology but Lacy knew a greater deal due to his years of studying the body, abnormalities, diseases, rehabilitation, and nutrition. Lacy communicated with the people far better than his boss and his methods were much more effective than the boss' methods. The boss would interrupt Lacy as he was helping people and told him to handle another task so the boss could work with the client instead of Lacy. The clients began to complain about the boss' behavior and demanded that Lacy be their only trainer. Just like the assistant manager at Alpha Beta, the boss at the Y wanted to meet Lacy after hours in a back office. They met and the boss told Lacy he didn't have nearly the education he had and was only getting treated so well because he was black.

"No," Lacy said. "I'm being treated well because I treat others well and I execute well."

"Bullshit, I can run rings around you Lacy," he said.

"Okay," Lacy said. "If you can run rings around me then why are you wasting your time trying to prove that to me? I get on a stage and win and once I've won I don't have to run around telling the other competitors I just beat that I'm better than them, you know why?" Lacy asked.

"No, why?"

Lacy said, "Because that would mean I didn't believe I really won and need to convince myself I won by rubbing it in their faces just like you're trying to do now. I've dealt with people like you my entire life, black and white and everything in between. You don't scare me and your education is impressive but your ability to use it sucks and that's why no one wants to work with you. We could work together in harmony and help each other, but I can see that will never happen, so if we're done here my ride is waiting for me."

"Just watch your step so you don't end up like the last guy in your position."

Lacy said, "And you watch your step so you don't trip over your own two feet." It was clear to Lacy this guy was a problem, but it was very evident that the management and customers saw Lacy's value and appreciated it. It was also clear that management was not happy with the boss and his arrogant attitude and behavior toward Lacy. Now, Lacy was closer to the club in La Crescenta so he trained his small group of private clients at that club and worked at the Y in between sessions. Since he still lived in the Pasadena area, he did his training for competitions at Imperial Health Spa where he met Trisha. She worked at the front counter at the club and was an aspiring actress and jazz and ballet dancer. She and Lacy locked eyes immediately, but Lacy looked away and went straight to the weight room. Later, he asked his friend Marcus who worked at the club to tell him what the girl at the front desk's name was.

"Oh, that's Trisha from Virginia Beach. She's new here."

"Really," Lacy said.

"She asked me questions about you after you walked by."

"Get out," Lacy said.

"No man, I'm not kidding. She asked about you."

"Yeah, but you know I really think I'm supposed to be with that girl from overseas."

"DOOOOOOOHH BROOOTHER! Give it up already," Marcus said. "That chick is long gone man. You two met at Aerobics and Nautilus Plus just before she returned overseas and you were barely friends, so what can you expect from her?"

"I know it seems stupid Marcus, but that day I was walking and only saw the profile of her face as she walked behind a car. The message was clear."

"What message?" Marcus asked.

"Naaah man," Lacy said, "you're going to laugh and call me crazy so just drop it."

"Well, I do think you're crazy for passing up so many wonderful women that want you, but go ahead and tell me the message you got."

Lacy said, "Keep this between us, okay?"

"Of course," Marcus said.

Lacy said, "That day I was walking to the gym and only saw the profile of her face but I got a clear message that she was going to be my wife and we are supposed to have children."

"P-P-P-PAAAHAHAHAHAHAHAHAHA! Maaaaan! Lacy you need a piece o' ass pronto because you're losing it."

"See," Lacy said. "I knew you'd laugh. When you guys ask me questions about your lives and about ladies I come through for you guys with the answers. Just like that time when that girl you liked kicked your ass to the curb and you asked me what to say and I told you and it worked. But, let me tell you or the guys what I see for me and you go stupid with the laughing. I have to work out." Lacy started to walk away.

"NO, Lacy. Wait. I'm sorry dude, you're right. You come through for us all the time...but man this is insane. She's on the other side of the world."

"That's another thing," Lacy said. "You focus on what may not work rather than what might work. I'm telling you right now she will be my wife and we will have twins. I'm telling you. I might date here and there but I will marry her even if it's only for the children."

"WHAT?" Marcus asked. "You are the least selfish person I know Lacy. How could you say what you just said?"

Lacy said, "Because I saw that I would have three children. Two children with one woman and one child with another but I don't see the women in the picture after the children are born. We either split or they leave."

"And you believe that woman from overseas is one of the women?" Marcus asked.

"Yes," Lacy said. "I believe I'll have twins with her. I've said since I was a child that I would have twin children."

"As wild and bizarre as it sounds Lacy, I believe you," Marcus said.

"It seems when I don't believe what you say it comes back to bite me on the ass anyway. Well, how will you contact her?"

"I've tried calling overseas but can't locate her."

"Well, until you do locate her please keep living your life and date and have fun along the way."

"I will," Lacy said. "I will." Then he went to train. Many months passed and he and Trisha finally went out a few times. One night she made it clear to him what she wanted, and age twenty-one was when he lost his virginity to her. She didn't want to see him anymore because she said he lied about being a virgin because there was no way a virgin could have known all that he knew about sex and what to do to please her. He tried to tell her that sex was talked about so much at his house and with elders that it just came naturally, but she wasn't buying it. Additionally, she was angry with him because he would not forget about the woman overseas. He told each woman he went out with or dated that there was a woman overseas that he would be with and if they saw that as a problem, not to go any further. It was so important for Lacy to be as crystal clear and honest about that because he'd seen so many men lie to women and didn't want to be that guy, although he didn't see the frustration that could cause women at that time. When Trisha's rent was due or she needed money for something she would contact Lacy using her sex appeal and it worked a few times, but Lacy quickly caught on and put an end to that connection. When Lacy was at the La Crescenta club, a girl named Sarah walked up to him and asked him out for New Year's Eve. Lacy didn't want to go. One of his clients was there and told Lacy to go ahead and go and have fun.

Lacy thought for a moment and realized he said "no thank you" to so many of her advances before, so he decided to say yes. Sarah was happy and went back to her workout while Lacy continued with his client and told his client he felt uncomfortable about the date. He and his client were pretty close, so his client reminded him that he was no longer a virgin and should not be so shy about meeting other people. Lacy reminded his client about the woman overseas and his client said when and if he met her again to deal with that then. Lacy said okay, but Sarah's energy felt different in comparison to many women he'd met. It was if there was a sadness or emptiness that she was holding onto. Two weeks before New Year's Eve, Lacy contacted Sarah and told her that he didn't want to meet for New Year's Eve. She was a little upset but said, "Okay, maybe some other time." Lacy said okay, and felt he'd done the right thing. When New Year's Eve passed, Lacy and Sarah saw each other at the club, and she invited him over for dinner later that week and he accepted the invitation. When he got to her house, she had food on the stove and the aroma was wonderful. She showed Lacy around her house and had a scrapbook in her bedroom on the bed and asked Lacy to sit with her on the bed to look through it with her. As they looked through the scrapbook she began crying and Lacy asked why. She said it was nothing, but Lacy asked again and she showed Lacy a news article of a guy she used to date. He was black and he was a physicist. She said he was much older than her and he broke her heart. Lacy told her that he was sorry to hear that. She told Lacy that he was the first person she had wanted to have sex with since that guy broke her heart. Lacy told her that he wasn't prepared for that and came just to have dinner and talk. She began crying and told Lacy she felt rejected by him and all she wanted was one night with him. Lacy told her that he didn't even have condoms with him so there would be no protection. She said there was no need for protection because she said the guy that broke her heart raped her and damaged her insides so she could never have children.

"What?" Lacy said. "What an animal. I'm so sorry for you Sarah."

"I didn't want to tell you that part Lacy, but now it's out," she said. "Lacy, if we spend the night together I promise never to bother you again if you don't want to be bothered, but I really need you now." Lacy asked about that new disease called AIDS.

"We don't have any protection." She told him that she gives blood regularly so she was clean. She began taking his shirt off and he resisted...at first. He told her he was still a bit new to sex. She told him she would teach him anything he needed to know.

Immediately, she wanted to get on top and he quickly remembered what Mom said about women on top bitching men out.

"Uhh, maybe we can start another way," Lacy said. She said okay, so she slid down and tried to put her mouth on him and he moved and asked her what she was going to do. She told him to relax but he couldn't. He could not get an erection because he was thinking about what happened between him and Randy when he was four. She tried to get him going for at least twenty minutes then slapped the bed with her hand and told him if he wanted to leave he should have just left and not play games with her.

He told her it wasn't a game. He said, "It's just not comfortable." He asked if they could just eat and talk and try again later. She said okay.

They ate and he really wanted to leave but he said he would try again, so he was not leaving. After they ate they went back to the bedroom and tried again, and once he got an erection she continued telling him that he didn't know how much them being together that night meant to her. She slid up and got on top of Lacy and he resisted at first, but she told him it was okay. She told him to relax and close his eyes. It was already dark and the only light was the moonlight shining through the window. He closed his eyes and she kept talking to him seductively, asking if he liked it, and he said yes.

"Do you really like it?"

"Yes," he said.

"Okay," she said. *SLAP!* Right across his face. He jumped up and turned the light on and asked why she did that. She said, "I'm sorry, I thought you might like that."

"Like it?" he asked. "I used to get slapped on a regular, so no I don't like that. What's wrong with you? You said you wanted sex then you slap the shit out of me. Mom told me about women like you."

"Baby, I'm sorry, really, I'm sorry," she said. "Come back and let me make it better." She went down on him again then got on top again and slapped him again. He got up to leave and she fell to her knees and began working on him orally so he stopped in his tracks. After a few moments, he picked her up and lay her on the bed on her back and they had sex and sex and sex and sex and sex. Afterward, she apologized for the slapping and said she had it done to her and thought he might be into it.

He said, "Never." He was in a rush because it was morning and he still had to go home, shower, and change. She thanked him for not rejecting her and for making her feel special again. He said he was glad they spent time together except for the slaps and he would see her at the club. She rarely went to the club anymore and he didn't see her for quite some time.

Lacy was waiting for Howard to get home so they could go out. He was making sandwiches for him and Howard to eat on the way to Hollywood while Howard's mom was on the phone at the dining room table. She was speaking with a girlfriend and was sharing her vacation stories about New Orleans. She said she had a great time then she mentioned how the "black gals waited on she and her friends hand and foot just like the good ole' days."

Lacy froze where he stood and Howard's mom noticed that Lacy's fast movements came to a quick stop and she looked at him and dropped her head. They just looked at each other for a moment until she got up and she and her friend went upstairs to her room to finish her conversation. Lacy and Howard's mom never spoke about that moment. Lacy didn't mention it to Howard but Lacy didn't want to stay there anymore.

A few days later when Lacy and Howard were talking, the phone rang and Howard said, "Yo Laaaace. It's for you."

"Me?" Lacy asked.

"Yeah, you, Mr. Popular."

"Who is it?"

"Someone named Sarah."

Lacy thought for a moment then said, "OOOH, Sarah. Sure." He greeted Sarah and asked how she was. She told him she was great and had great news. She said she was pregnant. "WHAAAAT?" Lacy asked. "That's great Sarah," he said. "I thought you couldn't have children."

"It's a miracle Lacy. It really is," she said.

"I'm so happy for you," Lacy said. "Who's the father?"

"YOU ARE, SILLY," she said. Lacy didn't say anything, he just looked at Howard with a blank look on his face. Howard asked Lacy what was wrong. Lacy said nothing. Again, Howard asked what was wrong as he stood up and moved toward Lacy.

"May I call you back later Sarah? Because I have to take care of something." He hung up the phone and told Howard that Sarah was pregnant and that he was the father.

"OOOOOHH FUCK," Howard said. "What are you going to do?" Lacy was quiet for a few moments, so Howard asked again.

Lacy looked him right in the eyes and said, "If that's my child there is only one thing to do man."

"Abort it?" Howard asked.

"NO! Take care of it and be the father I'm supposed to be." Howard sat down and told Lacy to think it over and how his bodybuilding dreams would be over. Lacy asked Howard to excuse him while he went to lay down and think things through. By morning, Lacy contacted Sarah and told her that he would be very responsible and father their child, but there was to be no marriage. She agreed and suggested they lived together to make the experience easier on everyone involved. He agreed. Word traveled fast about the pregnancy, and Mom told Marcel to tell Lacy that she wanted to see him. Lacy went to go see Mom at a different building since she moved around the corner from where she lived previously. As he walked up the walkway to her door, he remembered all the things Esta, Jasper, and various people along the way, including the older man on Lake Avenue, told him about being careful of those that may try to take things from him. Mom opened the door and told Lacy she was cooking and to follow her to the kitchen. When they got to the kitchen, he saw plates of food all over the counters and pots on the stove. Lacy asked if she was expecting a lot of company and she said Horace, Marcel, and Randy would be there soon along with Mr. Lincoln. "Ahhh. How's he doing?" Lacy asked.

"He's fine," she said. "So, you got that tramp pregnant I hear."

"We'll be having a child, yes," Lacy said. She continued cutting onions and didn't look at Lacy.

"Child?" she asked. "Is that what you think you're going to have with her? What have I told you and the other boys about women? She will take everything you have and more and you will be sorry Lacy. I guess you didn't see this in those dreams and visions of yours, did you?"

"Visions and dreams can help to a point but we have to use our common sense too and I just didn't pay close enough attention, but things will be fine."

"GOT DAMNIT LACY! Things will not be fine."

"Mom, I'd really appreciate it if you didn't yell at me anymore. I came because Marcel said you wanted to talk to me."

"You damn fool, I am talking to you. How many fucking times have I told you that you are too gullible and nice to people and they will see it as weakness rather than kindness."

Lacy said, "Yes, but those that see it as weakness and act upon it will only hurt themselves in the long run as you've seen. Everyone that has wronged me so far with no reason to do so has suffered great losses in health, mental state, finances, and happiness, and those that haven't yet will do too if they do not wake up and fix their selfish lives and behavior."

"I admit, you've been the luckiest person I've known in my entire life but luck runs out," she said.

"I don't mean to be disrespectful in disagreeing with you but God has been with me, not luck. Whether you or others believe it without hesitation or not, God is always present regardless of the outcome. Eventually, God deals with everyone one way or another at times least expected. So, those that see me as weak and are tempted to use me or take advantage of me will eventually pay the cost of their behavior in time. I'd rather be seen as weak and let the other person pay the cost rather than me pay the cost for being the jerk and ill-behaved one."

"Hmmm. Still the fool," she said.

"My child will be great and I will love my child as I should," Lacy said.

"Maybe you better leave because you make me want to vomit. And don't call me when that bitch takes all you have and gets you into trouble."

"Okay," Lacy said. "Please take care of yourself and say hello to the others."

"Uhmhmm," she said.

PAYING THE NEXT MAN

About this time, Esta began contacting Lacy more and more since she heard he was going to be a father. Although they didn't see each other often, Esta would phone Lacy from time to time and for a couple of years they saw each other on major holidays. Alexandra kept Esta well informed of the goings-on in everyone's life. As Sarah's belly began to show more and more, Lacy moved in as he said he would, and once the baby was born they all shared the same room since it was a small place. At that time, a gym called Flex opened not too far away and the owners came for Lacy at the Y. By that time, Lacy developed a private group training program at the Y for teens to educate themselves and motivate themselves early in life to adopt a better and healthier lifestyle. It was a hit, but Lacy wasn't getting any raises or bonuses and needed the money since he bought a car and payments were killing him. The owners of Flex told Lacy they heard about him and wanted to offer him more than the Y and they did. Lacy asked the Y if they could match the offer and they said no, so Lacy took the deal with Flex with the condition that he would take no salary if he could keep all of the money he made from his private clients. The owners of Flex took that deal quickly because they had no idea how many clients Lacy had. Once Lacy's clients began training at Flex and he gained even more clients, the owners wanted to change the deal and that was when Lacy knew it was time to open his own place. Within months, Sarah told Lacy that she wanted to get married so their son would not know he was born out of wedlock. Lacy said their son would be fine either way. No marriage. Sarah came home one day with a ring and told Lacy to wear it because they were getting married. Lacy told her to knock off the crazy talk and that he was not getting married. He came home one day to an empty house, and minutes later there was a knock at the door. It was one of Sarah's friends and she served Lacy with papers. It was a notice to appear in court with countless charges against him. Lacy jumped in his car that he purchased recently and sped to the police station on Briggs Ave in La Crescenta. He went inside and saw an officer and asked the officer if that paper was a gag, a joke, or prank, and the officer looked at Lacy and said it was very real and that he should arrest Lacy right there on the spot and take him into custody. He told Lacy that his pants were torn from hip to ankle and he needed to go home and change, otherwise, he would make an arrest. He told Lacy it was his lucky day and to get an attorney. Lacy tried getting a lawyer, but once they knew it was a white woman and a black man the lawyers told Lacy they didn't want to touch the case because they weren't confident they could win. One lawyer told Lacy to plead no contest, meaning he was not saying he did the crimes or didn't do the crimes, leaving doubt either way. He told Lacy that would be the best play or he would do a minimum of two years for what he clearly did not do. It was clearly all lies because the time frames and accusations were to have taken place when Lacy was training Stephen J. Cannell, world-renowned producer, director, and writer of 21 Jump Street, The A Team, and The Rockford Files, among many other shows. After they trained at Steve's home, they had dinner at Hamburger Hamlet in Pasadena near Steve's home to discuss training at Lacy's brand new training studio called Private Fitness by Lacy Weston. When Steve found out what happened and read the court papers, he was outraged and wrote a letter for Lacy in his defense and offered to show up to court. Lacy had many people give him letters of character

The night before court, Lacy woke up from a terrible dream. In his dream, he saw himself in a room with white floors, white walls, and a white ceiling. He saw people entering the room on a conveyor belt and the conveyor belt would stop each person in front of a man that sat at a table with small horns sticking out of his head and teeth that looked like a vampire's. The man at the table would say a few words to the person in front of him then the conveyor belt would move that person a little further down to another man that collected money from each person as they cried. There was also a man that stood by the exit door who would open the door as people left. The man with the horns kept looking over at Lacy because Lacy didn't want to get on the conveyor belt. The man stood from his chair and told Lacy to get on the conveyor belt or he would regret it. All of the people in the room told Lacy to get on the belt, including the man collecting money and the man that opened the door as people left. Lacy got on the conveyor belt and was moved in front of the man with horns and that man smiled at Lacy and said, "I don't care if you're right or wrong, you will bow to me. NOW PAY THE NEXT MAN!" Lacy paid the next man and as the third man opened the door for Lacy to leave, Lacy woke up. Lacy got to court and saw how things were handled and noticed people paying money to leave the room rather than be taken into custody. He noticed that the judge looked like the man in his dream with the horns and odd teeth. He also saw the collector of money and the man that opened the door as people left. When it was Lacy's turn to go before the Pro Tem, the Pro Tem didn't want to hear any of what Lacy had to say in his defense. He told Lacy to hurry up and pick guilty, not guilty, or no contest. Lacy tried to explain how it was all not true and tried to show the letter he got from Sarah as a confession, but no dice. The Pro Tem said many women wrote letters of regret that were not true and were forced by the guy.

Lacy said, "She wrote it because she lied and is trying to tell you that. She is sitting right over there and will tell you herself."

"Mr. Weston, guilty, not guilty, or no contest." The Pro Tem explained guilty meant Lacy would do time and that not guilty meant a trial by jury, which he didn't advise because if he lost he would probably do more time. He explained what no contest meant and as he explained, Lacy thought about the lawyer he spoke with that told him to plead no contest and just get on with his life and be more careful with the people he associated with in the future. Lacy teared up a bit because he hated, absolutely hated being accused of things he didn't do, especially when it involved bigotry and bias. He saw several white men that day walking out of the courtroom after admitting to doing terrible things. He pled no contest and got two years of probation and was told if he so much as spit on a sidewalk he would be arrested and do the two years. He was twenty-three years old.

He told Sarah, who was nearly ten years older, to never to speak to him again and they would have a mediator help with visitation. He put himself on house arrest and told all of his friends he was not going out for two years so if they wanted to see him it would be at home. He moved in with a long-time friend Randy, then moved into his own apartment a month later so he could have a place for him and his son. The only time he was out of his apartment was to go to work, to pick up his son and take him back, to the park to play with his son, or to the grocery store. For two years, Lacy focused hard and built his business, but there were some slumps here and there. One of which was when the lease of the first location was ending and the lessor didn't want to renew his lease because the lessor said a black man should be not making that kind of money. Lacy had to find a new location and he did, but the rent was four times as much and he only had enough money to last six months after the expenses of opening a new location and buying all-new equipment, since the current equipment was not his. By the time he was entering the second month of new rent, he went to pick his son up from daycare and the daycare mother said that the mother moved and his son no longer went there. Lacy knew this was a direct violation of his rights and visitation with his son. He tried calling Sarah but no response. He called a lawyer and the lawyer told Lacy that she violated his rights and he could take her to court but they had to find her first. The lawyer told Lacy that once they found her she would probably go to jail and Lacy's son would hold that against him in the future. The lawyer told Lacy he would try to locate Sarah but after weeks of trying, nothing came up. About two months later, Sarah contacted Lacy and told him that she moved to another state where she found a better job and told Lacy he could visit his son there. Lacy got hold of his lawyer and the lawyer told Lacy since they were dealing with laws in two different states the legal fees would go through the roof. He also told Lacy that she would definitely go to jail and reminded Lacy that his son would never forgive him if that happened. Lacy asked the lawyer over and over if there was another option. After more than an hour of the lawyer repeating himself, he finally told Lacy that he had seen many cases like his. He told Lacy the best thing to do was nothing and that Sarah would contact him when she got tired of their son asking for him. "Or, she will just get tired."

"I'm supposed to wait until she gets tired?" Lacy asked. "That could be never."

"Please trust me Lacy," the lawyer said. "All of the money you spend in court should be saved and used to make a better life for you and your son because you will go broke if you proceed. I can see your love for your son in your eyes and in your heart and I'm asking you to please not get financially drained due to emotions and out of fear that he is not safe." The lawyer told Lacy it would be very, very hard but it was the only way.

Lacy got up and said, "Thank you for your time," and walked out. He got to his car and went from lawyer to lawyer to lawyer and only one gave different advice. The lawyer told Lacy to move to the state where they were. Lacy told that lawyer he didn't want to be anywhere near her because of the false accusations from before. "I don't trust her at all and will never go where she is."

"Not even for your son?" the lawyer asked.

"If I were to go where she is in another state I risk losing my freedom if I were to be set up again, and then my son will have the same life I had. No. I will do what the other lawyers said. I will wait." Lacy became depressed and cried each night. His friends tried to cheer him up and told him that this was the first time in their lives they didn't see the Lacy smile they were used to seeing. He began to lose weight and work from three in the morning to nine o'clock at night to keep his mind off of the pain of not seeing his son. Howard noticed his weight loss and the terrible cough he had and drove him to Santa Monica and got him admitted to St. John's Hospital. When they saw Lacy, they immediately put him in bed and hooked up the IVs. They told Lacy he was severely physically exhausted and needed to rest. The doctor spoke with Lacy in private and asked what was going on in his life. Lacy broke down in tears and told the doctor that he completely failed his son and didn't know what to do. He told the doctor that history was repeating itself and his son would suffer just like he did. The doctor told Lacy he must calm down and try to relax. The doctor told Lacy that he would eventually see his son and they would have a wonderful relationship but that would never happen if Lacy continued his sleepless nights and overworking himself to numb the pain. He ordered Lacy to stay home for three weeks. He told Lacy to only get out of bed to go to the bathroom and to eat. Lacy stayed with Randy and Randy looked after him along with Howard and Marcus. Marcel told Lacy he felt very bad for him and said he could help Lacy with his customers since Marcel taught martial arts here and there. Since Lacy was concerned about paying his high rent he agreed and thanked Marcel for helping. Mom stopped by and told Lacy this is why she told him to abort the baby and if he did he wouldn't have gone through all that shit. That was not what Lacy needed to hear. That was when Randy told Mom that the doctor said that Lacy shouldn't speak much and must rest. Mom gave Randy an odd look and left. The next day, Lacy contacted Marcus and told him that he hadn't tried calling the woman from overseas. He said he would give it one last try and also said if he doesn't reach her he would stop trying altogether but that he believed he would find her. Marcus told Lacy to let that be the very last time so he could move on with his life. Lacy told Marcus that she was carrying the twins and he knew it.

Marcus said, "Lacy, you're supposed to be resting man, so maybe you want to call another time because you're talking crazy right now."

"You're right Marcus," Lacy said. "I'll rest and call later. See you later Marcus."

"Yeah man, I'll stop by later," Marcus said. Lacy called the overseas operator and gave her the woman's name and asked if she could locate her. For the first time in many, many calls that particular operator asked Lacy why he was calling for a person in another country because the operator had never experienced such a call. Lacy told the operator that he lost contact with his friend when she was called home for some type of emergency. He told the operator they never had a chance to say goodbye.

The operator told Lacy that she was staring at the number of the person he wanted and Lacy said, "Neeeeetoooo! I mean, wonderful."

The operator said, "I hope you and your friend have a great reunion," and gave Lacy the number. Lacy called the number immediately and a guy answered. Lacy asked if Felicia was there and the guy said she was away on business. Lacy wanted to ask the guy if he was Felicia's husband or brother but the guy interrupted Lacy's next sentence and said that Felicia would be back on the weekend. Lacy asked if he would let Felicia know he called and that he would call on the weekend. The guy said sure and they hung up. Lacy called Marcus and told him the news and Marcus could not believe it, just as Randy had a hard time believing it and everyone else that knew the story. That weekend, Lacy called Felicia and she told Lacy how glad she was to hear from him. She said she had just gotten home from a business trip and was in the middle of moving out of her ex-boyfriend's place, but she asked for Lacy's address and said she would write to him very soon. They said their goodbyes and hung up. Lacy just knew things would work out. Once Lacy was better and back to work, Marcel said he would like to continue working with Lacy but Lacy had always been against family working together in business, at least *his* family. After a few conversations, Lacy agreed, and within a few weeks, Marcel told Lacy that Mom said that he should ask Lacy for a partnership.

Lacy reached out his hand and asked Marcel for his key to the business and said, "This is where we part ways." Marcel asked him what the heck was going on. Lacy told Marcel that Mom had no influence over his business decisions and for her to make suggestions was too much for him so they were done here.

Shortly after that incident with Marcel, Felicia's letter arrived from overseas. Lacy called her all the time and they wrote letters to each other back and forth. Just as Lacy was approaching the sixth month in his new training studio, the movie "Terminator" with Arnold Schwarzenegger came out featuring Linda Hamilton, and she looked fantastic. She was on the "Donahue Show" talking about how she got her body in shape with a trainer, and overnight, Lacy's phone rang and rang and rang as people held onto the cards and flyers about his training programs he constantly put everywhere he could. By Christmas, Felicia arrived and they spent that Christmas together. The next movie that came out was called "Staying Alive" featuring John Travolta. He went on talk shows talking about how he got into shape with the help of a trainer, and Lacy's phone rang again and again and again, and that was when Lacy needed more hands on deck and put a call out for more trainers. That summer, Felicia visited and stayed for one month, then Lacy went overseas to meet her family and they were married months later. Shortly after they were married, Felicia was changing TV channels and Lacy asked her to stop when he saw Trisha from the Imperial Health Spa on the Playboy channel, topless and walking through a bar scene.

"Do you know her?" Felicia asked.

"Yes," Lacy said. "We dated for a very short time but it was long ago."

A few months after the marriage, Lacy was going to meet Felicia for lunch on Lake Avenue but when he arrived he saw police cars, a fire truck, and an ambulance, and wondered what happened. A man that recognized him from his ads told him that his wife was in the ambulance. Lacy ran to the ambulance and knocked on the back door. The medic asked what Lacy wanted and Lacy told him that he was told his wife was in the ambulance.

The medic said, "I doubt this is your wife because this is a white woman named Felicia."

"That's my wife," Lacy said.

The medic asked Felicia if that was true, and in excruciating pain because of her broken neck she said, "Yes, that's my husband, open the door." After months of rehab and medical visits, she healed. She didn't want to work for other companies anymore and asked Lacy if they could work together, but Lacy was against family working together in business. He knew that was true of his family but wasn't sure about his new family. This was an ongoing discussion for at least one year. Lacy was not at all used to asking for help outside of needing a place to stay like in the past. He also found it difficult to ask for what he needed, so he wasn't sure how to work with Felicia in a business capacity. Working with trainers and other business people came easy but working with someone he slept with was very new to Lacy. Much of this was dealt with when Lacy had four clients that he trained back to back. Three of the clients were psychologists and the fourth was a behavioral specialist. On the days when Lacy worked with those four clients, he would tell Felicia that he felt they were probing his head every second of those sessions and he was doing all he could to not let them in.

He said he was extremely exhausted by the end of those four sessions. The three psychologists were women and the behavioral specialist was a man. One woman worked in schools with teenagers and she would walk in the front door firing off questions.

"Hi Lacy. Wow! Look at all those cups in the trash can. You must be inundated with customers and so proud of yourself since you built this business from the ground up. Who taught you how to do all of this, your mother or father?"

Lacy looked at her then laughed and said, "Jack LaLanne." Of course, that was his way to get out of speaking about his parents. After that session, the next psychologist came in and mentioned how she had a challenging morning and asked Lacy how he handled challenging days and how his parents handled them. Lacy told her that he didn't remember how they dealt with challenging days. He said he dealt with challenging days by dissecting what was challenging about it, then dealt with that challenge appropriately. He told her that he also meditated and spent more time being grateful for each day than not, which lessened the degree of the challenges. She told him she admired his approach and outlook on life. The next psychologist would directly ask Lacy about his childhood and what it was like for him. Lacy didn't like talking about that. Lacy would mention all of his friends and the fun they had. The woman would press Lacy and ask him about the fun he had at home. Lacy told her he played board games inside and hide and go seek outside like most children did. "Why are you digging into my childhood so much?" Lacy asked. "Each time we train it seems to be the topic of discussion." The woman told Lacy she didn't want him to feel uncomfortable but she could tell he was holding onto so many secrets and pain, especially when she asked what he planned for Mother's

Day and Father's Day. She told Lacy that he got quiet when she asked about those holidays. She told Lacy that somehow, he learned how to tap into other people and help them release fear, pain, and reach great heights in life because she had heard nothing but praise for him all around town and in other cities. She told Lacy that once he was able to release himself from the past, he would be even more of an incredible godsend to the world. Lacy said, "I understand and agree with all that you're saying."

"BUT?" she said.

Lacy said, "But, I've spent my life hiding the truth from my closest friends and anyone that would ask the type of questions you're asking me." She asked Lacy why he felt he needed to hide from his closest friends. He said, "Because people talk and words would get back to people in my family. Also, boys are taught to keep quiet and not share these types of things, so I keep quiet. And, if I went to my friends or anyone each time I was not having a good time at home how long do you think friends would have lasted? Friends are great to talk to but no one wants to hear regular episodes of drama. That's what soap operas are for."

"Hahahaha. That's a good one Lacy, you've got a good sense of humor. So, have you shared your pain and frustrations with anyone?"

"Of course," Lacy said, "but in small, small doses."

"Who did you share with Lacy?"

"I would share with people that had similar stories because they would understand where I was coming from and I would understand where they were coming from."

"I see," she said. "Did you tell people that didn't have similar situations?" He said he found it easier to open up and share with women he dated or friends he met after leaving home that were much older than him because he felt they were mature enough to understand. "Would you feel comfortable sharing with me Lacy?" she asked.

"Would you feel comfortable sharing your childhood or embarrassing moments in life with me?" Lacy asked.

"Wow, I've never had anyone ask me that before Lacy. I guess I would not be completely comfortable sharing my life stories unless I trusted the person. I do trust you Lacy and really see why so many others trust you. I trust you Lacy, you can ask me whatever you like."

"I don't have any questions for you," Lacy said. "I just wanted to make sure the line of communication was clear and open on both sides."

"You're good at setting boundaries and I can see fairness is very important to you."

"It is," he said. She asked if he felt comfortable sharing anything he was feeling at that moment. He said, "Yes. What I'm about to say I've never said before to anyone so I hope we can keep this between us."

"You have my word," she said.

Lacy said, "You and the other psychologists and specialists keep asking me so many questions that it makes my head spin. It seems like you've all gotten together and decided to question me all day but I realize you all want to help me and I appreciate your help but it's hard."

"Lacy, if you don't mind let's not workout today. If you are open to it we can just talk because I feel like you are at a very important time in your life and you are about to break out of a very hard shell you've been in."

"I don't mind. Thank you," he said.

"You're welcome Lacy. What did you mean when you said it's hard Lacy?"

He said, "I mean it's not easy to discuss what you don't know."

"Explain," she said.

He said, "It's hard because I don't know the answers to many of your questions. I don't know who my real mother is and I don't know who my real father is. I've heard so many stories over the years that they could be anyone. I am the youngest of nine children I'm told but that isn't true. It feels like one day came and I existed in a house with a lot of people but I never had a connection to any parents and never called anyone Mom until I was four years old and that was slapped into me. I thought the word 'Mom' was a name like the name Lacy. I didn't know what it meant. In kindergarten when the teacher would read stories and talk about mothers and fathers I realized the word 'Mom' meant something entirely different. So, when I was told to call the woman that raised me 'Mom' I didn't feel a motherly connection, it was just a name. Most of the time I would just start talking and not call her Mom to avoid the very uncomfortable use of that word in regard to her. The worst part is that she recognized that I was intentionally not calling her Mom and I got beatings for it."

"Are you feeling angry or upset right now Lacy?" she asked.

"No, do I look angry or upset?" he asked.

"No. You seem fine but I want you to feel comfortable to let out whatever emotions you may be feeling."

Lacy said, "I heard Mom say over and over that she didn't go past the eighth grade and I heard others say that she was carrying on in the streets living the wild life since she was thirteen. I find it difficult to be angry or upset with an adult that is really a child in an adult's body. That doesn't mean I completely overlook all that has happened with her, but holding anger and resentment toward her isn't going to hurt or help her as it would only affect me and I don't need that."

"Right on Lacy," she said. "You have so much to offer the world Lacy and I hope you don't hide from all of those people that could benefit from knowing you. I believe you have a lot more to release and I am available if you ever want to set an appointment at my office to continue."

"Thank you," Lacy said. "I understand I've been holding secrets to avoid upsetting family with the truths I know. I've also been hurting myself by doing so and I promise you that stops today."

"Bravo Lacy," she said. "Don't rush yourself and just take your time."

Lacy said, "I won't rush but I also won't block up the dam that just burst. Thank you for allowing me to share with you and making yourself available if I need to speak with you. And, we will work out twice as hard next time to make up for today." He laughed.

"You are welcome Lacy, and yes we will," she said, laughing. Then she left. Lacy did a lot of thinking after that session. He thought of all of the questions he would no longer dodge regarding Mother's Day and

Father's Day since those two holidays caused more frustration for him than one could imagine. Because some people were extremely opinionated and projected their beliefs onto others like a bird crapping on someone walking below, Lacy would put on his imaginary raincoat and wait for the bird crap to drop.

"Sooo, Lacy what are you doing for your mother on Mother's Day?"

"Nothing, because we don't see each other."

"Wwwhhhaaat? That's horrible. What kind of a son are you?" or, "Heeeey, Lacy I bet you have something nice planned for Father's Day. You must have because you're a great guy so your dad must be great too."

"No, my father died a long time ago."

"OOOHHH, that's a shame."

"Will you spend it with your mom then?"

"No, we haven't spoken in years."

"OOH, honestly Lacy, I don't know if I feel comfortable training with any trainer that doesn't speak with his mother."

As Lacy would hear statements like that it became more and more difficult to hear. He would think of the times when Mom would tell him how she enjoyed seeing him upset or enjoyed the look of frustration on his face because it reminded her of his father. So, he would respond to people with, "Would you feel comfortable with your daughter meeting her rapist on Valentine's Day so that the rapist wouldn't feel alone that day?"

"How dare you ask such a thing Lacy?"

Lacy would say, "I'm saying the same thing you're saying to me but in your lack of compassion you just don't realize you're doing it. If two people don't speak, it's not up to you or anyone to judge either of the two. You asked me a question, and I answered by saying we don't speak and that should be the end of it." The other person didn't think the same and that was the last time they would speak. That particular type of conversation was part of a catalyst for Lacy to stop hiding from the world due to the past, and to use more tact in the process. Rather than saying, "MIND YOUR OWN FUCKING BUSINESS," he learned to say, "Mind your own fucking business." When Lacy got home that evening, he reflected on the conversation he had with the last psychologist and felt great about no longer hiding from the world. He always felt he could only go so far in life helping others if he wasn't honest with himself and others regarding his past. Now he felt like nothing was holding him back. He went to bed that night and woke up about three o'clock in the morning, just about an hour before his alarm would go off. He sat up in bed for a moment then he got up and stood still. Felicia asked if he was okay. He said yes. "I just had a dream that I was driving to work and when I looked in the rearview mirror I saw my son sitting in the back seat. He looked a couple of years older and said, 'Hiya Lacy. I'll be seeing you soon' and that's when I woke up." Felicia said that was an odd dream and told Lacy to go back to sleep. Lacy said he couldn't sleep because he knew his son needed and wanted him and would be calling soon.

"Is that what you really think?" Felicia asked.

"Yes," Lacy said. "There is no reason on this earth for me to have a dream like that otherwise. I've told you before there are dreams and there are messages and you have to know the difference. This was a clear message."

JOE MAXWELL

Three days later, Sarah contacted Lacy and said his son wanted to see him. It was agreed that Lacy would cover flights and accommodation in exchange to see his son. After that visit, Sarah told Lacy if he wanted to see his son again he had to pay for both plane tickets and for her hotel. Lacy said no. He said, "Now that my son and I have seen each other it will be difficult for you to block our desire to see each other again. I will pay for his ticket and he can stay with me but there is no reason for you to come. But, if you choose to come you can pay for your own ticket and hotel." That was exactly what happened. Apparently, Lacy grew tired of Felicia, friends, and strangers telling him how he was too nice and giving. Jasper's words, Esta's words, Mom's words, and the words of others were finally sinking in. When Lacy said no to Sarah he was actually thinking of the man he ran into on Lake Avenue many years earlier that told him to be careful because people would want to take advantage of him. He also thought of the history between him and Sarah and didn't trust being around her. He had no ill will toward her but he just didn't believe he could trust her. Lacy and his son were able to increase their visitation frequency through court and their relationship would grow over time. Having his son back in his life and knowing that his son knew 100% that he had a father that loved him, inspired Lacy to soar even more in life. Lacy began training more celebrities, writers, producers, and directors. He was featured on NBC News quite often with Colleen

Williams and that was a thrill for him because she was his client and friend. He was invited to the set of the hit TV show "Star Trek: The Next Generation" several times because his client Les Landau was one of the directors and Les' brother John, who co-produced "Titanic", was also a client. He opened three more locations in Pasadena, Studio City, and Hollywood about the same time he began training Zachery Ty Bryan from the TV show "Home Improvement". The Hollywood location was on the lot of Stephen J. Cannell Productions. Life was good and Lacy was having the time of his life. He and Felicia were doing great. When she first moved to the U.S., Lacy made it clear that he would never push her to have children and when she was ready to tell him and he would be ready and would not be an absentee dad. He told her that it broke his heart when his son was taken to another state. He told Felicia when they had children, "If for any reason we aren't together please know that the children come first and we must always be understanding and not put them through what my son went through." She looked at Lacy in an odd way as to why he would say such a thing.

She said, "I promise." Of course, Lacy believed wholeheartedly that they would have twin girls as the earlier vision showed him but it also showed him that she would not be around. He wanted to make sure he had her word so if the time did arrive where she would not be around, the girls would not suffer the absence of either parent as his son did. Many of their friends were having children so it was on both of their minds, but it was not yet time. They spent a lot of time going to visit Gus in Las Vegas where he lived and had a thriving security business. Gus and Lacy spoke all the time and one day Gus called to tell Lacy that he ran into a woman in her sixties at the grocery store that recognized him and said that she knew their family. He said that she wanted to see everyone and had a lot to share. Gus asked if Lacy could visit. Lacy said sure. That weekend, Lacy and Felicia drove to Las Vegas. Odessa and her husband arrived as well and Esta and her second husband later that day. The woman named Gertrude contacted Gus and asked if they could all meet with her right away because she got sleepy early and wanted to see them before she got too sleepy. Everyone drove to her home and she was very excited to see everyone. Esta had not arrived yet so it was Gus, Odessa and her husband, and Lacy and Felicia that showed up. Gertrude put out many chairs to accommodate everyone, and after the hugs, she asked everyone to sit down. She kept staring at Lacy and told him she remembered him as she smiled big. She immediately shared stories of how she helped Mom so much in the past. She said that she and Mom used to be best friends and watched each other's back, but they both did some prostitution and got into fights. She said one fight got so bad that Mom put just a touch of bleach in her wig. She said she realized what happened when her hair began falling out.

She spoke of the different fathers that all of them had then she looked at Lacy and said, "Now you know Esta is your mother, right?" Lacy looked at her and told her that he heard things over the years and noticed that they were the only two that looked alike. Gertrude said, "Lacy, your father is still alive and lives in Peoria, Illinois." Lacy was shocked and stopped breathing because everyone was staring at him.

Felicia said, "I thought you said your father was dead."

Gertrude said, "Oh baby, he had no way of knowing. He was so young that he just believed what he was told, so don't hold that against him." Lacy was still in shock. All those years of mystery and for what?

"What's his name?" Lacy asked.

"His name is Joe. Joe Maxwell."

"What? I spoke with that guy after I graduated high school. He was crying on the phone so I tossed the phoned down and didn't want to speak with him. Why didn't he just say who he was?"

Gertrude said, "Lacy, your Mom has long arms and knows a lot of people, good and bad. Everyone knows not to mess with her. Joe and your mom probably had an arrangement and he had to stick to the arrangement or deal. Do you want to speak with him?" she asked Lacy.

"Yes," Lacy said.

"Okay. I'll give you his number before you leave but you can't tell anyone I gave it to you or my goose will be cooked and I mean that. I'm doing this because no child should be on this earth and not know who their parents are."

"RIGHT," Lacy said.

"But Lacy, promise me you won't tell a soul where you got his number until I'm dead and gone or just say you found it on your own."

"Okay," Lacy said. Gertrude went on with her stories and when she got sleepy they left to let her rest. As they were leaving she said she was scared living by herself and showed them a huge poultry fork that she kept by her bed to protect herself.

Lacy thought that was odd because he saw Mom pull a similar poultry fork on Tex one day when he came home from school. *Must be a southern thing,* he thought to himself. When they got back to Gus' house, Esta had arrived and Odessa told her everything that the woman said. Esta was steaming furious and wanted to speak with Lacy right away. She began crying and told Lacy the story wasn't true and she was upset with him for believing a stupid old woman. She raised her voice and it seemed that she was angrier with Lacy than she was with the woman. Lacy couldn't figure out why she was talking to him that way instead of the woman so he told her that he did not need her to validate him and he was tired of the bullshit. He told her if she wanted to be in his life, great, and if not that was fine too because he was a grown man now and his life was good and he was rolling on. As she stormed out of the room, she told her husband that she was not staying there and she wanted to go back home to Los Angeles. Odessa pulled Lacy aside and told him she was sorry for mentioning to Esta what Gertrude said. Lacy said, "Odessa, it's not your fault. If I were in Esta's shoes and felt as guilty as she did I'd probably want to drive nearly three hundred miles back to Los Angeles too."

"Are you okay?" Odessa asked Lacy.

"YEEEES. I can't wait to hit the go-kart track and get some racing in."

"Boy, you're silly," she said.

He said, "Always and forever. For I am the professor, aka super genius, aka Lacy Dick Tracy, aka…"

"OOOOKAAAYYY! That's enough," she said. After a little more discussion about the goings-on of that day they raced go-karts, ate, and enjoyed the rest of the weekend. After the weekend, Lacy called the number for Joe, whom Gertrude claimed was his father. A man answered with a greeting for a barbershop. Lacy asked to speak with Joe Maxwell.

The man said, "He's not here but let me give you a number for him."

"Okay," Lacy said. Lacy called that number and a woman answered with a greeting for a diner. "Hi, may I speak with Joe Maxwell please?" Lacy asked.

"Oooh. Joe Maxwell?" she asked.

"Yes, Joe Maxwell," Lacy said.

"He ain't here. Who's calling?"

"His son Lacy," Lacy said. The phone went quiet.

"His...son...Lacy?" she said.

"Yes, that's right," Lacy said.

"Hold on, let me get a number for you."

"Okay," Lacy said. She gave Lacy a number and Lacy called it.

"Hello, this is Joe, who's calling?" Lacy froze and didn't know what to say. "Hello, speak up," Joe said. "Okay, well if there's nobody there I'm hanging up…"

"WAIT! Is this Joe Maxwell?" Lacy asked.

"Yes, it is young man, and I have things to do so if you have something to say, say it so we can stop wasting all this money on the phone company."

"Do you know who Lacy Weston is?" Lacy asked.

"Of course," Joe said. "That's my son. Who are you and how can I help you?" Joe asked.

"I'm Lacy."

"YOU'RE LACY?" Joe said.

"Yes, I am."

"OH MY GOD. HI SON," Joe said, as he began crying. This time Lacy didn't mind Joe crying as he did during that phone conversation after his high school graduation.

"Hi," Lacy said. Joe asked if Lacy was in town and Lacy said no. Joe asked how Lacy found him and Lacy told him it was simple. He said he used Joe's underground railroad by calling a barbershop and a diner. Joe laughed and asked when he could see Lacy. Lacy told Joe that he and Felicia would be going overseas in a week to visit family and they had a layover in Chicago for a few hours before going on the plane for the overseas flight.

Joe said, "Give me your flight information and I'll meet you at the airport."

"Perfect," Lacy said. They spoke for a few more minutes then Joe told Lacy that he despised paying phone companies so much money for what should be so much lower in cost.

Joe said, "Let's get off this phone and see each other in person soon."

"Cool," Lacy said.

"Now that you have my number you can call me anytime you want. I'm very glad you found me."

"Did you ever look for me?" Lacy asked.

"Son, it's a long story so I will share everything with you when I see you."

"Okay," Lacy said. "But, did you look for me?" Lacy asked.

Joe said, "Your mother made me swear not to ever contact you. I could only speak with you if she contacted me to talk to you or if you found me and contacted me yourself."

"We spoke after my high school graduation," Lacy said.

"That's right. Your mother called me and said I could speak with you but made me swear not to say who I was and that's why I was crying."

"I also spoke with you when I was ten years old."

"That's right," Joe said.

"And Mom went on a trip when I was a little boy. I stayed with

Odessa and Alexandra and the others went with her to Peoria, more than likely to see you," Lacy said.

"That's right. I had just gotten out of prison. Maaaaannn. You sure have some memory," Joe said. "But listen here, let's get off this phone and talk it all out next week."

"Until next week," Lacy said.

"Until next week," Joe said, then they hung up. That whole week, Lacy Dick Tracy was fitting more of the puzzle pieces together. It made sense why Mom refused to let Lacy get featured in those magazines and be placed on the cover of one back when he was in high school. Publicity like that could spread and inform many people of her past. It would also give Joe a better view of Lacy's life and it was clear Mom didn't want him to have that opportunity. The first two times that Lacy spoke with Joe when he was younger, he remembered that Mom spoke to Joe in a mean way just before she told Lacy to get on the phone. She was warning Joe not to slip up and say who he was. It was making more and more sense why Mom acted the way she did around the house. She was always hiding secrets and truths from everyone.

That was also why she purposely put one child against another whenever she saw them attempting to bond. She was afraid if everyone bonded that everyone would figure out the truth, that almost all of them had different fathers and that Lacy was not her son but her grandson, which would mean Joe molested Esta. The two pairs of shoes, Lacy thought to himself. Esta didn't steal two pairs of shoes. Mom disguised her pain and hatred for Esta by saying shoes, but really, she felt Esta stole the two men in her life. Esta would have been fourteen when Lacy was born and Joe would have been forty-three. No wonder Esta stormed out of Gus' house crying her eyes out that weekend. Was this something Mom allowed to happen based upon her ways or did Joe tiptoe in the middle of the night? He had to know for himself. A week later at the Chicago airport, Lacy was standing with Felicia where he told Joe they would be. After some time, Lacy felt his feet leave the ground and he twisted around to see who picked him up off his feet.

For the first time in his life, he saw a face that looked just like his. A voice came out of that face that said, "Hiya son."

"Wanna put me down?" Lacy said.

"OH, I'm sorry. I just got excited when I saw you and had to pick you up since I never had the chance when you were a baby." Lacy laughed and said he understood.

"Wow!" Felicia said. "You two look like twins."

"Yep, bald heads and all," Joe said. Lacy couldn't stop looking at Joe. "Son, you okay?" Joe asked.

Lacy got a bit emotional and said, "I've never felt a connection or seen anyone where I could actually say 'this is where I came from', so it's a bit of a jolt you know what I mean?"

Joe said, "I can understand that." Joe had a couple of friends with him that he introduced Lacy to, but they said they didn't want to interrupt their short time together so they walked away and Felicia sat with Lacy and Joe. Joe told Lacy to ask any questions he wanted and that he would not hold back on the answers. Lacy asked if there would be any repercussions from Mom if Joe talked. Joe said, "Son, you found me so she must keep her word now."

"Okay," Lacy said. Lacy asked Joe who his mother was.

Joe said, "Your mother is the woman you grew up with."

"No," Lacy said, "I mean my biological mother."

Joe paused and said, "I don't know what you mean."

Lacy said, "Joe, the way you're squirming around in your seat and acting fidgety is how Mom acts when she's uncomfortable. Why are you uncomfortable?"

"Does he always talk to people like this when he wants to know something?" Joe asked Felicia.

Felicia said, "I better leave you two alone," and walked away.

Lacy looked at Joe and said, "There have been so many lies and secrets and so much deceit, trauma, and pain caused by all of you so-called adults, and if you and I are going to stay in touch I want the truth. I don't care that I'm in a Chicago airport and that you drove one hundred and fifty miles to get here. Lie to me once about any of this and it will be the last time we talk."

Joe chuckled a bit and said, "You know son, you have such a warm personality and it's clear that you wouldn't want to hurt a fly, so when you speak this way it makes me chuckle and I'm sorry. Don't ever go to prison because you wouldn't make it in there."

"Funny," Lacy said. "You don't think I can make it in there but you proved you couldn't make it out here."

"Where on earth did you get that tongue of yours?" Joe asked.

"It was developed over time. Would you please answer the question? I am usually much more respectful than I am right now but I don't like being lied to and since you know Mom then you know why I have a problem with being lied to. You haven't been around and haven't seen all that went on and I'm not asking for payment or financial support of any kind like many sons and daughters might. I'm just asking for the truth. Who is my real mother?"

Joe said, "Lacy, please talk to your mother about that."

"I didn't agree to meet you in this place for you to tell me to talk to her."

"Lacy," he said. "I think you already know the answer. I promised your mother I would never tell a soul about any of that."

Lacy said, "It means a great deal to me when a person keeps their promises and agreements and if that's the way it is then that's the way it is. Protecting each other from being exposed to a world of deceit and hurt. I get it."

"I'm sorry son," Joe said.

"She would have been thirteen when she was pregnant with me," Lacy said.

Joe teared up a bit and dropped his head. "Do you hate me?" Joe asked.

Lacy said, "Man, I don't know you well enough to hate you and it's not in my nature to hate anyway."

"Son, may I come out to visit you and get to know you?"

Lacy looked at Joe for a few moments and said yes. "As long as things are kept on the up and up we'll stay in touch. As for those secrets, I now know what I needed to know, so that's that." Joe told Lacy his friends called him Perry so Lacy could call him Joe, Perry, or Dad, whichever he felt comfortable calling him. Lacy said Joe was fine for now. They said goodbye to each other and gave each other a genuine hug.

Lacy said goodbye to Joe's friends and thanked them for riding with Joe. "Don't mention it," they said, then Lacy and Felicia boarded their plane for their overseas trip. During their flight, Felicia asked Lacy if he was glad he met his father and Lacy said yes. He said it was good to meet someone that he actually had roots to and looked like.

"Being told you're someone that you're not isn't an easy gig to keep up once you know it isn't true." Lacy knew the guy they said was his father couldn't have been because his eyes and lips didn't match his. Lacy also remembered a road trip his family took once took to Las Vegas to visit Gus, shortly after he was stationed at Nellis Air Force Base. On their way home, they stopped at a diner somewhere in the desert and met some people.

One of the guys was supposed to be the brother of the guy Lacy was told was his father. His name was Butch and when he saw Lacy he looked very confused, then he looked at Mom with a look of disgust. He smiled at the others but Lacy could tell they had no idea who he was. Too many times Mom let the cat out of the bag and left him just enough crumbs to figure things out. Once, she, Horace, and Marcel were in her bedroom when Lacy was taking a bath. He must have been about ten years old. She called to him and told him to get out of the tub and go to her room, which was just on the other side of the bathroom door. He got out of the tub, dried off a bit, wrapped the towel around himself, then opened the door. She said, "Come in here," so he did. She told him to move closer. Horace and Marcel were laughing it up like hyenas as always. He moved even closer. "Remove the towel," she said.

"I'm naked underneath," Lacy said.

"I don't give a good got damn, you do what I tell you to do when I tell you," she said. "If I tell you to jump, you ask how high. Do you understand that?"

"Yes," Lacy said.

"Now, drop the towel."

"Yeah four-eyes, drop the towel," Horace said. Marcel just giggled. Lacy dropped the towel. "HE HAS HAIR ON HIS TESTICLES!" Horace said.

"YEAH! MORE THAN ME," Marcel said. Lacy didn't move a muscle. He kept his head still and moved only his eyes as he looked at Mom, then Marcel, then at Horace.

"You have something to say Lacy?" Mom asked.

"They can laugh all they want but I will laugh later," Lacy said.

"What does that mean?" Mom asked.

Lacy said, "Jesus once had to take his robe off to show himself and as I dropped my towel I felt a strong energy in this room that was very unhappy about them laughing." Marcel and Horace looked around the room and stopped laughing.

"Get that towel and get back in the bathroom and finish up," Mom said. Lacy finished up, then he went to the living room and sat in the rocking chair to think. As he sat there, he listened to the things Mom, Horace, and Marcel were saying. She lowered her voice a bit but Lacy still heard her say his father had a lot of hair down there too. His nickname was Perry.

"Perry?" Felicia asked.

"Yes, Perry. That clue she dropped many years ago paid off today."

"Are you going to contact your mother about this?" she asked.

"No. She'll contact me because she will be very angry that the cat's out of the bag and she will be afraid of the others knowing the truth."

"Are you going to tell the others?" she asked.

"No, Mom will warn the others and make up a story and say that I'm fabricating a story to get back at her but they will see right through her lie. I'm not going to do anything but keep living my life in forward motion." After their trip overseas, Lacy and Felicia returned home and Lacy was looking forward to getting back to work and building up his business further.

About two days after, he returned to work and was checking his voice messages, and found a very long message that Mom left for him. The message started off with, "YOU BLACK SON OF A BITCH." She went on and on about how Lacy had to go snooping and not mind his own business and added quite a few more curse words. Lacy ignored the message and didn't respond. Randy got in touch with Lacy and told him how upset Mom was and that Lacy should meet and speak with her.

Lacy said, "No. Games are over." Randy told Lacy there was a passage in the Bible that said you should honor your father and mother. Lacy reminded Randy that Lacy was the only one in the family that never talked back, raised his voice, or showed her blatant disrespect. "Now," Lacy said, "you go and look in the mirror and count the number of times you've stepped into a jail cell and tell yourself that same Bible passage."

"Fuck you Lacy. I'll get some people after you to fix your ass."

"Randy," Lacy said, "while you're getting your people, keep in mind if anyone even gives me a dirty look and tell me they know you I will unleash any and all feelings I have about you on your ass in a hellified way." *Click*, went the phone as Lacy hung up. That conversation with Randy silenced a lot of the noise that existed before and Lacy was able to completely focus on the business. He began developing fitness exercise products, workout videos, and a fitness and music album for children to inspire them to take care of their health. Lacy and Felicia bought a two-story home near the Rose Bowl, then had twin daughters just as Lacy envisioned all along. Joe came to visit their daughters and was very proud of all the things Lacy had done and was doing with his life. Joe did not like the way Lacy ate because Joe was used to frying everything and drank brandy. Lacy didn't like alcohol and since he didn't have anything Joe liked, Joe asked Lacy if he wouldn't mind taking him to his sister's house. "You have a sister out here?" Lacy asked.

"Yes. I believe she doesn't live too far from you."

"Okay, let's go," Lacy said. They got into the car and drove less than a mile away to his sister's house. "Has she always lived here?" Lacy asked.

"Yes," Joe said.

"Huh…" Lacy wondered. They went inside and Joe introduced Lacy to his sister. His sister gave Lacy a big hug and told him how happy she was to see him. She told Lacy and Joe to sit down. "I've been here before," Lacy said.

"Ohh, no you have not," Joe's sister said.

"Yes I have," Lacy said. "I recognize this room and the feeling I get as I sit here. I have definitely been here before."

Joe said, "Lacy that's impossible because you didn't even know my sister lived here."

"As a child I was brought here once or twice." Lacy said. Joe and his sister looked at each other. "That picture in the other room…that guy's name is Lorenzo, isn't it?"

"Why yes, it is," Joe's sister said.

"Yes," Lacy said. "I remember now. I went to the circus with a guy named Bennie…Lorenzo and Bennie are related. Mom couldn't pick us up from school one day so she sent someone to get us and the man looked just like you Joe. He wore a hat just like you."

"That was my husband," Joe's sister said. "Maybe you two better get going, I'm a little tired with my diabetes you know."

Lacy looked at both of them and said, "Okay." When Lacy and Joe got in the car, Lacy asked Joe if he remembered what he told him about being on the up and up.

"I remember," Joe said. "Lacy, I don't know where your Mom had taken you as a child and had no idea you'd been there."

"Didn't you and your sister speak?" Lacy asked Joe.

"Yes, we did, but we didn't talk about you or your mother."

"Doesn't all of this sound quite crazy to you Joe?"

"Lacy, I was in prison and when I got out I was way behind on all the things that went on out here. You were all the way in California and I was in Illinois. I'm being on the level with you...This isn't the way we came Lacy. Where are we going?"

"I need to stop by the store to get some fruit," Lacy said. "Do you want anything?"

"No. Well, maybe some brandy or sherry."

"Okay," Lacy said.

"Man, you don't drink a lick?" Joe asked Lacy.

"I don't mind having a glass of white wine once in a while but it's not my thing."

"You ever been high or drunk Lacy?"

"No."

"Man! What kind of life have you been living out here?"

"I have a lot of answers to that question that would be good for both you and Mom to hear. Got a minute?" Lacy said. Joe just looked at Lacy with a long face and Lacy burst out laughing and told Joe he looked like the horse from the old TV show "Mr. Ed." "Joe, if you don't want those types of responses from me then it's best not to ask those types of questions."

"You're right man, you're right," Joe said. They were parked in the Vons parking lot of the Orange Wood Plaza in Pasadena.

"Say Joe."

"What man?"

"If you don't want to discuss this just say so and I'll never ask again," Lacy said.

"Why did I go to prison is what you want to know right?" Joe said.

"Uh, I…Yes. That's what I want to know."

"I'll tell you," Joe said.

Lacy said, "Okay."

"Back in the day, I was rolling in money. I mean rolling. I don't mean to brag and I'm very ashamed of myself for not being there for you when I could have been. I was making a lot of money working two jobs. I was working at Caterpillar and…"

"Eastern Airlines," Lacy said.

"How did you know that?" Joe asked.

Lacy said, "Mom told many stories to her friends, Horace, and Marcel. I'd try to listen from the other room."

"OHHHH! You were eavesdropping," Joe said.

"Eavesdropping, trying to fill in the blanks of my life and learning what I needed to learn to survive the situation."

"I can understand that," Joe said.

"Please continue," Lacy said.

"Well, I worked those two jobs and saved up a good amount of money and decided to get a new car since the one I had was not going to last much longer. I like Cadillacs and went out one day and got one."

"Joe, I'm sorry to keep interrupting but I think I know the story about your car," Lacy said.

"You do?" Joe asked.

"I think I do. I'll go as far as I can and you stop me if I'm wrong. You went out and bought a maroon Cadillac and went home and a woman joined you later. You two ate and drank and when you woke up a few thousand dollars were missing from your pockets."

"YEEEESS! KEEP GOING, KEEP GOING," Joe said.

"You went to your car to drive to the woman's house to confront her but your car wouldn't start because someone poured sugar in your gas tank."

"That's right," Joe said. "Then what happened Lacy?"

"That's all I know."

Joe said, "After I realized sugar was put into my tank I went into the house and grabbed my pistol. I only meant to scare the woman. I got to her house and went up the back steps and saw her sitting at the kitchen table with a guy, laughing and carrying on. I pushed the door open and she jumped out of her chair and ran toward me and said, 'No Joe, please don't', and I was so startled that I squeezed the gun and it went off. The bullet hit her in the chest and her body shimmied down to the floor. Then the guy jumped out of the chair and rushed me, so I shot him and paralyzed him. I realized what I did so I walked right to the police station and turned myself in. Because I turned myself in I did a lot less time than I was supposed to do."

Lacy said, "You're the guy that Mom said was cleaning his gun and shot himself in the stomach and went to jail for it."

"Hahahahaha." Joe laughed and said he wished he shot himself in the stomach because those two people would be alive and he would not have gone to jail. "But Lacy, how did you know this story?"

"Joe, this may hurt and bring back a lot of pain for you if I tell you."

Joe asked, "You ever seen the movie Casablanca with Bogart?"

"Of course," Lacy said, "that's my favorite movie."

"If she can take it then I can too," Joe said. "Do you remember that line in the movie Lacy?"

"Of course. Ingrid Bergman arrived in Casablanca and ran into Bogart after breaking his heart years earlier. Bogart told Louis Armstrong to never play the song "As Time Goes By" in his bar ever again. Louis played it for Bergman earlier that day, so Bogart told Louis if she could take listening to the song after that heartbreak then he could too. 'Play it Sam. I said play the song.' Hahhahahaha. Louis' face cracked me up when Bogart caught him playing the song for her," Lacy said. "Classic movie for the books. When she left is exactly how I felt when Esta left. As Bogart said, it was a wild finish when Bergman left, and it was a wild finish when Esta left. When I first saw that movie, it made great sense to me and I think everyone in high school should have to watch it because the message is compassion and the world lacks that."

"Lacy," Joe said. "How are you able to speak of compassion after everything you've told me about the years when you were growing up?"

"Joe," Lacy said. "We are all here for a purpose and part of my purpose is to help others, and that can't happen if I play the victim. Many wanted me to play that character but I refused."

"Man, o man o man. Okay Lacy, back to the story. How did you know about my car and the woman?" Joe asked.

Lacy said, "Joe, you were set up."

"Set up by who?" Joe asked.

"You really don't get it, do you?" Lacy said. "Mom. She played all of you and all of us. She knew your daily routine and she knew you were buying a brand new car and would have a lot of cash on you. The woman who happened to meet up with you was Mom's friend. The plan was to stay with you until you passed out from drinking and then she was to leave. Mom was the one that took your money. The woman had no clue you had money in your pockets. Mom took your money then poured sugar in your tank and left."

"You're telling me I shot two totally innocent people Lacy?"

"That's the part I said would hurt."

"I lay in that cell feeling so much remorse for what I did and continually seeing the way that woman's body shimmied to the floor drove me crazy. Now, come to find out that they were completely innocent. But Lacy, she came to see me when I first went to prison and brought me a watch."

"A watch?" Lacy asked. "Joe, there's a funny saying in corporate America. At the end of your career they give you a watch when you retire so you can watch how much time you have left before you die. She bought you a watch with your money. It was a silver watch with a brown band, right?"

"Yes," Joe said. "Man, you don't miss nothin'."

Lacy said, "When you were in your cell with horrible memories running through your mind of that shooting, I was in a house with horrible stories I'd hear running through my mind."

"That's right," Joe said.

"Lacy, we'd better get to shopping before your wife wonders where we went."

"Let's go," Lacy said. As they were shopping, Joe offered to hold Lacy's hand cart and Lacy said, "No thank you. I've got it." As Lacy kept walking and talking to Joe there was no reply, so Lacy looked around and saw Joe standing near the oranges looking upset with tears rolling down his face. "What's wrong Joe?"

"Lacy, I've done nothing for you your whole life and you really don't need me at all. I can't even hold your hand cart for you."

"Sure you can. Here you go," Lacy said. "Joe, in prison, what would happen if you let people do favors for you?"

"OOOHH, Lacy. You never want to do that because guys that accept favors end up somebody's bitch or mule to pass drugs."

"That's how it was around Horace, Marcel, Randy, and Mom, so please understand I'm very conditioned and used to doing things for myself. I missed many wonderful opportunities in life because I couldn't open my mouth to help myself or to ask for what I wanted or needed. I missed out on a wonderful woman named Georgiana because I was afraid and couldn't get the words out. I've gotten so much better but still have work to do."

"Lacy, I'm in my seventies and I have never met a man like you in my life. It really saddens me I didn't see you sooner. You are a brilliant man."

"Thank you Joe, but I'm just a man wanting to do brilliant things."

"I'm very proud of you Lacy."

"Thank you Joe for sharing your past with me and allowing me to get to know you. It means a lot to me that you feel remorse for your past because I've never heard Mom admit that she feels that way."

"You're welcome, son." Lacy looked at Joe as if he was studying him. "Is it okay if I call you son?" Joe asked. Lacy looked around the room then looked at the oranges and realized the man in front of him needed to feel like his life wasn't all for nothing.

"Yes, I'd like for you to call me son," Lacy said. Then they hugged and headed home. As they headed home, Joe asked Lacy if he ever felt uncomfortable being a father. "Heck no," Lacy said. "I've been babysitting and taking care of Alexandra and Odessa's children since I was nine years old. I've had so much practice that it comes very easy and I've always wanted children so it's a breeze for me. I'd rather be with my son and daughters than be out with friends. I dig it Joe. I really dig it to the bone."

"I can see that man. Those children are going to be wonderful just like you."

"Thank you Joe, but please ease up on the stroking of my ego, it might be hard to get my head through the front door if you keep it up."

"Hahahah. Alright son." A few days later it was time for Joe to return to Peoria. As he and Lacy headed for the airport, Joe told Lacy he forgot to make a family tree for him so he would know his roots. Joe asked Lacy if anyone had ever told him to go back to Africa.

"Hahahaha. Of course," Lacy said. "I don't know many black people that haven't heard that before."

"Well, my mother was one hundred percent Cherokee Indian. Her name was Lucenda. That makes me fifty percent and you twenty five percent. The next time someone tells you to go back to Africa you make sure you tell them that you're already home and that they need to check their roots and return to them."

"Hahahahaha. Joe's got jokes. Pretty good Joe, pretty good."

"Oh, I'll keep you laughing for sure," Joe said.

WORTH IT

They laughed and spoke all the way to the airport, then Joe left. They stayed in touch for ten solid years and Lacy would send tickets for Joe until Joe could no longer fly. Joe died in 2005 due to cancer. He never sent Lacy the family tree, but that wasn't nearly as important to Lacy as his connection with Joe. Several years before Joe died, Lacy returned to the world of bodybuilding. One of his clients named Darla Longo came in for training at six o'clock in the morning and asked him if he ever considered competing again. Since they never spoke about bodybuilding, he thought it was odd for her in particular to ask that question because that wasn't their usual flow of conversation. He told her it crossed his mind from time to time. She told him he should get back on stage.

The next day, Sicilian Jimmie left a message on Lacy's business voicemail. They had not seen or spoken with each other in sixteen years since their lives were both in process. In Jimmie's voicemail, he told Lacy he was driving through La Canada and saw Lacy's name on a business and had to call him. He and Lacy got together the next day, Lacy's twin daughters' birthday. After his daughters went to bed for the night, Lacy and Jimmie spoke until ten o'clock that night. Jimmie was about to leave when he asked Lacy why he stopped competing in body-building. Lacy told Jimmie his son was born at that time so he wouldn't have had enough time to train, and he refused to use steroids. He told Jimmie that it was made very clear to him that he would not advance any further in that career unless he used steroids. Jimmie told Lacy that natural drug-free bodybuilding had grown and organizations like that didn't allow the use of steroids and that they tested for it. Lacy told Jimmie when taking a course to renew his personal training certificate, he ran into a guy that said he was a natural bodybuilding champion. Lacy told Jimmie he thought the guy was from the past like himself since they were both about the same size. Jimmie informed Lacy about many changes in the bodybuilding world since Lacy was so far removed from it due to his career. Jimmie told Lacy he should get back on stage. Lacy told Jimmie his wife dated a bodybuilder and hated the sport. "That has nothing to do with you Lacy," Jimmie said. "You were fantastic at it and should be out there grabbing titles like you had always wanted to do. Lacy, have you forgotten where you came from man? You had the fuck beaten out of you on a regular. Do you remember that time you took me to the school bathroom and locked the door and showed me your wounds from the beating the day before? Do you remember in Rocky when his wife wouldn't go to Russia with him but he went anyway and became champion? Laaaace maaan. You do what you feel is best but if anyone can make a comeback and tear up the shit it's you and it would be a damn shame if you didn't at least try to get what you've always wanted, the Mr. Universe title." Jimmie and Lacy spoke until two o'clock in the morning when Felicia came downstairs and reminded Lacy he had to be up in an hour to go to work, then she went back upstairs. Jimmie apologized to Lacy profusely for keeping him up but Lacy hugged Jimmie and thanked him for always being exactly who he was and never holding back his words for anyone. When Lacy got into work, one of the trainees gave Lacy a flyer and told him about a natural bodybuilding show that would be in Pasadena that coming weekend. Lacy went to the show, and as he watched the competitors he remembered the dream he had as a child about becoming a body-building champion much later in life. Lacy contacted Gus and told him he was returning to competition and Gus was thrilled. Lacy told Gus that Felicia would not like it, so Lacy told Gus that he planned to do a show in Las Vegas and if he won he would tell Felicia then and hopefully she would be on board with the idea.

Gus said, "Well if that makes sense to you then you do what you feel is best." Lacy gave Gus the date of the event and said he couldn't wait.

They hung up and Lacy called Gus back and said, "Gus, that's probably one of the stupidest ideas I've ever come up with in my life. I better just tell her."

"Hahahahahaha." Gus laughed and said, "I figured you'd be calling me back soon," then they both laughed about that for a while then hung up. Lacy always stayed in great shape so he was excited to get ready for the Mr. Natural Los Angeles. Felicia made it clear she didn't want to be married to a competitor but Lacy made it clear that it was now or never since he was thirty-five and had time since the business was going strong. Lacy made a deal with Felicia. He told her he would do this one show and if he won the entire event he would continue on for his pro card and finally go for the Mr. Universe one day. But, if he didn't get the overall title he would walk away forever. Felicia agreed. It had been thirteen years since Lacy was on a stage and he only had thirteen weeks to get ready. He watched current videos of competitors and used all of his knowledge about food and training to reduce body fat without losing too much muscle. He knew which foods to use as diuretics just before the show to look even sharper. When the show was over, Lacy was the overall winner. He continued on and won Mr. Natural California, Mr. Natural USA, Mr. Natural America three times in a row, Mr. Forever Natural Universe, and Mr. Natural Universe Pro. He was thirty-seven years old. By this time, Lacy and Felicia had divorced. Some speculated and said Lacy met someone else and chalked it up to an affair but that was the story people were used to hearing about male athletes and found it easy to believe. It was also said that Lacy abandoned his children and wouldn't pay to support them. But, some of those people that criticized him for being disciplined, running his business his way, getting back on stage, going through with the divorce, and living the life he set out to live came back to apologize when his daughters decided to live with him full time. Lacy learned early in life that people will say nasty things about you and do what they can to tarnish your name and your existence because they are the takers and haters of the world, but if you just keep going you will see the life you longed for will be waiting for you to enjoy in the future. He knew it was up to everyone to accept their life and take a stand for that life and how they wanted to live it.

Marcel once told Lacy that he and Lacy could never have a real relationship while Mom was alive because his allegiance was with her.

However, she moved in to stay with him and he kicked her out months later. While Randy was in prison he had a heart attack, so Marcel called Lacy and asked if he would give money to Mom so she could visit Randy. Lacy asked Marcel how it came to be that way, how even after all she had done for him and Horace they could not give her the money. He said they couldn't afford it, but Lacy knew it wasn't about them and what they could do or could not do. Mom was in need, and Marcel and Horace grew tired of taking care of her financial needs and thought contacting Lacy would ease their financial stress. Lacy said he would meet Mom and give her the money. They met a few days later at the Good Earth Restaurant in Pasadena. Lacy was not sure what to expect, so he alerted a couple of friends that worked at the restaurant that he was having a meeting and asked if they could keep an eye out for potential trouble. Lacy sat where he could see who came in the front door. Moments later, Mom walked in. They both saw each other and Lacy stood up to greet her. Neither of them knew what to do so they held hands then sat down. She watched his every move and he watched her every move. If his hands went under the table to fix his napkin she paid close attention and he did the same. It was clear she was nervous and expected some type of retaliation from Lacy, and Lacy thought she wanted retaliation since she found out about Joe. He asked what she would like to eat and she said nothing. He tried not to stare at the sorrow and pain he could see in the lines on her face. She couldn't look him in his eyes and he felt sorry for her and spoke only of current events in the world because he didn't want her to think for a second he would bring up the past. "You hear about Randy?" she asked.

"Yes, Marcel told me. Is he doing better?" Lacy asked.

"Yes, he is," she said, "but he's in that place you know?"

"I know," Lacy said. "Here's the money for the flight."

"DON'T GIVE IT TO ME NOW," she said. Lacy quickly surveyed the room looking for any signs of danger because he didn't know why she reacted like that. Then he looked at her and asked when he was supposed to give it to her. "Outside when we leave," she said. Lacy could tell the mood changed and it more than likely wouldn't get better so he suggested they leave. They went outside and he asked if it was okay to give her the money. She said yes. He gave her the money and she asked him to wait while she went to her car. He looked around, making sure things were safe, then she returned with a shoebox.

"What's this?" he asked.

"What the hell does it look like?" she asked. Lacy did what he could to avoid a confrontation with her because he didn't want that to be the memory for either of them from that day.

He said, "Show me what's in the box." She opened it and it was a pair of shoes.

She said, "I don't want you to ever be able to say I came to you begging for money so you take these shoes as an exchange for the money."

Lacy looked at her and said, "I met with you to be supportive of the situation so please keep the shoes."

"You aren't going to take the shoes?" she asked. "I didn't think you'd take them from me and that's why they're not for you. These shoes are for your son because you've never been my son, have you?" Lacy reached for the shoes and said thank you.

"I have to get back to work. I'll make sure my son gets them. Please take care of yourself and Randy. Goodbye Mom," Lacy said. Then he left.

Randy got better and was released from prison but went back to prison a few years later. After that last release from prison, he died a couple of years later. Esta died about eight years before he did. When Lacy went to Esta's funeral, many eyes were focused on him, and his daughters asked why so many people were staring at him. Lacy said, "Because they know I'm her son and they think I don't know that." One woman in particular kept watching Lacy, and when she noticed him staring at her she left the chapel, got into a white Mercedes, and drove away. Lacy asked around and got that woman's name, Christina. After doing some digging he found out where she worked and left a voice message for her. She contacted him and asked how he was able to contact her because her number was private. He asked if she remembered anything about Lacy Dick Tracy. She laughed and said yes. He said, "Well, nothing has changed." They agreed to meet at the Ontario Mills shopping mall in Ontario, California. They had lunch and spoke about Esta. Lacy told Christina that he remembered her always wearing knee-high socks. He told her that he always cried after church when Esta would walk him to the station wagon then leave with Christina to go wherever they went.

"Lacy," she said.

"Yes," Lacy said.

"Is there anything you want to know?"

"Yes," Lacy said. "You were one of her closest friends back then. Did you know she was going to leave?"

"Yes, I did."

Lacy said, "Then that's why you had a peculiar look on your face that day she dropped me off at Shirley's house. You and the others were in the car waiting for her."

"YEEEEES. I remember that," she said. "WOOOOOW! Lacy Dick Tracy strikes again. Esta was so proud of you."

"I know," Lacy said, "but she couldn't tell me why because she was protecting her hidden life from her other son and daughter."

"Are you angry with her Lacy?" she asked.

"No. I spent more time feeling sorry for her since she went through life hiding and I nearly fell into the same trap. I believe if she came clean and told me and her other children the truth she would still be alive. I believe her guilt and pain she carried for so many years caught up with her."

"I agree with you one thousand percent Lacy." Christina and Lacy finished their lunch and stayed in touch.

One day, Lacy was speaking with a man half his age that had gone to jail a few times. Lacy told the man about his past and the man said his own mother was a teacher so he had no excuse for his life being in shambles. Lacy told the man regardless of the woman's profession all women were teachers and if we listened and payed attention to the right things we could all learn something. Another man once told Lacy it sounded like he was raised like an animal. Lacy said, "We are all animals but we have the choice to rise above animalistic behavior or oppress the world with it as many well-raised individuals have done for centuries. If we can forgive ourselves and others, accept ourselves and others, work to understand ourselves and others, and try to learn from the lessons of our lives there's no doubt success and the ability to thrive will be waiting in our future." A woman told Lacy it was a shame that his biological mother left him in the hands of such a cruel and vicious woman who he was forced to call Mom. She said if Lacy were brought up in a wealthy family and was sent to the best schools with the best opportunities he would probably be one of the richest men in the world because of his mind. Lacy reminded the woman that the woman he called Mom lost both parents by the age of thirteen, never got past the eighth grade, hustled in the streets as a child, prostituted herself to survive, raised a house full of children in the best way she could, while struggling through a lifetime of pain and loss. He said, "It's through her deep pain, losses, and frustrations, combined with her strength, crafty mindset, perseverance, and her way of teaching that I learned how to survive in this world and thrive better than she did." Lacy told her if he could have his same mindset, visions, dreams, friends and helpers along the way along with the divine intervention he experienced, he would go through all of that hell again to have the children, friends, and life he now had today.

The woman looked at Lacy with much surprise on her face and said, "You really think going through all of that was worth it?"

"For the life I have today?" Lacy said, "Yes. She was worth it all."

ABOUT THE AUTHOR

As a child, Lacy's ambition annoyed many, and others just couldn't fathom his mindset. Although at age thirteen, Lacy knew that one day he would write a book, it was time, further life experiences, and maturity that inspired him to write *She Was Worth It All*. As a teenager, Lacy promised to open one of California's longest running fitness facilities and offer one-on-one training. Private Fitness by Lacy Weston is in its thirty-first year. For a long time, his goal was to become world champion. He is former Mr. Natural USA, three-time champion Mr. Natural America, Mr. Natural Universe Pro, and Natural World Cup champion. Lacy's deep concern for humanity inspired him to cowrite and produce the song *Transform Your Reality*, which is also the title of his earlier book. Lacy is a 100% devoted father of three and believes we all can make the world better or worse. He challenges people to pick a side.

Made in the USA
Lexington, KY
27 November 2019

57800691R00240